Animation RULES!

Book One
WORDS

A series of unillustrated lectures on the theory, practice, aesthetics, history and personal experience of the author in the world of animated film

Dan F. McLaughlin, Jr.

DEDICATION[1]

ADDRESS FOR RETIREMENT

Unaccustomed as I am to making retirement speech-I will just go with just some random thoughts - this is going to be short

The last film you some of you saw Claude the message to me was is if parents turn off the child the child can turn off the parents that has always been for me a basis for my teaching - don't block the creativity as Claude's parents did - keep the creative process alive and flourishing.

Wanted to give a person the same great rush - feeling I felt when I saw the first animated film I did. Which was a fire safety spot a cell of which I have hanging in my home office - give more

In the 60's and 70's animation was struggling to stay alive I am proud that I helped keeping it to stay alive until it is a major player in art today -

I will always remember the closeness and spirit of the workshop the students and their films over the years and their many accomplishments after leaving -

On the invitation it said The lizard has fallen

I thought for a minute it should be

The mighty lizard has fallen But that's not true

But in the workshop All lizards are equal

Tell story

Change it to this ending

Getting to get to step to stop to get it So a lizard has fallen

Landing on his feet

What I have tried to do to be a good teacher is to listen, be honest, be an example with actions not words - have a moral philosophy of life-all I can say is what Popeye said - I am what I am and that's what I am.

Future - will change but keep the core ideals and principles of the workshop - one-person - one film - individual films - quality - professional fee is done away with - and a return to free

---

1. Among the author's papers after his death was a copy of his retirement address. It was delivered December 9, 2007, at UCLA's Bridges Theater. This document was OCRed, and has not been edited in any way.

higher education

And now a short Poem When I started here in 58

I didn't know what to contemplate But I know that I've been in heaven When I depart in 2007

I would like to thank

My wife Marilyn, who is smarter than me but married me anyway

Mary and especially my children and grandchildren whose love and support has always been a solid anchor for me

Jutta

Bob Mitchell my friend who has passed away - who told me about animation - easy class sure B and one night a week - easy - he lied.

Bill Shull - who started the animation workshop in 1958 who I worked with for 12 years

Phil Denslow - who we work together for many years when there was just the two of us holding the workshop together - before the computer and after

Dug ward, - who holds the workshop together - who I have always been there for me Steve who has been a quiet support

Fellow teachers: Celia, Chuck, Richard, Valerie, Keith, Glenn, and Tom[2]

Thank all the students for all these wonderful years - my last word is: make good animation and be a good person

And now to a future of my own work - my book, my films, my poetry, and my painting and my wife

And the last last thought - if it can be done in live action do it in live action. That's all folks

Peace

Reason for going into teaching making my own films -

---

2. From top to bottom, Marilyn is Marilyn Powell. Mary is Margaret Serbia Powell. The children are Dan McLaughlin, Loren McLaughlin and Maura Weber. The grandchildren are Anna, Peter and Rose LaFollette, and Miles Weber. Jutta is Jutta Landa. Steve is Steve Engles and the teachers are Celia Mercer, Chuck Sheetz, Richard Edwards, Valerie Lettera, Keith Rouse, Glenn Vilppu and Tom Sito. Names of teachers provided by Celia Mercer.

CONTENTS

Chapter		
	Rules' Tale (aka Acknowledgments)	1
	Introduction	7
1	Idea	15
2	Storyboards	31
3	Timing	71
4	Sound	79
5	Layout	99
6	Technical Diversity of Animation	135
7	Animation	149
8	Post-Production	209
9	Distribution	217
10	Four Other Categories of Animation	231
11	Materials, Technology and Equipment	277
12	Making A Living in Animation	283
13	Teaching Animation	309
14	Pencil Test Assignments	333
15	Bibliography	355
Addendum One	A Brief Summary of Copyright Law	363
Addendum Two	Scriptwriting for a TV Series	369

RULES' TALE[1]

fig. 5-34

aka ACKNOWLEDGMENTS

Dan F. McLaughlin, Jr. died March 15, 2016, then I got this manuscript. My name is Dan McLaughlin. My Dad died that day in March.

Other salient points: Dad had been working on this book for decades. He had been making independent films for decades. He taught animation to 800 students and oversaw 700 films. That took decades, too. He had taken decades to complete films. Others had been completed in less time. For decades he had worked on The Book (this book). A few years before he died he had suffered a stroke. Before the stroke he had finished the words, and allegedly the artwork for The Book, which was "in the storage unit someplace." (In the time before the storage unit, the artwork had been "in the office someplace.")

Salient facts about me: I am the eldest and only son (with two younger sisters). I am a reference librarian. I have self-published several works of both fiction and non-fiction. In my youth, I made a few animated films using UCLA equipment, and later worked on a few of Dad's projects.

---

1. You know, reading this you might get the impression I did all the work in getting this book ready for publication as the heroic and solitary work of filial duty. Nothing could be further from the truth. Four of my father's UCLA colleagues, Celia Mercer, Phil Denslow, Doug Ward and Steve Engles provided prompt, courteous, thorough and comprehensive answers whenever Dad left tantalizing clues to the identity of a student or the intricacies of a process. Doug and Steve in particular deserve credit for going through the three boxes of potential illustrations I culled from my Dad's stuff, which I dragged up to the animation room at UCLA. (Doug consistently arranged for free parking, no matter how many times I showed up, and advised me on whether the item I had pulled from Dad's effects actually did illustrate a particular concept in Dad's text.) In many cases they had suggestions or alternatives to my initial finding that were much better. They also listened to the choices I made in regards to the entire project and offered helpful critiques and advice. Overall, basically anything I asked for from the UCLA animation community was quickly, and I would say lovingly, provided. Every time I asked for help or assistance from just about everyone, the answer was always preceded with some variation of "Your father meant so much to animation, and all of us, I would be happy to help."

So anyway in that kinda, "Hey this wasn't supposed to happen now/We all knew it was gonna happen soon" stupor soon after he died, my sisters and I gathered. At one point I asked, "So what about The Book?" One sister, who had been closer to him for the past couple of decades, said, "I think I have a copy of it." My other sister, who had been the closest of us all to him for decades, said, "And I think the art for it is in the storage unit someplace." We all laughed. "Mind if I take a look and see about getting it published?" They said no. "Any of it digitized?" I asked. We all laughed, again.

Next salient point: The words were way more done than the pictures. Rather quickly, my sister had gotten to me The Book in the form of a box containing various paper[2] drafts of the book.[3] After comparing them, I assembled and then OCRed what I think was meant to be the final version of each chapter. Basically, I chose the longest version of each chapter that had non-sequential illustration numbers, i.e. 5-17, 5-18, 2-47, 3-6, 5-19. I assumed that those versions reflected revisions of earlier chapters where the illustrations had been in order. In general, each subsequent version seemed longer than the one that preceded it, and had fewer notes made by Dad commenting on the text. Based on clues in the text, it looked like the last times various sections had been touched varied from 2002 through 2007.

Next salient point: Sections of the text that were completely outdated were intertwined with useful, interesting or relevant material. For instance, in the section on copyright (dated), there is a story of a student who left a piece of art for Elton John that attracted his attention and charmed him enough to give her the rights to one of his songs for her film. In another instance, in the midst of a discussion of current computer technology (very dated), he inserted a discussion of the artist as tool user vs. the engineer as toolmaker. It became clear to me that to simply delete the dated material would render the surrounding material meaningless and disjointed. On the other hand, correcting the dated material would be a daunting task outside the scope of my ability or time I wished to devote to this project. So I made an Editorial Decision: The text would stay pretty much as is, and any updates or corrections (which are extensive in many areas) would be made in the form of footnotes.[4] The only time I altered the text was when I attempted to corral his Hegelian-like sentences that suffer from a lack of pronouns or verbs or both. After I took a crack at at it, Kristina Haar proofread the book, and the author's granddaughter, Rose La Follette, indexed it.

Next salient point: Dad liked to repeat himself. Both verbally and here in The Book, he delighted in saying the same thing over and over. But since this book can plausibly be read non-linearly, I kept in almost all of the repeats.

Next salient point: I also assumed that at some point in time in the storage unit, I would find a box with "illustrations" written on the outside and filled with folders labeled 2-47, 3-6, 5-17, 5-18, 5-19. Alas,

---

2. Yes, paper. He even meticulously laid out several pages of tables with tabs which OCR simply could not handle. If there are any readers who are intending to leave a magnum opus behind for someone else to finish, remember, digital is good, label your drafts and leave the layout to the layout people.

3. And to be fair, there WERE a handful of floppy disks with drafts of texts and about 40 pieces of complete art. Also, his wife, Marilyn Powell, at the time of his death had a Word file of the introduction and first chapter that she emailed me from her home in Canada. Margit Schmitt also had variations of copies of these two files.

4. You know, there's always a section in these things where someone says something like, "I would like to thank X, Y and Z for their invaluable assistance, but all errors remain my responsibility." Well, in this case, not so much. This is Dad's book. Cleaned up, yes, but this is really his book.

this never really happened. However, as I climbed over and among the 120 boxes that filled the storage unit, I made an Editorial Decision:

First Editorial Decision: This book, The Book, would show the creative steps and, more important, the missteps that are made before the final project is put in front of an audience. Also, I decided to include things which are admittedly tangential to a book on animation but illustrated more of Dad's creative and professional life. The decision to show the author's drafts, missteps and rejection letters was made easier by the fact that the author was dead and not around to contest it.[5] Under the tangential category I have included, among other things, a letter that Dad sent President Nixon along with a copy of his film *Peace* (fig. 1-8). *Peace* had been shot on a protest day for the Vietnam War and consisted of people at Venice Beach saying, "peace." Dad sent a copy of the film to the White House along with a request that the White House provide back the North Vietnamese word for "peace." Under the process category, I have included a series of pencil tests from Dad's film *Claude* that nicely illustrate in detail how what looks so right in the final film is usually a result of considered thought and experimentation (fig. 7-78).[6]

Next salient point: While in many ways the author was a humble person (I would argue that the reason for his success as a teacher was his ability to transcend himself when considering a student's film and not impose his will or aesthetic on it), at the end of the day he was a UCLA professor who was used to things magically appearing because he was a UCLA professor and a heck of a nice guy. Among the things he thought would magically appear were images from major studios that he could use to demonstrate various animation techniques and styles. Consider his letter he sent to the Legal Department at Disney (fig. ar-1). Since Disney never got back to him, I made another series of Editorial Decisions:

First Editorial Decision (Art): First, I used a ton of art taken from the 120 boxes of Dad's stuff as illustrations, including art taken from films he never finished. Hence here seen for the first time is art from *Harry*, the story of a rather ordinary man who receives the answer to all the world's problems and a mandate to share it; and *Easter Island*, the story of what happens on Easter Island after the tourists leave. I used these images primarily as examples of storyboarding and character research.

Second Editorial Decision (Art): Rather than rely on or borrow images from others, I decided to simply ask the UCLA community to come forward again and provide images taken from their films to illustrate the diversity of the types of films that can be called animation. So I sent a series of emails to everyone who had attended Dad's service (held and hosted most graciously by UCLA—they even covered parking!) asking for artwork from their films. Phil Faroudja, Phil Denslow, Valerie Lettera, Jay Shipman, Celia Mercer, Brian Wells and Tami Tsark responded. I also reached out to Emily Hubley because her mother Faith Hubley and my Dad were close (fig. 2-34), and she responded with a scene from *Adventures of an* * as well as several corrections/suggestions of Dad's text that I had sent her. Jerry Beck responded with much useful advice and encouragement, and I also heard from Bob Dickson, longtime friend and filmmaker, and Maureen Furniss at CalArts.

---

5. It also helped that he saved pretty much everything from his life, including his first contract as a Hollywood extra at the age of 2 months and the Christmas cards he received from Disney animators.

6. Here is the first plug for the DVD of my Dad's films called *11 Films by Dan McLaughlin,* available through Pyramid Media (2004).

Third Editorial Decision (Art): I hired two incredibly talented artists to supply art that wasn't gonna come from anyplace else. Adam Holmes took Dad's rough sketches of the character Harry and then went through all the steps in designing a character and model sheets. Mike Schmitt took a rather minimal sketch showing a two shot and extrapolated from it a wide variety of camera angles and design elements. He also took the characters from *Claude* and used them to illustrate elements of design taken from classical painting. Both of these artists are available for employment.

Next salient point: While many of the above steps were being done, my lovely wife Vendi Elmen then designed the look and layout of the book, and then laid out the book in a program called InDesign combining over 250,000 OCRed words with over 1,000 individual illustrations. It sorta took over her creative life for about a year. We are, as of this moment, still married.

Penultimate Editorial Decision: I am self-publishing this book through CreateSpace, which allows me to set the price. Since this book was clearly intended by my Dad to be his legacy to the world of animation, I, with my sisters' consent, have decided to sell this book at cost.

Final Editorial Decision: So to keep the design easier (words in one book, illustrations in the other), to keep the physical size of the book a reasonable one for a paperback, to lower the costs of the individual books and to allow the inclusion of more art, I decided to separate the words from art into two physical books. You have in your hands the word book. The other book is called *Animation Rules: Book Two Art*, isbn 1541104048.

So that's basically it. I am sure this is not the book that my Dad had in his head. Nor should anyone regard each word or statement as gospel truth. But in retrospect, I believe this work is better because I went through 120 boxes of stuff rather than finding a neat folder or floppy disk that said "illustrations." What this book loses in topicality I think it gains in perspective in many ways. First, it reflects a moment in time when traditional hand-drawn animation co-existed with computers, and this book talks about both worlds as equally viable. Next, by considering the aesthetic through the ethical and ending up with the economic implications of the life of the animator, the book is filled with insights that transcend technology. Next, this book emphasizes process much more than final results, and shows the rejections and failures that even a successful artist has to go through to reach a final result. By seeing the failures, I believe the reader is better equipped to deal with and overcome them in their own work. Finally, this book has become much more of an homage to both my Dad and the UCLA Animation Workshop. For those of you who knew my father, this close relationship comes as no surprise. For everyone else, this book is an excellent memorial. As a son and a scholar, I am proud to bring this work to your attention. For all its flaws, this book is in his own words and is filled with his art. It is good. It is him.

Enjoy.
Or as he would say,
Peace.

Dan McLaughlin
Pasadena, California and Newport, Oregon
July, 2017

That said, the digital is in and film is out.
The Author

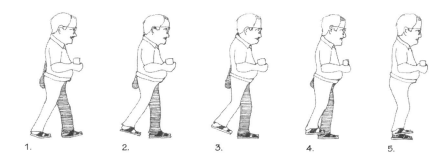

fig.7-16

INTRODUCTION[1]

"Animation is like a falling lizard; you have to step, to stop, to get it." That is the way one of my students defined animation in the 1980s when I was teaching in Jos, Nigeria. Think about it. My students at UCLA thought it was as good a definition as any other. The Falling Lizard became the animal totem of the UCLA Animation Workshop, and to this day, the weekend during which everyone is locked in to make a film is called "The Falling Lizard Weekend" (fig. intro-1).

The knowledge and information in this book comes from over 36 years of teaching at the UCLA Animation Workshop (fig. intro-2). The philosophy of the Workshop, which has been the premier graduate program in the world for the last 50 years, is "one person, one film." One person does all the work for the entire film.

The purpose of this book is to turn your personal vision into a reality. It will provide the information and guidance needed to make an animated film, complete in all its aspects. You will learn the principles of production that are the basis of all animation: traditional, digital, computer and interactive. You can use chapters individually or in combination if you want to focus on a particular specialization. This book will give you the necessary information to

---

1. As mentioned in the Acknowledgements, the author completed the manuscript sometime around 2007 and the text has not been updated for accuracy. All statements reflect the belief of the author at the time of authorship and may, or may not, reflect current reality.

prepare you for a life in animation.

The structure of the book will follow the essential stages of the production process from idea to storyboard, on to timing, sound, layout, animation, post-production and distribution. Other chapters will deal with the milieu of animation, from diversity in animation to making a living and teaching. The chapters are presented in the order for teaching a 10- or 15-week course. No particular style or studio will be emphasized.

OTHER DEFINITIONS

Animation is a new art form created in the early 20th century when the invention of motion pictures gave movement in recorded time to painting, graphics and sculpture. Today, animation is hard to define, as new technologies and experimentation have blurred the boundaries between animation and live-action film. You already know one definition: Animation is like a falling lizard; you have to step, to stop, to get it. Here are some more standard definitions, each of which is at least 90 percent accurate:

The dictionary definition (Webster's New World College, 1996), animate. To make alive, fill with breath 1. To give life to; bring to life 2. To make gay energetic, or spirited 3. To stimulate to action or creative effort; inspire 4. To give motion to; put into action 5. To make move so as to seem lifelike 6. To produce animated cartoon - adj. 1. living, having life, esp. animal life 2. lively, vigorous; spirited.

Animated cartoon: A motion picture made by photographing a series of drawings, each showing a stage of movement slightly changed from the one before, so that the figures in them seem to move when the drawings are projected in rapid succession.[2]

The Animation Guilds, Local 839, IATSE: Traditionally, the Hollywood Local has claimed jurisdiction over anything shot above or below normal sound projection speed or 24 frames a second. Today, the combining of live action and animation has complicated that definition. So union jurisdiction is decided by who makes 70 percent of the finished film, animation or live action.[3]

---

2. I was unable to locate a 1996 *Webster's New College Dictionary* (3rd edition, revised) to verify this wording, and this definition is at slight variance to the 2000 *Webster's New College Dictionary* Edition (4th).

3. I went to the website for Local 869, https://animationguild.org, and nothing on the website said anything like this. I contacted the union and gave them a copy of the above statement and received a very nice reply from Steven Hulett, the business representative. He said that there is no definition of animation anywhere in the current contract of Local 839. He said in general the Art Directors (Local 800) and Animation Guild (Local 839) continually tussle over who represents what. In his words, in general, 839 represents animated features and 800 represents animated effects in live-action features. He also added that most live-action visual effects work is non-union, although live-action storyboards are mostly union and done by Local 800.

The International Animated Film Association (ASIFA) definition: In its early days, the late 1960s, ASIFA's definition of animation was "a motion picture that only existed when it was projected on a screen." This meant that the animated film existed only as projected images (unlike those in a live-action film, which record an event that exists in real life). Today ASIFA defines animation as an art that "consists in creating moving images by using all the techniques, except live action."[4]

A common definition: Animation is film shot one frame at a time. Click, shoot a frame, move something, click, shoot a frame, move, click, 24 times a second, and you have animation.

In this book, animation is defined as the movement of the created image in recorded time.

THE BASIC CATEGORIES

There are presently five basic categories or areas of animation:

Traditional 2D. Hand-drawn or painted image. *Ta-Daa* (2016?) by Jay Shipman (fig. intro-3).
3D Stop Motion. Puppet or object animation. Chapter 10 (fig. 6-10)
Visual Effects. Animation used within a live-action film. Chapter 10
Computer. Animation that is digitally assisted or created entirely from scratch on the computer. Chapter 10
Interactive. Where the audience is part of the action. The computer allows the audience to interact with the animation. Chapter 10

This book will follow the production process of traditional 2D animation. Mastering traditional 2D provides you with the needed animation principles for the other categories. Anyone who aspires to do quality animation, whether traditional or computer, must first learn the principles of animation. In starting a character walk, the animation principles are the same whether the tool is a pencil or a computer. When you buy the computer, you do not buy the talent. Chapter 10 et passim will deal with basic skills and the different uses of the computer in animation.

Of the remaining four categories of animation, two have been around since the beginning. They are:

---

4. I went to the ASIFA Hollywood website http://www.asifa-hollywood.org/, and found nothing like this there. I contacted the organization and had a delightful email exchange with Frank Gladstone, executive director. He wrote that both he and longtime board member Jerry Beck did not remember either of the two definitions given above. He did say, however, that ASIFA's educational wing, the Animation Educator's Forum, came up with the following definition in 2011: Animation involves the creation of movements or performance using "frame-by-frame" techniques that are associated with artistic creation and production of the illusion of motion. For purposes of definition, such techniques, hand drawn, computer generated, stop-motion, augmented motion capture, etc., are distinct from those of "real-time" and "live-action" motion pictures.

3D Stop Motion Animation *Next Stop Judgement Day* by Jay Shipman (fig. intro-4).
Animation as a Visual Effect in Live-Action Films

The other two have arisen since the advent of digital media. They are:
Computer Animation
Interactive Animation

These four areas of animation have as their foundation the basic principles of animation that will be presented in this book. Only the production processes differ when different materials and tools necessitate a change. Examples are the addition of 3D lighting, to computer-created animation to computer capture of stop motion images through digital cameras, and these techniques then being used in the creation of interactive, story driven projects.

There are also distinct differences in the development of idea and storyboard for interactive animated projects, because the very nature of interactivity involves a non-linear approach to story creation rather a traditional linear structure. How the traditional production process is adapted to the needs of these other forms of animation will be a subject of that chapter. There will be an overview of the different production processes with an in-depth analysis only when crucial, such as the use of 3D lighting in 3D and computer animation, or the techniques used to combine animation and live action in visual effects, and the issues of non-linear communication in interactive animation are discussed.

WHAT IS AN ANIMATOR?

The term "animator" can have two meanings. One is the person who does the character animation and is the popular definition of animator. A character animator requires drawing, acting and timing skills. The other is an animated filmmaker who makes the whole film, an independent filmmaker. This book is intended for both.

TRADITIONAL ANIMATION PRODUCTION VS. TRADITIONAL LIVE-ACTION PRODUCTION

In traditional animation, a film is edited and timed in its final form before shooting begins. Ideally, the film is shot at a 1:1 ratio, and every foot of film shot is used in the finished work. In live action, far more film is shot than will ever be used because the film is completed in the post-production editing stage. The ratio in live action is often a 10:1 (10 feet of film shot for every 1 foot of finished film) or higher. This amount of footage is then edited down into the final film.

The four production stages for animation are:

Pre-Production: idea; storyboard; financing; selection of talent and sound (dialogue, sound effects, music), which is sometimes recorded before the animatic or filming of the storyboard; timing; and editing. (In Japan, sound is usually recorded after the film is shot.)

Production: layout; animation; exposure sheets or a frame-by-frame guide for shooting the film; filming; laboratory processing before or after sound mixing, or digital output of a "picture only" movie to be used in post-production.

Post-Production: Final audio synced with the picture. This includes music, dialogue and effects. In digital animations, this is also where fades and dissolves between scenes can be inserted. Final mixing is done and the picture is then locked.

Distribution.

Live action has four production stages, with the addition of a post-production stage before distribution, when the editing, music and effects are done.

The crucial difference between traditional animation and live action is that editing is done before shooting in animation. Since creating images frame by frame is usually more costly than shooting live performers, you have to know where you are going when you start your filmic journey. You create the images, the characters, their movement, the setting, and completely control their time and place in the finished film. In computer animation, you have greater control over the editing after the animation is done, but you still have to know where you are going.

TOO MUCH TO LEARN?

Please do not be overwhelmed by the amount of information you are asked to understand. In time it will all become clear. The logic of the process of animation will only really make sense when you have finished your first film. Continuing to learn animation can be a joy for the rest of your life. A good animator never stops learning. It is not going to be easy, but, hey, if it were easy, everyone would be doing it.

DO I NEED TO KNOW HOW TO DRAW?

No. You do not need to know how to draw in order to do good animation, and this book is written with that in mind. Concept and timing are essential, but not drawing ability. That said, it should be clear that being an animator of full-character animation, as in Disney features, requires a high degree of drawing skill and experience. However, there are many types of animation or jobs in animation that do not require draftsmanship. Two of the three most influential people in animation, Walt Disney and Norman McLaren, were never known for their drawing ability, nor were they hindered by this lack.

THREE LEVELS OF LEARNING

The first level is Information. This book will cover the first level completely, with all the necessary information needed for making an animated film.

The second level is Knowledge, which comes from receiving the information and using it to do quality animation. This book will help you achieve that knowledge.

The third level and highest level is Wisdom. This is the ability to take your knowledge and use it for good – to change people's lives for the better. This book can give you a foundation and instill in you the desire. The path to wisdom is usually traveled alone.

fig.7-85

QUOTES

"I can teach you, but only you can learn."
Lao-tzu (c.604-531 B.C.)[5]

"The greatest misfortune is when theory outstrips performance."
Michelangelo Buonarroti (1475-1564)[6]

"The best education is one that prepares you not for your first job but your last job."
Anonymous

"As long as your last job is not your first job."
The Author

"Animation has only two limits: exhaustion and your imagination."
The Author

"Where is the wisdom we have lost in knowledge?
Where is the knowledge we have lost in information?"
T.S. Eliot – Choruses from "The Rock"[7]

---

5. I was unable to find a source for this quote.
6. also attributed to Leonardo Da Vinci
7. T. S. Eliot." BrainyQuote.com. Xplore, 2016. 5 August 2016.

fig.7-61

CHAPTER 1

IDEA[1]

"Until you go too far, you don't know how far you can go."

Tex Avery[2]

"What interests me most in the production of animated film is that the person who creates it is the only one who can express what he feels, like a painter."

Animator Kihachiro Kawamoto[3]

"All true creation is a thing born of nothing."

Artist Paul Klee[4]

What Is an Idea?

Before the storyboard comes the idea. A quality idea is the most important part of your film. A simple formula is: good idea = a good film; bad idea = a bad film; no idea = a waste of film. Not only do you need a good idea to make a good film, but also, for the ease of production, your idea must be clear to you before starting the film. By idea, I mean the mental concept that is the creative core of your film. I prefer to use the word "idea" to encompass the entire range of

---

1. As mentioned in the Acknowledgements, the author completed the manuscript sometime around 2007 and the text has not been updated for accuracy. All statements reflect the belief of the author at the time of authorship and may, or may not, reflect current reality.
2. I was unable to find a source of this quote.
3. I was unable to find a source of this quote.
4. I was unable to find a source of this quote.

animation, from narrative to experimental. Other terms are more closely associated with the narrative form alone. Here are definitions of some of the terms that often overlap with "idea:"

Concept. A generalized idea of a thing or class of things.
Content. The substance of the film as opposed to the style of it. What the film is about.
Story. The sequence of events in the film that express the idea, content, concept, theme and moral.
Premise. The basis or basic argument for your film.
Theme. The topic or subject of your film and how you treat that subject. It should unify the entire film.
Moral. The message you want your audience to take away with them after seeing your film.

If your idea is character driven, narrative with character or animation narrative with strong character, then the character is part of the idea and just as important. The character must connect with the audience for the idea to be totally successful; the character has to pull in the audience. The audience must believe in and relate with the character or characters. Disney called this appeal. Appeal can be just as important for the antagonist as the protagonist. How many films owe much of their success to the evil character? The stepmother in *Snow White* comes to mind. The character can be the idea.

The idea can start with a question. In *WALL-E,* Pixar (2008), that question was reported to have been, "What if humanity left the Earth but forgot to turn the last robot off?" The full idea was worked out in the script. "Irrational love defeats life's programming" was the theme according to the writer/director, Andrew Stanton.[5] "What If" can be a good way to get an idea.

Reading the idea (concepts, content, stories, premises, themes, morals) behind any film is a good exercise because it can reveal the clarity and quality of the filmmaker's original idea. I can speak with complete assurance only about the ideas behind my films. In the examples that follow, I have used the filmmakers' description of their films, or my own and others' readings of them:

The Road Runner and Wile E. Coyote series, Chuck Jones, (fig. 2-40), Warner Brothers, 1949-1964. According to its director, Chuck Jones, the idea behind the series was to do a silent parody of chase cartoons. Later, when he developed the Coyote's character to carry the idea, Chuck used this quote from George Santayana to explain his character: "A fanatic is someone who redoubles his effort when he has forgotten his aim."

Daffy's Southern Exposure (Daffy Duck) (fig. 1-1), by Norm McCabe, 1942. Chuck Jones's analysis of McCabe's idea was a refusal to fly south. In other words, we all want to be individualists, especially Daffy (fig. 1-1).

---

5. Personal communication to the author?

In their book, *Disney Animation: The Illusion of Life*, Frank Thomas and Ollie Johnston (fig. 2-53) describe the story idea for *Dumbo*: "A baby elephant is considered a freak because of his enormous ears, until an enterprising mouse discovers a way to turn this liability into a startling asset."[6] More simply put, if you find the right circumstances or have the right attitude, what appears to be a negative can be turned into a positive.

Tom and Jerry, Tweety and Sylvester and *Bugs Bunny* (fig. 2-40). MGM and Warner Brothers, 1940s-present, various directors. My reading of the idea behind these three theatrical series is: By sheer cunning, the small, the weak and appealing defeat the big and strong.

Allegretto, Oskar Fischinger, German, 1936. A typical example of his work. Fischinger used the term "Absolute Animation" to describe his approach. By "absolute," he meant animation reduced to the absolute essentials of non-representational movement and form, as in modern abstract painting. Beauty without narrative.

Begone Dull Care, Norman McLaren, NFB, Canada, 1949. McLaren reduced animation to what he considered its essentials by drawing directly onto the clear film. The idea was that all you need is an artist and a little celluloid film to do animation.

Snow White, 1937; *Pinocchio*, 1940; *Dumbo*, 1941; *Bambi*, 1942; *Sleeping Beauty*, 1959; *Cinderella,* 1950 - In Disney's early features, the event that sets the film in motion is the loss or absence of the mother figure: a powerful theme in children's literature, perhaps the most powerful fear in a young child's mind.

Examples of the ideas behind my films:

Claude (1963). When the parents turn off the child, the child will turn off the parents (fig. 1-2). *God is Dog Spelled Backwards (1967)*. A Structuralist experiment in what is the shortest time the eye and mind can recognize continuously projected images. One-twelfth of a second or a new image every two frames is the answer — or in a humorous vein, if I took the Western World's greatest images with its greatest music, I should have the Western World's greatest film (fig. 1-3). *No Idea* (2000). You can be sitting on a great idea, but you will not accept it because you do not recognize any new ideas (fig. 1-4).[7]

When the idea for a film is written down, it should be no more than one or two sentences. Preston Sturges, the great live-action director from the 1930s and 1940s, would read a script only if it conformed to a certain format. The first page presented the title. If Sturges liked it, he then turned to the second page, which contained the idea for the film in a single sentence. If he liked the idea, he went on to the third page, containing a paragraph that elaborated

---

6. I am assuming the author is referring to Frank Thomas and Ollie Johnston. *Disney Animation: The Illusion of Life.* Abbeville Press, 1981. I cannot locate this quote in the book, however.

7. To listen to the author talk about these films, please go to http://danmclaughlin.info/talk.html. You can also purchase these films for your viewing pleasure from the DVD *11 Films by Dan McLaughlin* (2004), Pyramid Media.

the idea. Only after Sturges had read and liked the first three pages would he read the entire script. Similarly, in a pitch session, where you are trying to sell an animated series or feature to potential backers, you begin by telling them very succinctly the idea. The idea is the concept of the film that you can say in one sentence.

Many of the ideas behind film and TV today are formulaic ideas. For example, the tried and true "Boy meets Girl, Boy loses Girl, Boy gets Girl." Formulaic ideas will be discussed in the next chapter. But teaching the formulae, they are easy enough to learn, only teaches you to make formulae films. Which becomes boring. It is much better to make original films from original ideas.

A Question of Creativity

Where do quality ideas come from? In the Greek and Roman worlds, from Plato and Aristotle respectively, creativity was attributed to inspiration or imitation. In Western society, the source of inspiration has been attributed at various times to the gods, God, the muses, the subconscious, the universal unconscious, the zeitgeist, abuse of substances, impending deadlines, and so it goes. The artist is basically a telephone waiting for inspiration to call with a creative message to pass along to the rest of us. But in his *Poetics*, Aristotle allowed for the genius within -- creativity that comes from within, in other words. That is, some artists are more talented than others in their imitation of nature. This point of view, putting the individual at the center of existence, has been especially important in the last 500 years of Western society. The artist's inner turmoil and catastrophes, his ever-evolving states of mind, provide a source for creative outpouring in the arts. His theories of art, politics, religion or anything else, for that matter, influence the artist's vision. You don't have to specify a single source of creativity. Your job is to recognize a good idea.

A good idea often bursts upon you. This can be referred to as the "ah so" or "click" moment. As in: "Ah, so that is the answer." Or: "Click, that's it." The moment can be the genesis of an original concept or a solution to an existing dilemma. There is a story that Jack Warner once told a screenwriter named John Huston that he could direct the movie *The Maltese Falcon* if he could come up with a script by the next morning. Several attempts had already been made to turn Dashiell Hammett's 1929 mystery novel into a screenplay, and all had failed. How to come up with a script? Then the "click:" Huston called in his secretary and told her to hire as many people as needed to take all the dialogue in the book (and only the dialogue), put it into script form, and have it done by the next morning. She did; Huston gave the script to Warner; he loved it; and the next day John Huston became director of *The Maltese Falcon* (1941). Huston also had the good sense to give the lead role of Sam Spade to a former dancer with a slight lisp and a funny name.[8]

In the last analysis, creativity may *be* a mystery, and for many artists, discussion of it is taboo because they believe they will jinx the creative process by examining it too closely. But understanding, at least a little, may help you unlock your creative juices. Finding out how to be creative allows you to be more creative.

Inspiration can be a definite high that I hope readers of this book have experienced and are now ready to put into concrete form. But there is an old saying that art is 1 percent inspiration and 99 percent perspiration. I would amend that saying and claim that art is 10 percent inspiration and 90 percent perspiration. Constantly seek inspiration, but keep moving forward with analysis and deduction and inspiration will come.

Why do you need both inspiration and rational deductive thought to do an animated film? Because each contributes something the other does not. Inspiration can reveal new, surprising, exciting, original perspectives. But it can desert you at any time. Though it is a major contributor at the beginning of your film and can be fun, during the long course of production, inspiration is unpredictable and fleeting. Rational thought is more reliable. It can solve problems, as well as give a structure and schedule to your work. Backed by the discipline and principles of animation, rational thought allows you to move forward. It will get you through the long haul, the 8- to 16-hour days.

A Matter of Intuition

Why is Wallace in *Wallace and Gromit* mad about cheese? Is it because cheese just seems right for the character? And what if the moon was really made of cheese? Why is "Meep, Meep" the right sound for the Road Runner? (Actually, as Jones and the other members of the creative team were sitting around one day discussing the need for the Road Runner to have some sort of voice, Paul Julian, a background artist at the studio, was coming down the hall outside with a large stack of backgrounds in his arms. Because he could not see around them, he was going 'beep beep' to warn people to stay out of his way. The boys in the office heard this and Meep Meep was born.)[9] Intuition can provide such small, unexplained moments of perception. Unlike inspiration, it is a hunch, a sixth sense about something. Unlike rational thought, it does not provide an explanation for artistic choices that you make. When asked why, you reply simply, "I just like it that way." That's because intuition is counter-analytical. I caution you that relying on intuition alone can prove to be a weakness. I have seen students overuse it to justify their choices. That being said, if you have a strong feeling or hunch, go with it. You won't be happy if you don't, and if you aren't happy your work will suffer. At any

---

8. Again, I don't know where he got this story.
9. I assume this was a personal communication to the author.

point in the production process, all things being equal, intuition can help you on your way.

The same goes for taste. You like blue and you don't like red, so you choose blue. You like certain shapes. Taste is clearly allied to personal psychology.

Emerging Ideas

An idea can emerge fully blown. I call this working from the inside out. You have to expand the essential idea from the innermost core. When Michelangelo was furiously putting hammer to chisel, trying to release David from the marble, he had to know what he wanted. It would be impossible to change the position of David's hand or the tilt of his head after it was set in stone. But an idea also can emerge from a fragmented view of something wonderful. To realize it fully, you have to discover it step by step, through process. I call this working from the outside in. You have to keep molding, stripping and changing the outside until you get to the core. You find your complete idea through manipulation of the medium. That's what Picasso did in his later periods. He would start with a blank canvas and let the painting emerge, working from the outside in.

If you're in the tradition of Picasso, you'll have to rethink your creative process when you enter animation. Michelangelo provides a better model. In animation, you should have the complete idea by the end of the storyboard stage (fig. 2-8). Constantly revising images during the production stage would waste an inordinate amount of time and money, resulting in personal frustration and confusion. There are exceptions, of course. James Whitney took seven years experimenting and working through the production stage to complete his experimental animated film *Lapis (1966)*. And it was worth it. Whitney was committed to being an independent artist, and was quite willing to make the sacrifice of time and effort. However, in the traditional animation process, independent or commercial, the sooner you have your complete idea, the better off you will be.

At the very beginning, you should express your idea quickly in either a visual or written form. If in a written form, the visuals should be introduced as soon as possible. Animation is the on-screen performance of the created image. Small, rough drawings to get the idea down are called "thumbnails," and I recommend that you do many of them. Then start putting the thumbnails into a film structure, using rectangular panels with any dialogue or narration written below. You are now in the "storyboard" phase.[10]

In some forms of animation, where the concept and character design already exist and the action is mainly dialogue-driven (a TV series with a 'bible', for example), a script is written before the visuals of the storyboard. The format of writing an animation script for a TV series is discussed in Addendum Two.

---

10. To be discussed at great length in Chapter 2, Storyboards.

The Right Environment for Coming Up With Good Ideas

Some people think most creatively when they wake up in the morning. Others take hot showers, walk on the beach, write down random thoughts, research a specific area in depth, browse through libraries, bounce ideas off another person or group to get feedback (talking it over with a friend you respect is one of the best ways), get in the creative environment of a concert, poetry reading, art gallery or museum, or simply people-watch. When Disney handed out a new assignment, he would give the artist the next day off to think about the assignment in a relaxed and stress-free environment. Maybe a hike in the mountains would do the trick, or a visit to the zoo, drawing the animals, or just sitting around and staring at the wall. The old way of just sitting down and working on coming up with an idea, drawing and writing until you got it, still works. You will always be coming up with ideas during production, but make sure they are good ones before you use them.

A cautionary note here. If you think you get your best ideas when you're in an altered state, you're sure to be disappointed when you return to normal. The novelist and screenwriter Curt Siodmak (*Donovan's Brain,* 1953) told me this story. He was searching for an alternative to hard work and heard that drugs were the answer. So he locked himself in his studio, put a tall stack of blank paper next to his typewriter and ingested a fair amount of opium. Suddenly he had the world's greatest novel in his head. He knew the truth. Furiously, he typed through the night until the stack of paper was gone and then, exhausted, he fell asleep. Siodmak awoke hours later and rushed to the typewriter. The stack of paper was untouched, and the original single sheet was still in the typewriter. These words were written on it: "Life Is A Green Banana."

The most popular way to get an idea in the entertainment industry is to steal it. Dorothy Parker once observed cynically: "The only 'ism' Hollywood believes in is plagiarism."[11] It often results in a pale imitation, inevitable perhaps in a situation where turnover is rapid and the pressure is intense. How many times have Tex Avery's best gags been used by other people (fig. 1-7)? Which came first, *The Honeymooners* or *The Flintstones*? When my film, *Dog is God Spelled Backwards* (fig.1-3) was first shown on *The Glenn Campbell Summer Show* in 1968, kinestasis, the technique I invented, inspired a host of imitations that continue to this day. Be prepared for theft of creative output.

When is stealing not stealing? When it is called "paying homage to." The distinction is a difficult case to prove, as ongoing lawsuits in the industry attest. Still, there are films that deliberately evoke another filmmaker's work, and everyone is supposed to appreciate the reference. And it can be argued that, when you are setting out, the influence of another's style or approach can prove an educational experience. Just as a novice artist during the Renaissance was apprenticed to an established artist to learn his techniques, you can study your favorite animator's films, find out how and why they succeed, discover what you like,

11. Found this one. http://www.quotationspage.com/quote/32051.html

then incorporate your observations into your developing work.

The other side of the coin is how to protect your ideas. They cannot be copyrighted. Only the form of expression of an idea is protected. (See Addendum One (fig. add 1-1) on copyright and Chapter 12 Making a Living, the section on Ethics.) But you first must have an idea before someone can steal it.

PROBLEM SOLVING

John Dewey, the philosopher of education, created a six-step problem-solving method he called "reflective thinking." His method can be useful in the preliminary stage of developing your idea in animation. This analytical method can also be used when your idea is at the storyboard stage or in any other part of production:

- Define the problem by asking key questions. For example:

    What is the film about?

    What do I want to say with this film?

    Why am I making this film?

- Clarify the idea. Do further research and analysis.

- Develop possible solutions. Make lists. Do thumbnails (fig. 2-1) (small rough drawings). Use specific problem-solving techniques (see below).

- Choose the best possible solution and do a rough storyboard (fig.2-9).

- Test this solution. Test this board by first reviewing it yourself. Imagine it as a finished film. Be critical and find where it is weak. Then show it to others and get their reactions. Ascertain which of their reactions is most useful. Decide if the storyboard is good.

- If you are not satisfied, start over.

Other techniques that can be used to clarify a problem or develop a solution are:

- Make a list of all of the objectives of your film. Then rank them in order, making sure that the events in your board reflect the order of their importance.

- Make a list of points of information the audience needs to understand your film (fig. 2-63). Then, within the time frame of the film, do a graph of the release of this information to the audience. Use the graph to make sure all your story-points are released at the proper time. Do not have all the information at the beginning or at the end. That will produce a flat and boring film. Think of yourself as a magician revealing one story-point after another to an amazed audience.

- Research how others have approached similar problems. This usually means looking at other films. Use them as inspiration. Analyze and see what they did wrong or right so you can apply that knowledge to your film.

- Try out any of these different exercises on your idea:
    Use different combinations of people, places and time.
    Reverse gender.
    Substitute a dog for a man, the future for now.
    Change the levels of a character's intelligence.
    Put in silly ideas.
    Make fun of your idea.
    Break everything down into its basic elements and see if you can recombine them.
    Spit out ten or twenty ideas as fast as you can.
    Make the representational art abstract, or, if the art is abstract, make it representational.
    Free associate with your friends; brainstorm with people who know animation. Act it out; perform it.
    Take a rest; take a break.
    Try something different. Felix Salten, the Austrian author of *Bambi (1942)*, also wrote the immensely popular adult erotic novel *The Memoirs of Josephine Mutzenbacher*.

- Try shaping your idea as:
    an analogy - which is showing a similarity between two different things
    a metaphor - a figure of speech in which one idea or object is substituted for another (for example, the life of a carrot becomes a metaphor for human life)
    a parody - which is imitating the style of another work for comic effect or ridicule
    a parable - a story that contains a moral
    a satire - a work where the vices, follies, stupidities, abuses, etc. of human nature are held up to ridicule, contempt, sarcasm or irony
    irony - where a deliberate contrast is made between apparent and intended meaning for humorous effect (for example, "I really can't watch grass growing because it is too exciting")
    a drama, a comedy, a farce, an absurdist statement, an existential melodrama (fig. 1-5).

- Make the storyboard as short as possible. Just put down the basic idea: KISS, or keep it simple, stupid. Then add the embellishments you need to interest an audience.

- Show your board to another person and have that person tell a third person. Then have the third person tell you his or her version of your board and see how closely it resembles your original. Did you get your main points across?

- Always find a creative solution to a technical problem. This applies to all aspects of animation production. But, particularly in the early stage of developing your idea, do not let technical considerations, such as lack of resources, inhibit you. Create a way to do your idea without resources. Often it will make a better film.

- Do you really believe in your idea? Are you ready to fight for it? You must believe and fully commit to your idea. If not, it will be a hard film to make.

Bear in mind that there are three audiences involved in a work and that they all want something different. The first audience is the one that looks at it first, the creator or creators, who want to make a great film and achieve fame, fortune, love and personal satisfaction. The second audience has a personal or economic interest in the film and includes distributors, critics, exhibitors, marketing people, computer hardware and software companies, popcorn sellers, ticket-takers and DVD makers. (Filmmakers provide an income for thousands.) The third audience is the public or viewing audience, and what this audience wants or needs has long been debated: Is it entertainment, morality, escapism, beauty, catharsis, idealism or the filmmaker's blood? As you are developing your idea, you want to keep in mind the viewing audience and what you want it to think and feel.

When to Stop

There is an old story that it takes two people to create: one to sit at the piano and compose and the other to hit the composer on the head with a large hammer the second the work is done. Knowing the second your idea is complete is essential. It's easy to mistrust an idea and keep adding and changing until you turn it into an unholy mess.

When Not to Stop

It is very easy to stop before you have an ending or closure. But you mustn't; just don't let the film stop without closure. An idea can have a good opening without an ending. For years, I have carried around an idea about a little man named Harry who, one day, in the mail, gets the answer to all the world's problems. Unfortunately, I never got the answer myself on how to end his story and I never made the film (fig. 1-6). A good opening idea without an ending is like a single-panel cartoon without a punch line below.

If you don't have the ending now, it is very hard to get a good one during production. Do not leave the idea stage until you have an ending that completely realizes your idea.

QUALITY

The quality or excellence of your idea will determine the quality or excellence of your film. Every form of art or entertainment possesses varying degrees of quality. Classical music can be good or bad; so can rock, jazz and all other forms of music. Go to museums, concert halls, the theater, library and movie house, where you will find the best of the best examples that possess the highest moral as well as aesthetic quality. Ultimately, as artist and creator of your own film, you are the arbitrator. I remember once an old high school friend looked at one of my paintings and said, "Dan, I have to tell you this, I don't like your painting." I replied, "That's perfectly all right, Gordon, because it wasn't painted for you."[12] The founder of the UCLA Animation Workshop and a former Disney animator, Bill Shull, used to say, "Everybody likes their own brand of corn."

When your work is judged in public, don't let other people tell you what is good or bad. Often, their opinions are contradictory. Listen to them if they can help you, but never let them judge the entire work. A two-time Academy Award winner for best supporting actor, Thomas Mitchell, once said to me: "You can't believe them when they tell you you are good because then you have to believe them when they tell you you are bad."[13]

ANIMATION IDEAS VS. LIVE ACTION IDEAS

Animation is not live action. I have become famous for a comment I often make at the end of a student's storyboard presentation. "Shoot it in live action. It would probably be cheaper, quicker and more group fun." What I mean is, animation and live action are two different realities. If you don't use the special unique strengths and characteristics of animation and just copy live action, there's a 99 percent chance you will waste film.

Narrative is the most common form in animation, and it shares with live action the same narrative techniques: the continuity of storyline and editing (cutting, dissolves, wipes, fade-ins and –outs). There *are* at least two forms of narrative particularly suited to animation: bringing inanimate objects to life such as the toys in *Toy Story*, and giving animals human characteristics such as Bugs Bunny (fig.2-24), Daffy Duck (figs. 1-1, 2-24), Mickey Mouse, Donald Duck, among many others.

Following a long tradition in the literature of satire that is too disturbing for live action, human characters may be animated, as in the TV series *The Simpsons* or *South Park*. The distancing from reality that is part of animation allows the audience to accept comments on the human condition that would be unacceptable in live action. If live-action film is one step away from reality, the animated film is two steps away. This natural distancing makes art the main ingredient in the work.

Caroline Leaf's film *The Street* (taken from a well-known short story by Mordecai Richler, 1976) makes its own unique artistic contribution to the narrative. Because the images were painted

12. Sorry, I don't know who Gordon was.
13. This story I remember the author telling.

on glass while being shot, frame by frame, they metamorphose into one other. The flow of the narrative is continuous. The concept's complex. The art is beautiful.

Animation and Live Action Together

Since the early days of film, animation has incorporated live-action. In Disney's *Little Alice* series (1924), a real little girl interacts with the animation. And predominantly live action films have incorporated animation. *The Lost World* (1925) uses stop motion dinosaurs. Today, it is common for the line between live action and animation to be blurred, resulting in a new genre, a hybrid film. *Who Framed Roger Rabbit* (1988) is a good example.

If you plan to use live action in your film and you do not have a lot of live-action experience, get the best script, live-action director and actors that you can find. This is just what live-action producers would do if they were going to use animation in their film. Make sure that your reason for combining animation and live action is a solid one.

THE THREE SPHERES OF CREATIVITY

All animators should choose where to work and create. Not knowing your role can lead to frustration. There are three major areas in which you can be creative:

- You can be part of a larger whole (an ensemble) as an actor, musician or, in the traditional classifications of animation, as an animator, layout artist, character designer, background artist, etc. You are creative within the circumscribed role that you play.

- You create the overall structure for ensemble performance. Shakespeare wrote plays for a company of actors to perform. Beethoven composed symphonies for chamber groups and orchestras to play. There are no direct parallels to these roles in animation, but a studio, especially the early Disney studio, functioned as an ensemble and Walt was composer/playwright.

- You work alone, creating and doing the whole ball of wax, as Yeats, Cezanne and Joyce did in poetry, painting and literature. In animation, this kind of individual artist has become legendary: Norman McLaren, the filmmaker who started the animation unit of the National Film Board of Canada; Oskar Fischinger, the independent abstract animator, who worked in Germany and the United States; Frédéric Back, who made independent animated films for Radio Canada, the French arm of the national public broadcasting system; Jan Svankmajer, the Czechoslovakian Surrealist stop motion animator; James Whitney, independent American filmmaker . . . and maybe you in the future (fig. 6-16).

Limits

Normally, when you start an animated film, two avenues are open to you. You can make either an independent or a sponsored film. If you become an independent, you will experience few or no limits to your creativity. But you will have to concern yourself with money. Shirley Clarke, who was a leading independent filmmaker (*The Connection* (1961), *Portrait of Jason* (1967), used to say, if you want to make independent films, you have to be born rich or marry rich.[14] Clarke belonged in both categories. Other less-fortunate filmmakers have to hold down a second job, put a second mortgage on their house, teach, beg or starve in a garret. But, then, again, they did get to make their own films.

The more traveled path for an animator is that of the sponsored film (which I refer to generally as the "Hollywood" film). It comes with limits, especially on choice of idea or quality of work. In Hollywood, quality simply means a box-office hit, money means on budget and time means on schedule. You'll be lucky to achieve even one of the above. They tend to cancel each other out. Also, you can run into personal crassness and commercialism that can ruin the best intentions. I have always liked the story of the producer who, at the beginning of the Second World War, called Tex Avery (*Bugs Bunny, Daffy Duck*) into his office. Tex (fig. 1-7) had been doing films that cast Hitler in a negative manner (as only Tex could do). The producer told Tex not to do any more films that would "make Mr. Hitler mad, as we don't know who is going to win the war, do we?" (fig. 1-7) [15]

In the Hollywood film, the premise is usually given to you. You will have to be creative in turning someone else's good or bad idea into a quality storyboard and film. In this case, the problem-solving techniques that I outlined earlier in the chapter can come in handy. Bob Kurtz, a well-respected director of animated commercials, told me that his job was "to steal a good film" from the sponsor and ad agency. He described himself as a "Ninja animator."

RANDOM THOUGHTS

The important thing about having an idea is that it gives you direction and purpose in your work. You can have funny ideas (fig. 2-16), visual ideas, conceptual ideas, verbal ideas, money-making ideas, sexy ideas, erotic ideas, good ideas, bad ideas, emotional ideas, big ideas, little ideas, universal ideas, local ideas, cosmic ideas, political ideas (fig. 1-8), practical ideas, moral ideas, ethnic ideas, happy ideas, sad ideas, evil ideas, noble ideas, religious ideas, new ideas, old ideas, spiritual ideas, hateful ideas, loving ideas, negative ideas, scientific ideas,

---

14. I'm guessing as this is something she said to him, or what he remembers her saying to him.
15. Again, I have no idea where this story came from.

educational ideas (fig. 2-52), positive ideas, among a whole host of others. Ideas are fun and can lead to more ideas.

When people say there's nothing new under the sun, it usually means these people have never had any new ideas. Work on the problem, and the ideas will come.

If you have more than one idea and you have no preference, do the easiest. My personal belief is that if your idea does not make a positive statement about life, it should not be done.

What viewers take away from your film may not be what you intended. You cannot control response. If they love your film for the wrong reasons, do not mention your original idea. At least they got something out of your film.

There's no substitute for genius. Back in the '80's, when Artificial Intelligence was the hope of the future, I was invited to a conference on AI at the Massachusetts Institute of Technology. The conference sponsors were interested in developing AI programs for creating funny cartoons, and so they invited me to lecture on what made Bugs Bunny funny. They were expecting a formula. But when I stood up to speak, I announced, "What makes Bugs Bunny funny is very simple! It's two words: Tex Avery." I was never invited back.

(fig. 5-40)

OTHERS WHO HAD THOUGHTS ON CREATIVITY:

"Every act of creation is first of all an act of destruction."
Picasso[16]

But is an act of destruction an act of creation? Think about it.
The Author

"The vision of Christ that thou dost see
Is my vision's greatest enemy...
Thine is the friend of all mankind
Mine speaks in parables to the blind."
William Blake[17]

In other words, do not accept the obvious. The individual artist finds a unique vision.
The Author

"Love and patience are the elements to create miracles."
Frédéric Back, Animator [18]

Don't believe in miracles -- rely on them.
The Author

16. "Pablo Picasso." BrainyQuote.com. Explore Inc., 2016. 5 August 2016.

17. Blake, William. "58. The Everlasting Gospel." Bartleby.com. n.d.Web.

18. I was unable to find a source of this quote.

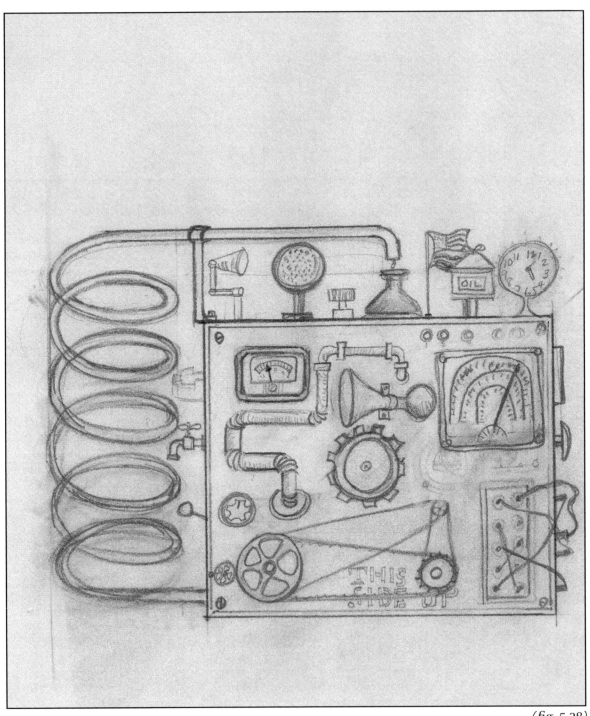

(*fig. 5-28*)

CHAPTER 2

Courtesy of the Dan F. McLaughlin, Jr. Collection

STORYBOARDS[1]

"The opera ain't over till the fat lady sings."
Anonymous

A storyboard is the creative idea in its visual form. The created images and verbal elements are put down in a structured format. The storyboard is the starting point of the production process, the first tangible and most important step in the making of an animated film.

The reasons you need a storyboard are:
- To create the visuals of your idea.
- To create the basic story structure with the shot and editing choices before layout.
- To start the timing and the style of your film, including the character design.
- To put your sound elements down, particularly dialogue.
- To keep the cost and time of production down and quality high.
- And most important, to make sure that your idea is presented in the clearest and most effective way possible.

We will first discuss the physical and technical, and then the content elements of the storyboard.

---

1. As mentioned in the Acknowledgements, the author completed the manuscript sometime around 2007 and the text has not been updated for accuracy. All statements reflect the belief of the author at the time of authorship and may, or may not, reflect current reality.

TECHNICAL INFORMATION

Physical Description

Storyboards start out as "thumbnails," small rough drawings that quickly capture your ideas on paper (fig. 2-1). Usually, the drawings are done on individual pieces of paper, rectangles with a ratio of 4:3. This prepares them for screen ratio: 1.33 horizontal to 1 vertical. Use the horizontal format (in painting called "landscape format"). Currently, this format is common to all film, though projection ratios may vary from wide screen (1.85:1) to cinemascope (2.35:1 or 2.55:1) to high definition (16:9) (fig. 2-2).

You can buy storyboard pads that are comprised of ready-made, detachable rectangles (fig. 2-3). Or you can make your own sheets of drawn rectangles, Xerox and then cut out the rectangles as needed (fig. 2-4). You can also quarter regular-size animation paper (fig. 2-5). Some studios, to save time later in layout do their storyboard panels on regular-size animation paper. I find it handy to use 5x3 index cards (fig. 2-6), which are close enough to the required 4x3 format.

Dialogue or narration can be written on the bottom of the rectangles--now referred to as panels--or contained in smaller separate panels below. Similarly, you can put music and sound information on or below the panels. Camera movements can be handled in the same manner (fig. 2-7).

Traditionally, storyboard panels are tacked with pushpins to a fairly large cork or tack board. This arrangement allows you to work in a non-linear way. You can replace or rearrange panels in any way until you have the final storyboard (fig. 2-8). It allows you, if the film is short, to step back and assess the entire film. If the film is feature-length, you can accomplish this a major sequence at a time. This is very helpful, as it is always hard to judge a storyboard as an entire film.

Graphite pencils, markers and blue pencils are the essential tools. Until Eberhard Faber stopped making the Blackwing 602, it was the standard pencil for all anima-tion (fig. 11-2). Since a Blackwing 602 isn't available anymore, a #2 yellow pencil will do. But try different pencils until you find one you like. Other tools include erasers, scissors, rubber cement, transparent rulers, copy machines, etc. Color is optional in the storyboard stage unless it is essential to your idea. Drawings should be kept simple through-out the storyboard process (fig. 2-9). Don't waste time on details.

If your story is character-driven, pin "model sheets" of the main characters at the end of the storyboard (fig. 5-3). Model sheets are three drawings of the full-body character(s), in poses three-quarter front, side and three-quarter rear. These can be detailed and in color. This way you do not have to spend time drawing the fully detailed character for each panel. To demon-strate what the final visual effect will be, pin up one or more pieces of finished art, including background, with the storyboard.

Sometimes it is easier to draw the characters or action first, and then place a frame around them. If the film is to be done in full animation, the character in the storyboard must be drawn in full (action poses), not limited, animation poses, otherwise the board will not reflect that the film is to be done in full animation.

It is a good idea to execute your early drawings in blue pencil. By doing so, you are free to experiment, make mistakes and save paper because you can go over the drawings with a graphite pencil for any final changes (fig. 2-10). A board is done and redone until you are satisfied, or run out of time. For his feature *Peter Pan,* Walt Disney had his story people produce a board a year for seven years before they gave him one that he liked. He had a special attachment to the story. As a boy, Walt played Peter Pan in a production that he and his brother Roy mounted in their parents' barn. Roy rigged up a pulley and ropes so that Walt could fly over the audience. The rope broke in mid-flight, and Walt used to say that he was the only Peter Pan who really flew.[2]

A question commonly asked is: "How many panels make up a storyboard?" The answer to that question depends on how many shots you plan in your film. You need at least one panel for every shot, though sometimes more panels per shot are necessary for showing additional poses or actions (fig. 2-11).

The term "shot" and the term "scene" are used interchangeably. However, in animation, they have been defined historically in the following manner:

A *shot* is an isolated action that begins and ends either with a cut, a dissolve, a metamorphosis, animated effect, title card or fade-out/fade-in.

A *scene* is a series of shots over the same background. For instance, cutting from a long shot to a close-up or cutting between shots of two different characters with the same background would be a scene. A background change means a scene change.

A *sequence* has been understood historically to mean a series of scenes encompassing the same plot issue or conceptual concern.

For example, in Walt Disney's film *Pinocchio,* the *sequence* of Pinocchio's setting out for school and being diverted by J. Worthington Foulfellow (Honest John) and Gideon starts with a fade-in of a complex multiplane truck through the village to Geppetto's house. Then it cuts to a matching *shot* of the front porch of Geppetto's house. The door opens, and Geppetto and Pinocchio come out. Then we cut to a *scene* of eight shots that are cutting back and forth between the shoemaker and the puppet over the same background. The *scene* ends with Pinocchio leaving for school over a new background. The *sequence* ends with Pinocchio going off to a career in "show business."

---

2. I don't know the source of either of these stories.

Disney's early features had an average of 14 sequences; the sequences in *Pinocchio* could be broken down this way.

1. Introduction. Jiminy Cricket, inside Geppetto's house, Pinocchio as puppet.
2. Blue fairy brings Pinocchio to life, Geppetto reacts happily.
3. Pinocchio goes to school and is waylaid by Honest John and Gideon.
4. Performs in Stromboli's puppet show.
5. Geppetto goes to find Pinocchio.
6. Stromboli locks Pinocchio in birdcage.
7. Jiminy finds Pinocchio imprisoned. Blue fairy releases Pinocchio.
8. Coachman, Honest John and Gideon confer.
9. On the way home, Pinocchio is convinced by Honest John to go to Pleasure Island.
10. Pleasure Island. Boys turn into donkeys. Pinocchio escapes.
11. Message from Blue fairy that Monstro the Whale has swallowed Geppetto.
12. Pinocchio and Jiminy go to save Geppetto.
13. Pinocchio finds Monstro the Whale and saves Geppetto.
14. Blue fairy makes Pinocchio a real boy for he has been "Brave, Truthful and Unselfish." End.

The number of panels of your storyboard should give a rough estimate of the timing of the film. If one shot represents a large percentage of the film, you should repeat the same drawing on the board to keep the timing accurate. At the same time, if there is a shot where the character is very active, do some extra panels to show the action rather than explaining it. As a point of reference, there are approximately 270 panels for a 22-minute children's TV program. The essential rule is that there are enough panels so that nothing important is left out.

At this stage, the board, usually rough, is called a "production board," and it can be shown to the production crew (writers, directors, composers, etc.) for input. If clients are involved, you should redo the production board in the most attractive and compelling manner possible for their viewing. Then it becomes known as a "presentation board" (fig. 2-12). According to legend, as a presentation strategy for new shows they were trying to sell to the network, the production team at Hanna Barbera studio covered the floor of the meeting room with painted cels. This forced network executives to walk on the artwork and think about it. They did, and they bought all the shows.

Design in the Storyboard

Visual design will be discussed fully in Chapter Seven, Layout. Some aspects of design are minimized in the storyboard process. Color, especially in production boards, is one such area except when color is critical to the content (fig. 5-24). Though in the storyboard stage, you could select the color scheme for your entire film by doing a flowchart. For example, your film could start with cool blues and greens and gradually introduce warm colors to reflect more intense emotions, culminating in an ending (fig. 2-63). The color flowchart could be used along with the flowchart for the center of interest to gauge the effectiveness of your film.

However, when designing your storyboard, certain design elements should be considered. They are:

- The framing of the shot by the camera.
- The composition of the shot.
- The editing or the ordering of all the shots. In animation, you edit your film before you shoot your film, although digital gives you choices later in the production.

The Framing of the Shot by the Camera

The camera can be fixed or mobile. Often, first-time animators unconsciously think of themselves in the theater, sitting in a specified seat in front of a proscenium stage. They don't move around in their imagination. Keep your camera fixed only if you have in mind a fixed viewer. But, if not, select different camera shots to express your more active vision. Perhaps use animation angles that are not rooted in reality. Animation shots are based on live-action techniques, but can go beyond them. For instance, you can locate the camera inside a character's head, peering out through the shape of an eye socket (fig. 2-13).

Here's an exercise you can do to learn the advantages of moving the camera. Your scene is of a cartoon man walking in the desert, dying of heat, with a buzzard circling overhead. If you present the scene in one, continuous medium long shot, it will lack emotion and interest. Instead, start with a master long shot of the man and the buzzard in the burning desert. Go to a medium shot of the buzzard looking down, then to a close-up of the man's face, expressing concern. Go back to the long shot. Cut to a close-up of the man's feet endlessly walking. Cut to his hands wiping his brow. Cut to a close-up of the hot sun shining down, then to a close-up of the buzzard. Go to a long shot of the man slowing down and staggering with the heat. Cut to his foot tripping over a rock. Cut to a moving POV shot of the ground rising up to meet his face as he falls. Dissolve to the man lying prostrate on the ground. Cut to a close-up of the buzzard, smiling, then looking surprised, Cut to the man holding a gun and firing. Cut to the man sitting in his den with the walls covered with mounted buzzards' heads. Moving the camera angle for each shot can maximize the impact.

Back to basic design of the storyboard. The camera frames these design elements in the shot: size, camera view, camera height and whether the space is 2D, 2½ D or 3D.

Size refers to the size of the main element(s) in the shot, with the human body as reference.

The live-action terms, also used in animation, describe the distance of the camera in relation to the subject.

Extreme close-up *(ECU):* A shot of part of a head, an eye for example. A dramatic shot (fig. 2-14).

Close-up (CU): A shot of the full head, to focus on a specific action or emotion (fig. 2-14).

Medium close-up (MCU): A shot of the head and upper body to the waist. Often used when two characters interact (fig. 2-14).

Medium (M): A full-body shot. When full-body action is required (fig. 2-14).

Medium long shot (MLS): The height of full body is no less than half the frame (fig. 2-14).

Long shot (LS): The full body is less than half of the frame. A master shot (fig. 2-14).

Extreme long shot (ELS): A shot of a city or the world. This is the really big picture (fig. 2-14).

Multiple shots (MS): Trucks and other movements of the camera that would cause the size to change within the shot (figs. 2-15, 5-38).

The tighter a film is shot, the more emphasis is placed on character or the action. Many beginning animators do not realize this and never use the power of the MCU, CU or ECU shots. Many directors use a master or establishing shot showing the location of everybody and everything essential when the story begins (fig. 2-16). The master shot provides a reference point for later scenes in the story.

The view of the camera is either:

- ***Objective,*** which is the view from the outside looking in (fig. 2-17).
- ***Subjective or point of view (POV),*** where the camera becomes a character in the scene (fig. 2-18). A dizzying roller-coaster ride from the perspective of the rider (the camera) is one example.

The height of the camera in relation to the subject is:

- ***High angle,*** the characters or objects are viewed from above (fig. 2-19).
- ***Level,*** the camera is at eye level (fig. 2-20).
- ***Low angle,*** the characters or objects are viewed from below (fig. 2-21).

Animation can be 2D, 2½D or 3D. If your film is 2D, you want characters or visuals to present one flat surface to the camera, so keep all surfaces in the art parallel to the camera. Characters in animation are often shown in profile, and the background is flat or non-existent. In the 1950s, this was the controlling aesthetic of UPA *(The Unicorn in the Garden, Gerald McBoing Boing)* (fig. 5-5).

To quickly achieve the effect of 3D, angle the camera so that two or more planes or surfaces are shown to the lens. In a room, for instance, show three planes--two walls and the floor (fig. 5-23). Characters have to be shown in at least three-quarter profile--a partial side and front view (fig. 5-6). To emphasize depth, have the line where the wall meets the floor angled differently from the bottom of the frame of the camera. Depth can also be suggested by overlapping characters or objects, adjusting their size in relation to the camera, or animating their movement toward or away from the camera. (A good trick is to draw a box and place the characters or objects inside it, making their scale relate to the depth of the box. Then erase the box (fig. 7-21). 2½D is a mixture of 2D and 3D techniques, which accounts for most hand-drawn animation.

The Composition of the Shot

According to *Webster's New World College Dictionary*, overall composition is an "arrangement of the parts of a work of art so as to form a unified, harmonious whole."[3] Is each shot designed to this end? If the film is a melodrama, does the shot reveal a dark and foreboding scene? If the film is a comedy, is the composition of the shot light, bright and crazy? If the film is about a single character, does the character cower as a Mr. Milquetoast or tower as the hero? Is he or she present in all or most of the scenes? Composition must support the idea behind your film, as well as illustrate its aesthetic.

At the storyboard stage, good composition anticipates the center of interest of every shot –where to focus the attention of the audience, in other words. The setting for the center of interest could be as basic as a clearing in a forest or a doorway (fig. 2-24). Making a simple design is usually the best approach.

Remember that shots should relate compositionally to each other visually, creating patterns. As an exercise, draw a series of panels showing the center of interest as a simple X. In each panel, draw arrows coming out of the X in the direction you want the action to go (fig. 2-25). You will see how the center of interest moves from shot to shot, through the transitions from shot to shot. Ward Kimball, one of the "Nine Old Men" of the Disney Studio, once demonstrated to me how much emotional impact can be achieved from a simple X. He made it spiral forward, getting bigger and bigger until it filled the screen. The early movies used this very pattern to capture the drama of sensational newspaper headlines.

Within the shot, the two basic elements of design are form and color (discussed in detail in Chapter 5). The components of form are line, size, balance, space and value.

The Editing

Editing is the sequential arrangement of the shots in your film and the transitions from one shot to another. In live action, you edit your film after your shoot. In animation, you edit your

---

3. Because the author used a 1996 *Webster's New College Dictionary,* (3rd edition, revised) in an earlier footnote, I am assuming that dictionary is the source of this quote as well. Unfortunately I have been unable to locate a copy of this dictionary to verify this wording.

film before you shoot. So you have to picture the entire film in your mindand decide your basic editing structure and strategy in your storyboard. With the introduction of digital technology, this situation may change as more editing is being done, especially fine-tuning and changes, during or after the shooting. (see chapter 5, Layout.)

Time (continuity) in editing narrative animation is handled in four ways:

- **Present time** - The events of the film are happening now and follow the logic of time moving forward. A shot that interrupts the normal passage of time results in a "jump cut," which is perceived visually. In one shot, a character opens a door and begins to exit. In the next shot, he's already on the other side of the door. The action is fragmented. Cordinate your shots if you want to preserve the illusion of real time.

- **Past time** - A flashback in time during the prologue to a film or during the film itself.

- **Future time** - A flash-forward in time.

- **Animation time** - Since animation creates its own time, it does not have to be logical. Animation time is used in narrative and experimental animation. In my film *Claude* (1963), the character wanders in and out of different times, without a sense of disruption or unreality (fig. 2-26).[4]

In the storyboard, start developing an editing style: fast cuts for action; slow long shots, with dissolves, for love scenes. For changing pace in an extended sequence, change rhythms from medium to slow or fast. Do a timeline of the flow of the film, showing these rhythms, that helps you control the pace of your film.

Visual transition is the change from one shot to the next. The following are the terms for visual transitions in animation:

Cut - Going from one shot directly to the next shot. This is the most common form of transition. A good rule is to cut on the action, any action, such as a hand movement, an eye blink, a fist striking. This helps to carry the flow and intensity of the film.

Dissolve - When one shot blends into the next shot. It is a fade-out combined with a fade-in. Commonly used to denote a passage of time or a change of location.

Fade-out, fade-in - When a shot fades to black (fade-out) and a new shot fades in from black (fade-in). Traditionally indicates a long passage of time or distance.

Wipe - A new shot comes in, wiping over the old shot.

Iris - A type of wipe that is circular. You iris in and out of black (fig. 2-27).

Optical Effect - For example, a swish pan. A swish pan is a movement done so fast that the visuals are blurred by the speed.

---

4. Two things. One, you can listen to the author talk about his films here http://danmclaughlin.info/talk.html Second, you can view *Claude* on the DVD *11 Films by Dan McLaughlin*.

Title Card - Written or animated. The dialogue in silent films is a good example (fig. 2-28).
Metamorphosis - The transition of one shot into another through ever-changing shapes.
Partial Transition - In animation, a transition can be accomplished just by changing backgrounds. You can dissolve out one background (city) and dissolve into another (country) behind your character as he's walking along.

Screen Direction

A character should always face or move in the same direction from shot to shot. Say that a character on the left side of the screen and facing right is talking to a character on the right facing left. They must stay on their respective sides of the screen when you cut back and forth between them. You apply the 180-degree rule, which is: You draw an imaginary line from the tip of one character's nose to the tip of the other character's nose and extend the line off the screen. This line is the 180-degree line (fig. 2-29). You can shoot from any angle you want on one side of this line, but on one side only, because if you alternate sides, the heads will flip-flop on the cut from one side to the other. Never cross the 180-degree line lest your audience get the characters confused or think they are not talking to each other. This rule also applies to a character leaving a shot. If she is moving from left to right and exits on screen right, she must re-enter on screen left. Otherwise the audience thinks the character has turned around or is a different character. Screen direction is often overlooked by people new to animation.

Keep direction consistent. A train going cross-country should always move from screen left or right. A convention of filmmaking is that a train traveling from left to right is going east and from right to left is going west (fig. 2-30, 2-31).

Sound

The three major areas of sound are voice, music and sound effects. In the storyboard stage, you need to know what kind of sound you want. Is the voice male or female, young or old, with a British or Southern accent, angry, happy or sad? Is the dialogue in dialogue or voice-over? Is the music original or already recorded? Is it classical, rock, jazz, folk, fast or slow? Are the sound effects in nature or an element in the music? Such questions should be asked at the very beginning. Sound must be part of your basic idea.

If you are working from a pre-existing soundtrack (a music video), all you have to do at this stage is roughly time out the track using some form of bar sheet (fig. 2-62). Later, for the actual production, you will need to time out the track carefully on exposure sheets (fig. 5-52). Listen to your track repeatedly. It can be influential in creating new images and ideas for your board.

Sound in animation is handled differently than sound in live action. In live action, sound is usually recorded at the same time as the action, and music and sound effects are added in post-production. In animation, any synchronous sound (synced to the picture) is recorded before the animation, so that the animator can match lips, body, and action to dialogue or music. This has been the method all over the world except in Japan, where animation is done before voice recording. The Japanese use generic lip positions so that different languages can be dubbed in for worldwide distribution.

Music and sound effects that don't have to be synced can be done either before or after animation. But it is not unusual to have the complete sound track (voice, music, effects) recorded and mixed before you animate. This is why it is important to make fundamental sound decisions at the storyboard stage. Since it is not limited by the visual, you can be very flexible and creative with sound. For example, the smacking of lips in a kiss can be heard as a loud explosion.

Sound can also aid in transitions. A voice says, "There's gold in them thar hills," before you cut to hills of gold. The music of the shot to come is played before the transition. The rattle of a rattlesnake becomes the chattering of teeth as you cut to a very frightened individual (fig. 2-27).

A Board Only, or a Script First and Then a Board?

The storyboard is a combination of your visual, verbal, musical, stylistic and editing strategies. It expresses your idea for your animated film, and is the traditional way of beginning an animated film. However, there is another way to begin, particular to television animation. In the 1950s, when children's TV programming was becoming established in the United States, it was easier and cheaper to begin with a written script. On a series, the main characters and storyline were set, and all that was needed for each individual show was a premise and dialogue. Then a storyboard was drawn to conform to this script. The concept and content are decided in the script and the storyboard is a visualization and layout of that script (fig. 4-1). You will find information on animation scriptwriting in Addendum Two.

In the written script format, the storyboard artist will board the staging of the characters, editing and camera shots to fit the determined time, content and established characters from the script. Most of the technical knowledge needed for storyboarding from a script is covered above.

One more point. If, for economic reasons, the storyboard is going to animators in different locations or countries, the director can add extra drawings to show the characters' key poses. This gives the director greater control over the animation. It is called "slugging."

History

Walter Lantz used a prototype storyboard in the late 1920s at Universal studio. But usually two people are credited with being the first to use boards: Ted Sears at the Fleischer Studios in 1930 and Webb Smith at the Disney Studios in 1932. Walt Disney established the use of storyboards in animation because of Walt's emphasis on story and character and the advent of sound. It seemed that Walt liked the storyboard panels that Webb Smith developed and pinned to wall, but did not care for the holes that the pushpins made in the stucco walls. Walt solved the problem by having corkboards made both mounted on walls and as moveable units. This is a process still used today (fig. 2-8). Disney was also the first studio to have a permanent story department.

The Computer and the Storyboard

The increasing use of the computer in the storyboard process has led to storyboards being drawn and timed within the computer and not going with the traditional paper panels. This means going directly from the idea to the animatic (an animatic is a timed sound storyboard on a computer program or tape and is the next stage after storyboard: Chapter 4 discusses the animatic) and has the advantage of saving time by cutting out a production step and having the sound and timing from the beginning. Also, the computer programs allow you to add moves and effects to the animatic. For 3D computer animation storyboards, the character and the location could be done roughly, so many angles and different shots can easily be tried. Also, having the storyboard as files allows you to change and add animation as the film progresses.

Some of the disadvantages are: Though the computer programs are non-linear so you can change or move a panel, at least for me it is not as easy as moving and changing panels as you are thinking, especially when the storyboard is being presented to other people. Also all the many bells and whistles, the tricks that can be done on the computer, can get you too involved with the technical aspects of the filmmaking instead of developing your idea. And it may be too much at the start of developing the idea to have to consider timing and sound.

Warning

Watch out for flying objects in the animation workplace. As I mentioned at the beginning of this chapter, pushpins are used to attach the storyboard art to a corkboard on the wall. When they are bored, animators have been known to throw pushpins into the board from several feet away. Animators at the Disney studio were so expert, they could stick pushpins to the ceiling. There were always several in the ceiling of the "Sweat Box," the room where storyboards were presented and dailies screened. One day, as Disney was walking to his seat, a pin fell from the ceiling and stuck in Walt's balding head. From that moment, throwing pushpins was frowned upon at the Disney studio. Another luminary in animation, Tex Avery (fig. 1-7), was blind in his left eye. Legend has it that he walked in front of a storyboard when animators were throwing pushpins and one caught him in the eye, causing his blindness. I have it from a good source that the story is not true. It was a paper clip that got Tex. Animators were shooting paper clips with rubber bands.[5]

CONTENT

What is your idea, your content? You should know it when you are at the storyboard stage and be able to state it in one sentence. For example, "A few brave men or women can win against all odds." Or, "Stupid people are funny." Or better yet, "A stupid coyote trying to catch a roadrunner is funny." Or, "There is not much hope for love, but love is the only hope."

Your film must say something about something through a story or a character, and you can determine whether it does very simply. Check the ending. If the narrative stops arbitrarily (with no closure), that means you don't have a clear idea of what you wanted to say. No ending, no content. If this happens to a student storyboard, I say, "Just tell me what your film is about in one sentence, and I can give you the ending." It works every time. Or when a student in my storyboard class announces that he's going to let the audience decide what his film is about, I know he's in trouble.

A storyboard is content in tangible form. You can see why knowing what you want to say affects the art you produce. Nothing exists until you put pencil to paper, but you're not just doodling. Unless you want to waste a lot of time and money, you better know what you want to say before you begin, and the storyboard is the way this is done.

Ninety-eight percent of animated films have to be storyboarded. However, a board may not be necessary if you're making an experimental film--particularly one that is created under the camera like James Whitney's *Lapis* (1966), which involved multiple exposures of basic abstract forms, or my own *God Is Dog Spelled Backwards* (1967) (fig. 2-32), where each different shot or image was conceived to be on the screen for only two frames.[6] Content was concept. Often, experimental films are not storyboarded because the process involved is one of exploration.

Such films do not rely on narrative. However, the majority of animated films do rely on the narrative either traditional narrative or animation narrative. Animation narrative adds the unique qualities of animation to the narrative.

---

5. The source of these stories remains with the author, now deceased.

6. Once again, two things. One, you can listen to the author talk about his films here http://danmclaughlin.info/talk.html Second, you can view *Claude* on the DVD *11 Films by Dan McLaughlin*.

TRADITIONAL NARRATIVE

Narratives in Western society began with the storyteller. Homer's epics, the *Iliad* and *Odyssey*, are fundamental to Western culture and staged religious events. Theater grew out of these events. Because it's closest in form to animation, I'm going to focus on theater.

According to the history, it all began in Greek theater in the sixth century BC, when the poet Thespis either introduced an actor onstage or appeared as an actor himself, performing beside the traditional chorus. When the playwright Aeschylus (525-456 BC) introduced a second actor, dialogue was born and the role of the chorus was diminished. Previously, actors spoke in monologues and addressed the audience directly. Then the playwright Sophocles (496-406 BC) brought three actors onstage. Dialogue became the rage, and theater as we know it today was fully launched. Perhaps Sophocles is to blame for all the out-of-work actors we have today.

Aristotle (384-322 BC) formed a theory of drama based on his observation of the literature and theater of his time. That theory, as it appears in his *Poetics,* has been interpreted and reinterpreted many times over the course of history, and furnished the basic structure of Western drama. The first principle of *Poetics* is plot, the arrangement of incidents. The second principle is character. These principles, Story and Character, developed in Greek theater, have dominated the narrative in Western society since then.

STORY

Story consists of content, which we have discussed, and the structure of the content. There are many variations of structure for the narrative. In *Poetics* Aristotle wrote, based on his observations of the literature and plays of the time, that the proper structure of the plot is beginning, middle and end, with the ending being the most important. Some of his other thoughts included the notion that length is fixed by the nature of the drama itself. If an action or incident makes no visible difference or is not an organic part of the whole, it should be left out. Of all plots, the episodic, in which acts succeed one another without probable or necessary sequence, is the worst. Plots are either simple, no change, or complex, change. A well-constructed plot should be simple in its issue. And a tragedy should be divided in this order: Prologue, Choric song, Episode, Choric song, Exode. Aristotle did not write on comedy, as it was deemed a lower form and not worthy of comment. It could be fun to speculate on what he would have said, maybe with an animated film in Greek.

The classical five- or three-act play is another structure. The concept of the five-act play was thought to have been started by publishers 100 to 200 years after Shakespeare's death as a way of putting his plays in an appropriate order. Various three-and five-act structure theories were developed, and are being developed today and can be found on the web or in books.

A simple structure has five major elements that are considered essential to a good story: beginning, middle, end, conflict and content. The beginning should pull the audience in, introduce the content and usually the conflict. The middle should develop the content through a release of information and action that keeps the audience involved (this is often the hardest part to do) and leads to the end. The end brings resolution and closure to the content. Here is an arbitrary formula for the percentage of time each element occupies: beginning 25 percent, middle 50 percent and end 25 percent. Conflict is often considered the necessary element in Western drama. Necessary because conflict drives the action, and without conflict you would have no drama. This is especially true in traditional narrative and animation narrative films. The experimental film often shuns conflict, and a lack of conflict may help define what is an experimental film. (Examples of conflict are sprinkled throughout the upcoming story section.) Content has already been addressed.

Another view of structure comes from Bill Scott (fig. 2-61), one of the best writers of animated shorts, who created most of Jay Ward's films. He also did the voice of Bullwinkle in *The Rocky and Bullwinkle Show* (1959-1964), and George in *George of the Jungle* (1967) and many others. He felt that any good story would have to go sequentially through these stages: arousal, hook, increasing tension, climax and release. Bill also felt that you needed a strong central character or characters.[7]

The "disaster" theory of structure, where the conflict and content are based on a disaster or potential disaster, is another alternative structure. The structure in this case would be: disaster or potential disaster, the resulting conflict; resolution. In the *Road Runner and Coyote* series (1949-1963), the pending disaster is that the Road Runner would be killed and eaten by the Coyote. Conflict starts when the Coyote, using the technological advantages of Acme Tools, tries to catch and kill the Road Runner. He never does and only succeeds in hurting himself. This leads to the content, "When you try to hurt someone else, you only hurt yourself." The subtext, "Don't rely on tools from Acme Hardware (fig. 5-31)," is revealed as the very alive Road Runner disappears. In the Disney feature *Snow White,* the disaster of the Mother's absence brings about the conflict with the Stepmother. A potential secondary disaster would be that Snow White would always be a maiden. The resolution is the demise of the Stepmother and Snow White's marriage. In *Pinocchio,* that the puppet is not a real boy is the disaster, which leads to the conflict of his trying to be a real boy.

A to B, or A to B to A, is the simplest story structure where B is the opposite (or in conflict) of A. Applying this structure to *Snow White,* you would get: At the start of the film Snow White is happy (A), then she is threatened with death and spends a terrifying night in the forest (B), she then finds security and happiness with the Seven Dwarfs (A), but then she eats the poisoned apple and is presumed dead (B), but is kissed by the Prince which brings her back

---

7. Again, I am assuming that Bill simply told this to the author at some point.

to consciousness and she and the Prince live happily ever after (A). A to B to A to B to A is the basic structure. The readily apparent premise is that "Love overcomes." In a contemporary reading, the premise could be that if you are a young girl, your ideal life should entail being passive, happily cleaning and cooking for the male. If you follow this role, you will be found by a handsome prince and live happily ever after (of course, the Prince in this case seems to like prepubescent girls who are dead). A secondary theme could be that a powerful woman (the Stepmother) will be consumed with hate and die a horrible death.

Popular sources for story structure are our cultural myths. Joseph Campbell, in his book *The Hero With a Thousand Faces,* examines the hero structures by the trials he must undergo to save his people. This structure has been used many times, such as in the *Star War* series in live action and recently in *9*, a thesis film by one of my students that is being turned into a feature film.[8]

A different kind of the journey structure is *Madame Tutli-Putli (2007)* from the Canadian National Film Board. Madame takes her life's luggage on a train journey analogous to the journey of life. In the journey, what happens on the way can be more important than the eventual destination.

Of course, you don't have to go to the end of a film to begin retelling the story. In *One Froggy Evening* by Chuck Jones (Warner Bros., 1955), a frog found in a time capsule sings and dances for his finder alone, who imagines great wealth from his frog. Twice, when faced with an audience, the frog freezes and the man is distracted, and he puts the frog back in the time capsule to be opened in the future.

A very old friend,[9] a writer of over 30 prime-time sitcoms, uses the structure of fairy tales for his writing. *The Three Little Pigs* (1930s) is a perfect example. It has conflict, a hero, a villain, an end, content and a middle. It also has a song that became the theme song of the Depression. Speaking of *The Three Little Pigs,* the number three seems to work well when repeating an action. In my film *Claude* (1963), the parents say their put-down of Claude three times (fig. 2-33). Three times just seems to work best for anything of this type: not two, not four. Uneven numbers also seem to work better than even numbers if the number is not three.

Another type of structure is the journey. *Jason and the Argonauts* (1963), in the quest of the Golden Fleece and the return home, is an example of the journey as the structure. In the journey structure, what happens on the way can become more important than the goal.

The legend of Sisyphus is a basic model of the cyclical structure, where the beginning of the film is repeated at the end and the film begins again, a never-ending structure. *Sisyphus*

---

8. This would be Shane Acker. The student film 9 came out in 2005 and was nominated for an Academy Award. The feature 9 came out in 2009.
9. Earl Barret

(1975), by Marcell Jankovics, Hungarofilms, is a beautiful film of the Sisyphus fable. *Zid (The Wall)* (1965) by Ante Zaninovic, Zagreb Studio, is another film structured around a never-ending cycle where the concept is to let someone else do the work but make sure you get the reward. Another example would be the recurring singing, dancing time-capsule frog in Chuck Jones's *One Froggy Evening* (1955).

Studying films can show how strongly graphed and structured animation can be. Andy Blaiklock, an animation graduate student, in his research found that the 57th minute was the time for the love song in Disney features.

A Hollywood cynic once said, "A story needs only humor, sex and violence."[10]

You could well ask, "What does all this structure have to do with me? I just want to make a film about cute little animals running around hitting each other on the head." However, structure is just as necessary in a one-minute short as in an hour-and-a-half feature. *The Simpsons* TV show is divided into acts. You need to bring order to chaos.

For some, the three most important elements of the narrative are: Story, Story, Story. Think of the animated features that have come out over the past few years. The failed ones had one thing in common: the lack of a well-crafted story. Some had great animation and a few had one or two interesting characters, but lack of story killed them all. Perhaps they did not heed Bill Scott's advice, who always felt that you needed at least three times more material in an animated feature film than a live-action film to compensate for the natural live empathy factor that exists in live action.[11]

ANIMATION NARRATIVE

This is when the structure of traditional live-action narrative is changed into a new narrative structure by the attributes and qualities of animation. This form of the narrative is particular only to animation. Animation narrative uses animation's unique power of creating its own images and time to give the viewer a new and different perception of traditional content. Using not only the traditional narrative sources of literature and theater, animation narrative also draws heavily on music, poetry, art and dance for its content and structure. Animation is a new art form that arrived in the 20th century by adding movement and time to the plastic arts. It is not surprising that a new form of narrative should accommodate it.

The most obvious and common source for animation narrative comes from the anthropomorphizing of animals, which is the giving of human characteristics or speech to the other living inhabitants of our planet. Animal characters have expressed human concerns in

---

10. I was unable to find a source of this quote.

11. Again, I am assuming this is based on personal communication between Bill Scott and the author.

stories at least since *Aesop's Fables*. Animal masks are part of dance and ritual in all cultures. Animated animals can easily act out basic emotions, such as a dog wagging his tail madly shows a joy that would be hard to capture in any other way. Animated animals can also make complex political or social comments, as in *Animal Farm*.

Other than the anthropomorphic animals, I am not sure there are any hard guidelines for the animation narrative, but there are many examples. Some are:

Les Jeux des Anges, by Walerian Borowczyk, France (1964). With minimal images of painted backgrounds of the WWII concentration camps and no dialogue, this film demonstrates that animation can produce as much horror of those camps as seeing images of the camps themselves. This work caused one of my students to say, "I really didn't like that film, but I will never forget it."[12]

Crac! by Frédéric Back, Canada (1981), is a 10-minute ode to love and the joy of humanity. Based on a story that he created for his children, this film's colored pencil art, its transitions of condensed passages of time and visual storytelling make it a tale that could have only been done in animation.

Gerald McBoing Boing, USA, UPA (1949), is based on the book by Theodor Geisel (aka Doctor Seuss)who had worked in animation. It uses sound effects and character in a new way that turns a handicap, a boy who makes sounds instead of words, into a blessing.

Balance, Germany (1989), illustrates the theme that we need to work together or we all lose. It is a stop motion film staged on a platform in space.

The National Film Board of Canada has developed an animation narrative approach that combines experimental materials for the visuals with traditional narrative and sound. This has proven very successful. An example is Caroline Leaf's *The Street* (1976), based on a short story by Mordecai Richler. She animated the film straight ahead by painting on glass underneath the camera as she was shooting frame by frame.

Faith and John Hubley pioneered the improvised approach in animation by recording their children doing their improvised stories as the content, and then animating them in a loose and free style. Faith later made films based on her visuals of pre-Christian myths[13] (fig. 2-34).

Final Thoughts on the Narrative and the Animation Narrative

The traditional narrative seems to work best in features and longer short films. Ben Jackson, a former student, once said that you need at least six minutes to develop a character (in the traditional sense). Conversely, animation narrative seems to work best in the short

---

12. Sorry, no one seems to know who this person is.

13. According to her daughter, Emily, Faith would prefer the term "ancient myths."

animated film that is the birthplace, and strength of animation. These two types of traditional and animated narrative exist in the short film form. So far the traditional narrative dominates the longer form.

Content of universal interest will reach a larger audience. Content based on topical issues may be forgotten before you finish the film, and local issues will have a limited audience.

As was mentioned, the traditional narrative described above is Western narrative. Other cultures, both current and past, can have a different narrative structure. If the film is intended for that culture, then you should consider using their form. When a folktale is taken from a culture with a different narrative structure and adapted to a Western structure, a problem could arise. Do you adapt it to a Western point of view and risk losing the essence of the tale? Do you use the different cultural narrative structure to remain true to the original, but by doing so you risk confusing a Western audience?

There is one test, a simple question, to see if the storyboard is for an animated film. The question: Can it be done in live-action? If the answer is yes, then it is not animation and perhaps should be done in live action or rethought for animation. Animation is a film form that could only be done in animation (either through the content or art or combination of both). It could not be done in live action.

CHARACTER

Character is basic to the Western narrative. It is just as important as the story. If your audience does not believe in or identify with your characters, your film will usually not work. Bill Scott always felt you needed a strong central character or cast of characters regardless of the story.[14] Chuck Jones (fig. 2-40) once said, "A plot without characters is like a tennis court without players."[15]

"He writes like he has heard about people but has never meet any." Bill Menger, screenwriter, talking about a fellow writer.[16]

Personality

To develop a character, you first create the complete personality of the character in the storyboards. Then you design the physical externals to fit that personality. Let the funny drawing come from the personality rather than trying to find a personality to match a funny drawing.

---

14. Again, another personal communication, I assume.

15. "Chuck Jones." AZQuotes.com. Wind and Fly Ltd., 2016. 19 Aug 2016.

16. I was unable to locate the source of this quote.

Below is a checklist, titled SEPARATE, to help in developing and defining the qualities of a character. The ingredients needed to make a character are:

- **S is Speech**. This involves their voice, more specifically the quality, the tone, the pitch and the gender, either male or female. It could refer to the speech pattern (Donald Duck or Elmer Fudd) or vocal style, as in pompous (Foghorn Leghorn) or accented (Pepé Le Pew - French(fig, 2-40), Bugs Bunny - Brooklyn), or lisping (Daffy Duck) (figs. 1-1, fig. 2-40).

- **E is Emotion.** Is your character happy, sad, mad or bad? The Seven Dwarfs, Dopey, Grumpy, Happy, etc., are prime examples as their names are their emotions. Often, this is related to their attitudes.

- **P stands for Personal History**. What is the educational, economic, regional, religious, family, ethical, moral, age, sexual orientation, etc., background of your character? How intelligent is the character? Also refers to a physical attribute of a character that drives the action, such as Mr. Magoo's near blindness or Dumbo's ears. In today's Hollywood jargon this is called the backstory.

- **A is Actions.** What are the defining psychological or physical actions or movements of the character? A distinctive walk is a common example.

- **R is Reactions.** What do the other personalities think of, and how do they act with the character? Are these perceptions different from the audience? Dopey was really the smartest of the Dwarfs; he got two kisses from Snow White but the other dwarfs did not think him particularly smart. I hope that by the end, the audience would feel he was the smartest dwarf.

- **A is Awareness.** This is how the character reacts with other characters, and what he thinks about the others.

- **T is Thoughts.** This is the character's philosophy; what are his main thoughts on life? Bugs Bunny is curious with a live-and-let-live attitude until threatened, and then it means WAR. Daffy is self-centered and believes in only taking care of number one, Daffy.

- **E is Events.** These are the events surrounding the character and their effect on the character(s). This would also include the place and time of the events. Examples would be *Der Fuehrer's Face* (1943), which places Donald Duck in Hitler's Germany.

This checklist can work for characters in any type of writing--plays, novels, live-action scripts, or it can help actors develop their characters.

A rule often quoted for drama is that a character must change. This is good for traditional drama, where conflict and change of character are deemed necessary, but in comedy, especially animation, the reverse is often true. The comedy comes from the character not changing, regardless of the situation. Some well-established characters and their personalities include Bugs Bunny, who when threatened will not change and therefore wins. His "this means war" is his answer to change. Daffy and the Coyote also never change and lose, and lose and lose.

A written description of the characters, their conflicts and their personalities is normally part of the model sheets or the animated TV series bible (the basic premise and characters of the series). You should do the same for your film (fig. 2-41).

To develop a character you should study people or actors. Take both from life and acting techniques. This quickly crosses over into animation, as the animator is an actor with a pencil. Good character animation is based on a well-developed character. Study people, observe how their characters are defined, and look for that little extra detail that clinches their personalities. Then take those observations along with everything else and put them into your animated character. Animated characters play only one role. Live-action actors play many roles, and we know too much about their marriages, divorces, trials, last films, etc. Animated characters belong to their own world and cease to exist outside of it. Snow White only plays Snow White. Bart Simpson only plays Bart, because that is who and all he is. This makes an animated character memorable. You can put across your idea by wrapping it in a character.

STYLE

Before we get into the physical appearance of the character, we must discuss style. During the storyboard stage, the basic visual style of the film, including the character, should be decided (fig. 2-47). This can be documented with some final art either in the panels of the storyboard, model sheets or as separate pieces of art from the panels. If it is separate art, then the visuals in the panels can concentrate on the content and not worry about the details of the style. Visual style not only includes the look of the characters, but also the look of the entire film. It is essential to have a strong visual style in which to clothe the content. The visual style will be the first thing an audience perceives when viewing the film, and will have a large say in how an audience views the film. The style must be finalized before animation is started. Style design is started in the storyboard stage and finished in the layout stage.

Sometimes the visual style is suggested by the content of the film or the backgrounds (fig. 2-35). Often, it is dedicated by your own strong art or drawing style. If you have a style of drawing, it is best to stay with it. Learning a new style, unless it is necessary for the making of the film, will take time and perhaps lessen the quality of the work. If the art style is open, first decide on a general direction. Is the film to be in a representational style, like a Disney feature such as *Snow White* (mostly) (1937), *The Lion King* (1994)? In a classical cartoon character style like Bugs Bunny? A stylized cartoon style like the *Simpsons*? A painterly style as in *The Man Who Planted Trees* (1987) or *The Street,* (1976)? An abstract character like *The Dot and the Line* (1965) or *Adventures of an* *(1957) (fig. 2-36)? A non-cartoon, *Frank Film* (1973) or *if my wings had dreams* (fig. 2-37)? An abstract non-character, *Begone Dull Care* (1949), *Allegretto* (1936) or *Street*

Works (1987) (fig. 2-38)? The most prevalent visual style, especially for character animation, is the humorous cartoon. The differences in styles in cartoons go back to the first two major animated films. *Fanstasmagorie* (1908) was simple, flat, cartoon, and non-narrative. *Gertie the Dinosaur* (1914) was complex, 3D, realistic and narrative. The style of the character will signal to the audience the type of animation to expect: a cartoon character, a funny cartoon; a realistic character, a realistic film.

If you have a problem finding a style, standard cartoon characters could be a good starting point. They could be cute, goofy, screwball, the bully, fat, thin, sexy, the professor, etc. These characters can fit into any style, but they can give you a direction.

After you have decided on a general direction of style, or while you are deciding, you can help yourself by doing the following:

- Research on style by watching other animated films, and looking at different cartoon styles in comics (fig. 2-39) and children's illustrated books. Study the history of painting, drawing, printmaking, sculpture and graphics, both from the East and West, for ideas. Then:
- Eliminate styles that will be too hard to do, either in time, cost or ability (fig. 2-50).
- Do many drawings, art or model sheets to try different styles.
- Then make a decision on a style that is most appropriate to the content.

If the film involves characters of one style over a background of a different style, it can become a concern. If the characters are flat, simple and cartoon and the backgrounds are 3D, detailed and realistic, they will clash. Both the characters and the background should look like they are from the same film (fig. 5-23). It is easy to overdo a background, as it is just one piece of art. A good example of background and character design meshing are the *Road Runner and Coyote* series from Warner Bros., especially the desert backgrounds. Disney spends considerable effort to make sure these two elements work together. One way to tie your character and background together is if you have a black line around your character and a black line around your background elements (fig. 5-25).

The tools you use often influence the style of the film. The traditional ink and paint on cels, drawing on film, colored pencils on paper, computer animation, painting on glass, moving backlit sand, cut-out paper, all will have their distinct looks, strengths and weaknesses. Knowing the look different tools give will help make an informed choice on style. Using a different or unusual tool or technique that enhances the content will often make the difference between a good film and an award-winning one. As an exercise, think of some wild and crazy way to do your film: old shoe buttons, dead beetles (has been done), grounded-up meat, broken dolls, dirt, wallpaper, anything. Color is a large part of style, and can increase or decrease the quality of the film. Color can be naturalistic or not, the film could be done in shades of one color, or the flesh could be purple (fig. 2-48,9).

Keep the style consistent throughout your film, unless the style changes because of the story, so as not to confuse the audience. Since animation is a total synthesis of all the arts, your choice of style will not only include the visual style, but the music, acting, the voice and movement (dance). Ideally, all these arts orchestrated together are the style. Style is very important in today's animation world, as many are looking for the next new, hot style. Animation style can go in and out of fashion overnight.

Character Design and Model Sheets

After the personality of the character is established and a style decided upon, the next step is to design and draw the character. Chuck Jones always said, "Designing characters doesn't start with a funny drawing. You start with the personality and let the design come from who the character is–you do not create a personality to fit a design. Good design comes from inside the character, not the other way around"[17] (fig. 2-40). The external physical description is a representation of the internal description. There is further discussion on character design in Chapter 7, Animation.

First, from the physical description of the characters in the storyboard, a series of rough drawings are done to establish the look and style of the character. When these "ruffs" (old animators' talk for roughs) are finished, they are cleaned up and become the model sheets that show the final forms of the character (fig. 5-3). They are the guidelines for drawing and animating the character. The animators need the model sheets for constant reference, so that the physical character will not change from scene to scene. Keeping the character on physical model is called "holding character" or "putting on character," and can take more time to do than the animation. A full set of model sheets for one character would consist of: (1) a verbal description of the character, containing the information mentioned in the previous section (fig. 2-41). (2) On one sheet of paper, a drawing of the character in three different poses: a three-quarter front, a side or profile, and a three-quarter back view. These three drawings are called a round (fig. 2-42). (3) One sheet of drawings of action poses (fig. 2-43). (4) Another sheet contains a sheet of facial expressions (fig. 2-44). (5) A color model sheet is on another page (fig. 2-45). Any of these sheets could contain information on how the character is constructed and any special instructions, such as "no dimples on long shots" or "mustache is one eye-width long." An important consideration here would be: Is the character designed in such a way that it can be animated? This means that the structure of the character is made up of basic shapes that can be animated and that the character is simple rather than complex. The basic shapes should be incorporated into the model sheet drawings (fig. 2-46).

---

17. According to Google, this is somewhere on chuckjones.com, but I couldn't find it anywhere on the website.

Ways to Design Characters

You can start by asking questions and arrive at the character by answering those questions. You should already have the answers to the personality of the character. Writing them down helps when you design the look of the character. Then ask the next basic question, is the character 2D, 2½D or 3D? Is character done in a contemporary 2½D cartoon style, like the Simpson's or in a traditional 3D cartoon style á la Disney? What are its proportions (figs. 7-55, 7-56, 7-58)? Where is it positioned in the gallery of animation? Is it a traditional three-and-a-half-head high cartoon character with a predominant feature(s) (fig. 7-51)? What is this predominant feature, the eyes or the nose? Does it look humorous? Does it relate to the dwarfs, elves and jesters of history? After answering these and other questions, start drawing using reference materials as necessary (fig. 2-47). Or you can just start drawing until you find a character you like that fits the personality for the content of the film, or that you just like. If you have a strong character drawing style, this may fit your temperament.

Using the character design of the current animation can make your character design no different from the rest. Often a film becomes a hit because the design of the characters is dramatically different from the past or current standard models.

An example of the logical approach to issues of character design is Disney's casting of little creatures, such as mice, crickets and sea horses, in prominent roles based on the "elephant theory" of character. That is, if an elephant crosses a room, it can do it in one or two steps, minimum time three seconds, and no time at all for any adventures. An ant, on the other hand will take thousands of steps to cross the room, perhaps even days, with opportunities for countless adventures. I know, I know, Dumbo was an elephant, but he was a little baby elephant and his buddy Timothy was a mouse. In the early days, Disney also designed his horses as cartoon horses, except the horse of the handsome prince, because not only was a cartoon horse easier to animate, but also every farmer in America would know how a realistic horse would move. "That cartoon don't move right, not like Old Nellie."

Another way would be to research successful characters from animated films, print cartoons, graphics or caricatures, and redo them until they look completely different.

If the drawing style or style of film has already been set, then the style of the character should follow. If the style of the film has not been decided, the style of the character could set the style of the film, including the backgrounds. The need for the coordination of styles of the character and backgrounds holds true except when using different art styles is the content of the film.

If the animation is planned to be full animation, this should be reflected in your character's model sheets and poses. They all should be done in movement poses or expression. No drawn, 3D full-animation character should ever be shown in a stiff pose or without expression.

The ease and time that will be taken of the animation is also a strong consideration in character design. Complex designs or prison stripes on clothing are examples of time-consuming and expensive animation, and ink and paint. When Disney was doing *101 Dalmatians* (1961) they had to address the question: How many black spots do you need on a white dog to make it a Dalmatian? They had figured that each extra spot would cost about $20,000 extra in animation, ink and paint (fig. 2-50).

Color

To get fresh color combinations for the character, use color palette books. Reflect on the emotional content of color; the black, white, and red of Mickey Mouse is considered the most pleasing color combination for children. A rough color version of the background that is overlaid with the color characters model sheets should be done. The background colors and the character colors must work together for the entire scene to have the right color balance. Be inventive with color; perhaps do the whole scene in one color (monochromatic), purple for instance (fig. 2-48).

The Ability of the Character to Be Animated Well

Whether a character and his action can be animated well or with ease is greatly influenced by the construction, modeling and anatomy of the character design. The basic body shapes should be so designed that they will be easy to follow in the animation (fig. 2-49). Find the simplest basic form in the object in order to do the first rough animation and adjust the basic shapes if necessary. Characters can be so designed or overdesigned that they cannot be animated well or economically (fig. 2-50).

Tips on Character

Do a set of extremes or major poses when you start animating to get more expression in your character (fig. 2-43). Try to do one pose that will tell the complete personality of the character. Make sure the character is drawn the proper size in its relationship to background (fig. 5-12).

An animated character in a series of shorts, either theatrical or television, will often change over time. Mickey Mouse started as a bad little boy and finally ended up as a very good boy, not only in personality but also in how the character was designed. He was more rodent like at the beginning and more soft, cute and babylike in his final form. Bugs Bunny's design changed over time, and his personality became less crazy and more Brooklyn smart.

Study people not only for the development of character, personality and good animation but also for the way they look. Different body and head shapes can lead to a good character design. I used to work with a man (he was a dealer in Tahoe) whose nickname was Hatchet

Head. His head shape was the foundation for a good character head design (fig. 2-51).

A character should have a conflict(s), a conflict that drives the content forward.

Each character should have its own physically distinct form, features, personality and movement. This will hold true whether it is a human or animal based character, or an inanimate object (like a sack of flour) or an abstract shape (a line). Examples of the latter are Chuck Jones's *The Dot and the Line* (1965) and Oskar Fischinger's *Study* series.

Marketing

The potential marketing or licensing value of a character, the toys, watches, clothing, etc., can add another factor in its development. Should you design or partially design a character for the marketing potential? It is a profitable market. Mickey Mouse merchandise still makes millions every year. A danger is if market value becomes the overriding factor in the purpose and look of the character, it could result in a poorly animated character for the film. The character may not be constructed correctly for movement, or not have the necessary personality for the story. A concern for animators is that unless they have it in a contract, they do not get or keep the rights to the character they design and have no share of this market.

VERBAL

The importance of words, either dialogue or the voice-over, is easily overlooked in the rush to put an idea into a visual form. The spoken word should be developed along with the idea and visuals during the storyboard process. It is traditionally written on pieces of paper pinned below the art. This way, changes can be made very quickly and the relationship between picture and sound is clear. Good dialogue should reflect or reveal the characters and their world, and keep the story on track and moving forward. It can be the primary way the conflict and premise are conveyed. Often, it is the most important element in the film. Award-winning films have been based on the written word, some with comedy records or a comedian as their source. *The Critic* (1963), by Ernest Pintoff and narrated by Mel Brooks, is one such film.

Frequently, dialogue is what you remember about a film. Who can forget the Daffy and Bugs dialogue in *Rabbit Fire* (1951) where Daffy has that immortal line: "I say it's duck season and I say Fire!" (Elmer fires. Daffy's bill is blown askew.) Daffy: "Hmmmmm" and later as Daffy addresses Bugs, "You're dethpicable! Yes, you're dethpicable ... and ...and ...very definitely dethpicable ...How a person can get so dethpicable in one lifetime is beyond me..."? The dialogue should always define and reflect the personality of the character as in live action. However, since the medium is animation, the dialogue can go places live action cannot. Daffy and Bugs can continue their dialogue after Daffy has had his head blown off and then reappears. This would be a hard thing for an actor dressed in a duck costume to do (figs. 1-1, 2-40).

If the script form of the standard TV animation (fig. 2-52) is being used, please see the chapter on making a living for information in this book. If you like the script format, a mini script can be done along with the visuals while doing the storyboard sketches. Having a written reference can be quite helpful. At some point in the storyboard process, the verbal will have to be put into a script form for the voice talent to rehearse and record (fig. 4-1).

Not all animators can write dialogue, and if that is the case, find someone who can write to work with you or use proven written material. Chuck Jones, early on in his career, wrote a letter to Walt Disney, and to his pleasant surprise received a prompt and friendly reply. This started years of correspondence between them. Years later, when Chuck was in St. John's Hospital, he saw Walt in a bed and they start talking. Chuck asked, "I always wondered why you answered me?" Walt replied, "Animators don't write too much, and I think you were the only one who ever wrote me."[18] Walt died a few days later.

The impact of words is summed up by Mel Blanc's gravestone inscription in the Hollywood Memorial Cemetery,

"That's All Folks"[19]

International Animation

There is a classification of animated films that have no voice track; their narrative is purely a visual narrative. I call this international or universal animation, a film that does not have to rely on a particular language to be appreciated and therefore can be shown anyplace in the world. This can mean added distribution for animators in countries with a small language base. *The Road Runner and Coyote* and *Pink Panther* series and the recent film *Balance* (1989) are examples of non-verbal visual narrative films.

Which First, Story or Character?

When starting a board, is your idea based on story or character? Either is fine, but don't forget the other. If your idea is story based, a good way of working would be to get the story as tight as possible and then work on developing the character as much as possible, especially during the animation of the character. Otherwise, you could end up with a good plot and weak 2D or cliché characters. A story change could always be made later if the fully developed character demands it.

Or, you can start with a character. A student of mine had a superhero, Stitchman, whose

---

18. A variation of this story can be found in Sampson, Wade. "Chuck Jones: Four Months at Disney." MousePlanet, 9 September 2009. Accessed 8 August 2016.

19. "Mel Blanc." Wikipedia: the Free Encyclopedia. 6 August 2016. Web. 28 August 2004.

superpower was that he can knit super-fast.[20] Or, you can have an ordinary person who can't recede properly, whose body doesn't obey the laws of perspective. The problem here is that you can end up with a great character and a weak or a cliché story. You need to develop a solid story before you start animating. Having a great story or a great character is only half of the battle.

As to the continuing argument of which is most important, the story or the character, I remember a lecture in the 1970s that Frank Thomas and Ollie Johnston, two of Disney's "Nine Old Men" and two of the finest animators who ever lived, gave at UCLA (fig. 2-53). In discussing the ending of *Snow White,* they felt that full character animation would be needed to end the film, but Walt disagreed and decided to go without full character animation but use still art and a narrator, and let the story carry the ending. Walt had his way and it worked (full animation would probably have been too strong, or perhaps he didn't have the time or money). Frank and Ollie are to this day not fully convinced. They felt that character was the most important and Walt felt it was story. At they end of the discussion, Frank, I think it was, grudgingly said that Walt may have been right, but he still was not too sure. This question will never be resolved. Though one fact is evident, it is better to have both rather than just one and one rather than none.

EXPERIMENTAL

Experimental is described in many ways: abstract, nonrepresentational, absolute animation, (used by Oskar Fischinger to describe his films), non-narrative, non-verbal, underground, avant-garde, stupid, boring, student and arty. Whatever it is called, many experimental animators share in common the deliberate shunning of the traditional narrative. The traditional holds no interest for them. Why keep repeating Aristotle's 2,300-year-old rules of drama? Why not find other ways to engage the emotional and the intellectual qualities in fellow humans? This probably holds true not only for animators, but all artists who experiment in any art. They want to do something different.

Since it is experimental, there are no hard and fast rules on what elements are used in experimental animation. Below are listed some of the concepts or underlying themes that could drive an experimental animated film. Experimental films often contain several elements such as structure, movement, techniques, music and belief system, but one element is usually the primary one. That is the one that drives the entire film. For example, it is a religious belief in James Whitney's *Lapis* (1966).

---

20. Again, another student's name lost to time.

Concepts or Elements That Can Underlie Experimental Film

Structure. Based on approaching content by using a film-making structure different from the traditional narrative structure. The new structure can be the concept. For example, the editing structure could be quite rapid, a cut every two frames, as in my early film *God Is Dog Spelled Backwards* (1967) (fig. 2-54). There could be no editing and nothing to edit as in *Red/Green* (1985), another of my films, which is a five-minute dissolve from a red color card to a green color card. This film also involves the changing color and texture of the screen. It becomes a moving-color field painting that relates both to the properties of film and theories of art (fig. 2-55).[21]

Movement. Abstract or non-representational images move in time to their own internal rhythm or to music as the primary emphasis. The flow of the movement gives it its aesthetic quality. In this approach, animation is conceptually and philosophically linked to dance. *SymphonieDiagonale,* done in Germany in 1924 by the Swedish artist Viking Eggeling, was the first abstract animation of this type. Also see Celia Mercer's *Street Works* (1988) (fig. 2-38) and *Fossils* (1999) (fig. 2-56).

Belief Systems or Emotions. Films that use experimental means to present an abstract vision of an emotion or a belief are in the category. An example is the visualization of the non-verbal religious tenets of Buddhism that were created by James Whitney in either of his films *Lapis* (1966) or *Yantra* (1955), or the films of Faith Hubley which are based on her visualization of ancient myths (fig. 2-34).

Music. Usually these films are known to the general public through such films as *Fantasia* (1940) or music videos. In its more experimental mode, it strives to create a new art form by synchronizing music and abstract animated-equivalent visuals into the same experience for the viewer. This is sometimes called visual music. Films of Oskar Fischinger, *Allegretto* (1936) and *Optical Poem* (1938); Norman McLaren, *Begone Dull Care* (1949) and *Lines: Vertical* (1960).

Theories of Art. An example of this would be animation based on the theories of Surrealism. Surrealism that portrays or interprets the workings of the unconscious mind as manifested in dreams. Surrealism is characterized by irrational, fantastic arrangement of content and material (fig. 2-58). Jan Svankmajer's *Dimensions of Dialogue* (1982) is a perfect example of an excellent animated Surrealist film. The foundation of Emile Cohl's *Fantasmagorie* (1908) was the philosophy of the Incoherents, a precursor to Surrealism. The Incoherents believed that insanity, hallucinations, dreams and nightmares were the sources of aesthetic inspiration. Abstract or non-representational painting is another major springboard for experimental animation. If you are stuck with the structure of an abstract film, I have found if you put your best shot last and your next best shot first and the rest in the middle and some good music, you should have a good structure.

---

21. *Red/Green* is also discussed here http://danmclaughlin.info/talk.html. Also, you can view *Red/Green* on the DVD *11 Films by Dan McLaughlin.*

Techniques. By techniques I mean when the tool or the technique is a primary source for the experimentation. A popular experimental technique is drawing or painting directly on film, for instance, Celia Mercer's *Scratch Film #1* (fig. 2-59) or Phil Denslow's *Madcap* (fig. 6-9). Len Lye and Norman McLaren were the first and still rank among the best in this type of animation. Len Lye's *Rainbow Dance* (1936) is an early example of a mixture of techniques, using printing on film and optical printing of live action to create an experimental work that was a commercial for the British Railway system. The techniques or forms from other sources can be adapted to do experimental animation. The abstract patterns of the kaleidoscopes duplicated in film or the abstract look of the computer-generated fractal images are two such examples.

Materials. An example of materials being the basis for an experimental film would be Pat O'Neill's spray paint on clear film loops that become a moving Jackson Pollock painting or Celia Mercer's *A Mystery Box* (2011) (fig. 2-60).

By definition, experimental animation means you do not know where you are going, especially when you start. It can help to speed up the experimentation if you have some sort of structure to underpin your work. This structure, which can later be dropped, should be part of the storyboard. Sarah Petty, a student of mine, took three years to do a semi-abstract film animated to an existing piece of music. Her next abstract film had no music structure to guide it, and it took her seven years to finish.[22] A basic structure of going from simple to complex and back to simple, or from medium to slow to fast speed, in the storyboard stage will help you go deeper into your experimentation. If you have done a series of abstract sequences and cannot arrive at their order in the final film, the easiest thing to do is to make your best shot the last in the film, make the second best shot first and put the rest in between.

Today many commercials and music videos use experimental techniques as a way of enhancing their visual to sell their product. Also, the ease with which the computer can create effects has generated more experimental work, especially abstraction, in animation.

Depending on the level of government support in a country, experimental animation can be fully funded to completely self-funded. Experimental is doing your own thing, not doing someone else's thing.

This quote by Santayana, paraphrased by substituting the word animation for poetry, expresses the philosopher's view of the creation of an experimental work. "Memorable nonsense, experimental animation, or animation with a certain hypnotic power, is the really primitive and radical form of animation. It launches a new direction--the animator who creates a symbol or an entire film as a symbol, must do so without knowing what significance it may eventually acquire, as he or she is conscious at best only of the background from which

---

22. IMDb has her name as Sara Petty. According to the Alternative Projections website, which also has her first name as Sara, *Furies* was released in 1975 and *Preludes in Magical Time* came out in 1988.

it emerged. This animation is pure experiment and it is not strange that 90 percent of it should be pure failure." [23]

MORE THOUGHTS ON STORYBOARDS

Humor

Most people think that animation has to be funny. This is true especially in the United States where the term "cartoon" stands for humorous animation. People will pay to laugh, and animation with its graphic possibilities can be funny. Because of this, the market in the U.S .was oriented to funny animation to make money, and so the cartoon was born. Also, children love animation, so in the public's eye animation was cartoons for kids, especially when TV started marketing toys. Of course animation can be any genre, not just comedy, but a book on animation should mention humor.

What is humor (fig. 2-61)? That is a question that opens a whole can of worms with no answers or rules. If there were rules for humor, then everyone could be funny and we would be laughing all the time.

All I can do is make some general observations about humor. They are:

- A humorous person is one who can say something funny, say something normal in a funny way, or do something funny.
- Humor often involves someone dumber or different than you. With today's political correctness, dumb is about the only thing left because they don't realize they are being laughed at.
- Humor often means something bad happens to someone else. It can involve different social or economic differences. If a bird defecates on an upper-class snob dressed in top hat and tails, that's funny. But if the same bird does it to a little blind beggar girl, it's close to tragic (except for the people who are sick).
- Verbal humor is often culture or language based, and doesn't translate well into other languages or cultures.

Physical humor, pantomime or slapstick is international as it appeals to all peoples.

Timing is important to animation. Timing is not only important in the delivery of humor but also the interval between gags. This is why visual humor can keep you laughing, because you don't have to hear what is funny, you just have to see it.

---

23. George Santayana, Little Essays Drawn from the Writings of George Santayana (New York, Charles Scribner's Sons, 1921) 151-152. Found in googlebooks 27 August 2016.

In earlier days, they would show a film to a test audience in a theater and see what was funny. The best way to tell what is funny is to let the audience decide. Storyboard presentation can give you a clue.

Go against accepted ways--like pigs singing "The Pirates of Penzance." Something out of context can be funny.

Some gags are more violent today, for instance, when a cat gets run over by a steamroller. In olden days, the cat just became paper thin and usually popped back into shape. Today, the cat gets run over by a steamroller and there are blood and guts all over the place.

Toilet training probably explains why gags about bodily functions--defecating and urinating are funny for some. Social mores against passing gas, vomiting, picking your nose and eating it explain what some find funny.

Why is it that a dog peeing on a fire hydrant is always funny (for most people)? Funny people often make funny films. Study Chaplin's silent comedies. Comedy is not action but reaction, the result of an action.

Titles and Character's Names

The main titles and character's names should be part of the storyboard from the beginning. They are important elements of your film that can be easily overlooked. The main title is normally the very first thing your audience will read about your film. Ideally, the title should be the embodiment of your film. It can save time and animation by putting the audience immediately into the film, by raising certain expectations. If the title were *Maura*[24] (fig. 15-1), the audience would probably expect a character-driven film about a character named Maura. Descriptive titles such as *Skeleton Dance, Walking, The Snowman* and *Balance* are all films that deliver what the title promises. Conversely, by deliberately not delivering what the audience expects from the title, you can set up the audience for a comic or dramatic effect. To jumpstart a funny film, Warner Bros. titles from the Golden Era employed puns: *Rabbit Hood, Porky Chops, Nothing but the Tooth, Odor of the Day, Don't Give up the Sheep, Rabbit Fire, Canary Row, I Gopher You, Cat-Tails for Two, The Hole Idea, Fast and Furry-ous* (the first *Roadrunner and Coyote*, 1949), *Sandy Claws, No Parking Hare* and *One Froggy Evening*. These also show the depths of punning that animators can sink to.

It is important to find the right name for your character. There is a story that in the original manuscript of the novel *Gone with the Wind*, the editor suggested only one change, that the lead female characters name Pansy be changed to Scarlett. Indeed, "Frankly, Pansy, I don't give a damn" does seem to lack something. Another story, closer to animation, is when Walt

---

24. This is also the name of the author's youngest daughter, Maura Weber.

Disney came up with a mouse character to replace Oswald the Lucky Rabbit, he first wanted to use the name Mortimer Mouse, but his wife persuaded him to use the name she felt was better, Mickey.[25] "Mickey Mouse" also is an example of the use of alliteration (the repetition of an initial sound, usually consonant or cluster, in two or more words of a phrase) and is very popular for animated characters: Porky Pig, Donald Duck, Daffy Duck, Koko the Kop, to name a few.

Titles and character's names in general should be memorable and easy to remember, short for space on the marquee and, if educational, should have the right title for reference in a catalogue. If a title or a character's name is a fabricated word, it should not have an embarrassing meaning in another language. The copyright symbol is always included at some place in the titles (fig. add 1-1).

If a storyboard does not have a title and its maker cannot think of one, a good way is to ask them what is their premise? If they can answer this, they should have a title.

Timing

A good storyboard should give the timing of the film to come. Watch the balance of your board in terms of time; do not let a couple of drawings represent half the time of your film. Even if not much is happening, which may be a problem in itself, and no new panels are needed, copy the panels enough times so that they represent the timing of the film. A timing guide or bar sheets could be done now as well as later (fig. 2-62).

To help with flow and rough timing of the film, create a simple timeline. A timeline showing the length of each scene or major sequence, in terms of seconds, of the entire film will illustrate the visual balance of the film. Does all the action happen in the first 10 percent of the film? Does it all happen in the last 10 percent? Does the film have a steady dramatic build until the climax at the end? A timeline allows you to spot an imbalance very quickly. A timeline showing the use of color is also a positive tool at this stage. Graphing out the major color of each scene or sequence in terms of time allows you, among other considerations, to choose the emotional color flow of the film (fig. 2-63). As an example, you could have your quiet colors at the beginning and the warm, hot colors at the end.

Presenting the board by timing it with a stopwatch as you tell the story is one way of getting the rough timing of the film. Acting out the board and timing it is another way. Some animators will run their hands over the panel as they present the board with a good watch. Recording the board presentation is a very good way of not only getting a good sense of the timing, but also of whether the board works or not.

---

25. Wikipedia agrees.

Censorship and the Audience's Reaction to the Film

Your content or style will often contain ethical, social, religious or political considerations (fig. 2-64). This can lead to concerns you should be prepared for. They include: People who share your ethical or moral position will like your film, but people who are opposed to your position may not like your film, regardless of its quality. Depending on the film's distribution system, educational, religious, political, ethnic, cultural and pressure groups may object to your film, even work to forbid it. You might be surprised to know that my film *Claude* (1963) in which Claude causes his parents to disappear (fig. 2-26) was banned from distribution in various library systems, including all in the state of Colorado, in the early 1970s. An example would be on network television what would their Standards and Practices department (these are the people who decide what is correct) approve or not approve? These are some of the TV network restrictions on animation from the 1970s. *1.)* No hitting in the face, or on top of the head. *2.)* No falling on head, although backsides are OK. *3.)* People in cars must wear seat belts, and children must be in car seats. *4.)* Helmets on motorcyclists. *5.)* Do not have heroes destroy property without adding a line or indication they will repair or reimburse for the damage. *6.)* No ropes or binding around necks. *7.)* No grabbing around necks. *8.)* No holding by neck. *9.)* Include minorities in supporting roles, not as villains or in demeaning jobs. *10.)* Never put a character in automatic washer, dryer, oven, etc. [26]

The worst aspect of the censorship issue is self-censorship. This is when you censor yourself because you think someone else may censor you. Do not let anyone pre-censor you based on what you think they may think. You might be surprised how far you can go, especially on cable or independent films.

Another issue is to be aware of the subtext of your film. You may inadvertently be promoting a moral position you do not endorse. This can be especially true with gender issues. A common example is that only the male character or characters can be heroes, never a female character. Double-check your board for offensive sub themes. If it is offensive, you can change it and take the offensive nature out, or can you make it even more offensive. Some artists believe their role is to offend the audience; others believe their role is to help and educate an audience. Regardless of your role, you should be prepared to assume responsibility for your film and the audience's reaction to it.

Being prepared for the audience's reaction to the finished film is a factor in determining the content of your film. A student once presented a storyboard for a very depressing film. I asked him if he was prepared for a depressed audience and he said yes, no problem. The day came when the film was done, he did an excellent job on it, and it was shown to an audience of 30 people. It was usual after the screening to stay and discuss the film, but this time as soon as the lights came up everyone bolted for the exits. The filmmaker was shocked. "Why

---

26. I was unable to find a source of this quote.

did they all leave, don't they like my film?" "Oh they liked your film," I said. "Too much. They were depressed as hell and just wanted to get out into the sunlight. I warned you."[27] Another student had a great storyboard where in a pinball machine, the ball is a rolled up a nude woman and all the obstacles in the machine are penises. She did a fine job on the finished film. It was too good, in fact. She saw it and did not want it shown. Only I got to see it for her grade and then she destroyed it. Too bad. It would have been the hit of the festival circuit.[28]

Cause and effect. Your film will have an effect on an audience and you caused that effect. Be prepared for it.

The Animator's Block

Animator's block refers to the blocking or stopping of the animation production process at some point along the way for hidden emotional or psychological reasons. It is often disguised as indecision and excuses. Personal blocking most often occurs at these points with students: the storyboard stage, the layout stage and the last moment before shooting. Why this happens I do not know. Perhaps it is a fear of failure or a fear of finally seeing what your finished film looks like, and you are naked on the screen. I also do not know how to get someone unblocked and back on production. Encouragement, support, deadlines, fear of a failing grade and visits to a psychologist have all been tried. Sometimes they work; sometimes they do not. If a person really does not want to finish a film, nothing on earth can make him or her finish it. Rollo May's book *The Courage to Create* addresses this issue. Actually, the title says it all. It does take courage to create.

PRESENTATION OF THE STORYBOARD

Audience for Boards

There are some people who do not show their boards to an audience and go right into production, but the majority of filmmakers show their boards. Filmmakers present their boards either to improve the quality of the film, to cut down costs by finding the right direction or, given the necessity of the funding process, to get the backing of a client, backer or studio people.

There are two kinds of boards for two different kinds of audiences. The first is a production board, which is a working board for people in the studio who will be making the film, such as the director, music director, voice actors, animators, and layout or background artists. Since

---

27. While I can think of a few incredibly depressing films through the years, the exact identity of this film and filmmaker shall remain anonymous.

28. This one I think I would have remembered if the author had mentioned it.

this board will be seen by professionals who know the process, it can be in a rough form, although it should have some color examples of the finished art and character model sheets to indicate the basic style and colors. A presentation board can also be used for this audience.

Second are presentation boards (fig. 2-12). They are done in the most lavish way possible, with full color, sound, etc. The purpose of this board is to sell your project to the client. A client is anyone who has the money, or the control of the money, to make your film and/or the money to pay you to make a film. A client could be a producer, a sponsor, a charitable organization, a rich patron, an investor, a cable network, a fine arts grant, whoever and whatever. As clients often do not have a working knowledge of animation, this board should be well-designed and eye-catching, with finished-looking art, perhaps suited to your client's tastes. You can be very creative here on your presentation, dazzle them, and use any medium possible. An animatic could be used in lieu of a presentation board. The point here is to sell the film to the client with the strongest possible pitch (to present anything in Hollywood is to "pitch it." a term perhaps related to the old-time circus pitch). So how do you convince them, your audience, that a few pieces of paper will become a great film?

On Your Feet

First of all, be positive, witty and brief. Do not be negative, dull and long-winded. Look your live audience in the eye and say, "This is the best goddamn board in the world!" When you present a storyboard, tell them a story and act out the character(s). Do not ever say how terrible the board is, how you could not get an idea and how everything about you is really stupid. If you tell them negatives, they will believe you and will hate your board, though they may feel sorry for you. Do not ever explain the board. If you have to explain anything, you are already in trouble. Entertain them if entertainment is your goal. One of the best examples of a board presentation is a tale about Walt Disney and his original presentation of the *Snow White* storyboard. Walt had been an actor, playing Peter Pan in a hometown presentation as a child and later doing Charlie Chaplin imitations. In fact, some of the people then at Disney felt that Walt was a better comedian than Charlie, but that stage fright kept him from appearing in front of the camera. As the story goes, Walt presented the *Snow White* board to the animators who would be doing the film. He acted out every role to give them the range and depth of the emotion he wanted in the film. He did so well that at the end, many of the hard-bitten veterans of animation had tears in their eyes and a smile on their lips.[29]

Speaking of tears in the eye, it is best not to cry when presenting your board. The audience may feel sorry for you, but it will not make them like the board better. One on my students always cried when he presented his board. At the end he was sobbing, and had to be led out of the class

---

29. Wikipedia agrees.

by his wife, who he always brought to his presentations.[30]

As you present your board, listen to comments, but try to distinguish between the good and the ugly. Try to remember only the suggestions, negative or positive, that help. Think on your feet, ask questions and milk the audience's brains. If you are quick enough, you can make changes and be creative during the presentation. This will get the audience more involved and often makes your idea stronger. If you can, take notes or tape record the comments. During the presentation, talk to your audience and look people in the eye, especially the ones who are falling asleep. Face the audience, not the board. Stand on the right side of the board, the audience's right. This forces you to face the audience, and your position will reveal the panels as you move from panel to panel. A pointer can be helpful. All this is assuming you will have the board mounted on a wall. However, be prepared in case it is not. I remember once presenting the storyboard for the titles of the film *Where's Poppa?* (1970), where the only place to present it was on the floor. The director, Carl Reiner, and I crawled around as I did my pitch. Luckily he saw the humor in the situation, liked the board and I got the job (fig. 2-65).

Practice presenting your board and tape your presentation if you can, so you can see it as an audience would. On tape, you can see its strengths and weaknesses from a distance. As a bonus, you can see if you have personal idiosyncrasies when presenting: scratching in inappropriate places; excessive use of the words "you know" or "and then," or "like;" and nervous tics. A little practice can make these habits part of the past and turn your board presentation into a joy. Make your presentation unique. Acting classes can help, as presenting a board is in part an acting job. Come up with something unique to make your board memorable. A Ph.D. student in anthropology at UCLA once presented his board in a wet suit that was made up to look like a flayed Mayan sacrifice victim. He also dressed up as a 15-foot blue marlin.[31] If you are doing a presentation, be aware when you have sold it and stop. A very common mistake is to go on too long and you lose the sale.

I have found it a good practice when teaching storyboard to always ask the presenter five basic questions. They can also work for a pitch.

- Title of film
- Projected length
- Intended content
- Intended audience
- Intended sound

(The third and fourth points above are only used to allow the audience to respond specifically to the stated goals.)

I also find it helpful to have everyone write comments, and give them to the presenter at the

---

30. Sometimes it's best not to ask any questions.
31. Since Dad didn't give him a name , I decided not to persue it.

end of their session.

You must believe in yourself and your board. If you believe in your board, really believe, your audience cannot help but believe in your board.

The Reaction of the Audience

Different audiences will have different reactions, and it is to your advantage to read and understand these reactions. I had a friend and distributor once whose reaction to my boards had 100 percent accuracy as to the future film's audience reaction. Every one of my boards that he hated became a wild success, and every one of my boards that he loved became an utter failure.[32] A friend like this can be very valuable; if you find one, keep him. You can always tell what is wrong with someone else's film, but it is very difficult for you to tell what is wrong with your storyboard. This can be a good reason to listen to other people who have smarts and no agenda. You have to make a judgment on the audience's comments as to which ones will help the film, and which ones do not. Be selective; if you take all the audience's suggestions you would end up with a mess. The audience cannot do your film. Also, think of the motives of the audience. They can have their own motive, which is their self-interest. People may be asking you, "What's in it for me?" especially if it is a sponsored film, and you will need to answer that question before you will get their support. An audience can really be tough. In live action, there is an old story of an executive producer in the 1930s who after reading a script from a producer under him, would tell the little producer that the script was fecal matter, spit on every page and throw the pages covered with his spittle on the floor. The little producer would then have to get on his hands and knees, pick up each sheet and wipe the spit off of it with his hand, arrange it in order, slam it on the big producer's desk and say, "I don't care what you say, I want to make this film." The big producer, ego stroked and dominant position assured, would then OK the project. Another producer who was in charge of animation at a major Hollywood studio did not possess any humor. Luckily, he hired a good story man to sit with him during the screenings of his unit's film to tell him if they were funny or not.

In the golden days at Warner Bros., there would be a weekly meeting to discuss the current storyboards. In those meetings there was only one rule: You could not say anything negative. If you want to have a productive and creative storyboard session, this would be the rule to follow. Often, negativity in a storyboard session is only a disguise for a personal attack or for personal gain. Concerns should be expressed with a possible solution, not in a negative manner. A positive presentation will leave everyone in a highly creative and dynamic mode. Always schedule a meeting before lunch or quitting time to guarantee that it will be short and productive.

---

32. I think I know who this is, but some things should be kept private.

Networks - If you are pitching a concept to a network, be prepared to wait. Usually they will offer you a six-month option for a little amount of money. This is to their advantage because : 1. It makes your idea unavailable to other networks; 2. It gives the development network people a never-ending job. If they keep saying no they have a job with no risk. If they say yes to the film, then they have to work and may lose their job if the project turns out bad. Another trick of the networks is an option contract, meaning that any money they put into the development has to be repaid before you can take your idea to another network. This is so your idea is effectively dead for other networks. Never sign a contract with that in it.

Afterward

After your board presentation, immediately write down your thoughts and reactions as well as those of the audience (fig 2-66). It is a good idea to take notes during the verbal comments if you are not taping them. Review your notes or tape recording. Think about them and other comments. Which ones would help your film? Which really have nothing to do with your film? Is there a general misunderstanding about any part of your idea? Did your audience get confused? Many times, in presenting your board to a group you will see the idea with a new insight that can be used to enhance the film. Almost always the board will have to be redone once or twice.

FINAL THOUGHTS ON STORYBOARDS

The three most common problems for first boards are:

- The proposed film is too long and complicated.

- The film is done in one shot. Many beginners never consider or understand the necessity of using the language of film, editing.

- The film lacks an idea that leads to the lack of content. The telltale signal of that is the lack of an ending.

Do not leave part of your film undone in the storyboard and plan to fill it later. Doing it now will save you time later. It is fine to have poetic sections that do not have literal meaning, but they must have a power of their own or drive the film forward. Plan to spend some time coming up with your idea. Take time off to do it, relax, use rough thumbnails at first, and try to get the visual stuff down from the beginning. Adaptations are fine, but you must add your viewpoint; otherwise why do a film? If you have a narrative form, does it follow the rules of that form? Are the story or character elements complete? Is your premise clear? Know your strengths and weaknesses when you start on your first film and concentrate on your strengths, whether it is idea, story, character, drawing, a film sense or a strong point of view. You can work on your weaknesses later but avoid them now. If you are good at comedy and not drama, stick with comedy.

When audiences are asked what a film means, they will often say the film means nothing and is a waste of time. How many times have you or your friends, when the lights go on, said, "I had no idea what that film was about." Or, "I didn't understand that film at all." Audiences come to a film to be entertained, either high or low entertainment, not to waste time trying to find a content when there is none. There has to be something for them to figure out, and the clues to that are in the content of the storyboard.

Make sure you have the copyright clearances for anything you use in the film before you start production (fig. 2-67).

Always ask yourself the question that has for years struck terror into the hearts of my students: **"CAN IT BE DONE IN LIVE-ACTION?"**

Doing your first storyboard can be very frustrating because you are being asked to create an animated film before you have done one, and usually before you understand animation. It may take you several animated films before you become proficient at doing boards. A good idea is to do several different boards before you do your first film. Also, doing a very short silent animated film, approximately 15 seconds long, is very helpful. Many people avoid the board stage because it is hard or they do not have an idea, but starting your film with a board, except for some experimental animation, is still the best way and often the only way to achieve a good animated film.

When you finish your animated film and what you see on the screen is all yours, it is one of the best feelings in the world. You have made your own film, and no one in the world can take that accomplishment away from you (fig. 2-68).

fig.7-49-8

OTHERS ON CONTENT

"Gulley: Half a minute of revelation is worth a million years of know nothing.
Cokeky: Who lives a million years?
Gulley: A million people every 12 months."

The Horses Mouth by ***Joyce Cary*** [33]

"There is no money in poetry,
But there is no poetry in money."

Robert Graves [34]

"Painting is silent poetry and poetry is painting that speaks."

Simonides of Ceos (500 BC.) [35]

"You are taking your audience on a journey."

Bernie Lucht, Canadian Broadcasting Corp. [36]

fig.7-49-9

33. I was unable to find a source of this quote.

34. "Robert Graves." BrainQuote.com, Xplore, 2016. 29August 2016 (fig. 2-69).

35. "Simonides of Cleos." Wikiquote,. 15 July 2016. 29 August 2016. The Quote as given there is, "Painting is silent poetry and poetry is painting with the gift od speech."

36. I was unable to find a source for this quote.

CHAPTER 3

(fig.2-5)

TIMING[1]

Time in animation is created.

The author of Wily Coyote, Chuck Jones, once told my class, "I found that if the Coyote fell off a cliff, I needed 18 frames for him to disappear and 14 frames later for him to hit. Thirteen frames didn't work, and neither did 15 frames; 14 frames got the laugh."[2] In animation, one frame, one twenty-fourth of a second, can mean the difference between a laugh and silence.

Time in animation is calculated in frames, seconds, minutes or footage. A frame is one image with 24 frames per second in film, 30 frames a second in NTSC tape, 25 frames a second in PAL tape and a little less than 30 frames a second in High Definition Digital. Animators use the abbreviation x to denote frames. Footage is the length of film, 16x in 35mm and 40x in 16mm. In silent 35mm, film 16x = one second. In the silent days, 35mm footage and time were the same, so the time of a film was counted in footage. But when sound came, in 24x per second was needed for sound projection, so time was not counted in footage though footage was still used to calculate how much work an animator did daily or weekly and payment for freelance animation (fig. 11-3). Film frames and seconds will be used for timing in this book.

---

1. As mentioned in the Acknowledgements, the author completed the manuscript sometime around 2007 and the text has not been updated for accuracy. All statements reflect the belief of the author at the time of authorship and may, or may not, reflect current reality.
2. I was unable to find a source of this quote.

Time in Animation

In animation you create and control the time in three areas: they are:

- ***The timing of the action within the shot.***
  The most common is the timing, in terms of frames, of the action and reaction of a character or between characters. Also, there is the timing of the lip sync or the timing of the mouth and of the acting of the face and the body, including the shrug of the shoulders, to the recorded words (fig. 7-70). A good example of timing without dialogue would be the sequence that started this chapter: when the Coyote makes eye contact with the audience at the moment he realizes that he is about to fall (one of the rules in animation is that a character cannot fall until they realize that they are no longer on solid ground) and registers hopelessness before he exists stage bottom. The next shot is of the Coyote falling into that very deep canyon and then the final shot with the timing of the explosion. The timing of the action helps establish the personality of the character.

- ***The timing of each shot or panel.***
  Each shot in the animatic should have enough time for reading the action and working with the time of the other shots, particularly the shots on each side. If each shot is the same length, it can be repetitive and dull. Better to have a lively rhythm for the sequence of shots: two seconds, five seconds, four seconds and four seconds, etc. This is important in creating the rhythm that helps sets the emotional, dramatic and comedic ebb and flow of the film (fig. 3-1).

- ***The time of the film.*** Three circumstances will govern the total time.
  When the time is preset by the delivery system: TV commercials by their paid time slots, a Saturday-morning TV show averages nine minutes of commercials and 21 minutes of story for a 30-minute slot. Features, by tradition and economics, have to be a minimum 75 minutes. An animated song is preset.

  When part of the time is preset, voice or music, but the rest is up to you.

  When you set the entire time, as there is no preset time. The timing within each shot can be the building blocks used to determine the length of the shot, and the shots the building blocks for the total film.

How to Determine Timing

You can learn to create timing, but it does help if you have a natural sense of timing. Timing is the essence of comedy. If you can tell a joke well, you already have a good intuitive timing sense. A musical background also helps, as music timing shares some of the basic principles such as tempo and changes in tempo of animation timing.

The easiest way to learn to determine the length of time for a shot is to act out the action in the shot in seconds. Say the shot consists of the character picking up a glass, drinking from it and putting it down. Act it out, in front of a mirror if possible, with its emotional content. Use your whole body even if only your arm, shoulders and head are in the shot. After you have rehearsed the action several times and have it the way you want it (Charles Chaplin would do a simple scene, like reaching into his pocket for keys to open a door, literally hundreds of times to time the right action for the character), time the complete movement by using a stopwatch, the second-hand sweep on your watch or by counting seconds. I usually find that counting one a-n-d two, or one Mississippi two Mississippi, will give you a fairly accurate count on seconds.

Other timing methods include letting your fingers act it out, imagining the actions of the shot or running your fingers over the rough drawings as the action is timed. Speak the dialogue or narration as you do the timing. If you are a good storyteller, you could time your verbal description. Taping actors doing the action or taping them in the recording session will you give a very close timing reference.

Say the shot consists of picking up a glass, drinking and putting it down. Timing it, I found that at a leisurely pace, it took about eight, seconds or 192 frames.

After you have the rough timing, do the key or main drawings for the action and start timing the animation. Adjust until it is right.

Timing Patterns in Animated Films

There is no formula for timing but patterns do emerge. These are partially based on the style (frantic vs. lyrical) and type (full animation vs. limited) and movement (simple vs. complex) of the film. These timing patterns can be seen if we study the past in animation. I analyzed eight award-wining films both for average number and length of all shots, plus at the end the average length for two of the most used types, **M** and **MLS**, of shots. To refresh your memory a Medium (**M**) shot is a full body shot. In a medium long shot (**MLS**), the height of full body is no less than half of the frame (fig. 2-14). The films are:

NIGHT ON BALD MOUNTAIN (1933). Alexander Alexeieff and Claire Parker, France, 7.9 minutes. 56 shots, average length of shots = 202 frames or 8.4 seconds. (NBM-a)

NIGHT ON BALD MOUNTAIN (from FANTASIA, 1940). Disney, USA, 13.8 minutes. 69 shots, average length of shots = 288 frames or 12 seconds. (NBM-d)

SONG OF THE PRAIRIE (1949). Jirá Trnka, Czechoslovakia, 20.8 minutes. 274 shots, average length of shots = 110 frames or 4.6 seconds. (SOP)

THE STRANGE CASE OF MR. AND MRS. DONNYBROOK'S BOREDOM (1981). David Silverman, USA, 4.5 minutes. 45 shots, average length of shots = 143 frames or 6 seconds. (DB)

BALANCE (1988). Christoff and Wolfgang Lauenstein, Germany, 7.2 minutes. 103 shots, average length of shots = 101 frames or 4.2 seconds. (B)

TECHNOLOGICAL THREAT (1988). Bill and Sue Kroyer, USA, 3.6 minutes. 69 shots, average length of shots = 75 frames or 3.1 seconds. (TT)

CUCKOO (1988). Velislav Kazakov, Bulgaria, 2.7 minutes. 27 shots, average length of shots = 146 frames or 6.1 seconds (C)

SAND DANCE (1988). Richard Quade, USA, 3.2 minutes. 23 shots, average length of shots = 203 frames or 8.5 seconds. (SD-q)

The average length of time for the two most common shots of these films in seconds [medium (37 percent) and medium long (24 percent) or 61 percent of the shots] is:

Film	NBM-a	NBM-d	SOP	B	TT	DB	C	SD-q
M	5.8	5.9	4.4	4.0	3.4	6.7	4.4	8.4
MLS	11.6	7.8	5.0	5.5	2.4	7.2	9.5	12.3

Their average length was a tad over five seconds for a medium shot and a little over 7 seconds for a medium long shot. These are not rules, just patterns, but they may be of some help as a reference. More information on the percentage of type of shots is in Chapter 5, Layout.

TIMING AND SOUND

Sound is recorded, transferred, listened to and written down in terms of frames using a computer. This frame count is called "reading the track" and is used for timing the animatic, the animation and the film. Chapter 4, Sound has more information on this process. The timing of sound is required in these basic sound groups:

- Voice timing is needed in two distinct areas. For dialogue, the words are synced to the lips and the character (fig. 7-70). For narration, or voice-over, the words are put in sync with the action.
- Music timing is needed for the length, accents and mood change of the music. Sometimes you need the tempo or beat to sync with the action as in a walk cycle where each beat is one step.
- Sound effects timing is needed for the accent and the length of each specific effect such as an explosion, the flush of a toilet, etc.
- Written language timing is needed for titles and sub titles to be read: Read them aloud slowly. Time them once, and time them with a stopwatch.
- Syncing sound and picture in general. We see things before we hear them, as the speed of light travels faster than the speed of sound. You hopefully see the lightning before

you hear the thunder. For animation, this means that you could put the action a frame or more before the sound to make the sync more like what we expect. This can apply to explosions, lip sync, etc. One story is that some early Disney features had the sound dropped two frames back.

BAR SHEETS

Bar sheets are forms designed to write down the first timing for your film and are a way to plan the timing of the film. The animators at Warner Bros. in the 1930s and 40s could time out a six-minute film (the length the studio dictated) entirely from bar sheets.

Bar sheets arrived in the early 1930s, right after sound, and look like blank music sheets. They are divided into four horizontal lines, which represent different film elements: action, dialogue, effects and music. These are changed to fit the needs of the film, camera moves, color changes, etc. The vertical divisions break the horizontal down into time units; one second or 24 frames is a common designation. These time units should be consistent. A running total time is written at the end of each bar. Scenes and sound accents are flagged above each bar where appropriate. The bar sheets are done in pencil (fig. 2-62).

Bill Hurtz, who ended up as the final co-director on the feature *Little Nemo Adventues in Slumberland* (1989) (this feature holds the record for the number of directors who worked on it), came on the project after many years of rewrites, revisions and massive changes in the animation. It was a mess. Bill showed me the bar sheets he made to put everything into order and the film back on track and finished. They were the best bar sheets I have ever seen. Bar sheets are being replaced by animatics, but they are good training for the discipline of animation.

ANIMATICS

An animatic is when the storyboard panels are timed in seconds and recorded in sequence. This real-time film preview, or storyboard reel, was developed at the Disney studio in the 1930s. Disney did not stop with the storyboard reel, and during the production would replace the panels with pencil test animation, and finally the finished ink and paint animation. Since some scenes were done before others, looking at a Disney feature in the middle of production ranged from seeing storyboard panels to finished scenes with an evolving sound track.

The term "animatic" began replacing the expression "storyboard reel" in the 1970s for TV commercial storyboard reels. Those animatics were used for client approval or test audiences and usually included color, a sound track and some movement. A European term for a storyboard reel is "Leica Reel."

A digital animatic is done today, where the panels are scanned or drawn into the computer. The digital allows for quicker changes in timing and images. The animation can then be constantly updated, as Disney did, which helps keep the quality high during production. This is one of the most exciting developments that digital technology has brought to animation.

After you have timed the shots from your storyboard, you will end up with a list showing the shots and their times. Check this list to see the pattern of timing or rhythm. Does it have a slow beginning pace that speeds up to a smasheroo climax, or is it boringly even all the way? Does the time flow fit the content and mood of your film? Editing the animatic until the timing is right will save time and money later in production.

There are two types of editing, linear and non-linear. In non-linear editing, in either film or digital, if you change or drop a shot, you do not need to change anything else in the film. Premiere or Final Cut Pro are two non-linear computer programs now available for animatics. Non-linear editing on film, cutting and taping together film, takes longer. In linear, electronic tape editing, if you change or drop a shot, then you will need to redo the rest of the tape to compensate for the length change.

An animatic allows the embryo film to be shown for an audience's reaction. If shown to people who are unfamiliar with an animatic and have only seen finished films, their comments may be less than helpful. You can always beef up your animatic by adding movement, putting in posed animation, adding more art and laying in a full sound track.

A final story on comedy timing. Jack Benny, a famous radio comedian of the mid-20th century, had this sure routine. Benny, whose character was known as the world's champion miser, was accosted by a hold-up man who said, "Give me your money or your life." There follows a pause of 18 seconds, and the hold-up man repeats his lines. A very brief pause, and Benny replies, "I'm thinking, I'm thinking." His timing resulted in the longest audience laugh in radio history, 47 seconds.[3]

Creating time is unique to animation. The success or failure of your film will depend significantly on its timing. The next production stages are sound and layout.

---

3. I have been unable to verify this claim. According to Wikipedia, the laugh was five seconds. Another Jack Benny joke got at least 32 seconds of laughter. "Jack Benny." Wikipedia, the *Free Encyclopedia*. October 9, 2016, Web. Accessed October 9, 2016.

QUOTES

"Time is that wherein there is opportunity."

Hippocrates (c. 460 – c. 370 B.C.)[4]

"When a man sits with a pretty girl for an hour, it seems like a minute. But let him sit on a hot stove for a minute, then it's longer than any hour. That's relativity."

Albert Einstein[5]

(fig. 7-33)

4. "Hippocrates." _Wikiquote,_ Web. September 2, 2016.
5. "Albert Einstein." BrainyQuote.com. Xplore Inc, 2016. 13 October 2016.

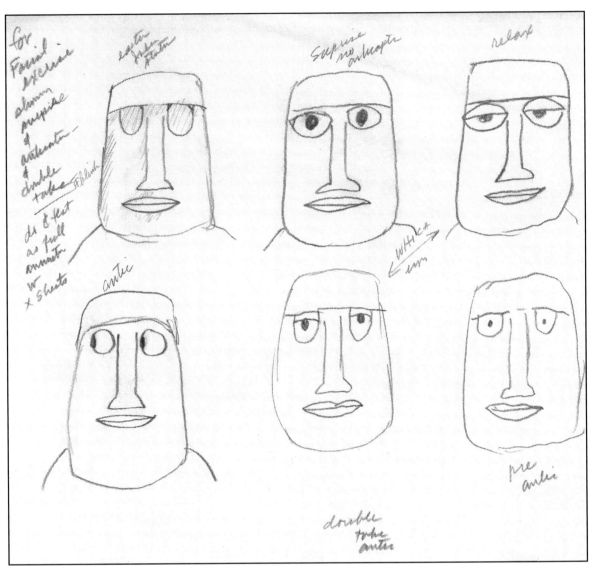

(fig. 2-47)

CHAPTER 4

Courtesy of the Dan F. McLaughlin, Jr. Collection

SOUND[1]

Description

In animation, the creation of the sound starts with the idea, parallels the creation of the visual elements and ends when the picture and sound are joined together to become the finished film. Though the sound process exists as a separate production process, it does interact constantly with the visual, especially in terms of timing, and each area influences and strengthens the other during all stages of the production. But any sound that is to be synced with picture is normally recorded before the animation is started.

THE THREE AREAS OF SOUND

- *Voice.* There are two basic types of voice work. The first is narration, or voice-over, where the speaker is not seen, related to the voice of the gods in Greek drama. The second is dialogue, words spoken by or between characters. Animating the recorded words to a character speaking is called "lip sync."
- *Music.* Music can be either original or pre-recorded. The animation can be synced to the music as in Disney's *Silly Symphonies* or *Fantasia*, or in Sara Petty's film *Furies*. Alternatively, the music can be composed to the finished picture. Animators often forget in their rush to animate the importance of music. It adds an emotional nonverbal underpinning that cannot be achieved in any other way.

---

1. As mentioned in the Acknowledgements, the author completed the manuscript sometime around 2007 and the text has not been updated for accuracy. All statements reflect the belief of the author at the time of authorship and may, or may not, reflect current reality.

- ***Sound Effects.*** Sound effects can be realistic, recorded live or from a sound effects library, or they can be nonrealistic, created by using your voice, strange instruments or the computer. Your composer could incorporate the sound effects into his music. If the effects are tightly synced they should be recorded first, but if the sync if rough they could be added after the picture is done. However, you should know the approximate length of the effect, let's say an explosion, by timing a sound effects record for example, so that the animation is not too far out of sync. Sound effects, usually written as SFX will enhance the overall mood and purpose of the film.

The production stages of sound are:

- Acquiring each of your sound elements. This can either be an original recording or a pre-existing recording.
- Transferring the original sound, if needed, to a digital form. Each sound element, voice, music, effects and multiples of each, if needed, will be on a different track or level. Then:
- Listen and time each sound track to find the exact frame count for the sounds that you need to synchronize (sync) to the animation. This is called "reading" or "timing" a track. Some editing may be needed at this stage. The timing is put on exposure sheets for the animator.
- Edit the tracks so that all the sound elements are timed and placed in the final sequence for the mixing of the tracks. Bar sheets, animatics, pencil tests or the finished film are your guides at this stage.
- Mix all the different tracks (voice, music, sound effects) onto one track. Then play picture and sound together for review.
- Prepare the sound, now fully mixed on magnetic track, for a composite finished film. This is necessary today as long as a film is the final result. It is not necessary if the final is digital and tape recording.

WHEN THE SOUND IS DONE IN ANIMATION

For live-action sound, the standard practice is to record the voice during the filming. Music and effects are added in post-production. Animation is quite different. The sound, especially the voice, is best recorded before the animation begins, as this allows the animation to be done in sync to the sound. (This is not done in Japan where the voice is done during post-production.) With this basic rule in mind there are these three choices as to when to do the sound during production.

1. Doing all the sound first in pre-production. In this case, the complete sound track would be done before animation. The disadvantage of doing this is that you are locked into your sound and therefore the timing to your animation and have little opportunity to change the

timing, however quite a bit can be changed today digitally. The advantage to doing all of the sound first is:

- The complete track is a source of inspiration for improving the quality of the timing and animation
- With the timing done, it cuts down production time and cost spent on working on the timing.

A former student became a leading producer of "clip shows," which are the putting together of clips of various films around a central theme. *The Best of Donald Duck* would be an example of a clip show. In his first job, he and several producers were given shows to do for a TV clip series based on different aspects of Hollywood films. Phil quickly became the best director by bringing in quality show under budget and before deadline by using the animation techniques of (1) storyboard, and (2) doing the sound first. He was done while the other directors were still editing hundreds of feet of film.[2] A variation of all sound first would be to record all the sound together at one time, as is done in live radio. This recording stage can be done after the storyboard and bar sheets are finished, or after the animatic.

2. Doing all the sound last, in post-production, after the animation is shot. This is difficult, especially if you have voices, as they would then have to be recorded to fit the filmed generic mouth movements. Good voice talent is needed to do this type of dubbing, putting voice in after the film is shot. Japanese animation is done this way if you would like to see how it looks. The rest of the world records the voice first. If there is no voice, music and effects can be done at this stage, particularly if the music is composed to the film. Dropping in a recording of music not made for the film is difficult to sync properly and only occasionally works completely.

3. Doing some first and some last, both pre- and post-production. This is the most common approach in sound production. TV animation would have the voices recorded and edited before the animation, and the music and effects added and mixed with the voices in post-production. Disney, at least in the old days, would do the voices, a piano track of the music and perhaps a scratch effects track in pre-production and then do the final music and effects and mix in post. A good way to do it would be to have all the tracks, voice, music and effects done and in the pre-mix stage in a digital based sound system. A rough mixed track could be done for reading the track and for mood. Keeping the final mix untill post would allow changes to be made during the animation stage. The mix can be done to the finished animation for the maximum result.

---

2. I think this is Phil Savenick.

THE CREATION AND RECORDING OF SOUND

The decisions on sound should begin in the idea stage and finalize in storyboard. Are the voices female or male, young or old, with or without an accent, dramatic or soothing, etc.? Is the music classical, rock or rap? Is the mood happy, sad or noble? Decide the sound effects and how they will be done. Sound design the entire film. Bar sheets and animatics are used for the timing of the sound.

Voice

Select or cast the talent, the actors or actresses, according to your concept. It is best to get professional voice talent. The professional talent will have recorded samples of their voices to listen to, or you can do a scratch recording of voices you like and to compare. Check out any local theater or comedy shows for the right voices. If in the Los Angeles area, put an ad in Drama-logue.

If you use non-professional talent, cast them using their regular voices, rather than asking them to act or create a voice. Non-professional talent will often get tired after two or three takes, so try to get a good recording in these first takes or have them come back a different day. This is especially true with children. Professional actresses do many of the children's voices for this reason. Also, if reading from a script, non-professional talent will often sound like they are reading. If they do this, try having them act it out as they record it. They are then using their bodies and movements to get into the role.

When you have cast the people, show them the storyboards (fig. 2-12), model sheets (fig. 5-3) and any animatics or animation. Explain and discuss what you want from the film and them. If they want to do something different for you, listen to them, because often they come up with something better. But you are the director; be diplomatic, and when you record do it both ways, yours and theirs, but do yours first. You can decide later which to use. To gain experience in directing, take an acting class. From the class you learn that one of the most important things in acting is for the actor to know what the director wants. The voice director needs to tell a person, "I want this and this type of character voice," or "this and this type of reading." This worse thing an actor can hear is a director saying, "I really don't know what I want, but I will know when I hear it (sure), just give me something." The actor must know what you want, or they can be there for days trying to get it right. Treat the talent nice, be sure they are comfortable, have soft drinks, chairs, coffee, etc. When directing the voice talent, you can use the timing from the bar sheets (fig. 2-62) or animatic to give them direction on how to deliver the lines: fast, slow, a long pause there, and stress this word or section. An old studio method is to film or tape the talent when they are recording to use as a resource for the animation. They did this for Phil Harri's Baloo character in *Jungle Book* (1967) so the animation is pretty much how Phil Harris acts in real life. To see how much

Phil Harris contributed to the Baloo character, please read about it in *Disney Animation, The Illusion of Life* by Frank Thomas and Ollie Johnston.[3] It is a classic example of how a voice talent can add immeasurably to the animation with his or her acting talent.

Music

Decide the type and style of the original music you want for the film. If you are not the composer, you will need to find a composer. A composer can not only do the music but also see to its recording, either on a computer, a single instrument or an orchestra. If possible, the finished music should be in a digital format. Discuss the film and the storyboard with the composer. Explain clearly what you want the film to achieve. A composer may make suggestions and ideally becomes integral to the creative process. Listen to him but remember it is your decision and your film. Often a composer will suggest a particular instrument to go with the mood you want. There has been a tradition of associating certain instruments with specific genres. Examples are:

- *Humor:* bassoon (middle/low), oboe (middle /high), clarinet, bass clarinet (low), xylophone.
- *Narrative Background:* Combined strings and woodwind (middle).
- *Drama:* strings (low), french horn, trombone, woodwind (low), english horn (low), bass flue, (low), contrabass clarinet (low), piano.
- *Silence:* anywhere, any time.
- *Science Fiction:* moog synthesizer, yamaha organ, female soprano voice, vibraphone (haze effects) percussion (effects), strings (harmonics, flute (high).

The registers mentioned–high, middle and low–when used will change the perceived quality of the instrument. For example, a violin in the high register will be spirited, melodic, arresting. In the middle register it will be warm, romantic and compassionate. In the low register it will be dark, dramatic and morose.

Talk with your composer about the mood, instruments, relationship of the music to certain characters (whether each character will have its own musical theme) to certain scenes or actions, and the tempo and tempo changes you want. The film tempo chart is at the end of this chapter. The tempo of music is important not only for the quality it will bring to your film, but it can also speed up or slow down your animation. During the process, the composer should do some samples for you to hear. The composer can, in the music he writes, put in many if not all of the sound effects needed for the film. Decide when you are working with a composer if this is a good choice for your film.

---

3. Frank Thomas and Ollie Johnston. *Disney Animation: The Illusion of Life.* New York: Abbeville Press, 1981. pp. 407-408.

Sound Effects

Prerecorded sound effects can come from a sound effects library or disk, which can be purchased commercially, or from a sound effects studio. The actual sound can be recorded, for example a door closing (which often doesn't sound right), or other objects can be recorded to give a similar sound. For instance, hitting two pieces of wood for the door or hitting two coconut shells together to produce the sound of horse hoofs. If nonrealistic sounds are opted for, try doing the sound of a door closing with your vocal chords. That kind of sound is fun to do and may be completely different from the one expected and have a comedic effect. Try out different ways and things. Sound effects editors spend many hours coming up with different ways to get a sound to sound like a sound. Children's musical toys are a source, as well as a simple large sheet of cardboard as well as a thin metal which when shaken can produce a fine storm effect. The computer can generate sound effects or modify existing ones. As mentioned before, the composer can incorporate sound effects into the composition. Doing all or some of your effects as part of the score can unify the sound. A "Foley stage" is used to do live sound effects. This is a space in a recording studio that has various materials to do sound effects with such as gravel or sand for walking or doors for closing. These effects can be done and recorded in sync while the film is being projected.

RELEASE FORMS FOR YOUR TALENT

All your talent, voice and music, should sign a release form giving you the rights to their work that is done for your film. If it is a student film and their work is gratis, you should give them major screen credit and a free VHS copy of the film for their portfolio. For beginning music and voice talent this can be very important, as they need a film to showcase their talent. They may need you more than you need them. If a release form is not obtained, the talent could demand money and threaten a lawsuit if the film received some financial consideration. A sample release form is in Addendum One: A Brief Summary of Copyright Law (page 367).

THE TECHNIQUES OF RECORDING AND THE OTHER PRODUCTION STAGES OF RECORDING

Using a sound studio will give you the best quality, as it has all the equipment needed for recording. It could also have a Foley stage. The studio will come with a professional sound person to do the recording, which leaves the directing of the talent to you.

If you are doing the recording yourself, you will need a digital tape recorder, a good microphone, digital tape and a very quiet room to record in. If time is limited, the recording can be done directly into the computer that is being used for the mix. A good mike and tape are essential, as any poor technical quality in the recording will always remain. Try to use a proper recording area, a sound stage or a scoring stage. Reading the lines to set the right recording levels is done before you start recording. If there is only one mike and more than one person, they will have to share that one mike. The best is one mike for each voice. If there are multiple mikes, a mixing board, where all the input from the mikes are mixed, will be needed. When using a mixing board or a single mike, it is far better to have someone else operate that equipment rather than you so that you can concentrate on directing the talent.

The actors need a clean, double-spaced copy of the script with each line numbered for retakes (fig. 4-1). Mounting each sheet on a stiff board can cut down on paper sounds. On a take, that is a recording that is intended to be used, let the talent record the whole script all the way through, even if they make a mistake. If it is a good take but there are mistakes, the actors can just re-record those lines, usually called retakes or pickups, which are listed on the script by number, until they are right and they can be edited in later. Identify each recording or rerecording at the beginning of each recording to make it easier to edit later. An example is, "The Secret, August 28, 2005, take 17, pickup line 34." Mistakes can be fixed later, but what is most important is getting the reading you want. Keep directing the actor and recording them until the right reading is achieved or everyone gets exhausted. Sometimes you can never get it right and will have to recast. One vice president of an animation company who was in charge of recording had a very well-known live-action actor in to do the voice on a public service show. She said, "He had a great smile, but that didn't help the recording." So after the 37th bad take on the first line, they both agreed to use someone else. If you are using non-professionals, rehearse before the recording outside of the studio so that when you come in, everyone is completely prepared. Professionals will not need a great amount of rehearsal time and can rehearse in the studio. But you don't want to spend all your studio time rehearsing and it can tire the talent. An old radio trick for hearing the voice quality you are getting is to close your eyes while the person is recording or on playback. You can concentrate solely on the voice.

As mentioned before, as the director it is most important to know what you want, so the actors will know and you will know it when they get it. If the recording does not come out well, do not use it just to make the talent happy. It is your film and your responsibility to make it good, so when in doubt throw it out. Telling actors or composers you cannot use their work is difficult, but you have to let them know. Be sure to thank them and tell them they did a fine job, but it just is not what you need. Make such a decision early so that you will have time to do the casting and recording over. The Disney feature *Robin Hood* (1973) had the main voice redone when they were halfway through animation. They found that redoing the voice so changed the character that they had to take the time and money to redo the animation. You will need the best possible sound right from the beginning; if the original recording is of poor quality or does not do the job, it will only get worse.

Transfer

This is when the original source is transferred to the editing/mixing system. You normally will be transferring several different sources. These would be the separate voices, the music and the effects tracks. The two editing mediums are 16mm magnetic track (old process) or digital information in the computer (new process). You would transfer your cassette, reel to reel, DAT, CD's, DVD, DY, DVC or whatever is the current technology. Get the best available CD's, tapes, etc., possible of pre-recorded material to 16mm magnetic or into the computer. Keep the volume constant when you change the levels in the mix. Why choose one way over the other? The reasons for using magnetic track are: (1) the sound must go on magnetic track, after the mix, for a composite print in film, and (2) you experience the old traditional process. Reasons for choosing the computer are, and (1) the process is faster; (2) the quality of the sound does not deteriorate during transferring.

EDITING AND MIXING

Sound editing is putting the different sound elements in their proper places on each individual track. Mixing is the combining of the edited tracks into a single final sound track. Submixes are combining several tracks, the music for example, into one for the final mix. Bar sheets, animatics, mixing sheets or the finished film can be the guide for the editing and the mixing. In editing, the most important track, the voice, is normally edited first. Then the other tracks are edited or laid in. For example, you could edit two voice tracks, one music track and three sound effects tracks so that sound in each track is in its proper timing and place, and all tracks are in the proper timed relationship to each other. In the old days, editing and mixing were manually two different operations. Today, using the computer systems, you are often mixing the film as you are editing the sounds, as all the tracks are synced together digitally. These tracks are usually checker boarded into different levels, allowing the artist to apply numerous effects to the tracks besides levels of volume. Other effects include to slow, speed up, echo or play the sound backward. Fade-ins and fade-outs are also controllable and their speeds can be adjusted.

If you are doing your editing on 16mm mag track, you will need single-sprocket leader for spacing (the blank areas between sounds) and head and tail leaders.

You may want to use work tracks for your rough editing and save your original mag for the final edit.

You may need ambiance sound, usually called a presence track, for any parts of your track that is without sound. The complete absence of sound will sound strange. Examples of a presence track would be birds, wind, etc., for a country scene; city noises and freeway noises for an urban scene; and a presence track without any describable sound, the faint hiss of an air conditioning unit, for an interior scene. To get a sample of interior ambiance sound, for later duplication and use, record 30 seconds of silence at the beginning of your recording.

When you do the final mix, make sure that the music and effects levels are not so loud as to drown out the voice(s) tracks. This often happens, as you know the voices so well that you can hear them even though the music drowns them out for the intended audience. It is also a good idea to never let the composer mix the tracks. The music and effects tracks are mixed at a lower level under the voice track level when they are on together. The music and effects tracks can be at a normal level when the voice track is not present.

The final mix, with all the different tracks put onto one track, means the sound is done.

Timing or Reading the Track

This is when you put down the exact timing of any sound and its location in terms of frames, needed for animation on your exposure sheets (fig. 5-52). You normally start your count from zero before the first frame on your exposure sheet. Done in pencil, the frame count for a short film will run from zero to the last frame count on your film on the extreme right-hand side of the exposure sheets. On longer films, or films that are shot in sequence, each sequence can be timed as a total unit. For a total footage count of a longer film, bar sheets can be used.

Before you start reading the tracks you must first decide what sounds need to be read for syncing to your animation, and if this reading needs to be to the exact frame or will reading a block of time be sufficient. Example, you may need only the location of the complete word or you may need to break a word down into its various units–vowels or stresses. On the computer the frame count will be read off the screen. On 16mm mag track you will read it off a sync block, a moviola or a flatbed. The count will be in feet and frames, so you must convert to just frames for writing on the exposure sheets. There are 40 frames to a foot.

Negative Cut for a Film

After the film has been shot and all the sound is one digital element, the sound must be put into the proper form for the laboratory to make the final or composite film print. Before that is done, the magnetic sound track and the work print should be projected together in a mix room to check the sync and quality of sound. This is called "interlock." If everything is OK, the next step today is to transfer the digital sound track to a magnetic track. Then the original negative and work print, with the proper leaders and instructions, are sent to a negative cutter who will prepare the negative for the composite print. During the same time, the composite magnetic track, at least today, has to be made into an optical sound track. Then the synced optical sound track and cut negative are sent to a film laboratory for the composite print. A composite print has both sound and picture on the same piece of film. Together at last! You could also go to composite on digital and not go to film. This is less expensive. Today film is still the preferred medium for quality, some festivals and preservation. To make a video copy from film, you would make a digital master and then make video copies from that. If the work is in the digital format, it can go directly to video or be shot to film for a composite film print.

FILM TEMPO

The composer may need to know the primary beat or tempo of the film, scene or character (as in a walk cycle) that the director wants. Since musicians, and metronomes, work by the minute, you must convert frames per beat, the animator's timing or pacing, into beats per minute, the musician's time or pacing. The formulas are:

$$\frac{\text{Frames per minute} - 1440x}{\text{Beats per minute}} = \text{Frames per beat}$$

and

$$\frac{\text{Frames per minute} - 440x}{\text{Frames per beat}} = \text{Beats per minute}$$

Beat/Minute	Frames/Beat
40	36
60	24
72	20
80	18
90	16
103	14 (approx.)
111	13 (approx.)
120	12
144	10
160	9
180	8
206	7
240	6
360	4

The terms for tempos, the speed of the music, range from slow or Largo (40-60 beats per minute) through Larghetto (60-66), Adagio (66-76), Andante (76-108), Moderato (108-120), Allegro (120-168) to Presto (168-200), the fastest.

DRAWING SOUND ON FILM

If you want to experiment in drawing sound on film, these are some of the rules:

Pitch marks per frame x 24 frames a second = Cycles per Second /(CPS) i.e. 16 marks x 24 = 384 CPS or G above middle C

Lines across the frame equal the most sound impact. Lines drawn at an angle equal less volume. A beat is a big repetitive noise. Configuration determines timbre (what it will sound like).

See the drawing on sound film of Norman McLaren for more information. Oskar Fischinger also did work in this area.

SOUND EDITOR

In an animation studio, the sound editor's job is usually to edit the tracks, and create and lay in the effects and music. Treg Brown at Warner Bros. was considered the most innovative sound editor in animation.

FINAL THOUGHTS

Consider the effect of the verbal in visual comedy. When you have a verbal with the visual comedy, you have to stop laughing so you can hear the next line. In silent comedy, you do not have to wait on the verbal to get to the next laugh, so you can get a continuing comedic effect. I know a projectionist who thought the Marx Brothers were dull and unfunny. Working in the project booth, without the response of the audience, he could never understand why after a funny line there would be a stop of everything for a few seconds. This would kill the laugh for him. Only when he saw the film with an audience did he realize that the dead space in the film was there for the audience to laugh. The Marx Brothers' earliest films had been stage plays so they knew where the laughs were and timed their films accordingly. He now enjoys their films. This is a consideration in developing a nonverbal comedy storyboard. Two modern examples are: *The Road Runner and Coyote* and *The Pink Panther*. Another advantage of leaving out the language is that your film can be distributed internationally, which can greatly increase its audience. Of course, sound effects then play a vital role.

Since in animation sound is recorded separately from the action, it can be much more flexible and creative. It does not have to be handicapped by reality. This happened at the beginning of the sound era in live action. The recording of the spoken word necessitated a static camera shot, which resulted in the domination of dialogue and the subjection of the visual. This was not necessary in animation and animation did not become the slave of dialogue, at least until television. It had remained unfettered during transition from silent film to sound, using both the visual and the verbal in any mix. This is one reason why animation was so great during 1930s and 1940s, or as it is called, The Golden Age of Animation. In *Steamboat Willie* (1928), the first popular sound animated film, it is very apparent that Disney used sound to free up the visual. You can exploit the free use of sound in animation as an advantage, not only in the actual sound design but also in its fusion with the visuals and your idea.

When every action is accented by a sound it is called Mickey Mouse Sound.

(fig. 2-43)

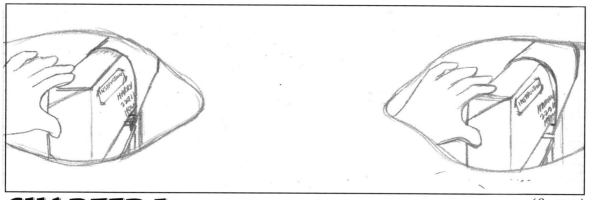

CHAPTER 5

(fig. 2-13)

LAYOUT[1]

Layout is the design, both technically and aesthetically, of the animation (especially character) and background of the entire film. Layout is divided into two interacting parts. The first is the Design layout or the look of the film. The second is the Technical layout or how to achieve the design. Layout can be done by pencil or digitally.

Layout is the major design and technical stage for the visual look and animation of the film. It must be done before the animation. Enthusiastic novice animators who forget this rule start animating right after the storyboards. This means redoing some or all of the animation. Good preplanning allows you to do your best animation and can save time later in the production process.

Professionals who do layout are called layout artists. They parallel these live-action professions: editor, art director, director of photography (lighting and cinematography), costume designer, set designer, special effects supervisor. Layout artists also assume certain duties of the director such as the blocking of the actors. The animation director is responsible for the layout of the film. Building on the storyboard sketches, layout includes:

- Deciding the final design and layout of the animation (fig. 5-1).
- Deciding the final design and layout of the backgrounds (fig. 5-2).
- Deciding the final combination and integration of the animation and the background layouts (fig. 5-1).

---

1. As mentioned in the Acknowledgements, the author completed the manuscript sometime around 2007 and the text has not been updated for accuracy. All statements reflect the belief of the author at the time of authorship and may, or may not, reflect current reality.

- Deciding the final character model sheets (fig. 5-3).
- Deciding the final design elements of the shot, composition and color, the art direction (fig. 2-33).
- Deciding the final editing of the film. Maintaining the screen direction (figs. 2-29, 2-30, 2-31).
- Deciding the final staging and dramatic flow of each shot and the entire film (fig. 2-63).
- Doing the exposure sheets as needed (fig. 5-52).

The layout process for traditional animation is taking the rough storyboard sketches and redrawing them in the proper size for standard film format. Physically, the work is done on regular-size (10½ x 12½) animation (fig. 7-4) or pan length (10½ x 25 or 37) paper. An animation table and disk, a field chart (fig. 5-36), animation paper, pencils (some colored) (fig. 11-2), drawing tools (rulers, etc.), exposure sheets (fig. 5-22) and erasers are needed. For digital layout, a drawing tablet is needed.

Before doing the layout, try some variations (inspirational, atmospheric or stylistic) of the storyboard panels. This could lead to a better film. The first task in layout is choosing the field size of the shot. Then the design decisions above are done.

You may wish to divide the work by laying out the animation or character elements before the background elements. The animation is everything that moves and the background, or BG, is everything that does not move. In a professional studio, the layout unit is often divided in this way. Both can be done together or the animation done first, it depends on the studio. The combination of the background elements and key animation poses in one pencil drawing will constitute the finished layout. When all the shots of the film, along with all the necessary nitty-gritty technical information on exposure sheets, are finished and laid out in sequential order, the layout of the film is done.

First we will discuss the design of the film followed by the technical layout of a traditional animated film shot on an animation crane. The layout of a digital film follows the same principles.

DESIGN

Camera, Editing and Composition

This section is a more detailed explanation of the design information in Chapter 2.

Storyboard - Some definitions again:

- *A shot* is a continuous action that begins and ends with either a cut, dissolve, metamorphosis, animated effect, a title card, or a fade-out/fade-in.
- *A scene* is a shot or a series of shots of the same environment. In the old days, each background was a different scene.
- *A sequence* can be a shot, a scene, or a series of shots or scenes with the same story or conceptual concerns.

The elements of design in animation are:

- **Camera** - the framing of the shot by the camera.
- **Editing** - the sequence of the shots and the change from one shot to another.
- **Composition** - the interior composition of the shot, including the composition of the animation.

CAMERA

Many of the camera rules in narrative animation come from live-action precedents. An animator should know these, as most audiences feel that live-action rules are the standard for all films. In live action, the camera shot is decided during the filming though some excellent directors, for example Alfred Hitchcock, would storyboard their shots. Setting up the shot on the spot gives the director and director of photography some creative freedom; they need only follow the script and provide minimum coverage for the editing. Some directors, for example John Ford, claimed they would film their shots in only one way so the editor would not have any choice but to cut it Ford's way. Having been an extra on a couple of Ford's films I would have to say I did not see any evidence that would support that statement.[2]

In animation the camera shot is decided in layout with the layout artist taking the place of the camera, using the live-action principles for a foundation. As one becomes more experienced in animation, the live-action rules can be supplemented or replaced by animation techniques and principles. Some of you may instinctively be there already.

The elements that are dealt with in the framing of the shot by the camera are: size, camera view, camera height, subject angle to the camera and movement. (Illustrations of these elements are in Chapter 2, specifically fig. 2-13 through 2-21.)

Size

The size of the main element(s) in the shot with the measuring stick being the normal human body. These are fairly standard definitions; different studios can have their own variation.

- **Extreme close-up (ECU)**: a shot of part of a head, an eye for example (fig. 2-14).
- **Close-Up (CU)**: a shot of the head (fig. 2-14).
- **Medium Close-Up (MCU)**: a shot of the full head and upper body to the waist (fig. 2-14).
- **Medium (M)**: a full-body shot (fig. 2-14).
- **Medium long shot (MLS)**: the height of full body is no less than half of the frame (fig. 2-14).
- **Long shot (LS)**: the full body is less than half of the frame (fig. 2-14).

---

2. To hear the author talk about his time as a Hollywood extra, please go to http://danmclaughlin.info/talk.html. Also, see fig. 5-4.

- *Extreme long shot (ELS)*: a shot of a city or the world (fig. 2-14).
- *Multiple shots:* Pans, trucks, pantographic movements and combinations of these movements that would cause the shot to change within the shot (figs. 2-15, 5-39).

These shots are often used for these actions or attitudes:

- *ECU* - very dramatic, mouth opens in a scream, eye gets cut open with a razor blade.
- *CU* - focus on individual or specific action, person speaking, picking up an apple. CUs add dramatic emphasis and cut down on the labor of animation.
- *MCU* - the characters are more important than BG, you can clearly see the expressions and gestures, good for two to three people. Often used for a two-shot (two people interacting). The staging rules for a two-shot should be learned for doing narrative animation.
- *M* - when a full-body shot is needed. As in Tex Avery's *Red Hot Riding Hood* (1943).
- *MLS* - where the full body has to move, dance. A Fred Astaire shot.
- *LS* - the entire area of action, the master shot or an establishing shot.
- *ELS* - to show the scope of the setting or event, the end of the world or the birth of the universe.
- *MS* - the most complex one I can think of is the truck to Pinocchio leaving for school.

As mentioned in the Chapter 3, Timing, I have done quantitative research on the percentage of different kinds of shots in films. The films that were my sample are:

- NIGHT ON BALD MOUNTAIN (1933). Alexander Alexeieff and Claire Parker, France, 7.9 minutes. 56 shots, average length of shots = 202 frames or 8.4 seconds. (NBM-a)
- NIGHT ON BALD MOUNTAIN (from FANTASIA, 1940). Disney, USA, 13.8 minutes. 69 shots, average length of shots = 288 frames or 12 seconds. (NBM-d)
- SONG OF THE PRAIRIE (1949). Jirí Trnka, Czechoslovakia, 20.8 minutes. 274 shots, average length of shots = 110 frames or 4.6 seconds. (SOP)
- THE STRANGE CASE OF MR. AND MRS. DONNYBROOK'S BOREDOM (1981). David Silverman, USA, 4.5 minutes. 45 shots, average length of shots = 143 frames or 6 seconds. (DB)
- BALANCE (1989). Christoff and Wolfgang Lauenstein, Germany, 7.2 minutes. 103 shots, average length of shots = 101 frames or 4.2 seconds. (B)
- TECHNOLOGICAL THREAT (1988). Bill and Sue Kroyer, USA, 3.6 minutes. 69 shots, average length of shots = 75 frames or 3.1 seconds. (TT)
- CUCKOO (1988). Velislav Kazakov, Bulgaria, 2.7 minutes. 27 shots, average length of shots = 146 frames or 6.1 seconds (C)
- SAND DANCE (1988). Richard Quade, USA, 3.2 minutes. 23 shots, average length of shots = 203 frames or 8.5 seconds. (SD)

The films and the frequency of the different shot size usage for each film are:

Film	NBM-a	NBM-d	SOP	DB	B	TT	C	SD
ECU	0%	0%	0%	0%	0%	0%	0%	0%
CU	11%	6%	11%	6%	6%	40%	7%	7%
MCU	2%	7%	36%	17%	16%	11%	7%	4%
M	36%	22%	35%	51%	36%	36%	44%	39%
MLS	30%	33%	13%	21%	22%	13%	37%	25%
LS	7%	17%	3%	4%	4%	0%	4%	25%
ELS	5%	4%	0%	1%	0%	0%	0%	0%
MLS	7%	10%	3%	0%	17%	0%	0%	0%

Most Common Shots:

- Medium Shots (M) ranged from 22 percent to 51 percent per film for an average of 37 percent.
- Medium Long Shots (MLS) ranged from 13 percent to 37 percent for an average of 24 percent.
- The M and MLS accounted for 61 percent of all shots.

Others:

- MCU - ranged from 2 percent to 36 percent for an average of 12.5 percent.
- CU - ranged from 11 percent to 40 percent for an average of 12 percent.
- LS - ranged from 0 percent to 25 percent for an average of 8 percent.
- ELS - ranged from 0 percent to 5 percent for an average of 1 percent.
- ECU - none - 0 percent average.

Notes on Shot Usage

For a traditional narrative film, many directors consider an establishing or master shot (fig. 2-16) essential to let the audience know where everything is and to make sure later shots are easier to understand. They are also aware that the closer the shot, the more emphasis there is on the character, art or object. Many beginning filmmakers never use MCU, CU or ECU because they are afraid to let the audience too close to their characters or art. This can make the film too emotionally cold or make characters that do not come across. The closer the audience gets, the more empathy can be generated. A traditional concern in animation is that in getting too close on graphic material allows the audience to see that it's just really a bunch of lines and puddles of paint, but audiences are more sophisticated now and are able to accept the graphic part of animation. CUs will take a little more care, time and details but they can be well worth it.

With the size of the shot decided, the next step is to place the camera. The three considerations are: camera view, camera height, and subject angle to camera, or up, down and all around.

As an example, say you have a scene of a family in the kitchen where the two kids are trying to get their way. In the storyboard it is all in a master shot, but you break it up into different shots in layout. Starting with the master shot of the kids pleading, you then cut to a CU of the father saying, "no way," cut to down CU shot of little girl saying, "But please dad, you promised;" cut to MCU of mom looking annoyed at her husband and saying, "Sorry honey, but daddy doesn't always keep his promises;" then cut to low MCU angle of father saying, "OK, you can jump off the bridge;" cut to MLS of kids dancing happily. You have now laid out the scene for maximum effect and minimum amount of animation.

Camera View is either:

Objective Camera. The view is from the outside looking in. The events are not the viewpoint of anyone within the scene but are the audience's point of view. Called the fourth wall in theater. Tex Avery was a master at breaking the fourth wall, where suddenly a character or a sign would directly address the audience, usually with a satirical comment on the action (fig. 2-17).

Subjective Camera. The camera places the viewer in the scene. A roller-coaster ride shot from the roller coaster or when the camera shows you what a character sees; the character looks off screen, reacts, and then you cut to what they see. Another subjective view is a point of view shot (POV), where the audience is looking directly through characters' eyes (fig. 2-18).

Camera Height - The height angles are High, Level and Low

High Angle. The characters or objects are viewed from above. Good for a sense of location. Can make the audience feel superior to the character (fig. 2-19).

Level. The characters or objects are viewed from the eye level of the character. The common angle in animation is also the least interesting (fig. 2-20).

Low Angle. The characters or objects are viewed from below. Can be very dramatic, threatening or omnipotent. It can make a shot far more interesting (fig. 2-21).

Subject Angle to Camera

The character or visual can either present one surface to the camera, which will make the shot flat, or two or more surfaces, which implies depth in the shot. To achieve a flat effect, keep the camera straight on and all surfaces in the art parallel to the film in the camera. Characters are customarily shown in profile. The background is flat or non-existent. Good examples of this approach are the films from UPA during its heyday as their philosophy of animation style was: Film is flat, art is flat, the screen is flat and therefore the animation is flat (fig. 5-5).

To achieve a depth effect, place the camera angle so that two or more planes or surfaces are shown. In laying out a room, for instance, you would show three planes: two walls and the floor (fig. 5-34). To emphasize depth, have the floor line angled different from the bottom of the frame line. If you place a character in that space you would, by the laws of perspective, have to put them into at least a three-quarter profile pose and they would have to present at least two surfaces to the camera, side and front (figs. 2-19, 5-6, 14-3). This is one reason why on model sheets a three-quater profile pose is drawn, not a full profile (figs. 2-42, 5-3). If one character upstages the other, one stands closer to the audience and looks at the one farther from the audience so all the attention is on the character up stage (fig. 5-7). This is a dirty trick in the theater but a good trick in animation, as it has created the illusion of depth by the subject's angle to the camera.

Other Shot Terms

- *Insert shot* - an insert of written or printed material. A letter, a sign, a newspaper, etc (fig. 2-28).
- *Dutch shot* - Extreme camera angles, crazy tilts. When the vertical axis of the camera is at an angle to the vertical axis of the character or object (fig. 5-8).
- *Neutral shot* - a shot without x, y screen direction. Moving directly away from or into the camera is one such shot. Also could refer to a shot that is neutral to an action, an eye, a face or a dog. These can be very useful for editing your way out of a dilemma, just put it in when the screen direction goes haywire. Shoot some extra neutral shots when you shoot your film as a backup (fig. 5-9).
- *Pan shot* - a moving shot across the landscape or following the action. Animation uses the same term (fig. 5-39).
- *Dolly, zoom shot* - moving in or out. The term truck is used in animation (figs. 2-15, 5-38).

Additional Thoughts

Many first-time animators unconsciously think of themselves as an audience in a theater, locked in their seats, looking at the fixed proscenium stage. This view can limit their film to a series of static master shots. If static shots are germane to your central idea, stay with it. Otherwise select different camera shots, compositions and transitions that best express your vision. Cutting and moving the camera are the structure of film. Just as an exercise, arbitrarily change the type, size, view, height and subject angle of a series of shots to see what it does for your film.

First do a floor plan (fig. 5-10) and a master shot (fig. 2-16) when you do a layout. This tells you where the characters and background elements are in relationship to each other so that you do not lose them in the layouts. It can also be helpful in planning out your camera angles, making sure you don't cross over the 180-degree line.

The normal screen ratios are the rectangular or landscape format. This is different from the common vertical or portrait format in painting. For those who come from a painting background, this may be a little difficult at first. Sometimes it's easier to draw the characters or action first, then draw the frame or background around them (fig. 5-12).

Arrive at a philosophy on the use of the camera. Chuck Jones had a rule that he would do a camera shot in animation that could not be done in live action, as a camera in the middle of a blazing fireplace. This brings up the use of the animation angle rather than the camera angle.[3]

The animation angle is not based on the reality of the camera. It can use the principles of the live-action camera, but it goes beyond them; a POV could really be inside a person's head and looking out through his eye sockets (fig. 2-13). There is a marvelous shot in Caroline Leaf's *The Street* (1976), as two men stand talking on a balcony and the audience's view pans around the surrounding buildings in a pure movement that is unrelated to any known reality. UPA films had some flat graphic design shots that made 99 percent of live-action camera shots look pale and insipid. Develop your own approach, it is a matter of taste and what camera style is best for your film, but as long as you are in animation you might as well use animation (fig. 5-13).

MOVEMENT

Movement is animation. Movement and its flip side, non-movement, are essential in animation. Movement in animation, though all related, takes on different forms. The movements we are discussing here are the relationship of the basic movement of the image and the camera to the shot, and the basic direction of movement within the shot. The use of these forms of movement can add value to any film, but are often overlooked in the storyboard and layout stages.

Relationship of movement and camera to the shot

- Camera still, image still - static, still, a painting.
- Camera still, image moving - emphasis on the image and its movement.
- Camera moving, image still - to show a location, place, pans, trucks.
- Camera moving, image moving - most active.
- Two or more of the above in the same shot but at different times. This can cause a change of pace.

---

3. I believe this is one of those many personal communications to the author.

Direction of Movement: x,y,z. This can be either the camera or the action within the shot

- x = horizontal (quiet)
- y = vertical (more active)
- x + y = diagonal (most active)
- z = move away (animate or truck out), move towards (animate or truck in)
- Combinations of x, y & z movements
- It is possible there is another movement -- the circular.

An analysis of number four, the Z-Axis movement, will serve as an illustration of why knowledge of direction of movement is important.

What is meant by Z-Axis animation? It is animation that elicits a sense of forward motion or forward acceleration, or, in computer jargon, Z-Axis motion. This is from the reference to the Cartesian coordinate system of analytic geometry in which X designates the horizontal axis; Y, the vertical axis; and Z the third axis of dimension or depth. In traditional animation, Z-Axis is commonly referred to as animating in perspective. This is difficult and usually avoided because an object moving in perspective is difficult to animate and is constantly changing speed in relation to the viewer. The closer the object is to the viewer the faster the speed, the farther away the slower the speed. This makes Z-Axis animation time-consuming and costly. In addition, not all animators have the ability to do Z-Axis animation and a good one can be hard to find. All of these factors combine to make Z-Axis animation the least used movement in traditional animation. Conversely, it is one of the cheapest and easiest movements to do in computer animation, the fly-through or fly-by, for example. Two animators in traditional animation who did Z-Axis animation well were Ub Iwerks, especially in *Plane Crazy* (1928) and Bill Littlejohn. Bill Littlejohn (fig. 5-14), today the oldest freelance animator working,[4] has developed a particular form of Z-Axis animation, that of moving the viewer in a forward, rapid ever changing journey that is of the highest aesthetic and kinetic quality. This is especially true in his Tiger Paws and Rain Tire commercials from the 1970s (fig. 5-15). In one of the Tiger Paws commercials, Bill animated the cat coming over a top of a hill from the tiger's point of view. He animated the tiger's front paws extending out in front and moving down to grab the road. After the screening to the New York advertising people, the head copywriter jumped up and said, "Those paws have to go!" Bill asked why, they seemed to work very well. "Too well," said the copywriter. "They made me sick, gave me motion sickness, and we will have half of America throwing up after we broadcast it." Bill argued and argued, but the paws went. Imagine a 30-second animated spot done so well in Z-Axis animation that it

---

4   Bill Littlejohn died September 17, 2010.

would have made half of the United States sick.[5] Bill's Z-Axis animation is helped immensely by his years of experience as a pilot. What is more Z-Axis than landing a plane? If you have such a background or experience, draw on it for your animation.

Z movements when we are moving forward, either as a point of view (walking) or as a spectator (as in a moving car), and fast-forward movement seems to induce within us a more kinetic response than a more normal speed forward movement. Why? In the human evolutionary history, the consensus among anthropologists is that humans evolved from an arboreal primate form similar to the modern gibbon. Gibbons swing arm over arm from trees, grasping branches from the underside in a mode of locomotion called "brachiation." Brachiation is very physically demanding and requires a brain that must be capable of orchestrating the rush of information received by the body projectile as it is hurled forward from branch to branch at the highest speed achieved by any primate, and it includes calculating the parabolic of its trajectory. In human history, and now on foot, moving fast-forward was either chasing game or a fellow human, or running from the same, and being very careful as a misstep could mean death. With the advent of the domestication of the horse and the invention of the internal combustion engine, the human on land has turned this faster-forward motion into a passion for thrills. Many sports have as the primary movement the Z-Axis motion: horse racing, surfing, skate boarding, running in track, riding on a roller coaster, or just the pleasure of motoring fast through a spring countryside in a sports car.

Cinema has used this Z-Axis movement from its conception. One of the earliest cinematic visuals includes a shot from a camera mounted on a cowcatcher. This type of forward movement continues in today's car chases, Luke's flight through the fabricated canyon of the Death Star in *Star Wars* and the high-velocity jumps into hyperspace. Also, Z-Axis movement functions differently to the edges of the screen. Whereas the X-horizontal and the Y-vertical movements are cut off by the edges of the screen, the Z-Axis is unbounded and motion along it is unrestricted, and it's size is constantly changing to the edge of the screen.

This predilection toward Z-Axis motion seems to be hardwired into our brain. If we duplicate that sensation in animation, we will have a very positive and powerful visual response. One that best mirrors the exhilaration and freedom of animation.

EDITING

Editing, as mentioned before, is the sequential arrangement of the shots in your film and the transitions from one shot to another. In layout, you will double-check your editing decisions made so far, change if needed and refine them. Editing, the structure of film, like the structure of language, grammar, has a set of principles. The first set concerns the continuity of the shots.

---

5. Another personal story told to the author?

Time Continuity

Present - The events of the film are happening now and follow the logic of time that is moving forward. If time is not compressed, as in a scene, the editing is called continuity cutting. Time, in editing, is usually compressed in a film. Thus time in animation can go from little or no compression, as in *Gertie the Dinosaur* (1914) or *The Big Snit* (1985); to sometime compression, as in *Snow White* (1937) or *The Dover Boys* (1942); to large time compression, several generations, as in *Crac!* (1981). Audiences are used to short cuts in cinematic time and readily accept them as long as the continuity is logical.

Past - A flashback in time either during the film or the prologue.

Future - A flash-forward in time.

Animation - Created time, not reality-based time, breaks the laws of physics and time. Normally found in experimental animation. *Begone Dull Care* (1949), *Allegretto (1936), God Is Dog Spelled Backwards* (1967) (fig. 1-3), *Sand Dance* (1988), all create their own screen time. The only logical time is the running time of the film.

Space Continuity

This is somewhat parallel to time continuity. The locations in present time should follow a logical order. If you are in a city, you should remain in a city. Past and future should have the correct look and the transition to them should be clear. The audience should never have to ask the question, "Where are we?" In animation this rule can be broken if the content calls for it. The lack of space continuity was one of Chuck Jones's running gags in *Duck Amuck* (1953).

Direction Continuity or Screen Direction

Screen direction means that a character should always face or move in the same direction when you transition from shot to shot.

If one character is on the left side of the screen and facing right and is talking to another character that is on the right facing left, when you cut back and forth between them they must stay on their sides of the screen. The one on the left stays on the left. The one the right stays on the right. You keep them where they belong by applying the 180-degree rule which is: If you have two characters in a shot and you plan to cut between them, you first draw a line that goes from the tip of one character's nose to the other character's nose, now extend that line. That line is the 180-degree line, and you can shoot from any angle you want on one side of the line, but on one side only. You cannot shoot from the other side of the 180-degree line or the heads will flop from one side to the other on the cut. Never, ever, in traditional editing, cross the 180-degree line (fig. 2-29). Also if you do, the audience will get the characters confused or think they are not talking to each other. The audience can get lost or think you are a beginning filmmaker. The same problem will occur if you cut from a front shot to a rear shot and cross the line, unless you have the character centered. Simple, yes, but this is one of the most common rules a person breaks on his first board or film. Always think of the 180-degree rule when you are cutting around in the same scene. This rule applies when a character leaves the shot. If a character is moving from left to right and exits on screen right, then if you pick them up in the next shot they must enter on screen left so they will still be moving left to right. Otherwise the audience will be confused, thinking the character has turned around or is a different character. If you get yourself up a box canyon on this, throw in the neutral shot (fig. 5-9) -- eye, apple and cosmic explosion -- between the two mismatched shots and the audience may not notice. The last rule on screen direction involves screen direction in travel. The rule is an elementary one: Always keep the direction consistent. If a person is on a train going from Los Angeles to New York the train should always be going from left to right (fig. 2-30). When the person is returning to Los Angeles from New York, the train should be moving from right to left (fig. 2-31).

It is very easy to lose your audience when you are cutting between characters talking to each other or exchanging looks. Make sure the characters are relating properly so the audience knows where they are or that the relationships do not look odd. The shots must match the direction of the character's "look." An example would be if two characters, one sitting and one standing, are speaking and you are cutting between them (of course, observing the 180-degree rule) so that the character sitting is looking straight ahead and not looking up at the standing character when alone in the shot. The audience could easily think the character is looking at the other person's crotch (fig. 5-16).

A *Jump Cut* is when you jump ahead of or behind the present time in continuity cutting. Most jump cuts occur when the character jumps ahead in time on the cut from one shot to the next shot. A common example would be reaching for the doorknob in one room as the character exits the room in the first shot, and then cut to the next shot in the other room with the character already in the room just closing the door. You must exit a character before you can cut to him entering a new shot. It is up to your sense of timing if you want to give a frame or two on the empty space after he leaves and before he enters or you cut just as he leaves and exactly when they enter. A jump cut backwards would be if you had a person exiting a room through a door and he was halfway through the door when you cut to the next room and the door is still closed and there is a beat or two before it opens. To avoid jump cuts you use matching action. The action when you leave a shot will match the same action when you are in the new shot.

On a *Cut In*, a cut into part of the previous shot, usually a close-up of the center of interest. If you move only a very little distance you will cause not a jump cut, but more of a bump cut. To avoid this, when you cut in on a character or object always travel a longish distance.

Of course, rules like the ones above can be broken, especially in animation narrative or experimental film, but you should only break them after you know them and then only to do a better film. Now a few more terms used in editing to end this section.

Matched Cuts - present time, a continuous flow of action from one shot to the next.

Cut Away - to a shot that is not a continuation of the previous shot.

Cross Cutting - parallel cutting of two or more actions in an alternating or checkerboard format. "Cut them off at the pass" "or meantime back at the ranch" type editing.

Cutting on Action - a popular way of cutting; you cut on the action, rather than a hold, like a door opening to start a scene or closing to end a scene. This will keep the action moving and it may mask any problem you have with the cut. Even cutting on something as small as an eye blink can keep the action going.

Cut to - cutting to a specific action or subject-as in "cut to close up."

Matching Shots

The entire composition is not only very important for the shot, but is also important for the editing. In cutting, do you want the composition to remain basically the same? On the other hand, do you want a smooth change to something somewhat different? Will a new center of interest replace the old center of interest? These are decisions that are very important to rhythm, flow and continuity of your film. To control the match on the transition, there are three elements that need to be considered.

- The elements of composition; Form, balance, line, size, space, value and color.
- The elements of the camera; size, angle, subject angle.
- The element of mood; keeping the mood of the film at that point, or changing the mood.

Since you control these elements, there should be no problem in matching them. Just be sure, as you are creating all of the above, that you are thinking about the editing and matching the shots. When I say match, it need not be smooth, as you may want a visual shock match for its dramatic effect. The best cut for shock that I have ever seen was watching the live-action film *Black Orpheus* (1959). The scene was a beautiful, sun-drenched day high up above Rio de Janeiro, with slow, panning shots of the white and brightly colored houses. Suddenly there was a cut to the interior of an ambulance, going a hundred miles an hour, with it red light lashing madly and its siren shrieking down a black tunnel at night. The cut literally knocked me back in my seat. I found out about 20 minutes later they had put the wrong reel on at the changeover. It was a mistake, but what a creative one.

As an exercise for controlling matching shots, do a series of your panels just showing where the center of interest is, a simple X with arrows for the direction of movement will do (fig. 2-25). When you look at these panels you will see how the center of interest moves from shot to shot. Does it add excitement and interest to your film, or does it just stay in one spot and become boring? This exercise will allow you to control this basic visual flow of your film. The invention of this approach has been attributed to Ward Kimball (fig. 5-17) in his early days at Disney.

The emotional influence of a sequence can be affected by the editing. An example is the "Kuleshov Effect," where the juxtaposition of shots can alter the intent of the scene. Example, a medium close-up of a character looking at something off screen, followed by a shot of a beautiful woman, ending with an extreme close-up of the man's eye conveys an emotion, but if you substitute a shot of a casket for the woman you change the intent of the scene. A prime example is the montage or the editing together of discrete or contrasting shots to convey an idea or emotion. A battle montage composed of quick shots of soldiers fighting or an earthquake montage composed of shots of people in an earthquake.

There is one last thing I want to mention: eye movement or scanning. Only in motion pictures do audiences move their eyes. TV audiences do not move their eyes as the screen is so small. In motion pictures the eye can be constantly traveling, hopefully under the control of the filmmaker. Because the eye is constantly scanning, you have to be aware of where the eye is when you cut. When cross cutting on two talking heads, you must keep the eyes on the same level. If the line between the eyes is not at the same level, it will cause the audience to lose the rhythm of their eye scan, and they will have to jump up and down as well as across, which will cause a subtle disruption of the scene for them. The same goes for a gunfight. Keep the guns on the same level. This may seem a minor point as eye movement is often not considered a principle in editing, but if you want smooth editing, you should be aware where the audience's eyes are looking and in what direction they are moving as you transition to the next shot. One type of cut on screen direction that can cause confusion in the audience is when a character exits screen right and then to match the direction he has to enter screen left. This causes the eye to scan from right to left, which can break the flow of the movement. It is best to put another shot in between the two so that this does not occur (fig. 5-9).

This is the visual part of editing; the timing of editing (how long a shot should be) is in the timing chapter.[6] As you review the timing you should be starting to develop a timing style: fast quick cuts, or long slow shots, or changing rhythms medium, slow or fast. If you do not have a sound track to sync up to, use your bar sheets and timing flow charts. Do the cuts work well with the timing of each shot? Does the whole film have the pacing you want? You could supplant your story sketches in the animatic with finished layout drawings to get a very clear feeling of how well the structure and timing of your film works, and you can see each of your

---

6. Chapter 3.

decisions as a part of the total film idea.

TRANSITIONS

A transition is the method of change from one shot to the next shot. These are the methods available in animation. Plan your type of transition to help your content and timing.

Cut - Going from one shot directly to the next shot. It is the most frequently used form of transition. Called a cut because the film is actually cut, then taped or glued together.

Dissolve - When one shot blends into the next shot. It's really a fade out superimposed over a fade in. Originally used to denote a period of time or a change of location. They can range from short dissolves, a few frames, to very long dissolves. I once did a film that was an eight-minute dissolve from the color red to the color green.[7]

Fade Out, Fade In - This is when a shot fades to black (fade out) and then a new shot fades in from black (fade in). Traditionally indicates a long period of time or distance, but it is a definite separation of the scenes or of time. Can be of varying lengths.

Optical Wipes - The new shot coming in wipes out or over the old shot. Comes in a myriad of patterns and directions.

Irises - A particular optical wipe, where you iris in and out of black or iris a new shot over an old one. The black iris was used effectively in silent films (fig. 2-27).

Optical Effects - For example, a swish pan. A swish pan is one done so fast that the visuals are blurred by the speed. A popular TV show would cut in a stock one- to two-second swish pan as a transition when they wanted to keep the pace frenetic. It worked very well, especially coupled with a sound effect.

Title Card - Written or animated. Title cards are one of the oldest film traditions; they were the spoken word in silent films (fig. 2-28).

Metamorphosis - Or the change of one shot into another through ever-changing, often abstract, shapes.

Partial Transitions - In animation, transitions can be accomplished through changing only part of the scene. Because most animation is shot on different levels, you can change one of the levels and not disturb the others. You could dissolve out one background (city) and dissolve in another (country) behind your character as they are walking along.

Animated Transitions - a form of metamorphosis where the transitions is controlled by using animation. It can be hard to tell it is a transition as the animation works as a transition. It is a good place to use "animation thinking."

---

7. This film is called *Red/Green* (1985). You can listen to the author talk about *Red/Green* here http://danmclaughlin.info/talk.html. Also, you can view *Red/Green* on the DVD *11 Films by Dan McLaughlin*. See also fig. 2-55.

Sound Transitions

Is the use of the voice, music or sound effects to aid in the visual transition? A voice could be describing the next shot, "There's gold in them thar hills," as you slowly dissolve to hills of gold. The opening of Beethoven's 5th could set up a cut to a superhero or a little confused puppy dog or the rattling of a rattlesnake turning into the chattering of teeth as you cut to a very frightened individual. Sound seems to work better if it happens before the picture appears. The audience is able to understand each in turn, which is helpful since we see quicker than we hear.

"Zero cut" means that you have planned a transition so that in case you have to reshoot part of your film, you do not have to reshoot the entire film. Example, if all the scenes in your film were connected by dissolves, you would have to reshoot your entire film if there was a mistake (unless you had an explosion, a good place for making a cut). But if you put in a cut or two or a fade-out/fade-in, you would be adding zero cuts to your film, places where you can cut without making the images in the edited negative of your film jump around, thus making it easier to edit for reshoots. Information about hands-on editing is covered in Chapter 8, Post-Production.

A quick review of editing:

- What scene or shot will go where/when for the maximum impact of story or content?
- Can the audience follow your film? Or will the structure of your film confuse them?
- Does the composition work with the transitions?
- Is the screen direction correct? Did you cross the 180-degree line?
- Do you have a good combination of long shots, medium shots and close ups?
- Do you use good angles in your shot selection?
- Does the editing rhythm follow the emotional content of the action? In a simple sense, fast cutting with short shots for action or chase scenes, and longer shots with dissolves for romantic or lyrical scenes.

COMPOSITION

"An arrangement of the parts of a work of art so as to form a unified, harmonious whole," *Webster's New World College Dictionary*.[8] The composition within the shot of an animated film must do two things: one, support the film, and two, be aesthetically pleasing within the content and style of the film. Once again, there are two compositions within a shot, which together make up the total third, final composition. The first is the composition of the back-

---

8. Because the author used a 1996 *Webster's New College Dictionary*, (3rd edition. revised) in an earlier footnote, I am assuming that dictionary is the source of this quote as well. Unfortunately I have been unable to locate a copy of this dictionary to verify this wording.

ground or anything that is not being animated (fig. 5-2). The second is the composition of the animation. The third is both together (fig. 5-1). The composition of the background is usually done after the path of action or composition of the animation has been laid out (fig. 5-12). The following elements of composition apply both to background and animation and to the total shot. The purpose of a good composition is to focus the audience's attention on the center of interest, usually the action. The audience then looks where the artist wants them to look.

FORM and **COLOR** are the two basic components of formal composition in animation. The components of **FORM** are:

Balance, or the equality in all the parts, is a state of equilibrium. Balance can either be **symmetrical** or **asymmetrical**.

Symmetrical means that both sides of the screen are equally balanced, therefore the whole shot is balanced. A dead-in-the-center head shot, a centered bull's-eye target. The effect can be static, dramatic, formal or quiet.

Unless you want this particular effect it is better to have **asymmetry**, or balance through tension. The sides are formally out of balance, one side formally stronger than the other, but balanced by other means. A large stationary object in one area can be balanced by a small moving object in another. One bright color can balance a large gray mass. Placing your main character higher and closer than anyone else, but balancing her by the weight of the other characters. The headshot, instead of being straight on, is put slightly to one side or the other and is balanced by the larger negative space on the other side. If the character is on screen right looking at something off screen left, looking into the large space gives more room for the look and balances the shot even more. If the character is looking off screen right and it is on the right, the shot will be out of balance and will look very awkward as there is no place for the character to look. Now the question, which side of the screen is the best to place the head of your character? The right side is normally preferred because in European cultures we read left to right so the eye would read across the screen to the face on the right side and stop. Our eye movement would balance the shape of the head.

But how far to the left or right and how far above or below the center line to place the head? Are there pleasing points and lines of reference? Yes. The Greeks had them and called it "The Golden Section" or a:b=b:(a+b). Today we can use a grid system to find these sweet points. For a simple grid system, divide the screen into thirds horizontally and vertically. The four points and lines that occur will give you four very acceptable points and lines for visual reference. An illustration in still art would be the painting *Madonna with Child and Two Angels* c. 1465 by Fra Filippo Lippi, where the upper two points frame the Madonna and Child and the main angel is placed on the bottom third line, making a very fine asymmetrical composition (fig. 5-19). Another illustration would be Rembrandt van Rijn's *Self Portrait as a Young Man* (1634), where the two vertical lines frame his face and his eyes are on the upper line, which then creates the asymmetrical balance (fig. 5-20). Dividing the screen *into* thirds makes it immediately asymmetrical as you break up the even half-and-half division. Using thirds (or any uneven number) is a known technique in art. The rule of threes means having three cows, three trees, three ships, not two in a painting. It works in animation and timing also. For instance on a moving hold it is better to have three trace backs rather than two, as two will give you a too-mechanical look. But there will be more on that in the next chapter.

A more complex grid system is the 6-10. This is where you divide the screen into 10 equal units both vertically and horizontally. Now the sweet points and lines are on the sixes, counting in from any side. This may work better for film, because of the TV cutoff and you don't want to get to close too the sides.

If you have one center of interest, the balance of the composition will be judged on how well you manifest asymmetrical focus on that center of interest. If you have two centers of interests balance them with care. Occasionally a composition will have one character speaking in the extreme upper right-hand corner to another speaking character in the extreme lower left-hand corner for a dramatic balance. So dramatic that the audience will take so much time moving their eyes back and forth they will lose what the characters are saying and doing, especially if they are doing it at the same time. The film demands balance in its still art, its moving art and in the sum of the total film.

Line

We are not talking about the use of line in drawing, a contour, a curving, and a thick and thin or broken line, etc. Rather we are talking about the types of lines created by the composition. It could be a line of direction caused by a group of shapes or a shape. The combination of a strong horizontal horizon line, repeated by a strong horizontal line created by the roofline of house, and supported by a horizontal line of clouds will give you an intense horizontal composition. It is conceptually a composition of quiet rest. You would design a basic vertical, diagonal or Z-Axis (and time too) composition in the same way. Or it could be the invisible line that the eye follows through the composition, an implied line created by the formal composition. *Mother and Child* by Diego Rivera (1926) has an invisible line that guides the viewer's eye in a circular movement through the body of the mother, through her face down to the child, through the child, back to the body of the mother to repeat the movement (fig. 5-21). This line could be circular, triangular, straight or any other line of direction. In this type of line there is also design consideration for where the eye enters the path of the eye movement. This entry point could be a strong color, an expressive hand, the look of the eyes. Another line would be the line created by the movement in the animation, which should work with and within the lines of the formal composition. And last there is the line that defines the form, forms and shape, both individual shape and the shape of unified forms. An illustration of the use of unified forms would be *The Holy Family* (c.1504) by Michelangelo Buonarroti (fig. 5-22), where the three heads form an inverted triangle near the top and the clothing of the Madonna forms a triangle with her head at the top near the bottom that interlocks with the inverted triangle near the top to focus the audience on the main subject matter. This is also a good example of how the delineating line is intertwined with volume, space and the guidelines in each of the following components of form. Here is a small sampling of the perceived emotional attributes of line types.

- Straight lines = strength
- Soft curved lines = lyrical
- Sharp curved lines = laughter
- Long horizontal lines = rest. But **if** done at a low camera angle they can be very dramatic.
- Strong vertical lines = activity, action
- Strong diagonal lines = the most dramatic, eye catching. Sharp lines = liveliness.

If you want a more conceptual view of line, I would recommend Paul Klee's *Pedagogical Sketchbook*. "Line on a walk" or "a line is just a dot taking a walk"[9] are some of his thoughts on line that can open up new ways for you to approach line and design.

Size - The different aspects of size are:

- **Mass** - either a shape like a head or several characters grouped together as a mass. If large, mass can dominate the shot.
- **Shape** - a property of line (or is it the other way around?). Can either be the shape of the mass, hard = angular, soft = sensuous, or a delineating shape. Please see the example in Line.
- **Scale** - the proportions. It can either be the size of one object or character in relation to another, or the size of the character or subject in relation to the background. Are the proportions correct and stay correct or are they distorted for dramatic or aesthetic reasons?
- **Volume** - the amount of space inside an object, like inside a bouncing ball. It should remain the same, except when changed by outside forces.
- **Weight** - clouds are light, and cannonballs are heavy. Each will have a certain presence in the layout based on its weight.

---

9. "A line is a dot that went for a walk." Paul Klee. BrainyQuote.com. Xplore Inc., 2017. 22 March 2017.

Space

2D, 2½D or 3D - discussed in Camera Height. Which to use should have been decided in the storyboard stage. Nevertheless, double-check if there is a doubt.

Negative and Positive Space - Positive space is taken up by something, a tree, a character, an abstract shape, anything. Negative space is the space between positive spaces (fig. 5-13). For instance, the open space between the tree and the outhouse. Both of these spaces have a form, and how these forms of positive and negative space balance and interact are relevant to the composition.

Perspective - The art of design or drawing in depth. Perspective is the appearance of the object or the animation in the shot as determined by its relative distance and position. This is a complex subject. It will be taken up as a separate item later in this chapter and also in Movement in the animation chapter. The conceptual aspects of movement in perspective or Z-Axis animation are discussed in the Movement section of this chapter (figs. 5-33, 5-34, 5-35, 5-41, 7-21, 7-79, 14-3).

Value

Value refers to the areas of light and dark in the shot. Color theory uses the term in the same way. Value can refer to masses of **light** and **dark**, or patterns of light and dark and all the shades of light and dark inbetween. Value in a shot can range from extreme difference between light and dark, called **high contrast**. At the other extreme the value range could have very little difference, called **low contrast**. The tonal values audiences are normally attracted to are the brightest or lightest value surrounded by dark values. Due to the contrast between light and dark, a bright object will appear to come toward the audience in a composition.

General Thoughts

The key words in composition are **center of interest**, the place or area where the composition focuses the attention of the audience. The components of form, used properly, help achieve this goal. The stage is set for the action. It can be as simple as an actual framing device, a door or window (fig. 2-17). Or boundaries set by trees forming a space in the center (fig. 2-24), a long corridor focusing the eye in the center (fig. 5-34) or an isolated character on the screen without a background. The composition should also empathasize the story, the aesthetic and the content of the film. It should enhance the mood and atmosphere of the shot. Is it a happy, bright shot? A dark and sad shot? A dramatic shot?

One of my former students did very dramatic layouts for his film. Extreme camera, subject angle and Z-Axis layouts were his forte. A very high angle long shot of a city street, a low angle very deep shot of a carousel or a gazebo were some I remember. He never did finish his film as he was hired by Disney and soon became one of their top layout people. He is probably still doing very dramatic layouts if he hasn't retired.[10]

Bigger can be better, as seen in modern painting. The bigger the actions, the clearer the actions. I will never forget a story one of my painting teachers told us. He did very small paintings of delicate black lines on a white background, which he would always hang unframed. Once, he could not find his painting in a group show; he looked and looked throughout the whole exhibition and did not see it. On the last time around, he found it: he had thought it was a crack in the white wall when he had passed it before. The next day he was painting 8x10-foot canvasses filled with large contrasting jagged shapes of black and white.[11]

One theory of composition is to have nothing in the shot but what is needed for the shot, a chair to sit in, a door to go through and a book to read, and eliminate everything else. A dependable test for the background composition is that if you take something out, does it hurt the composition? If it does not, why leave it in? The only answers would be for atmosphere or mood, or if your natural style encompasses a rich, detailed, abundant visual approach. Especially if you conform to the South Pacific art style, where based on religious beliefs, every inch of space is filled with complex art. *The Book of Kells* is another case in point. Following the less is more philosophy will keep it simple. A good way to check the simplicity and readability is to look at your shot and think what you would see in it if you were driving at 65 mph and your shot was a billboard that you would only have a couple of seconds to read. Normally, the best the billboard can say is "Drink Coke." Simple.

There should be nothing behind the animation that will cause visual confusion. Bright colors, complex details, too much contrast and the background the same color as the character will all distract from the character and the action (fig. 5-23). An analogy would be the use of a spotlight in the theater to showcase the main character.

COLOR

Color is the other part of composition. Below is the terminology for the characteristics of color and some of the color principles that you will be using when you are composing with color. The tool you will be using is a 12-part color wheel available at most art stores.

Hue - The name of a particular color: red, brown, violet.

---

10. Another name I cannot find.
11. I have never heard this story before, and I don't know the art teacher in question.

Tint - Color plus white. Most colors used in animation, particularly in characters, are tints. Most animation, notably comedic, uses bright, light colors. Not only for mood, but also because colors may be deadened through the technical process of recording, processing and distribution.

Tone - Color plus grey. Used when you want tonal values, as in a background for low contrast. See Value under Form. In the 1950s, when there was only black and white TV, some TV animation was done in color so that it could be shown in reruns when color TV came in. At that time, there was a nifty little lens that allowed you to view your color setups and see how they would look in values of grey. If you could find one of those today, it could help you set your tonal values in your colored film.

Shade - Color plus black. Very dark shades should be used only when you don't care if the color turns black to the eye during the technical process. This is a very common mistake on first films, using deep rich dark detailed shades, which look great as still art, but when they are projected they are a dull dead black hole with no detail.

Key Color - The dominant color. Often for the main character or form, or at least part of them.

Neutral Grey - Combination of black and white. Can quiet down a too-active shot, as can tone when used judiciously.

Chroma - Intensity, or the brightness or dullness of a color. See Tint. Certain colors next to each other will change their intensity. Complementary colors next to each other spur each other to maximum intensity. Sometimes called saturation.

Value - The lightness or darkness of a color.

Primary Colors - Red, yellowy and blue. Cannot be mixed from any other colors and from which the other colors are mixed.

Secondary Colors - Two primary colors mixed together, which will give you orange, green and violet.

Tertiary Colors - Or intermediate colors. Colors that result when a primary and secondary color are mixed together.

Warm Colors - Reds, oranges, yellows.

Cool Colors - Greens, blues, violets.

Earth Colors - Brown, dark shades of blue, green, and blue-violet.

Complementary - The color opposite a color on the color wheel. When complementary primaries are used, red/green, blue-orange, yellow-violet, you will have the most contrast. When they are next to each other, they will be the most vivid. Referred to as complementary harmony. If their pigments are mixed together, they will yield a neutral gray black.

Spilt Complements - Using one color and the color on each side of it. Red violet, red and red orange. Creates another color harmony.

Diad - A system of two colors that have one color between them. Red, orange. Color harmony.

Triad - Color systems that have three colors equally spaced from each other. The three primary colors, red, blue, and yellow, is one example.

Tetrad - A contrast or system of four or more colors.

Analogous - Using the shades, tints and tones of colors that are at 90-degree angles on the color wheel.

Monochromatic - Using only the shades, tints or tones of one hue (fig. 5-24).

Acromatic - A color system without color, just black, white and grays.

The choosing of colors can be one of the most intuitive or subjective decisions made in the animation production process, as most people favor certain colors and some have a highly innate color sense. For those not lucky enough to have the talent to pick the right color (I don't), here are principles and processes to help us.

To help select your color scheme, do a color time flow chart of the entire film so that you have color unity throughout the film (fig. 2-63). This will give you the key color or colors of the film as well as each shot. Your film could start with cool colors, blues and greens, then the gradual introduction of warm colors and end completely in the warm range. The film, at least from the colors, would start cold and sad and gradually build to a warm happy ending. Using this stage as a guide, you select a range of colors for your characters, keeping in mind that the colors you assign each character will give them a certain ranking and also support or work counter to their personalities. You next will do this for your background, working off the colors you have decided for your character or foreground action.

Next, make color models of your characters first by using color markers, color paper or pencils on paper. Then put the colors on a cel with cel paint so you can see it the way it will look when shot (fig. 2-45). To avoid wasting cels, ink the outlines of character on one cel and apply the colors on the back of a second cel. This way you don't have to ink an outline on a cel each time you want to check a color. Bear in mind a couple of things when you are selecting the colors for your character. Since you will have to paint each cel, a very-time consuming process, you can save time by limiting the number of colors; five to nine is a good range, one or two is even better in each character. If you can also duplicate any of those colors, the white for the shoes and eyeballs, the same green for the shirt and the shoes, you will cut down the painting time considerably.

On the skin tones do you want natural colors, no color or non-natural colors? On *Sesame Street,* (figs. 6-15, 13-3) the intended audience was the 2½ old inner-city child, so he had to be able to identify with the characters, which became a consideration for the animator when deciding the colors. Also, if the skin tones are too dark, it will make it very hard to see the details.

Any colors that you see at this stage will be slightly duller in the finished film unless you plan carefully. To get an idea how the film and tape will affect the colors, look at the color models while squinting your eyes. This is best to do when you look at a complete setup of a shot, say four levels of cels with a background below (fig. 5-47). If you look at each level separately, you are not taking into account the density of the overlaying cels. A background by itself can be quite bright, but with four cel levels on top it will be quite dull. You may need to increase the intensity of your colors to compensate for cel levels. The basic principle we are dealing with here is that you must check your original art against how it will look when finally viewed, and if there are problems, correct them now in your art. Don't hope the laboratory can correct it later with their color filters because they can't.

Character or overlay object colors tend to be bright and warm (reds, oranges, yellows) with light value and tints, especially the key color, so that they come forward and can be seen. White seems to jump out the most, and used naturally in the eyes (especially in big eyes) will direct attention to a character's face. Background colors tend to be cool (greens, blues, violets) and with darker values and shades. This can help imply depth (if wanted), puts the background behind the character, and lessens the chance of a color clash between character and background. However, sometimes a pop of bright color behind the main character can add an emphasis to the action. Bright colors convey more weight than dark colors. If the paint on cels is a different kind of paint than the paint used on the background boards, you could have two different color looks. Be careful. One way to avoid this problem is to use cel paint for the background painting. If you have a black outline on your character, putting that same black line around the objects on your background board will tie both the colors and composition of foreground and background together (fig. 5-25). To do a black line on the background, first do the black line on a cel and then put it over the background (fig. 5-26).

You may want to study the uses of color in Western painting. Johannes Itten's book *The Elements of Color* is an excellent condensed version of the different color schemes used by painters and schools of painting. It is also a good source for a more theoretical approach to color.

To paint a character for a night shot, try using darker shades of the same colors (fig. 5-27). How to unify colors in a group can be a special problem. The Pirates, the Lost Boys and the Indians in *Peter Pan* (1953) are a good example for study on how to handle this issue.

Below is a sample of the range of different opinions on what are the emotional or other mental attributes of a particular color. You can use these as reference when you choose colors to enhance a character's personality, a background atmosphere or a shot's mood.

Red: Warm, aggressive, heavy, anger, war, love, communism, blood, passion, energy, fire, heat, when coupled with black gives the impact of violence.

Orange: Warm, aggressive, fall season, life, lively, oranges.

Yellow: Warm, aggressive, enlightenment, understanding, sun, joy, youth, spring.

Green: Cool, receding, jealousy, nature (there are more values of green in nature than any other color), spring season, bile, eternity, water, fresh, soft.

Blue: Cool, receding, light, passive, peace, winter, water, sky, reverence, truth, justice, water, ice.

Violet (Purple): Cool, receding, mystery, terror, royalty, mist, darkness, shadow.

White: Purity, cleanliness, frank, cold, snow.

Black: Neutral, night, emptiness, death, evil, somber, strength, sophistication.

Color can have social or religious meaning. In China, white is a sign of mourning. In Catholicism, white is reserved for the Pope and crimson for Cardinals. And in Westerns, we all know who the guy in the black hat is.

No color choice is made in isolation. Each color is part of the color harmony of a character, a group of characters, a background, a background and a foreground, a shot, and a film.

Composition in Time

As mentioned in Editing, all compositions must work in and with the time flow of the film. Every shot is composed with this in mind. A time flow chart and a storyboard will help as a structure, but the best yardstick will be the animatic.

Props

A prop is anything in the shot that does not represent a living thing and is not part of the basic background. It could be the teapot that the tea is poured from, a sword in a duel, a car driving down a street. It usually moves at some point. Props are designed with model and color model sheets (fig. 5-28). Be sure that they match the style of the rest of the film. If a character will need to touch the prop, but not move it, it should still be on a cel, not a background. Otherwise the painting difference between a background and a cel could make it look odd or unnatural.

Style

Review your style. Do you have a style? Are you developing a unique and original look? Or are you emulating an established artist or animator? The categories of styles include: cartoon, realistic, symbolism, painterly style, current style, photographic, abstract, etc. Sources for style research include: other animation, paintings, graphics, photography, comic books, children's books, illustrations, etc. If you choose a style from these sources, make sure it can be adapted to the rigors of animation.[12] Be sure to do at least one complete setup, cels and background in the color and style of your final film, as early as you can in the process, so you can see the final look. This is very important; you do not want any unwanted style surprises when the film is done.

Color Character Model Sheets and Color Background Model Sheets

Review your character model sheets and do color model sheets (figs. 2-45, 2-48.1). Fine-tune them by asking these questions: Is the style constant? Are the characters designed and built for animation? Can they work as poses in your layout? How many colors are in your character? Can you do that many colors given the time and budget constraints? Is the scale of one character to another consistent? Has the emotion or personality of your character changed since the storyboard and sound stages?

Do you need to redesign your characters so their acting can mirror these changes? Make copies of your model sheets so that you always have one handy for reference. In a long film holding character or to put on character your animation can take more time than the animation itself. This one reason computer 3D animation can be faster because the character is always on model.

The characters as a line drawing for the pencil tests (fig. 7-79) often look different from the characters when they are ink and painted (figs. 1-2, 2-33). Inking onto cels or cleaning up the drawings for the computer will change the line quality. The painted cel with its volume, mass and color will give more weight and bulk to the animation. It's the nature of the beast, but you can get a glimpse of the future by looking at the drawn model sheets and the color model sheets (figs. 2-43, 2-44, 2-45). Before they Xeroxed cels at Disney, and just looking at the pencil tests, you would see animation that would rock you (this is not to disparage the inkers at Disney in those days who had a marvelous line, especially using a brush). Xeroxing the drawing can help keep the animator's original line quality.

Do a rough color version of your background and overlay it with the color characters. So the background and the character colors work together for the entire scene.

Film vs. Video - the Screen vs. TV Set

There are different aesthetics involved in the way you view film (a big screen) and video (the TV box). This can affect the way you layout and design your film. There is the size factor. In

---

12. An interesting apporach was taken by Jay Shipman with his film *Chasing the Light* (2014). For this film he painted a sweries of 36" x 36" oil canvases. He then photographed each painting and then in Photoshop drew the characters as another layer, and then used Premier Pro to composite the painting frames with the character frames (fig. 5-29).

the large theater screen, you have the monumental quality. Big is just better, in itself. You also have space for more background action, animating several different characters or panning over a full landscape. Video, since the screen is smaller, uses more close-ups and full head shots. Designing for TV is sometimes called the art of the close-up, which can mean an emphasis on dialogue and acting. The TV can use Z-Axis movement effectively, as it is the one movement that is not bound by the edges of the picture (fig. 5-15). Of course, x and y movements can be done in TV, but the eye does not scan them with the same awareness that it does movement on the big screen with its wide sweeping landscapes, as the eye does not move. Today's new screen size is that of handheld receivers, whose popularity and aesthetics are still being debated.

There was a quality difference but with digital high-definition TV, better delivery systems, larger screens, DVDs and the big film venues going digital, the gap is rapidly closing and it is not considered that much of an issue.

Perspective in Layout

Perspective is putting art and animation in natural depth, or what the eye naturally sees. Once you have decided to work in depth, 2½D or 3D, you can create depth either through conventional linear perspective or through the illusion of design and movement, or a combination of the two.

Linear perspective relies on fixed viewpoints and on straight-line projection to vanishing points (figs. 5-33, 5-34, 5-35). Linear perspective can serve to put your permanent background or stage into the correct depth and serve as a reference to your animation in depth. I will briefly go over the principles of linear perspective, but to learn perspective well, you should take a class or get a book and practice. It is not too hard. In linear perspective, the picture plane is the sheet of paper on which you draw. The horizon line is where the sky and land you're standing on appear to meet depending on your eye level. If you look straight ahead, the horizon line will be at your eye level (fig. 5-30). If your eye is above, the horizon line will be lower (fig. 5-31). If your eye is below, the horizon line will be higher (fig. 5-32). The ground plane is the land you are standing on. You use one, two, or multi point vanishing points to build the framework of linear perspective. In one-point perspective, the vanishing point is one point on the horizon line. This point is your center of vision. All lines at 90 degrees to the picture plane and parallel to the ground line will converge at this point regardless of where they originate on the picture plane (fig. 5-33). Two-point perspective is two vanishing points, one on each side of the picture plane. Lines converging at these points will give you two sides of a square or rectangle, which is the most the eye can see (fig. 5-34). Multi point perspective includes two-point angular with multi vanishing points and three-point perspective (the third usually being the vertical) (fig. 5-35). You would normally use one-point perspective in animating on the Z-Axis. More on that in the next chapter.

Some methods to give the illusion of depth through design are: overlapping objects; showing more planes, especially planes in depth; animating between or behind objects; on object in the distance using less detail, clarity and weight; use receding colors and lighter tones for distancing; and awareness of perspective scaling (size progressively diminishes the farther away it is) (fig. 2-24). Pans in Layout - Technical explain how different pan speeds can achieve the illusion of depth (page 123).

Decide if the depth is shallow, medium, deep or unlimited? In the *Road Runner and the Coyote* great depth was obvious from the start with the design of the landscape. Later many of the gags depended on depth, such as the Road Runner coming toward the Coyote Acme trap or the Coyote falling into that very deep canyon. The UPA style was quite flat and 2D.

Lighting

The basic lighting in traditional animation are the two lights used to illuminate the flat artwork. Any lighting in the film is done in the art. The only variation is the occasional use of a bottom or under light. Because of the effort and cost, traditional animation rarely attempts to reproduce the lighting of the real world. This is one of the major aesthetic differences between traditional 2D animation, without lighting, and 3D stop motion or animation where the molding by light of a 3D object gives the shades and tones of shadows with the effect of a 3D world. If 3D lighting is attempted in 2D traditional animation, it is usually a shadow or shading that is put on one side of a character or a ground shadow (fig. 7-76). The shadow or shading of a character can be done by using a marker on the top of the cel, carefully painting or cross-hatching a shadow area in (this must be done very precisely as the edge of the shadow area, if not perfect, can creep all over the place and become an animated area that draws attention to itself), or by applying the multiple exposure technique used for ground shadows. Ground shadows are normally created through multi exposure as in the opening sequence of *Snow White* and will be discussed in the effects animation section of the Animation chapter. A discussion of 3D lighting is in Chapter 10.

Special Effects in Animation

Special effects are water falling, rain, wind, and fire, and they are laid out in the same manner as any other aspect of animation. Because they often use multi camera techniques to enhance the effect, their layouts can be more complex. Discussion of special effects animation will be in the next chapter and the use of animation in live-action visual effects will be in Chapter 10.

Animation Layout

First, in the proper field, the last pose or key frame in the path of movement of the animation will be roughly drawn. Next, rough in the first key frame or pose. Then add as many key poses inbetween these two poses as needed to give a clear picture of the movement. You start with the end position so that the ending, usually the most important part of the animation, is well staged and doesn't go off the screen, which can happen if you just start animating with enthusiasm from the start position and in your excitement run out of room. If there is trouble with the bunching up of the action within a single layout, putting in another shot, probably a close-up, should handle it. Follow the principles of strong poses and clear silhouettes when you lay out the action.

Background Layout

One (12½") (fig. 5-2), two (25", for pans) and three field (37" for pans) are the standard lengths of backgrounds (BGs). They can be longer, as long as your roll of BG paper, but these are the standard lengths. Backgrounds are laid out like animation. Done in pencil first, usually blue. Some studios have a policy when laying out BGs especially pans, to do the graphics that will be on the BG in red pencil and rough in the positions of the animation in blue pencil so that the BG artist will know where the animation will occur (fig. 5-39). Normally you do a rather detailed layout of the BG, taking into account where the animation will be and such technical details as pan speeds, starts and stops, the beginning and end of trucks, where the animation and the BG will come into contact, etc. (fig. 5-1.7). A standard mistake of first-time filmmakers is to do the BGs first, before the animation, and then find that the BGs and the animation do not match in action, color or composition (fig. 5-12). They are then faced with the choice of whether to do the animation or the BG over or have a terrible-looking film. A film could consist of only background shots. There have been several beautiful films that only use the background of time-lapse nature shots. The background could dominate the film as in *The Game of the Angels* (1964) by Walerian Borowczyk, where the space or background of each shot is a metaphor for the content of the film. A good question to ask is: Does the background occupy a place and time in the known world? Has the research been done to authenticate the details of that time and place? After both layouts have been done, you combine them for the finished layout (fig. 5-1).

KISS or Keep - it - simple – stupid. It is a positive way to approach good layout.

The technical part of layout follows: much of it is boring, but necessary.

LAYOUT - TECHNICAL

The technical layout chapter deals with the mechanical limits of the tools, traditionally the animation crane and now the computer. All the drawing/artwork created must be done to technical specifications or limits. Exposure sheets are the record of all the technical information needed for the film in relationship to the timing for the shooting. The technical terms used in this chapter are the traditional ones used for the animation crane and film. These technical issues will change in the digital, but the basic information and ultimate result is the same. Different terms used for the same technique may vary from studio to studio. The technical issues concerning layout are:

Field Chart

A field chart, normally the first tool used, is the guide used to determine the size of the area on the paper where your artwork will be created (fig. 5-36). A 4 field = 4" across, 8 field = 8" across, 12 field = 12" across, 7.28 field = 7.28" across, etc. The field chart is at a 1:33 to 1 ratio, roughly 4/3, so a 12 field, for example, is 12" x 8 7/8". The basic position of a field is at center and is noted by the abbreviation FC, or field center. The compass points of North, East, South, West are used to determine the direction of movement from center. If the field or the center of the camera view is not at center, the position is noted by giving the center by using the coordinates of the field chart as well as the size of the field. A center point of a 4 field that is 3 fields south and 6 fields west would be written as 4F 3S & 6W. A field is usually divided into 100 units per inch for planning movements or location of the field center. An example of that usage is 9.28 FC, 2.2N, & C (C for on the center line East and West). When going "off center," the edges of the field size cannot extend beyond the parameters of the field chart, a 12FC. A 6F, 8E & 10N would be beyond the edges of the field chart and a part of the crane bed would be filmed. A 90-degree rotation will give you a vertical pan field, which is limited to an 8½FC as you are rotating on a 4x3 rectangle. Diagonal fields are constrained to a limit of a 7FC at 45 degrees.

In the technical procedure of screening on NTSC, an area around the perimeter of the field size equal to about 1/6 of the entire field is lost. This is the TV cut-off. Though the problem today is not as bad as it was in the old days of TV, it is still advisable for the main action of the animation to stay within the TV safe parameters. The safe TV cut-off for a 12FC is a 10FC (fig. 5-37). If a digital film is played on an NTSC monitor there will be a cut-off, but if it is played on a computer monitor there will be no TV cut-off. A cel placed under the layout paper and marked with the field TV cut-off for the field you are using will prevent this error from occurring. One time, on a *Sesame Street* Spot, I thought I had done a great layout but was in such a hurry to animate that I did not consult a field chart. And lo and behold, when I checked it just before shooting, I was losing half of the animation to the TV cut-off. There was no time to reanimate and ink and paint, so I had to overshoot the art. The spot still looks lousy 30 years later. There is even a smaller cut off for a safe title area; an 8 field area shooting on a 12 field is a safe field for titles. The TV cut-off can affect your editing and timing on pans and animation going off the edge of the screen followed by a cut. Do you cut when the animation goes off according to the field chart or the TV cut-off? If you cut when it goes off on the field chart, there may be a few frames of empty screen. If you use the TV cut-off, you may cut before the action leaves the screen. All I can say is, take your best guess.

Trucks

Changes in field sizes can be accomplished by:

- *Cuts* - just cutting from one field size to another.
- *Dissolves* - dissolving from one field size to another, see the section on dissolves.
- *Trucks* -Trucks are accomplished by physically moving the camera into or away from the artwork. All trucks, and all camera moves, are filmed on one's (one frame at a time), not on two's, three's, four's, etc., unless a stylistic jerky effect is desired. Even if the animation is done on two's and three's, the crane movement must be on one's. The laws of the persistence of vision will cover any problem in this case (figs. 2-15, 5-38).

Exposure Sheets for Trucks

The field size and NEWS (north, east, west, south) coordinates are indicated on the exposure sheet to inform the camera operator where to set the camera. The information, always written in pencil, goes in a box in the camera instruction column and is written well before the frame where the action is to start. You draw a straight line from the box to the starting frame. A wavy line with a start and stop arrow is drawn in the camera instruction column for the entire number of frames over which a camera action takes place. This tells the cameraperson that they are to be working. This is done for pans, trucks, dissolves (with a special format box, see below), pantograph movements and other camera instructions. It is best to use the full amount of frames on the exposure sheets for animation, pans, trucks, etc., so that changes and checks can be made frame by frame.

The information needed in the instruction box for trucks is as follows:

- Starting field size and NEWS coordinates as needed.
- Ending field size and NEWS coordinates as needed.
- Time in the number of frames for the truck.
- Type of truck (if needed), as in Slo In, Slo Out.
- Speed of truck. This is determined by the distance moved each frame. Different cranes have different ways of calibrating distance. A common way is to divide the distance between each field into 100 units. If the truck was moving at 10 units per x, it would take 10x's to move a field. This is a fairly fast truck (fig. 5-38).

There are four types of trucks you can do in relation to speed:

- A **SLO IN, SLO OUT** truck starts out very slow so that there is no bump at the start of the truck, it builds gradually to speed and then slows down at the end so that you do not notice when it stops. The old Disney formula was a 1/3 (SLO IN), a 1/3 (CONSTANT SPEED), a 1/3 (SLO OUT). This type of truck (or pan) is usually used when there is action or a hold before and after the truck.

- A **CONSTANT SPEED** truck moves the same distance for each frame for the entire truck. A constant speed truck will move faster at the smaller field and slower at the larger fields. Trucking in from a 12F to an 11F, the camera is only moving one-twelfth to one-eleventh of the field, a relatively small move given the total area. If you are trucking from a 5F to a 4F, the camera is moving from one-fifth to one-fourth of the total screen area. As you because as due to the relative field sizes.[13] If the speed is the same, you appear to be moving three times faster in a 4F than at a 12F. A constant speed truck (or pan) is usually done for the entire shot. If the transition to the scenes surrounding the truck is a dissolve, the truck should run all the way through the dissolve.

- The third type of truck, the **EXPONENTIAL** truck, compensates for the fact that the closer the camera gets, the faster the object appears to move. This compensation is accomplished by trucking (or moving) the camera faster at the 12F and slower at the 4F. It is used for very long-distanced trucks -- 30F to 2F, or when doing back-to-back matching trucks. On the SLO IN and SLO OUT trucks and the exponential trucks, the distance of the move per frame is written on the exposure sheet for each frame.

- A fourth type of truck would be a **COMBINATION** of different types of trucks. For example, start a truck with a SLO IN and end it at constant speed on a cut.

This is how the information in the box would look:

80x Truck
from 12PC
to 4FC
at 10 moves per x (for a constant speed truck)

Or:

32x Truck
from 5.72F 3N & 6E
to 10.28F 1S & 1W
with SLO IN & SLO OUT - As indicated (fig. 5-52)

A way for you to rough in the truck is to use a mask or a mask made with your fingers and move in or out, fast or slow on the layout, counting seconds to yourself until you get what you want.

---

13. I really have no idea how to edit this sentence.

PANS

Pans are camera moves that are used to convey movement across the screen. Whereas in live-action filmmaking a pan is accomplished by (1) panning (rotating the camera on its tripod) the camera across a landscape or (2) a dolly shot, where the camera is moved along tracks, car, a wheeled tripod or some such device. In animation the camera is stationary, so the illusion of the panning action is accomplished by physically moving the artwork on peg bars on the bed of the crane, across the field of the camera. Pans are drawn to the required length in layout either on long pan paper or sheets of animation paper taped together.

A pan can be horizontal, vertical or diagonal (fig. 5-39). The simplest pan is just over a single level, say, a landscape. More complex is to pan the background (BG) and not the overlay(s). An example of this would be a walk cycle on a cel (a moving dolly shot in live action), where the legs of the walking character move but the position of the character remains fixed, and the trees in the background slide across the screen. Or you could reverse that and pan the overlay(s) and not the BG (a held camera with a character or object entering the scene in live action) so that the object on the overlay moves in relationship to the sides, or you can pan both the overlay(s) and the BG. If you have some elements panning and some not panning, they must be on separate peg systems, usually top pegs for one and bottom pegs for the other. Some cranes can support up to four systems of pegs at once (two top/two bottom). You can have three pans moving at different speeds to give the illusion of depth. A foreground pan at .25, the middle pan at .10, and the distance pan at .01 would give you a depth illusion as you would get when driving across the desert at high speeds and looking out the side windows: The objects at the side of the road whiz by while the cacti 200 yards out move sedately across the scene and the mountains in the distance barely move at all. Matching pans and animation requires great care in the layout stage to avoid later mistakes.

The information required in the pan instructions is:

- **Material(s) Panning** - the number(s) of the cels or BGs that are moving.
- **Direction** - it is either left or right.
- **Time in Frames** - this is the length of time of the pan; 24x frames = one second.
- **Speed** - move per frame in terms of one-hundredths of an inch. Example: .03 = one-thirty third, .05 = one-twentieth, .10 = one-tenth, etc. These examples can give you an idea of speeds relative to action. A crawl title at an 8FC would be .02 or .03. A slow walk at 12FC would be .05 per frame and a brisk walk would be .10. A fire engine going full speed at a 12FC would be .80 per frame. They can be constant speed, or SLO IN and SLO OUT or a combination of the two.
- **Distance** - This is the number of inches or fractions thereof from center start to center stop. The C Stop is marked either on the top or bottom edges of the panning material. The C Stop measurement is always taken from the vertical centerline of the field chart. The distance is from the center of the starting field to the center of the ending field.

All together this would read, in your information box, as: Pan BG 12 left for 96x at .10" per frame = 9.60". The order of the information really does not matter, but all the information has to be included (fig. 5-40).

To arrive at the time, speed and distance information needed in the pan instructions, first decide what is the given information for these three elements. The time for the pan could be set by the sound track. The distance may be set by art that cannot be changed, as in a photograph. The speed, fast or slow, may be decided by action. A rough sense of the time can be arrived at by moving a field mask or a rough rectangle of your hands over the art from center start to center stop and counting seconds. If two of the three elements (speed, time, distance) are known, the third element can be found by using one of the formulas listed below. In the formulas below for figuring out the distance, speed and time, time is noted as frames, speed is movement in of 100ths of inches per frame and distance is the total movement from C Start to C Stop on the art in inches.

Use this formula when you have the speed and time to get your distance:
speed times frames = **inches**

Use this when you have distance and speed to get your time:
inches divided by speed = **frames**

And this if you know your distance and time:
inches divided by frames = **speed**

For instance, if you are panning an object all the way across, including in and out of the screen, and the field is a 12F, you know the distance of a 12F is 12" across, and if the width of the object is 2" then you add the width of the character to the field, 12" + 2" = 14", and that is the distance required. Now you want this to take 140 frames (almost 6 seconds). You would divide 14.00" by the needed information. Of course it does not always work out this neatly, but you juggle the different elements about till you find a good solution.

These formulas will give you a constant speed pan. Like trucks, constant speed is usually used when you come into the scene panning and leave panning. A SLO OUT, SLO IN pan would usually be used when you start or end a pan within the scene. A SLO OUT, SLO IN will get rid of any bumps or jerks at the start and stop (unless you want one for a special effect). SLO OUT or SLO IN pans can be worked out mathematically (using a calculator) based on the information from the above formulas or from computer models. The old Disney formula for a SLO OUT, SLO IN pan was a 1/3 SLO OUT, a 1/3 constant, and a 1/3 SLO IN.

An object panning at the same rate on a small field and a large field will appear to be moving faster on the smaller field, and slower on the larger field. For example, if you pan a dot across a 12F at .10 it would take 120X's, 12.00" divided by .10 = 120x's. 120x's = 5 seconds. At a 4F a dot panning at .10 = 40x's, 4.00" divided by .10 = 40x's. A second and two-thirds or three times faster than at a 12F.

You can give the appearance of a continual BG by using a 3F length BG with head and tails hookups. This is when the last 12F is painted the same as the first 12F, so that you can just repeat the same 3F BG pan, switching from the end of the pan back to the beginning for as long as you want. You can pan this BG forever.[14]

The illusion of twinkling stars can be achieved by poking several pinholes in a piece of black artwork. When the artwork is underlit, the light shines through, revealing tiny specks of light upon the black field. To make the "stars" twinkle, create a "garbage matte," a cel with scribbled black lines, and pan it under the black artwork at .10. On successive frames, the random scribbles eclipse the pinholes and then reveal the light, so the illusion of a twinkling nighttime sky is created as you pan.

Complex pans with many levels of animation are time-intensive when shooting. Plan accordingly. A note on the direction of movement: Many pans move from left to right, this is somewhat arbitrary but probably based on the fact that most European languages read from left to right and our eyes are familiar with that movement. Before the collapse of the Soviet Empire, the camera-people in the Eastern Bloc were taught to always have the character or action moving left. When you are panning BG with a held character it is usual to have more space in front than behind, as that will create the illusion of more space to walk into, making the walk more natural.

It is a mistake to do the finished art for panning backgrounds or the animation for the pans before doing the layouts. The art of the panning background has to be planned in layout so that it fits the requirements of time, distance, and speed of the pan. If it is not it will probably have to be done over.

FADE IN - FADE OUT - DISSOLVES

A *FADE IN (FI)* is achieved when the film "fades" from black to a fully exposed image. This is achieved by opening the shutter on the camera a small amount for each frame shot.

A *FADE OUT (FO)* is achieved when you "fade" from a fully exposed image to black.

A FADE IN is often used at the beginning of a film and a FADE OUT at the end. If you FADE OUT one scene and FADE IN another scene as a transition, depending on the length of the fades, it usually stops or slows down the action and traditionally

---

14. Doug Ward would like to add the following comment: "You should add that 3F = 3 Fields in width. A repeat pan could be 4 or 5 fields in width if you have more variety in the background. This is to keep the famous plant stand from reappearing so many times behind Fred Flintstone when he's chasing Barney through his house. The first and third fields need to be identical, same artwork, same painting in the same location on, the start and ending fields. The field in the middle is the only one that can differ."

represents a passage of time.

A **DISSOLVE** (DISS) is a FADE OUT combined with a FADE IN over the same frames of film. A DISS is done in these steps:

- FADE OUT one scene by closing down the shutter one frame at a time until the shutter is completely closed. The start frame for the DISS must be noted on the exposure sheet.
- When the shutter is completely closed, put the camera motor in "reverse" and wind the film back to the frame where you started the FADE OUT. It is helpful to wind back past the starting point, and then switch the camera back into the "forward" position and click off frames until the starting point is reached. This technique serves as a reminder to place the camera back into the "forward" position when the shooting is resumed. If the camera motor is not put into forward, you will FADE IN over the frames that precede the FADE OUT of the DISSOLVE and continue to shoot over already exposed film, thereby ruining the film.
- Change the artwork.
- FADE IN over the same frames, with the new art, of the FADE OUT by opening the shutter one frame at a time as the shooting progresses.

For writing dissolve information on exposure sheets, you will need in the information box the length of the DISS and what art is going out and coming in. The box is before the event (the DISS). In the camera column you diagram a FADE OUT over a FADE IN. In the level columns you will show what is going out and coming in, the animation. You can just DISS out on action while leaving the others the same. An example would be to DISS out the background, say a city into a countyside, while the walking character remains the same. You can run animation through a dissolve, it just means you have to shoot it twice. Make sure that the frame count on the side of the sheet reflects the length of the DISS (fig. 5-52).

The exposure on every frame of the DISSOLVE will always stay at 100 percent. For example, when your FADE OUT exposure is at 30 percent of the available light coming through the shutter, the corresponding FADE IN exposure is 70 percent of the available light. Since these percentage values together represent a multiple exposure on one frame of film, the frame will be exposed with 100 percent of the available light. Most cranes are mechanically equipped to accurately accomplish the following length FI, FO and DISS:

4x, 6x, also as DISS could be considered soft cuts or can be used instead of animation when done as back to back DISS.

8x, 12x, 16x DISS is a very short DISS and can also be used as a form of limited animation for complex art with back-to-back DISS.

24x, 32x, 40x, 48x, 64x - most common dissolves.

Other lengths and longer FI, FO and DISS can be done.

Only about the middle third of each dissolve will have a double-exposed image, as the images fading out or fading in will dominate the beginning and ending thirds. Multiple dissolves back-to-back will give an animating effect that is a good technique to employ when the art is complex and animating could be difficult or sloppy because of moving lines or colors. Holding a dissolve in the middle creates a true double-exposed effect. If you shoot your film to have dissolves done in the laboratory, you must shoot the length of the entire DISS plus a few extra frames on each end so that a full DISS can be made.

ROTATIONS, SPINS, WIPE OFF AND PANTOGRAPIDC MOVEMENTS

Rotations are done in degrees (360 in a circle), and direction of the move "South to East" (S to E) or "South to West" (S to W). Sometimes this is called clockwise or counter clockwise. On the exposure sheet the distance of the rotation move for each frame is in degrees. A notation in a rotation information box on your exposure sheet would read like this: "24x Rotation south to east at 2 degrees per frame from zero degrees to 48 degrees." (fig. 5-52)

On a rotation the whole scene, the frame, will spin or rotate. Rotations can be combined with a pan for a special effect. For example, the illusion of a rocket taking off can be achieved using a vertical pan and then doing a rotation to give the illusion of leveling off.

A spin is accomplished by rotating the material, not the camera, so that only part of the scene rotates. Examples include a clock hand moving rotated by a pin or ducks in shooting gallery rotated on a large cel. You can also rotate a robot (fig. 5-41).

A wipe-off or scratch-off is when you create the animated illusion by physically removing elements of the artwork from the cel. A line disappears or shrinks. You need to use material that can be removed without leaving a trace. Airbrushing water-based paint or a grease pencil will work. Backlighting a clear line on a black field and covering the line with a bit of black paper on each frame can create the same illusion. A guide of the wipe-off movements is needed for a forward or reverse wipe-off.

A reverse wipe-off will give the appearance of something growing. For example, to make your name appear as if it is being written on the screen, successive frames are shot off with the camera in reverse, after you have advanced it forward with the shutter closed, as you incrementally erase part of the name from the end to the beginning of the word. When the film is played in forward motion, it appears that your name is being written on the screen. In straight-ahead animation such a scene could wobble all over the place. You can also use the backlight technique here.

A pantographic movement is executed by moving from one set of coordinates in the field to another set of coordinates by moving either the animation crane bed or the camera mount, north/south and east/west each frame (fig. 5-42). An example would be moving over a photo-graph (fig. 5-43) or piece of art (fig. 5-44). Quite often used in motion graphics.

MULTIPASS

The multi pass is used in animation and in animation as a visual effect in live action. The various uses and techniques of multi pass are covered in Chapter 10 in the Animation as a Visual Effect in Live Action section. I advise you to read it as part of this chapter (pages 249-256).

ROTOSCOPING

Rotoscoping is the projection of frames of live action or animated footage onto a working surface with peg bars so that it can be traced onto paper or cel. Rotoscoping can be used to: (1) learn animation (Richard Williams said he learned animation by rotoscoping an entire *Road Runner and Coyote* short), (2) turn the traced live action with little or no change into animation (this is called motion capture in digital rotoscoping), (3) become a reference for the movement of the animation (fig. 5-45) (Marge Champion, then a student at Fairfax High, was the live-action reference for *Snow White*) and (4) register the animation to the live action for visual effects or to combine live action and animation in the finished film. The Fleischers patented the technique in 1915 and used rotoscoping by filming Dave dressed in a clown costume for the acting of the rotoscoped animated Koko character. For an expressive example, see *Yellow Submarine* (1968), *Lucy in the Sky with Diamonds* number, the basis of which was a live-action dance couple from a Hollywood film.

NUMBERING, LEVELS, AND FOLDERS *(all the little bookkeeping stuff)*

There is no standardized way of numbering the art. Just make sure that everyone involved with the film -- camera operators, checkers -- understands the system. The numbering system that is written on the cels and backgrounds is also written on the exposure sheets so duplication in the numbering system must be avoided, as that will cause confusion during shooting. Breaking it down into scenes helps avoid this and using a scene notation is helpful in a longer film, Sc.1, A-1, or M-1, Sc.1. Backgrounds are normally called BGs and usually carry the needed numerical order of their use, BG-1, BG-2, or the scene, BG-1 Sc.1, BG-2 Sc.1 The same holds true for consecutive cel numbering, except for the term BG a different alphabetical system is used. For a short film I prefer to use the first initial of the character or art; Sc.1, M-1, M-2, etc., for a character called Maura. WS is used for weird shape, R for rain. This tells me immediately what is on the cel. Other systems could just start with A and move through the alphabet until AA is needed. Always do the numbering in the lower right-hand corner for bottom pegs (fig. 7-78) and the upper right-hand corner for top pegs (fig. 7-77).

Decide on which level each cel or series of cels will be. The background is normally on the bottom level. The first or number one level will be on top of that, and then the second level, etc. (fig. 5-47). You normally do not want to go over five levels, as the cel density will darken the background and lower levels of cels. You also decide here what cels/BG go on either top pegs or bottom pegs. It is better to have cycles on bottom pegs with any held cels that must be over the cycle on top pegs. On pans, the moving elements must be on a different set of pegs than the held elements. The moving BG would be on top pegs, while the held cycling cels would be on bottom pegs.

Use folders to keep scenes in order with each scene in its own folder (fig. 5-48). On the front of the folder you can put a checklist for any or all these things – number of scene, storyboard, layout, key animation, rough animation, finished animation, ink and paint – so that each step can be checked off when it is completed. In a two-character scene, each character could have a folder. Do a list of all of the scenes in order and a checklist of what is done and what needs to be done so that you can always tell where you are in the production. If you do not do this, you will waste a lot of time finding stuff and getting it set up each time you start working.

TITLES

The technical parts of titles concern type size, face, readability and timing. Size in type is given in points, 72 points equals about an inch high. The higher the number, the bigger the type. Newspapers run about a 10 point type. Thirty-six point is about the height of half a field on a field chart. For main credits, 36 point is good if you want a medium-size type when shot on a 12 field (all the advice I will be giving you will only work if shot on a 12 field). Eighteen point is the lowest I would go, especially for a TV screen, where it could be hard to read. Forty-eight to 96 point are reserved for producers and stars who want their names in bigger letters than anyone else. If you design titles for movies or TV, this will be in their contracts. For size they get the biggest type or no one else can be bigger, so you end up with different type sizes for different jobs that people do on the film or show. This means you will have to design a whole range of type sizes to fit everyone's egos. The other thing that may be in the contract is whether they get a 100 percent card, which means only their name on the screen, a 50 percent where they share the screen with someone else, and so on (fig. 10-4). Once I did titles for a feature in which both producers wanted his name to come first. Try designing that sometime, it's hard to do.

Type Face is what the type looks like; this paper is being typed in 12 point Times. It is a typeface with serifs, the fine cross stroke termination of letters. This is 12 point Geneva, sans serif, no cross strokes; this is *Geneva in italic* or slanted. Fancy or elaborate typefaces can be hard to read. Complex action going on behind or next to the titles can also make the titles hard to read. Having the titles on too short a time can make the titles impossible to read. In the old days, reading the titles aloud twice would give everyone enough time to read the title. Today, people have been trained since childhood in reading off the TV screen, so reading aloud once is fine, but you must read it aloud. For titles you should not only shoot inside the TV cut-off, but to make sure, shoot inside an 8FC, which is called the safe title area when shooting on a 12FC.

How do you get the type ready to shoot? You can hand-letter it on cels or a board, or there still may be some letterset or press-on type around to put on cels (fig. 5-49), or you could print it out from the computer and shoot it that way. You could have a line negative made which will give you black letters on a clear cel that you can put over the artwork or a negative made which will give you clear letters on black and you can double pass it in.

Since the titles are the first thing the audience will see of the film, you should take some care with them. If you have sloppy or last-minute titles, you can already put the audience in a negative mood toward your film. The titles could be involved in the first action of your film. This is not a bad idea, because it makes it harder for people to cut the titles off and either take credit for the film or show the film without your credits on them. For your own titles, you would probably have your credit at the beginning with other key people; composer, voices, etc. Have the "thanks to" at the end. This seems to be the pattern on all titles: major names at the beginning, lesser at the end, often in a roll title. This is OK, but do not let your end titles go on too long or they may destroy the mood of your film. A way to avoid that is to have some action or vocal going on over the end credits. If this is your film, what title do you give yourself: filmmaker? A film by? directed, written, animated by? Emphasize the role in the film that you want to continue in the future. If you put filmmaker, you can confuse people in Hollywood. Make sure you have your copyright logo in your titles. When it is the last title, as in Hollywood feature films, it is usually surrounded by "bugs," which are the various union's and guild's logos that are represented in the film and contractually have to appear in the credits. Often a fade-in and fade-out are used at the beginning and end of a film.

PRODUCTION PLANNING

Production planning is where you attempt to achieve the optimum for the first two basic factors that govern any film production, money and time, to get the best out of the third factor, quality. Each of the first two affects the third, and rarely do you have enough of either. Therefore, in the production planning process, you often end up balancing one against the other to achieve the third. Rarely do you achieve the optimum for all three. In fact, there is an old saying in Hollywood that you can never get all three, you are lucky to get one. To give quality a chance, the budget (money) and schedule (time) must be carefully planned.

Budget

This will include the cost of the raw stock and processing for the film, and the workspace. The workspace is not only the animation tables and art space, but the editing, computer, sound equipment, and the camera and crane. There is the cost for the paper, tools such as pencils, brushes, markers and other supplies specific to your needs (fig. 5-50). Check Cartoon Colour Company for prices; it's probably your best single source. For commercial work, the labor cost will depend on the going rate, union or otherwise, the budget, the status of the talent, and any type of participation in the profits. It is best to hire someone who knows, a production manager or producer, to oversee this aspect.

Scheduling

You will need to plan a complete production schedule (fig. 5-51). First schedule the time to finish the film you storyboarded. How many hours a week can you work on your film? How many hours will it take you to do your film? How many feet or seconds can you layout or animate or ink and paint a day? You can take your daily completion rate for each process and multiply. Add them all together and you will have a rough idea of the total time it will take to complete your film. Then break down the total time into a schedule for completing each phase. If you find you do not have time to do the film as planned, often the result of an overly ambitious project, you will have to rethink your film to keep the quality and fit the time. Some common truisms in scheduling are: Ink and paint takes a long time, so schedule at least two or three times longer than what it takes to animate. Build in extra time for unexpected technical difficulties that throw you off schedule. Try to work as many hours as possible at one time. Eight-hour stretches are good, just like a regular workday.

Next, using your scene list to work out a schedule for when each scene will be done and stick to it. Animation is very labor-intense and Murphy's Law applies.

In a studio, the production manager or coordinator is the one who oversees the production pipeline and makes sure everything is done and on time.

EXPOSURE SHEETS

How exposure sheets are used is scattered throughout this book (fig. 5-52). You will start using them for all your animation starting with the pencil tests. They become the complete shooting plans for the film and are, with the art, in one sense the film. The cameraperson follows the instructions on the exposure sheets to shoot the film. Decisions in shooting are not made during shooting. (There is a type of animation that is created under camera without planning that is done by some independent animators.)

For the frame count, the exposure sheets are read from right to left. The frame count is written outside the printed edge on the right and represents the frame that has been shot. The next to be written in are the camera instructions (in the wide column) and next are the levels (a series of narrow columns). The bottom level is the first column, the second level is the next column to the left, etc. Try not to go over five levels. The last two columns on the left deal with dialogue (timed and written down) and notes. Exposure sheets are read from top to bottom in terms of time/frames. Each horizontal line represents one frame of film. It is best to use the full amount of frames on the exposure sheets for animation, pans, trucks, etc., so that changes and checks can be easily made. Only condense frames on an exposure sheet when you have a hold. By reading across the exposure sheet you know which frame you are at and what materials are to be shot. By reading the information in the camera instruction column, you know how the material is to be shot in relation to the workings of the animation crane (fig. 5-52).

Information needed in the camera instruction column: The field size and NEWS (north, east, west, south) coordinates are indicated on the exposure sheet to inform the camera operator where to set the camera. This information is always written in capital letters in pencil and goes in a box in the camera instruction column. This information box is placed before the frame where the action is to start. You draw a straight line from the box to the starting frame. An information box is required for pans, trucks, dissolves (with a special format box), pantograph movements and other camera instructions. A wavy line with a start and stop arrow is drawn in the camera instruction column for the entire number of frames over which the camera action described in the information box takes place such as pans, trucks, etc. This wavy line tells the cameraperson that they are working. For multi passes just tape two sheets together so that they match up, and by dividing sheets by colored pencil you will have columns for each pass.

Shorter films are usually shot from beginning to end, so you would start your frame count on the sheets at zero and end on the last frame of the film. Longer films usually are shot a scene at a time, and each scene is started at zero and the last number is the last number of the scene. The film is then cut together in the post-production process.

If your exposure sheets are correct and have been checked and you shoot carefully one frame at a time and make no mistakes, your film will be shot perfectly. Sometimes exposure sheets are called X sheets and in England they are called dope sheets, but that is the English for you.

The Computer in Layout

In 3D computer animation, layout can be done in a 3D world after it is digitally constructed. But the initial set is layout first with traditional means and concerns, and then the final layout can be done after the animation is done. In *The Incredbles* (2004) the gumball scene was set completely up and the shot selection was done with all the elements done. This use of the computer gives greater flexibility in the editing and timing of the film, but still you need the basic layout to be done in the preplanning.

THOUGHTS

I do not have any good quotes on layout. Layout is not the most glamorous part of animation, but it is the foundation and architecture of the entire film. Please keep in mind these rules during layout.

- A good layout puts across your concept and the animation.
- A good layout must support and respect the timing.
- You must do the animation layout and the background layout before the animation.

(fig. 5-12)

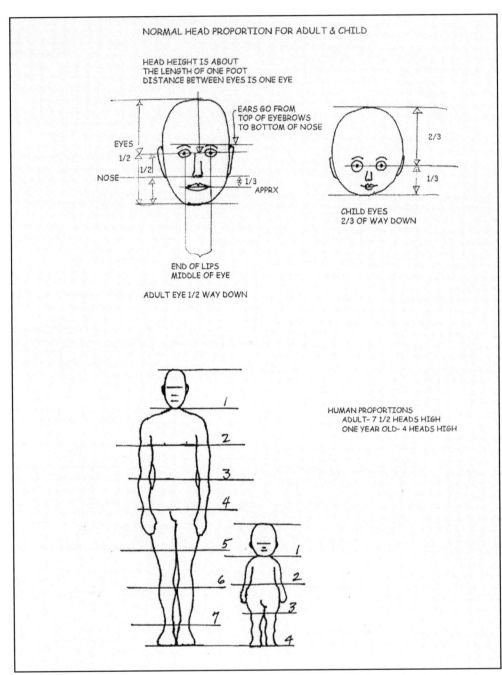

NORMAL HEAD PROPORTION FOR ADULT & CHILD

HEAD HEIGHT IS ABOUT
THE LENGTH OF ONE FOOT
DISTANCE BETWEEN EYES IS ONE EYE

EARS GO FROM
TOP OF EYEBROWS
TO BOTTOM OF NOSE

EYES
1/2
1/2
NOSE
1/3
APPRX

2/3
1/3

CHILD EYES
2/3 OF WAY DOWN

END OF LIPS
MIDDLE OF EYE

ADULT EYE 1/2 WAY DOWN

HUMAN PROPORTIONS
ADULT- 7 1/2 HEADS HIGH
ONE YEAR OLD- 4 HEADS HIGH

Courtesy of the Dan F. McLaughlin, Jr. Collection

CHAPTER 6

(figs. 6-1, 6-2, 6-10)

TECHNICAL DIVERSITY OF ANIMATION[1]

Animation has many techniques. You should decide which one to use when you start your film. Today the common techniques used commercially are hand-drawn cel and 3D computer. But there many more to consider and most are listed below. Tomorrow there may be more as animators are constantly surprising us with new or changed techniques. Many films, like Disney's *Fantasia* (1940), will mix two or more of these techniques. Some techniques are not as popular as others. *L Idee*, a film made in 1932 in France by Berthold Bartosch was the first, and probably the last, animated film done with woodcuts.

THE MOST BASIC TECHNICAL CATEGORIES

- **Traditional 2D:** Two-dimensional handmade drawn or created images.
- **2, 3D Stop Motion:** Three-dimensional handmade puppet or model animation.
- **Visual effect:** When animation is used within a live-action film.
- **Computer:** The computer is the primary tool used to do the animation.
- **Interactive:** The audience not only views but also interacts with the animation.

1. As mentioned in the Acknowledgements, the author completed the manuscript sometime around 2007 and the text has not been updated for accuracy. All statements reflect the belief of the author at the time of authorship and may, or may not, reflect current reality. Also, I never spoke to my father about this book, so I really have no idea what he meant by the pathway documents or how they were meant to be used. I have merely reproduced what was in the written text that he left and leave the interpretation to you.

Traditional Animation Techniques

Drawn on paper or a non-transparent surface and shot on an animation crane or scanned into a computer:

- Drawn on normal paper with pencil or ink. Everything must be on that sheet of paper, including the background, no levels. Examples: Emile Cohl's *Fantasmagorie* (1908), Winsor McCay's *Gertie the Dinosaur* (1914), Tami Tasik *A Frog He Would A-wooing Go* (1990) (fig. 6-1).
- Drawn on paper with charcoal, marker, pastels, etc. Sara Petty's *Furies* (1977), Norman McLaren's *La Poulette Grise* (1947).
- Drawn or painted on paper but then cut out and attached to a cel with some form of rubber cement. This allows the use of multiple levels and a separate background. Dan McLaughlin *Epiphanies* (1968) (fig. 6-2)
- Drawn on paper for backlighting with two to three levels of paper. Faith Hubley's films *Starlore* (1983), *Hello* (1984).
- A printmaking process such as woodcuts. *L Idee* (1932).
- Printing devices such as stamps, stencils. *Mothlight*, Stan Brakhage in an experimental film attached dead moth wings to clear film with clear Mylar tape.

Done on cels or transparent material and shot on an animation crane:

- The traditional ink and paint, with the ink outline on the top of the cel and the color paint puddled on the bottom side within the outlined space, as seen with Brian Wells *All Aflutter* (1997) (fig. 6-3). Allows the use of up to six levels and a background. Almost any film from Disney, Warners Bros and MGM from the 1930s and 40s was done in this technique. Because of its flexibility in economics and production, it is the most common technique used in animation today. Celia Mercer's *Swimming* (1986) (fig. 6-4).

- Paint only, no outline. Walerian Borowczyk's *Game of Angels* (1964), Alexander Petrov's, *The Old Man and the Sea* (1999).

- Outline ink, wax crayon, china marker, grease pencil, or marker only. Bill Littlejohn's *Tiger Paws* (n.d.) (fig. 6-6).
- Frosted cels for use with pencils. Frederic *Back's Crac!* (1981), *The Man who Planted Trees* (1987).
- A marker for paint color and backed with white paint so that it becomes opaque. Murakami Wolf's *The Point* (1971), the first feature (an hour long) done for prime-time TV.
- Painting on glass. Dave Fleischer's *Popeye meets Ali Baba and His Forty Thieves* (1937): The animation was on glass, which was in front of a 3D model background. George Dunning's *The Flying Man* (1962).
- Multi-plane. Instead of one animation base of platen, moving pegs and lights under the camera on an animation crane there are several of these stacked on top of one another. Usually used with cel animation. Disney's *Pinocchio* (1940) is a prime example.

Existing materials shot on an animation crane or created on the computer:

Photographs. Often used in documentaries. Colin Low and Wolf Koenig's *City of Gold* (1957) from the National Film Board of Canada is an excellent example.

- Kinestasis. Non-sequence shots, often photos or reproductions, filmed at a very fast rate, one to five frames per image. My *God Is Dog Spelled Backwards, or 2000 years of art in 3 minutes* (1963) was the first complete film in this technique (fig. 6-7).[2] Frank Mouris's *Frank Film* (1973), which is also a collage film, won an Academy Award.
- Collage. Cutting up magazines, etc., as in Biographic's *Do It Yourself Cartoon Kit* (1961).

Under the Camera or computer - Created images

- Unjoined cutouts that are top light. Portions of Ernest Pintoff's *The Critic* (1963).
- Joined cutouts with string or pivot rivets that are top light. Gianini and Luzzati 's *The Paladins of France* (1960).
- Silhouette animation. These are joined cutouts that have backlight only so they appear as a silhouette or a shadow play. Lotte Reiniger's *The Adventures of Prince Achmed* (1926).
- Sand, rice, graphite, etc. Richard Quade's, *Sand Dance* (1988).
- Liquids, using a backlight shallow dish with oils and liquids. James and John Whitney's *Celery Stalks at Midnight* (1937). They also did a film using the pendulum at the Griffith Observatory as the drawing tool so that the motion of the Earth drew the animation.[3]
- Felt on a felt board or rubber on magnetic rubber. One of the sequences of Norman McLaren's *Canon* (1964).
- Thin chains or strung beads. Tsvika Oren's *Experimentations* (1970s).
- Paint directly under camera. Caroline Leaf's *The Street* (1976), Joan Grantz's *Mona Lisa Descending a Staircase* (1992) , Celia Mercer's *Bad Dream Girl* (fig. 6-8).

Horizontal artwork

- Pinscreen. Alexander Alexeieff and Claire Parker *Night on Bald Mountain* (1933) and Jacques Drouin's *The Landscape Painter* (1976).[4]
- Wax cutting. Oskar Fischinger, experiments with shapes in cast wax that is filmed when sliced off. Oskar also experimented with silhouettes of thin metal (1920s).

---

2. Two things. One, you can listen to the author talk about his films here, http://danmclaughlin.info/talk.html. Second, you can view *God is Dog* on the DVD *11 Films by Dan McLaughlin*.

3. Some Internet sources give a year of 1951 for *Celery*. I can't find any mention of this other film.

4. Most online resources list Drouin's film from 1976 as *Mindscape/Le paysagiste*.

Working directly on film:

- Paints, inks, scratching, etc. Norman McLaren's *Begone Dull Care* (1949). Phil Denslow's film *Madcap* (1991) was made by drawing on clear 16mm leader with Magic Markers. Then it was printed as a negative to reverse the images. *Madcap* was awarded first prize in the Experimental Animation category at the '90 L. A. Animation Celebration. Also won First Prize in Animation at '91 Ann Arbor Film Fest (fig. 6-9).
- Character drawing on film. Robert Swarthe's *Kick Me* (1973).[5]
- Drawn sound on film. Norman McLaren's *Hen Hop* (1942).
- Exposing objects on undeveloped film. Man Ray, I believe, did this in the 1920s.[6]
- Airbrush. Pat O'Neill's *Screen* (1969).

Rotoscoping (tracing existing live action or animation):

- For realistic looking animation (fig. 5-45). Used throughout most of Ralph Bakshi's later films. Used in computer animation and is usually called motion capture.
- Aesthetic animation. Ryan Larkin's *Walking* (1968), George Dunning's *Lucy in the Sky with Diamonds* number from *Yellow Submarine* (1968).
- Used to match live action and animation. MGM, *Tom and Jerry*, and Gene Kelly sequence in *Anchors Aweigh* (1945).
- Used by beginning animators to learn animation. Richard Williams said he learned animation by rotoscoping an entire *Road Runner and Coyote* short.

3D stop motion (Real objects):

- Articulated puppets or models, typically made out of plasticine (modeling clay), cloth or cast latex, that are supported by a skeleton of wire or ball and socket that is called an armature. Also can be made of wood with movable or replaceable parts. Kihachiro Kawamoto's *Oni* (1972), Nick Park's *The Wrong Trousers* (1993), George Pal's *Tubby the Tuba* (1947). Another example is taken from the UCLA Falling Lizard Film *Pirates vs. Ninjas* (fig. 6-10).
- Everyday or unusual items. Anything that is 3D and that can be moved is a potential star. Films have been made using household furniture, cut-up vegetables and embalmed beetles. *The Invisible Moving Company* (1914), Jan Svankmajer's *Dimensions of Dialogue* (1982), Ladislaw Starewicz's *The Cameraman's Revenge*, (1912).
- Pixilation. Shooting a live human figure one frame at a time in different poses. Norman McLaren's *Neighbors* (1952), and *A Chairy Tale* (1957), Mike Jittlov's *The Wizard of Time and*

---

5. Looking at the film on youtube, it looks like the copyright date in 1975.
6. The internet seems to agree.

Speed (1979), Paul de Nooijer's *Transformation*[7] are good examples of pixilation.

- Changing camera speed
- Time lapse. Rower growing, beach changing, clouds flying across the sky, stars (Bill Mitchell).[8]
- High-speed photography. Slow motion.
- Sculpting in flat clay, a bas-relief.
- Special combinations. Jimmy Murakami's *When the Wind Blows* (1986) was a combination of animated characters over a 3D model background.

Visual effects:

An animated visual effect is any visual element that is added to a live-action film after the original shooting of the live action. The optical printer was the tool used to create multi-exposures necessary for these combinations. Now the tool is digital computer. Some examples are:

- The combination of animated and live-action characters. A blue or sodium screen process was usually needed for this process. From Willis O'Brien's *King Kong* (1933) and Disney's *Mary Poppins* (1964) to *Who Framed Roger Rabbit* (1988).
- As part of a live-action film for a realistic effect. For a visual effect that is too expensive or dangerous, or just impossible in live action.
- Taking live action out of realism and making it a fantastic or fantasy world. From the mundane, the frame-by-frame removing of the wires that hold up a flying Superman, to the epic worlds of space or the interior world of a weird mind.
- The optical printer can be used as a tool to create the entire content of a film. By using the techniques of special effects in an artistic or experimental manner to create a complete film. Norman McLaren's *Pas de deux* (1968), and Pat O'Neil are two filmmakers in this format.

Motion control:

- A computer controls either a vertical or horizontal animation crane and the artwork or model. The Star Gate sequence (art) and spacecraft (models) in *2001, A Space Odyssey* (1969).

---

7. I think the author might mean *Transformation by Holding Time* by Paul de Nooijer (1976).
8. http://www.blueskyfootage.com/Cinematographers/Bill_Mitchell

Computer

- The computer assists in the production of traditional 2D (drawn) animation. Examples of this type of animation are the recent Disney animated features *The Lion King* (1994) and *Atlantis: The Lost Empire* (2001). Drawn on paper but then scanned and colored in the computer as in Jay Shipman's *One Final Encore* 2016 (fig. 6-12).
- The computer is the primary production tool for 3D character computer animation. An example of this type of film would be *Toy Story* (1995). The predecessor of 3D computer animation is 3D stop motion.
- 2D computer animation that can either be 2D character animation like *South Park* or 2D motion graphics. In 2D motion graphics, archival art or film and effects are used to create moving graphics. Easy to see examples of this type are inexpensive TV commercials.
- The computer is also used in stop motion, special effects, and interactive animation to fit the special technical needs of those fields.

Interactive

Interactive means that the audience is an active participant in the process. It is made possible by the computer. Interactive is divided into two spheres, static and dynamic.

- Static. Example, a website or a datebase. The audience controls the entire process.
- Dynamic. Example, a game. Where a possible number of events can happen at any time. The program in the computer is active in the process.

All the animation techniques mentioned can be used in these interactive digital spheres.

PATHS OF PRODUCTION

These are current paths of production in traditional 2D animation:

- The film is done in the traditional way with pencil and paper, ink and paint on cels or some other hand-done method and shot on an animation crane and it comes out on film. This is the production path followed in this book, as it is the best way today to learn animation.

The Common Production Pathway for the Traditional Camera Animated Film

		Idea		
		Storyboard		
		Animatic	Bar Sheets	
Budget	Character Model Sheets	Layout		Sound Sources Selected for Music Effects & Voice
Production Schedule				
				Recording the Sound especially any synced sound
Exposure Sheets		Rough Animation and Pencil Test		
	Backgrounds			
				Transferring Sound to Digital Editing for Timing and Composition
		Cleaned up Animation		
		Ink and Paint		
		Check		
		Camera		
		Lab for Development and a Color Work Print		
		Interlock Viewing and Corrections if needed		
				Final sound as needed
		Negative Cut		
		Sound and Neg. Cut to Lab. for Composite Print – First Answer Print		
		Film Done		
		Distribution		
		Fame		
		Fortune		
		Personal Satisfaction		

- The film is shot on the animation crane but composited in digital. This saves the lab costs of film.

Production Pathway for the Traditional Camera Animated Film but Composited in Digital

		Idea		
		Storyboard		
		Animatic	Bar Sheets	
Budget	Character Model Sheets	Layout	Sound Sources Selected for Music	Effects & Voice
Production Schedule				
				Recording the Sound especially any synced sound
Exposure sheets		Rough Animation and Pencil Tests		
	Backgrounds			
				Transferring Sound to Digital Editing for Timing and Composting
		Cleaned up Animation		
		Ink and Paint		
		Check		
		Camera		
		Lab for Developing and a Color Work Print		
		Interlock Viewing and Corrections if needed		
			Final Sound as needed	
		Telecine to the Digital		
		Composite Sound and Picture in Digital		
		Digital Film Done		
		Distribution		
		Fame		
		Fortune		
		Personal Satisfaction		

- The film is done with pencil and paper and scanned into the computer for painting and the other necessary production steps needed to arrive at a finished digital tape. If a film is desired, the digital files must be shot on film.

Production Pathway for the Traditional Animated Film but Digital from the Ink and Paint On

		Idea		
		Storyboard		
		Animatic	Bar Sheets	
Budget	Character Model Sheets	Layout for the Computer	Sound Sources Selected for Music	Effects & Voice
Production Schedule				
				Recording the Sound especially any synced sound
Partial Exposure Sheets		Rough Animation and Pencil Tests		
Backgrounds - Traditional or Digital				
				Transferring Sound to Digital Editing for Timing and Composting
		Cleaned up Animation		
Exposure Sheets		Complete Pencil Test of Animation		
		Scan into the Computer		
		Digital Ink and Paint		
		Composite Picture in Digital		
				Final Sound as needed
		Composite Sound and Picture in Digital		
		Digital Film Done		
		Distribution		
		Fame		
		Fortune		
		Personal Satisfaction		

Production Pathway for the 3D Computer Animation

			Sound Sources Selected for Music	Effects & Voice
		Idea		
		Storyboard		
		Rough Character Models - Rough Layout - Rough Backgrounds		
		Animatic		
Budget			Sound Sources Selected for Music	Effects & Voice
Production Schedule				
				Recording the Sound especially any synced sound
		Characters Constructed		
		Character Rigged for Movement		
		Rough Texture and Color (can be turned off)		
Timing		Animation		
Backgrounds Constructed				
		Color		
		Lighting		
		Finish Texture		
				Digital Editing for Timing and Composting
				Finish Sound
		Composite Sound and Picture		
		Digital Film Done		
		Distribution		
		Fame		
		Fortune		
		Personal Satisfaction		

- And for one of the many pathways for Visual Effect in a Live-Action Film, see chapter 11.
- And a possible pathway for Interactive Games, see chapter 13.

For current 3D animation, including visual effects, the film could be done either in film or digitally. However, visual effects are almost all done digitally.

- Last, a pathway for an experimental animated film.

Pathway for the Concept Film

		Idea		
		No Storyboard		
		Production in whatever technique		
		View		
		Call it finished, redo or move on		
		Possible distribution		
		Fame		
		Fortune		

STYLES

A student in animation should be constantly studying art and style history, as almost all the styles used in animation have come from the older arts: music, painting, theater, dance, drawing, literature, poetry and sculpture. Today the art styles used in animation could be grouped into three main categories: (1) realistic/naturalistic, (2) caricature/cartoon and (3) non-representational or abstract. Which style is chosen should fit the idea for the film.

GENRES

Genres are the classification given to different types of stories as distinguished by the subject, theme, or style. Examples of the narrative genre would be: comedy, romance, Western, mystery, musical or a combination, i.e. a space Western or a romantic mystery. In animation the most prevalent genre is comedy; some others are: action hero, family, kid, prime time, music video, feature, art, and even the sick and twisted series. There are non-narrative genres such as documentary or experimental.

Animation, especially in the short form and in the United States, is thought of as only one genre, comedy, and until recently only for one age group, children. The short, funny, animated "cartoon" for kids was pretty much the standard for animation. It was the one genre that generally turned a profit. Not until Disney did the feature *Snow White* in 1937 did the general audience look at animation as more than a short cartoon comedy but as a feature love story of a young girl's coming-of-age story done as a musical. However, it was still considered a film for children.

In the 1950s and 1960s television broadcasters further defined animation as for children only by their scheduling of animation for children on Saturday early mornings and late afternoons. "Kid Vid" became electronic babysitters and created a very profitable advertising revenue stream. In other countries, even though children's animation was key, animation was often taken more as a serious film form and other genres were successfully done. Europe and Japan are two good examples. The restriction of the genres in animation was abetted by the old Hollywood attitude that considered the use of animation appropriate in only these three areas:

- Where something was too big or small to film in live action
- Where symbolic representation was needed.
- The fantastic or fantasy.

Today, with the advent of computer animation, yearly theatrical release of multiple features, cable TV, interactive (games), anime and prime-time series, the number of genres accepted in animation has grown and has contributed to the expanding world of animation. A major development is the combination of animation and live action into a new film form. To many, however, there still is the perception that animation should only be funny.

The animated documentary is a documentary that is done mainly or completely in animation. The content is the event that the film documents. A typical animation documentary uses still photos to replace live action that is not available. *The True Story of the Civil War* (1957)or *City of Gold* (1957) are examples of this form, which is still not widely recognized as an independent entity.

Animated Commercials are films whose purpose is to sell a product. They use various animation techniques along with the principles of salesmanship and persuasion. Frequently the animation is very experimental and can give the animator an opportunity to be visually creative. The Muratti marching cigarette commercials done by Oskar Fischinger in 1920's is an early example as is Bob Mitchell's CALM anti-perspirant cartoon (1971) (figs. 6-14, 2-52).

Animated Educational films cover a wide range. From the classroom to *Sesame Street* (fig. 6-15)to health care, animation is an effective teaching method.

THE FUTURE

Answering these questions will help you predict the future of animation. Will new techniques be found? Can you find one? Will there be less technical restrictions? Will there be no differences between live action and animation? Will there always be a difference? Will the director of the future have to know both forms? Will (if not when) we be shooting on digital film? Will a new major film form, that combines live action and animation so neither dominates, arise?

As part of the questions above, what impact will the UCLA Walter Lantz Digital Animation

Studio have on the future production of animation (fig. 13-5)? The experimental super workstation was based partially on this concept–that animation is unique in the field of motion pictures as one person can essentially do a complete film: write, direct, act, set design, light, color, edit, voice and music. This is very rare in live action, the exceptions being the early comedians, Charlie Chapin Buster Keaton, and later Jacques Tati and Mike Jittlov (fig. 6-16). Only in the commercial area, where the egos and incompetence of producers and the demands of the so-called marketplace have forced the Taylor method of the assembly line on animation, has animation gone away from this unique strength. Sometimes this has led to disastrous results. The Walter Lantz Studio is an attempt, and so far a very successful one, at strengthening the individual creator's role in animation and perhaps even bringing that unique strength of individual talent back into the commercial world of animation.

Trying different techniques is fun and a break from doing the same technique ad infinitum. It can also lead you in different directions that will improve your ability as an animator and a filmmaker.

(fig. 6-16)

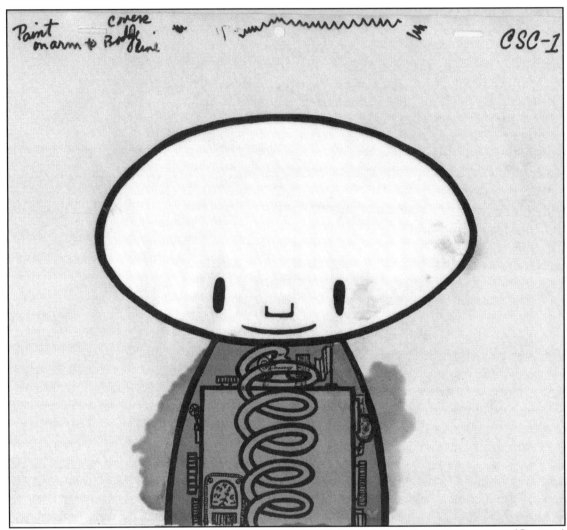

(fig. 7-77)

CHAPTER 7

(fig. 7-11)

ANIMATION[1]

"Any idiot that wants to make a couple of thousand drawings for a hundred feet of film is welcome to join the club."
Winsor McCay, Animator, c. 1910-1920[2]

"Animation is not drawings that move, but movement that is drawn."
Norman McLaren, Animator, late 1960s[3]

Anything can be animated; moving a pencil around on a table and shooting it one frame at a time will become an animated dancing pencil. Animation on this basic level is simple, but consistently good animation is complex. Learning to animate well takes hard work, patience and commitment. The principles of animation discussed and illustrated in this chapter are the beginning.

---

1. As mentioned in the Acknowledgements, the author completed the manuscript sometime around 2007 and the text has not been updated for accuracy. All statements reflect the belief of the author at the time of authorship and may, or may not, reflect current reality.

2. "Winsor McCay." AZQuotes.com. Wind and Fly LTD, 2016. 01 December 2016.

3. BrainyQuote has it slightly different: "Animation is not the art of drawings that move but the art of movements that are drawn." "Norman McLaren." BrainyQuote.com. Xplore Inc., 2016. 1 December 2016.

WHAT IS IMPORTANT

Movement between the frames is more important than what is on the frame. The timing of what happens between the frames makes good animation.

METHODS TO LEARN ANIMATION

Sitting down, animating with pencil on paper and then shooting it, is the best way to learn to animate. It is labor- and time-intensive until the principles are firmly understood and you are producing good animation on a consistent level. Doing the exercises in this chapter is a beginning.

Rotoscoping (fig. 5-45). Copying other animated or live action frame by frame is not a common way to learn animation. But it can help with difficult animation, as in animating a long, flowing dress of a dancing woman. Richard Williams is said to have learned animation by rotoscoping an entire *Road Runner and Coyote* short.

Computers. Perhaps someday the principles of animation can be learned on the computer, but presently there are two major drawbacks: 1. Computers are not flexible enough a tool. 2. You have to learn the computer software, including rigging the character for 3D, before learning animating. Some of the latest 2D software, with drawing on the screen, holds promise. Computers, like pencils, cannot do animation. A person does the animation. You don't buy the talent when you buy a computer.

THE THREE BASICS OF ANIMATION

- *Timing*
- *Speed*
- *Holds 16 frames*

They are related. Timing is the varying of the speed of the movement and holds are a stop in the movement. This rhythm or changing of the timing supports the action. If a character puts his or her hand on a hot stove, it will come off fast and slow quickly, and then shake violently in pain. If the same character is raising his or her hand to catch a fly ball in the outfield, the hand will track the ball slowly, rise, then catch it with a fast movement and hold it up for all to see. Unless you are doing a robot, always keep changing the speed and holds to bring life to your animation. The timing of the scene can tell you how many drawings you need to do. One second equals 24 frames in film and if you are doing the standard one drawing for every two frames that means 12 drawings. So a simple three-second scene will need 36 drawings. Timing it to the action may take 22 drawings.

To help you find the length of a scene, imagine it in your mind or by acting it out by moving your hands on a sheet of paper with a stopwatch or a metronome. Mime it using a mirror, or if you have the sound use exposure sheets. The action must be on long enough to be seen and understood. Art Babbitt, one of the great Disney animators, felt that you needed at least 16 frames for audiences to see a complete action.

Timing, speed and holds will be covered in exercises #1 and #2.

THE THREE METHODS OF ANIMATION
(or Where Does the Next Drawing Go?)

All drawings are done on single field punched animation paper registered on an animation disc with a light source.

- **Key or posed animation.** This is the method used by most animators. You first draw the extremes, the last and first drawings of the action, also known as the keys or key poses (fig. 7-13). Do the last drawing first so the animation will end up in the proper place with the right expression. Next, flip the extremes to see if the animation is correct and redo if needed. Then do breakdowns, the main drawings in between the keys and flip. When you get the movement or emotion you want then do the drawings in between the breakdowns to fill out the time. In the production method developed at the Disney studio, the animator did the key poses, the assistant animator cleaned them up and put them on model and may have done some of the breakdowns, then the breakdown animator did the breakdowns and finally the inbetween animator did the remaining drawings or inbetweens. Where the breakdown drawings are spaced is important for correct speed. If drawing #1 is one extreme and drawing #10 the other, then where does #5 go? It may be only a short distance from #1 for a slow start movement or very close to #10 for a fast start. To draw #5, place a blank paper over #1 and #10 to use as reference on the underlight disc for roughing in #5. Flip, correct, flip, and then do #3 using #1 and #5, and #7 using #5 and #10 for reference. Flip, correct and finish by doing the inbetweens in the same manner. The walk exercise is a good example.

To help plan and to communicate to others, do a timing chart on the first drawing to indicate the variations in the speed and where the breakdowns go of the movement. This chart would have the numbers of the first and last poses and a vertical line between them that would be marked off at intervals with the in-between numbers to show whether the animation is to be slow or fast by the distance between the marks. If the action started slowly, the middle would be a third of the way down the chart.

The key poses are your most important drawings as they show the complete personality or the attitude of the character or action. Use a blue pencil at the beginning and clean up with a graphite pencil (fig. 2-40). Work rough and loose, animating only the basic forms (this is when you realize how important it is that a character is designed to be animated)(fig. 2-46). Do none of the details (eyebrows, fingers) or secondary animation until cleaning up and putting on model.

- **Straight-ahead.** Just as the name implies, you do the drawings in order, starting with the first until you reach the last. To figure out where the next drawing goes you can guess, eyeball or mark the positions on a separate sheet. You could flip the first drawings to see if they work, make corrections, flip the next batch, check, correct and continue this way until the end. A problem with this method is that the animation can end up off the edge of the paper before the action is completed. This technique is for experienced animators or those who can visualize ahead.

- **A combination of straight-ahead and key pose.** The key frames, the extremes and the main keys, and perhaps breakdowns are done. Then the inbetweens are done straight-ahead. This can be the best of both worlds, the control of the key poses and flexibility of the straight-ahead animation. It can give life to animation that is becoming stale.

THE TWO TYPES OF ANIMATION
Full animation
Limited animation

- Full animation means full continuous movement. An example of full character animation is any of Disney's features where the main character is completely redrawn every time. In experimental animation, the films of Oskar Fischinger, where each frame is redrawn, is a good illustration. Full animation is time consuming and expensive. *The Katzenjammer Kids: Still Stranded Synopsis:* Two boys on a stranded ship in the North Pole play a trick on the crew, with the aid of a little bear (fig. 7-1).

- Limited animation uses less drawing than full animation, thereby limiting the movement. Most TV animation is limited and is achieved by various methods, including only animating the mouth and not the head for lip sync, using flat 2D pans for the walk cycle, trucking in and out on a static shot to imply movement, exaggerating and holding the key frame, overuse of cycles and letting the dialogue take the place of animation. The National Lumber commercials excelled at this (fig. 7-2). There is a type of limited animation that is done only with key poses. In a unique film, *La Jetée* (1962), each shot is only one key held frame of the original live-action shot.

Standard ways to enliven limited animation are eye blinks, eyebrow raises, simple head movements and a standard set of cliché facial expressions. Today, Kid Vid is an example of very limited animation. Programs, at the low end, will have only a few thousand drawings for a 20 to 22 minute show. The high end would be over 20,000 drawings for the same time.

In the 1950s and 1960s, examples of limited animation were UPA's (United Productions of America) flat 2D animation, Hanna-Barbera's use of poses and educational animation. Limited animation is less expensive than full animation but it can still be effective. *Rocky and Bullwinkle* and other Jay Ward productions are perfect models.

Motion Graphics. In non-character animation, limited animation is used in animating photos, still art, paintings, etc. Examples are *City of Gold* (1957), the Weston Woods storybook films and *The Games of Angels* (1964).

Limited, full and motion graphics can all be in the same film. And now the exercises.

EXERCISES IN THE BASIC PRINCIPLES OF ANIMATION

These are the exercises for the first class in animation. The exercises include five pencil tests, a 15-second film and exposure sheets. Many of the principles of animation are covered through the exercises.

PENCIL TEST ASSIGNMENTS

In the first course, these exercises are given each week with the lectures and readings. The lectures will cover the normal animation production process and the pencil tests illustrate the principles of animation. The lectures and pencil tests are not parallel; when the animation lectures are reached, the student will have had several weeks of pencil test animation. This allows the student to understand the complexity and interdependency of all the elements of animation.

At UCLA, a Teaching Assistant will digitally shoot the finished pencil tests at one time for ease of viewing (fig. 7-3). The students can shoot tests on their exercises to see the animation immediately. In the old days, your pencil tests were shot and developed on film, a delay of a few days to a week. It is somewhat like hitting the keys on a piano and hearing the notes days later.

BOUNCING BALL - Assignment #1 (fig. 14-1) also see pp. 334-338

The bouncing ball exercise, which covers the principles of squash and stretch and the control of speed, is traditionally the first exercise in animation. Its origins are lost in the dark and murky beginnings of animation.

In this exercise you will be creating the illusion of a bouncing ball. A drawn circle will appear as a bouncing ball by the way you time, move and space it. A bouncing rectangle was added about 40 years ago to increase the learning qualities.

The tools used are a No. 2 yellow pencil or a comparable soft-lead art pencil (fig. 11-2) and a Sharpie or equivalent. The materials needed are at least 30 sheets of punched animation paper (fig.7-4). The equipment needed will be an animation disc and desk.

At the start, a circle (ball) falls into the screen from the left (this direction is chosen because European languages read from left to right), hits an invisible ground line, immediately changes into a rectangle, bounces once as a rectangle, hits the invisible ground line again, changes back into a circle and bounces off the paper (fig. 7-5). You will do this in 24 sequential drawings on paper bottom-hole-punched that registers the paper on the bottom pegs. In the old days (the 1920s and 1930s) animators on the East Coast used top pegs to register their paper and animators on the West Coast used bottom pegs, claiming it made it easier to flip and check the drawing. We will use bottom pegs.

The first drawing you do will be the layout of the path of action of the bouncing ball. Horizontally divide the paper roughly into thirds and mark the two points in the bottom third of the paper, not too close to the bottom and about a third of the way from the sides. These are your invisible hit or contact points. Then draw a path of action that follows a normal arc between the two points and a half arc going on and off the paper. Everything you want seen on the screen should be inside the 12 field center (12FC). The borders of the 12FC are roughly one-quarter of an inch in on the top and the sides and 1½ inches in on the bottom of the paper (figs. 7-5, 14-1). If you have a field chart (fig. 5-36), place that on your disc so that you can see the edges of a 12 field. Draw all the way to the edge of the paper to allow for mistakes in shooting.

Next, mark off the 24 numbered positions for the ball/rectangle on the arcs of the layout. The positions are marked to mimic the force of gravity, which pulls us down (the Earth sucks). The speed of the ball slows at the top; gravity is starting to pull it back and faster when going up or down (fig. 7-6). One way of the two ways to change the speed of the ball is to vary the spacing between the drawings. The greater the distance between the drawings, the faster the movement; the smaller the distance between them, the slower the movement. Simply put, to move a ball fast you will use less drawings, to move a ball slow in the same distance you will use more drawings. So to give the illusion of gravity, there will be fewer balls going up and down (faster) and more balls closer together at the top of the arc (slower). Also the ball moves faster coming out of the hit to imply the force that gives the bounce. The shape of the ball or rectangle will be stretched somewhat when going into or out from the hit point, and will squash flat on the bottom and bulge on the sides at the impact point. This illustrates the principle of squash and stretch, which gives the animation life. Then draw the appropriate circles or rectangles over the position marks on the path of action. This exercise is done as straight-ahead animation. The rest of the exercises can be done in any of the three methods of animation you choose.

Using the light box on your animation disc and using a pencil or Sharpie, copy these drawings to individual sheets of paper. Do not use a ballpoint pen; its line will be too light when filmed. Your drawings will have more life if you keep them loose and rough. Do not go insane trying to make each one perfect. However, if you are a perfectionist, at least use the lid of a jar for the circle and not a compass. Number each piece of paper in the lower right-hand corner as you trace. When you are done, put the 24 punched sequential drawings in order and your name sheet on the top, and paper clip together and hand in to be shot. Each name title will be shot for 12x with 12x of blank paper shot between each student's work. Twelve frames are chosen to get students used to the length of a half of a second, the march time beat in music and usually the minimal time needed to read an image on the screen.

The other way to change the speed of the action is to shoot your drawings at different rates: 1's, 2's and 3's. This will be done for this assignment. Shooting at three different speeds will also give you an idea of how to arrive at the amount of screen time needed to make an action believable. When the 24 drawings are shot on 1's, the action will last one second on the screen. When shot on 2's, the bouncing ball will be on the screen for two seconds or 48x. On 3's it will be on for three seconds or 72x. Which of the above timings looks correct as a bouncing ball crosses the screen? Does one move too fast or too slow? Do all three look acceptable? In that case, which speed fits the intended action the best? These are the kinds of basic questions animators constantly ask themselves.

The animation in this assignment will be on the screen for six seconds or 144x. This exercise should only take a couple of hours. You will not need to do exposure sheets for this assignment.

Since it is fundamental to animation, let's review the two ways you control the speed of movement.

The spacing between each drawing

The distance between each drawing will determine if the animation moves slow or fast and if it is accelerating or decelerating. The greater the distance between each drawing, the faster the movement. The shorter the distance between each drawing, the slower the movement (fig. 7-6). Most animators and computers use this method.

The number of frames each drawing is shot

The three basic shooting times for continuous, smooth animation are one, two, or three frames per drawing. Shooting on 1's, 2's and 3's is another way to control the timing (speed) of movement. 1's are used for fast action and runs and computer animation. Most animation is shot on 2's, which cuts the amount of drawings in half (at 24 frames per second, 1's = 24 drawings and 2's = 12 drawings). 3's use less drawings (eight drawings per second) but is felt to be not as smooth as 2's. These rates can be mixed to make the movement slower or faster within an action. For example, the animation can be on 2's, then a 3, then a series of 1's, then back to 2's.

All mechanical moves, pans, trucks, dissolves, etc., are shot on 1's otherwise there will be a slight jittery effect. It is not necessary to do the animation on 1's when this happens; use 2's for a walk cycle on a pan and the two rates will work together. At four frames or more per drawing, the movement will be jerky. A few animators shoot on 4's or 5's, and this is acceptable to them. History note: In silent film, animation was done on 1's as silent film was projected at 16 frames per second so only 16 drawings were needed.

A good way to get a sense of the time needed for any action is to move your finger or an object over the path of action at the speed you want and count seconds to yourself until you feel the proper time. Then convert that time from seconds to frames and divide by two, and discounting any holds (shooting for 4's or more), will tell you how many drawings are needed. Traditional hand-drawn animation is done on 2's; computer animation is done on 1's. Perhaps that is one reason that computer animation looks different from traditional.

The other aspect of movement, non-movement or holds, will be covered in the second assignment, the asterisk.

Now that you can control the speed in animation, how do you apply it?

The four basic types of speed in movement are:

Even Speed Movement. The spacing between each drawing and the frame rate is the same. As this speed is constant and unchanging, it gives you animation that lacks life. Living beings are not robots and do not move at an even speed.

Slow to Fast Movement. The spacing between drawings is close at the start, Slo (Slo is often used by animators as an abbreviation), and grows farther apart to speed up. Or the frame rate could change from 2's to 1's also. This movement, Slo to fast, is used for animation out of holds, in character animation to go from a Slo take to a fast reaction, and in this exercise from the Slo gravity pull at the top of the arc to the fast falling.

Fast to Slow Movement. The spacing between the drawings is farther apart at the start and is closer together at the end. The frame shooting ratio can also change. Examples of a fast to Slo movement would be when a character quickly removes his or her hand from a hot stove, easing into a hold, or in this exercise the change from the fast up to the Slo arc. A very experienced animator once said she always used either Slo to fast or fast to Slo to go into or out of a hold, and it usually didn't matter which, but it was absolutely essential to do one or the other.

Any combination of 1, 2 and 3, slow, fast, even, slow, even, fast-slow and fast. When used in combination, you can get a rhythm and flow to your movement.

And now back to the exercise.

When the numbered drawings are in order starting from the top, it is called a cameraman's stack, as the cameraperson will put the whole stack on the pegs of the animation crane and remove them while shooting. The number sequence that starts on the bottom is an animator's stack, making it easier to flip the drawings. You should start flipping your animation to see how it works with this exercise. A good place to check is the squash and stretch of the ball. If you do not see the animation at first, do not be discouraged. Look at one spot in the action and keep flipping until you see it move. This will get your eye and brain in sync, and then you should be able to see the whole sequence within a few more flips. Some animators say this is the most exhilarating experience in the whole animation process, the first time that you see your animation come alive.

The audience will know what kind of ball it is by how it bounces. A tennis ball will hit and bounce as in this assignment. An Indian rubber ball would bounce higher, a glass ball will shatter and break, a ball of wet dough will sort of go "splot" and not bounce too well, while a shot put will hit, bounce very little and roll away. A high or low arc can also create an illusion of the weight and type of ball. This holds true for any object; the way it reacts to physical laws will define it. You do not need to draw a ground line as when the ball hits and bounces an imaginary ground line is defined. The viewer will make this association because of previous experience.

A common mistake for beginning animators is not enough squash and stretch (fig. 7-52. "More squash and stretch" is a quote frequently heard in a critique of animation. Squash and stretch gives weight and gravity to the animation. You can put in speed lines, lines behind the object to give the impression of speed. But not too many or for too long, or else they will give the ball a hairy tail. You could add a moving ground shadow, keeping the light source constant.

For this assignment the circle and rectangle are 2D, no shading because the drawn cross-hatching will jiggle all over the place and distract from the bouncing object. The assignment is to learn animation, not rendering. Do not animate in perspective. Make sure the volume, the size, remains roughly the same. When an object changes size, it gives the impression that it is moving away from or toward the audience. If the size changes randomly, it will look like it has life or is poorly animated. Do not rotate the rectangle; it is hard to control the edges and is too advanced for this assignment. Do not put a face on the ball or rectangle, it is a cheap gag, used to hide the fact you cannot do the exercise. With more complex animation, the basic shapes and movement are animated first and then the details are added. Pretty drawings can waste time and effort.

One thing this exercise illustrates is exterior animation, moving an image through space. Interior animation, movement within the object, will be in future assignments. Even though everyone will be doing the same exercise, each bouncing ball will be different, and this difference is one of the strengths of animation.

This exercise introduces:

- The important principle of controlling the speed of movement by changing the distance between drawings and by shooting on 1's, 2's or 3's.

- The principle of squash and stretch. The squash and stretch principle is used throughout animation. It could be the basic movement for a human or an animal jumping, leaping or bouncing. Osamu Tezuka, a great Japanese director, made a very good film based on squash and stretch, which he called Jumping.
- The logic for the changes in speed of movement, in this case gravity.
- The process of doing a layout, with the timing and movement planned before starting your animation.
- The audience's acceptance of an instantaneous metamorphosis, justified by the action of impact, when the ball changes to a rectangle and back.
- The audience's acceptance of the nature of the bouncing ball, and the audience's rationalization of an invisible ground line.
- Flipping the drawings to see if the animation works.
- Seeing the relationship between sequential drawings on paper that turns into your first (for most) animation on a screen.

This is the basic pencil test exercise in animation. The first computer animation was a bouncing ball done at MIT in 1950 by a chap named Saxenian.

ASTERISK (TIMING AND HOLDS) - Pencil Test Assignment #2 also see pp. 338-341

For this assignment animate one simple shape anyone can draw, an asterisk*. The reason for using a simple shape is no student is worried about drawing ability or uses drawing ability to fake the assignment. The purpose of this exercise is to introduce the creation and the control of time by animating an asterisk at various speeds of movement and will stop or pause, a hold, at least once. Any shot for four frames or more without movement is a hold. Even in full animation there are holds: all the characters will hold except the main character or there is a slight hold for anticipation or emphasis. In limited animation, there are many holds where nothing is moving.

If timed correctly, holds can be more important than the movement, as it defines, accents and anticipates the movement. Holds interrupt the movement and therefore have a different impact than continuous movement. A hold is a pause. We pause in speech, in movement, in thinking, in music. A hold is a blank space in a painting. Life itself is a series of stop and go, pause and movement.

Holds, done in a pattern, can add beats or a rhythm to the animation. A common mistake of a beginning student, who in his or her desire to learn full character animation, is that he or she become drunk with animating nonstop movement, forgets that holds accent the action and display the character's emotion, and ends up with continuous animation full of sound and fury signifying nothing.

For this exercise the type of movement is up to you. The movement can be slow to fast, fast to slow, sequential and flowing, random and poetic, staccato and jerky, following a path of action or not. It is inherently an abstract movement, but it can be an abstract mimic of a character's movement (a pause then a fall and bounce). Paul Klee said, "A line is just a dot taking a walk[4]." In this animation, you take an asterisk for a journey.

A requirement of this assignment is to have at least one 12x hold. This assignment is 72x long (three seconds) and outside of the holds, the animation should be done on 2's. If you have a 12x hold and the rest are on 2's you will have 31 drawings. Drawing and shooting on 1's can make the shooting too long. Use a simple exposure sheet, the instruction sheet used for shooting, to note where the hold starts and ends and how long it is. You can do other holds of varying lengths. On the exposure sheet (fig. 5-52), note the number of each drawing and how many frames each drawing is shot.

As the class progresses, you will be exposed to doing more complex exposure sheets. By the end of this class you will write out a complete animated film on exposure sheets. Even if you are shooting the animation yourself you must do this, as exposure sheets are integral to animation. Unless you write it down you will forget what you have shot 10 minutes later and exposure sheets will tell you. On exposure sheets you see the entire timing sequence, and it is far better than putting the number of frames to be shot on each sheet. Exposure sheets are in common use the world over. I had a student who went to work at a studio in Paris. He didn't speak French but found this no problem in animating, because exposure sheets were a universal language, even in Paris. In the world of animation, if you know exposure sheets you rule. Exposure sheets are done in pencil and you will use exposure sheets for the rest of your exercises.

Keeping the pencil test assignments short and controlled will help the student understand the value of one frame and give them one-frame acuity, a mark of a good animator. To paraphrase Godard, "Animation is truth 24 times a second."[5]

The purpose of this exercise is to control a singular unchanging object in time and space. Do not change the shape of the asterisk (spinning on a hold is OK) or have more than one a trick. If you animate what is happening within the trick, you will miss the purpose of this assignment. Please, no funny faces or cute little spiders. There will be plenty of time for that later. Please, no hold for the entire assignment. That is a still picture.

---

4. Paul Klee. BrainyQuote.com. Xplore Inc. 2017. 22 May 2017. "A line is a dot that went for a walk."

5. "Photography is truth. The cinema is truth twenty-four times a second." Jean-Luc Godard. BrainyQuote.com. Xplore Inc., 2016. 9 November 2016.

Animators often use a blue pencil for the beginning layout and animation (fig. Extra-2. Punch), then go over rough sketches with a graphite pencil for the final drawing. Using a colored line first to distinguish the many preliminary sketches from the finished graphite drawing is a more efficient way to animate and saves paper. This exercise is a good place to start using a blue pencil (fig. 2-10).

Plan the path of action; use the bouncing ball test as an example. Do several different options of staging the action. A path of action would include: the rough start and stop marks, poses of the animation, and any variation in height and width for perspective. The pattern of the animation could reflect a sung musical beat or bit of music. You can mark on the path of action the drawing positions of the animation, all or just the keys to plan the speed, or on the bottom of the keys use spacing charts to communicate the timing. A spacing chart shows the space between each drawing (fig. 7-6).

A cardinal rule on timing is to vary the speed of actions in a scene. Change your pace before it becomes boring and detrimental to the purpose of the action. This change of speed brings rhythm and reason to the animation. The change in timing will bring contrast, perhaps even conflict, to the rhythm. The changes of the rhythm should always support the action. Be sure to consider animating easeing in and out of the hold. Practice flipping the animation.

Holds

There are three types:

A hold is when the action stops and freezes. Any shot that is four frames or more without movement is a hold. It could be a four-frame hold of an extended finger for emphasis or several seconds of a key pose. It is commonly used in limited animation.

A moving hold is a cycle of a traceback of the character. Discussed below.

A pause or semi-hold where there is a pause in the main action with secondary animation taking over. An example would be a running character who stops and looks around with a facial or eye reaction, an eye blinking. Or an action where only the main character is moving and everything else is held. Conversely, hold the main character while all the others are moving. This puts the focus on the main character.

In this exercise you can do the first two. To do a regular hold, just stop the animation for 12x by noting a hold on the exposure sheet.

To do a moving hold, when you are afraid your held object will look too static, cycle tracebacks. A traceback is a copy of the original done as closely as you can. Copy each traceback from the original, otherwise they can vary too much and give an unwanted movement. A three-drawing traceback cycle is common (fig. 7-7), as two drawings will look mechanical and three drawings cycled in a random order, 1, 2, 3, 1, 3, 2, etc., will give a random movement. Also you could cycle the arms for a spinning asterisk. You could draw the asterisk larger or smaller for one drawing and cycle the original and different-size drawing for a pause, or draw the second drawing a little ahead of or behind the original one and cycle them. Anything you can come up with that will give the effect of a pause.

The hold is an indispensable tool for varying the animation and making the intent of the animation work. It can be the pause that defines the intent of the scene or character with the needed anticipation. Do not be afraid to hold a pose for what seems like a long time.

Cycles

You can use cycles. Cycling is when the animation is repeated to create the action. If you animate your * arms moving in a circular pattern in five sequential drawings numbered as 1, 2, 3, 4, 5, and then you repeated those numbers on your exposure sheet, 1, 2, 3, 4, 5, 1, 2, 3, 4, 5, 1, 2, 3, 4, 5, the cameraperson would shoot the same cycle three times and the * would rotate three times. If you went 1, 2, 3, 4, 5, hold 5, 4, 3, 2, 1, then the * would move around once, stop and then move around once in the opposite direction.

When you draw the inbetweens between the arm positions on the asterisk, the first drawing should be less than halfway to the other arm. If it is more than halfway, it will appear to move backwards as the eye will register the shortest movement as the direction moved. This is why a spoke wheel can look like it is moving backwards. In Westerns, when this would happen, a clump of mud would be put on a spoke so the eye could follow it in the right direction. When rotating your asterisk, two inbetweens will work well between the arms, with each moving less than half the distance to the next drawing. The most common cycle is the walk cycle. Please see Exercise #5 for an explanation of a walk. Rain, snow, flowing water and fire are often cycles. Cycles are often overused in animation, especially as a cost-saving device, and can cause a scene to go flat. Cycles were used for the very first time in animation in 1914; 44 percentage of *Gertie the Dinosaur* was cycles, especially in the moving holds that keep Gertie alive, the "Gertie Stomp." McCay also developed the key-pose method of animation, which he called the McCay Split System. Winsor McCay not only pioneered animation but also invented ways to cut out the drudgery. Out of respect for Winsor you should try key pose animation for this exercise. Do the key drawings first, flip them, change if necessary and then do the inbetweens.

Movement in Perspective

You do not have to remain in 2D space for this exercise, you can move the * in 3D. The rules of movement in perspective are (1) an object moving toward you keeps moves faster and bigger and (2) an object moving away from you keeps moving slower and smaller. Speed decreases as the object moves away and increases as it gets closer. A jet high in the sky will appear to be moving slowly even though it is moving 500 mph, while a car going 80 mph in front of you will be moving fast.

Animators commonly use these two layout methods to calculate the placement of the drawings. In 3D speed change, the middle drawing is not halfway between the first and last drawings.

- Use the first and last positions of the total distance. First draw a line for the height of the first and last positions and lines connecting them, then draw a line connecting the top and bottom of each position. Where these lines cross will be your midpoint of the move. You continue to repeat this procedure until you have all the positions of the move for the animation. It is good for a hit-in-the-face action. But the closer moves may be too fast to be read.

- Do your front drawing and then put the next position back where you want it. This slows the movement of the closer positions. Then draw a line from the top of the first position through the point where the middle line and the second vertical line meet, continuing the line until it meets the bottom line. This will be the third position. Continue this method until you have all the needed points (fig. 7-21). This will take more drawings than method one and is good for showing a character's action.

With these guides, using a box based on the outer side limits of your object will help keep proportions of the moving character. Use a field chart as a guide (fig. 5-36). Perspective can be exaggerated for good effect.

Back to the Assignment

You can have the asterisk leave the screen by exposing a blank sheet. The blank screen will become anticipation of the *'s re-entry. Any pencil test exercise, within the limits of the exercise, can be a test of animation for the final project. This exercise can take more than two hours if done with thought. Any of these exercises can be faked in less time. They are very easy to spot, as they look terrible.

In this exercise, timing is emphasized to create a feeling for timing and rhythm. This assignment concerns:

- The introduction of creation of time and how to do timing.
- Introduction of pauses or holds.
- How simple exposure sheets are done.
- The principle of pose or key animation can be used.
- Flipping the drawings to see if the animation works.
- Use of blue pencil technique.
- How cycling is done.
- How animation in perspective is done.

Handout and exhibits: Written assignment and exposure sheets with different configurations of pauses will be tacked on the board. Total length = 72 frames.

STORYBOARD FOR THE FINAL PROJECT - Assignment #3 also see pp. 341-343

This assignment, the midterm, is to do the storyboard for your final 15-second film. The storyboard assignment is given early on so you can rethink or redo completely and still have time to finish. Do each storyboard panel on 12F paper so that you have the beginning of layout. Depending on your concept, eight to 15 panels should suffice (fig. 2-5). You should have a different panel when:

- The BG changes
- Something new is introduced
- To display complex or dramatic action (fig. 2-11).

It can be drawn, pencil or marker, but the lines should be dark enough to be seen from a distance. Do it in color if it is important for the concept. If the film is to be character-driven, character model sheets should accompany the board (fig. 5-3). A bit of the finished art could also be helpful.

To time the film, do a vertical timing guide by marking off each of the 15 seconds and then filling in a description of the action (fig. 2-62). If the film is too long, then overlap the titles and action to gain time, start timing the film from the end and when 15 seconds is reached start it (many opening shots are unnecessary), or drastically redo your board for the 15 seconds. This is a good exercise, as animating within a set amount of time is always a headache in animation: either you do not have enough time to do the animation right or you have too much time for the action.

Points that should be reviewed are:

- Reread the first three chapters of this book, especially Chapter 1: Idea, even though the film is only 15 seconds long. You probably will have time for just one idea.

- This is the chance to express your own vision: humorous, artistic, creative, political (fig. 7-9), or ?

- Take some time and put in some effort to come up with the idea. Disney would give the day off to someone who had received a new scene so that he or she could give it his or her full attention.

- Make sure the timing is not too quick. Give enough time so your audience can see and understand the film by doing a timing guide.

- Use your areas of strength: timing, ideas, drawing, acting, writing, color, etc.

- Emphasize the area where your interest lies. Be it content, movement, character animation, humor, background painting, story, experimental, etc.

- A story is not required; the film can be purely visual.

- Seek inspiration from the other arts. Art for images, music for timing, poetry for ideas, dance for movement, etc.

- Make a strong style statement.

- Stress quality, but if you make quality a stressful issue, then the issue of quality can become a block to creating. Stressed is desserts spelled backwards, so go figure.

- Be careful that the film is not too difficult or complex to be finished in the available time. As a test, think how long it is going to take to make the film, and then double it and that will just be half the time necessary. An animated film cannot be done overnight. The requirements for the final, a 15-second film, are given in the syllabus (pp. 314-316). From now on you should be working on your final, especially within the different pencil test assignments.

The board will then be presented to the class. After the pitch, the other students will give you their written comments. A handout, like the one below, will be given out:

WHAT TO DO AFTER YOUR BOARD PRESENTATION

Presenting your board to a group can give you new insights. Taking notes during the comments will give you a record after the excitement of the moment has passed. Consider carefully the written comments: Which ones help? Which ones have nothing to do with your film? Is there a general misunderstanding about any part of your idea? Is there any one element of your board they all like, something you could give a larger role? Focus on what you want to say and eliminate confusion.

Consult with the teacher, TA, friends. Rework your board; it is a rare board that cannot be improved. You can do a completely new board.

Start the production as soon as possible by using the timing guide and your panels to do an animatic. Redo until the timing is right and the shots are on long enough to be understood. Then rough-in the main blocks of time on your exposure sheets (fig. 5-52). The finished animatic may be presented to the class as an assignment or shown to the teacher or TA.

You now have the idea, the visual board and the basic timing for the best-ever 15-second animated film. The next stage of the production process is the layout. Please read the Layout chapter for a detailed breakdown. The major steps are given below:

- In pencil (fig. 11-2), using a field chart (fig. 5-36), do the rough and then the final composition of all your shots on regular animation paper. This will include:

> The field sizes; the camera, size, view and height; the subject angle; and the movement.
>
> The editing; screen direction, transitions (matching cuts, dissolves, animated or metamorphosis)(fig. 5-1).
>
> The form and color of your composition.

- Calculate the technical moves when doing the layouts of the trucks and pans (fig. 5-40).
- Do some final art to see how the finished film will look, especially in color. Try some different art, techniques and styles to see if you can improve the visuals (fig. intro-3).
- Do the character model sheets in color (fig. 2-45).
- Do the staging of your animation, including your key animation poses. Be sure to have layouts for both the animation and the backgrounds (fig. 5-1).
- Do all the little technical details: levels, scene numbering, etc. Plan your budget and schedule your time (figs. 5-47, 5-50, 5-51).
- Add information and the calculations for pans and trucks to your exposure sheets (fig. 5-40).
- Do not forget to do the titles. They are included in the 360-frame limit (fig. 5-49).

The layout is the planning stage for the animation and must be done before starting animation. Without a layout, you often will become lost as you animate and be forced into reanimating or settling for poor animation.

Finally, animation. Remember these rules as you put pencil to paper:

- You animate with your mind, not your hand.
- You are doing movement that is drawn, not drawings that move.
- Timing makes the animation work.

You normally start animating the key poses first, rough and in blue pencil. Then flip and pencil test the drawings (fig. 7-79); restage and/or reanimate the action if necessary. Do the breakdowns and inbetweens. If you have a character, use the eyes for acting; blinks help (fig. 7-11). Fill in the exposure sheets when you are happy with a pencil test and then clean up in graphite pencil, putting on model with the details of figure and clothes and secondary animation (figs. 7-45, 7-46). Fine-tune the final exposure sheets (fig. 5-56). If you are not doing drawn animation but photos, cutouts, collages or another style, change the process to fit your technique. Work on the backgrounds and make sure they match your animation (fig. 5-12). BGs can be finished now or later.

Now do the final art of the animation. This could be ink and paint on cels, color pencils or markers on paper, or a combination of art techniques. If you use colored pencils, work within a 6x to 7x field to save coloring time. Budget a few days for ink and paint, as it is a very time-intense process. Finish the backgrounds. Clean up all the materials and do a final pencil test.

Schedule a final check of all the materials and exposure sheets with the TA a day or two before you shoot. If the TA does not check you, it will count against your grade. If you miss your scheduled time, there may be no time to reschedule and you could receive an F. The TA or technical supervisor will guide you during your shoot. A copy of your film will be available after the screening.

ANTICIPATION - Assignment #4 see also pp. 344-345

Anticipate: to look forward to; expect *Webster's New World College Dictionary*.[6] The right anticipation of the timing and animation before any action will make it be clearly seen and understood. If the audience is looking elsewhere on the screen or the animation happens too quickly, the action will not be seen or confused. When the Coyote, in the *Road Runner and Coyote* series, runs off a high cliff and keeps running until he realizes that he is no longer on solid ground, he anticipates his fall by looking at the audience, shrugs and then falls. If he just ran off the cliff and fell, it would not be as funny or effective.

Anticipation will focus the audience's attention on an action that is about to happen and may be as simple as a long or short hold, like a 15x pause before a character makes a decision. Or starting a long movement left with a countermove of two to three drawings to the right. Or raising one eyebrow before speaking, or as exaggerated as a baseball pitcher drawing way, way back and windmilling 10 times before he throws a strike. Or when a Tex Avery character needs to exit fast, he or she jumps into the air, spins his or her blurring legs, leans one way, then runs off the screen in from zero to three frames, leaving only speed lines. In the last two examples, 80 percent of the time was spent in anticipation.

Anticipation is frequently used to start a movement, a weight shift in the direction moving, a coil and strike like a snake, and a squash and stretch (fig. 7-52) for a jump.

For this assignment, animate an anticipation of an action from your final project, the example of a teakettle boiling over (fig. 14-4). The exposure sheet examples for the teakettle will include the use of a forward and reverse cycle for building tension, illustrating how different timings of the same drawings can achieve different types of anticipation. Another anticipation exercise is the hatching of an egg (with a surprise inside?). Also illustrated is anticipation by first moving in an opposite direction: A character or object first moving left before moving right. For longer anticipation, a pause or traceback could be used in the opposite-direction move.

Use the key pose or method of your choice to animate and do a layout of the animation. Practice your flipping. The assignment is 72x long on 12FC. Maximum 36 drawings. Exposure

---

6. Because the author used a 1996 *Webster's New College Dictionary* (3rd edition. revised) in an earlier footnote, I am assuming that dictionary is the source of this quote as well. Unfortunately I have been unable to locate a copy of this dictionary to verify this wording.

and name sheets are required.

Handouts and display: Exposure sheets and examples will be tacked on the board.

ACTING - Assignment #5 see also pp. 346-347

The purpose of this pencil test is to animate a facial expression of emotion or an action (fig. 7-10). A change of expression could be considered going from one self-evident pose to another. An emotion could be crying, laughing, anger. An action could be going from normal to surprise. Use a character(s) from your final project.

Think about the possible ways a face can express a thought or an action without being based entirely on live action, but on your imagination, the eyes changing to dollar signs or the opposite sex. Do character model sheets of facial expressions to establish the character's attitude. How many of the features (eyes, nose, mouth, etc.) do you need, all of them or just the ones needed for the action? Animate the thought first, and then the action based on the thought.

First come up with the idea, then do roughs of the face and the extremes of the action. Keep the drawing loose for the basic animation. Acting it out in a mirror can help. Do a basic timing, including holds, on exposure sheets. Next do a layout of the animation, getting the face in the right size and placement on the screen. Then begin the animation using the keypose method (blue pencil is optional) and the basic forms, the head with a centerline and an eye line. Do your breakdowns and inbetweens after the keys pass the flipping test. Clean up and put on model. Shoot on the pencil test unit with exposure sheets.

If you are not using a reality character, you can design any style of face you like, big nose, big ears, whatever works for your character. The animation for this type of character need fit only your imagination. Do not be timid. If your face is based on cartoon standards, you can use established cartoon expressions. Since this is an exercise, check out different styles of art or drawing. Change your art if you find something better.

In normal adult head proportions the eyes are located halfway down the face (in a baby, the eyes are a third of the way from the bottom), the bottom of the nose is halfway between the eyes and the tip of the chin, and the mouth halfway between the bottom of the nose and the tip of the chin. The eyes are one eye apart, and the middle of the pupil when in the middle of the eye projects straight down to show the end of the lips. The height of the ears goes from the eyebrows to the bottom of your nose. Use these simple proportions to keep the features correct for head movement, or as it is called, "holding" character.

Examples of head proportions (fig. 7-58, 7-59).

Eye Blinks

The eyes, sometimes called the windows to your soul, are a major component of animation acting. This is one reason animated characters often have very large eyes. Eye acting can be as simple as moving the pupil to show thinking or looking, or using an eye movement to anticipate a body movement or action. Eye blinks are used to add life to the character. A standard blink is: eye open, closed roughly a quarter of the way down, halfway down, then fully closed. Reverse it on the way up. This will work on 1's or 2's. After the blink, bring the pupil back to a different spot to add to the effect.

An old Disney trick to turning the head from side to side was to dip the head and blink the eyes in the middle to get away from a full front view that stops the movement.

Or eye uses include: use the top eyelids to show emotion and drop the lower lids for an effect, use walleyes or crossed eyes for a comedy effect, using a blink before an action such as speaking to show thought, and using an eye blink before a cut. Always keep both eye movements linked unless for a comedic effect. For realistic blinks, you should curve the eyelid to conform to the rounded shape of the eye, curved up when above the halfway line and down when below.

Illustrations of eye blinks (fig. 7-11).

Eye blinks are the secret weapon of the animator.

When Mickey Mouse was first designed he had shoe-button eyes. This later proved animating his expressions difficult; to look to the side his whole head had to be turned, you just couldn't shift the pupils in the eye. So after many meetings they decided to give him eyeballs, but then the problem arose: Would the public accept Mickey with eyes and a pupil? Since Mickey's merchandising kept the studio alive, they couldn't take a chance on losing Mickey. At the final meeting one animator said he had the solution, first do only one eye with an eyeball and if the public accepted that, do the other one. Walt said that was a dumb idea, let's go with both.[7]

A Take

A take is a character's reaction to an action. It should reflect the situation. Do a very extreme take (you can't go too far, e.g. Tex Avery[8]). Usually you make the start of all takes fast and the secondary action (clothes, etc.) animated to emphasize the take. The timing of the take is very important. A double take is two takes, one after the other, with the first one normal and the second one extreme.

Example: *Easter Island* double take. This has two reactions, the eyeballs popping out of the head and then the mouth dropping to the chest (fig. 7-12).

Expressions

Simple drawing principles used for major facial expressions are:

---

7. Another story I can find no record of.
8. I think this is just a trueism.

Laugh - corner of mouth up and back, lift upper lip causing furrows in cheeks, eyes narrow and lines around eyes lift up and deepen.

Anger - eyebrows drawn in and down causing a strong vertical fold between eyes, mouth turns down with furrow around corners of mouth.

Smile - partially close eyes, mouth curves up, furrow under eye and around mouth and nose.

Surprise - mouth drops open, elongated furrows on side of mouth, top of eye and eyebrows arch up, furrows in brow move up.

Fear - mouth partially closed and contracted, furrows on brow slant down, upper eyelid lifts.

Pain - upper eyelid partially closed, mouth slightly turned down, eyebrows turn down and up, cheek lines almost straight down.

To accent an expression change, do not go directly from one expression to another, but use the principle of overlapping action by adding a breakdown drawing or two anticipating the action. Examples:

Change to anger with first the eyes, then the mouth anticipating the anger. Do inbetweens for the proper timing.

Change to smile with the eyes anticipating, then the jaw drops, then the smile and inbetween.

Change to laugh with eye blink first, then eyes, then laugh, then inbetween. (fig. 7-13)

Don't do this just to be clever; make sure that it helps emotion.

Back to the assignment

This assignment is 72x to 96x long on a 12FC. Name sheets and exposure sheets are required. Handouts and display of various examples of cartoon-face emotions should be available. Use the character(s) in your final project in this assignment. In this exercise, your animation will bring an emotion to life.

WALKS AND OTHER FORMS OF LOCOMOTION - Assignment #6
see also pp. 347-350

The assignment is to animate a walk. Use a character from your final project because even if the character does not walk, animating a walk will help develop him or her. If your project does not have a character, walk anything you like: a realistic or cartoon character (possibly from the comics), male, female, child, an animal (four legs are hard), fingers, blobs, stick figures and/or centipedes. In animating a walk, you are animating a character moving through space and within itself (the head, arms and legs).

Walking is so natural, we never think about how we do it; this makes walks hard to do. This assignment takes more time than the other exercises.

All walks are different, and with 6 1/2 billion people on Earth this means there are 6,524,682,850 different walks. The good news is that all walks are based on the same principles, which are the human structure and the effect of gravity. When we move forward from one place to another, to keep from falling we need to keep a center of gravity or balance by placing one leg in front of another in a continuous cycle. One step with the right leg followed by a step with the left leg for a complete walk cycle. This exercise is to do such a cycle. The rest of this section is to discuss or show the many types of walks (but not nearly a billion).

HOW TO DO A WALK

I will explain how to animate a walk in space, a walk in place, runs, and then other forms of walks or locomotion. All the animation described, except for runs, is based on one drawing shot for two frames (on 2's). The runs are based on ones (1's), one drawing for each frame and 2's. In computer animation, most 3D and 2D walks are done on 1's but can be done on 2's to give it a more traditional animation quality. A simple step-by-step procedure for animating a walk in space is:

A Walk in Space

A walk through space is animating how we normally walk. Each drawing of the character will be drawn forward in a different space except for the base of the pivot foot. The character will constantly change its position in relation to the edge of the screen and the background.

Design the Character

Decide how many heads high is the character (figs. 7-47, 7-55, 7-56).

Decide where (if needed) the joints or pivot points are for the hips, knees, ankles, shoulders, elbows, wrists. This allows you to keep the limbs and movement consistent from drawing to drawing. Draw the character at its contact points. It should appear to be in balance (figs. 7-35, 7-46).

Decide the angle of the body during the walk. This can be based on the speed of the walk or run.

Design the character in two stages. First, do either a simple stick figure or the basic structure of the character. Use this model to do your basic walk. Then, after the basic walk is achieved, do a second model over it of the character with clothes, features, all the bells and whistles.If the character uses a different-than-normal walk pattern (rubber hose or limbs without joints, straight legs without a knee joint, etc.), design your character accordingly.

Best to use a blue pencil to start and a stack of paper, as it can take many drawings until the right ones are found.

Speed

Decide on the speed of the walk. The speed of the walk is determined by the number of frames per step and the number of frames per drawing. A complete walk cycle is two steps, one left leg, one right leg. Doubling the number of frames for a step gives the total number of frames, the speed, for a walk cycle. The total number of frames divided by 2's (one drawing equals two frames) will tell you how many drawings you need. A common walk is done in march time, a step every half-second or a complete cycle in a second (Hup, two, three, four, Hup, etc.). The speed of the walk will be influenced by the action, character design and personality. To get a rough time of the walk, walk your fingers, or moving a drawing of your character while counting seconds can give you a rough timing. Common step times are:

4 frames per step = fast run = 4 drawings on 1's = 1/6 of a second per step, 8 drawings per cycle = 1/3 of a second for a cycle.

6 frames per step = run = 6 drawings on 1's = 1/4 of a second per step, 12 drawings per cycle = ½ second for a cycle.

8 frames per step = fast walk or slow run = either 4 or 8 drawings depending on shooting on 1's or 2's = 1/3 of a second per step, 8 or 16 drawings = 2/3 of a second for a cycle.

12 frames per step = march time or a normal brisk walk = 6 drawings at 2 frames each = ½ second per step, 12 drawings = 1 second for a cycle.

16 frames per step = a slower walk = 8 drawings at 2 frames each = 2/3 second per step, 16 drawings = 1 and 1/3 seconds for a cycle.

24 frames per step = slow walk = 12 drawings at 2 frames each = 1 second per step, 24 drawings = 2 seconds for the complete cycle.

32 frames per step = stroll = 16 drawings at 2 frames each = 1 1/3 second per step, 32 drawings = 2 2/3 seconds for a complete cycle.

Drawing the First Step of the Walk Cycle

- Put down a ground line.
- Using the basic character model, draw the hit or contact points for the step. The contact point is when the front foot first hits the ground and the foot behind is just leaving or about to leave the ground. The distance from the back foot to front foot is the distance

the character moves each step. This position is your extreme drawing. Mark off the placement of the front foot, as this will be the pivot foot and remain in this one position for the entire step cycle.

- Start inbetweening the step by first drawing the crossover or middle position. To get the middle position you need to get the two extremes of the cycle–the first drawings of each step. On a 12x/6 drawing step do, drawing 1 and 7 so that the inbetween between them is crossover drawing 4. It would look like this: 1, 2, 3, 4, 5, 6, 7. A 16x/8 drawing step cycle would look like this: 1, 2, 3, 4, 5, 6, 7, 8, 9, with 5 the key inbetween. Be sure to keep the contact or pivot foot secure. Using the center of the hips as a reference point can sometimes help to keep the body from swaying unnaturally.
- Do the rest of the inbetweens.
- Do the arm positions now or after the leg cycle is done and tested. The arm positions are at their widest position at the feet's extreme positions (though some animators like the next position). The arm movement is opposite to the leg movement to maintain the body's balance. Right leg forward, left arm forward. Opposite arm, opposite leg.
- Add gravity to your walk to make it natural and avoid a floating walk by doing an up-and-down movement in the walk. The lowest down position is when the lead foot is completely flat. The highest position is after the crossover. This will give a curved line going up and down that will be reflected in the head, shoulders, hips, etc. The extent of up-and-down movement will depend on the personality of the character.
- The walk in space always has the contact foot (the pivot foot) nailed to the ground. A common mistake is moving the planted foot forward as the body is moved forward. This will cause a strange skipping movement.
- It helps to put the character model under each drawing to hold character. This can be on a smaller piece of paper.
- Flip and redraw, if necessary, each drawing. Good animation has snap to it when flipped. Flip the whole step.
- Pencil test the first-step animation.
- Always number the drawings.

Drawing the Second Step

After drawing the complete first step, you need to do the same cycle for the other leg. If you have sliding peg bars, simply move the sliding peg bar with the first step on them to the new pivot foot placement so that the new drawings can be placed on the opposite pegs and copied. If you don't have a sliding bar, go to the top pegs for the new drawings and slide the proper drawing to be copied under the new paper and do your best. You can repeat this process for each step called for in the walk ,but it is a good idea to do 5, 6, 8 above for the first complete cycle, get it right, then do the total number of cycles. You could end up with alternating top-and bottom-pegged steps which you can redraw on one set of pegs during cleanup. You have now done a complete walk cycle in space.

A Good Way to Check

On a table lay out the one step in a row, then using the numbers as a guide, lay out the other step directly below and see if the positions match. If they do not, flip and redraw as necessary.

Pencil Test the Complete Walk Cycle

Finish the Rest of the Walk. Do as many drawings as you need to fit the time or distance required for the walk.

Add Additional Actions. Actions could include singing, pointing at the stars, talking to another character, etc. Add the details (features, clothes, hair, etc.) and secondary animation (dress or coattails swinging or snapping the fingers). When designing a new character, it may be best to do each detail separately, the arm action, the acting, the shoes, etc., getting each cycle action correct and not getting confused with too many details. Flip and pencil test each action.

Put on Model, Clean Up and Pencil Test the Entire Cycle

Illustrations of Walking in Space

Female adult walk cycle. A 12x/6 drawing step, the first half of a 24x/12 drawing complete walk cycle. Women have a different walk than men, as they have a different pelvic structure. Another reason could be for social reasons or clothing issues (high heels, tight skirts, etc.). A difference commonly noticed is the posterior motion, where the buttock of the leg leaving the ground and starting the crossover will move up and then down as the leg moves forward. A looser arm swing is also common, as well as the stomach being somewhat forward. If the breasts move up and down, it will be in counter motion to the up and down of the body. Body up, breasts down, body down, breasts up (fig. 7-14).

Male adult walk cycle. A complete 32x/16 drawing walk cycle with a slight up-and-down motion. Drawing 17 added for the next step position (fig. 7-15).

Cartoon adult character of the author walking with a beer and a slight up-and-down motion. One step 16x/8 drawing for a 32x/16 drawing cycle. Drawing 9 added for the next step position (fig.7-16).

A Walk in Place

A walk in place is a fake walk. The character is drawn in the same place, with the pivot foot drawn sliding back as the moving or free foot swings forward. It is the same motion as walking on a treadmill. The advantage of a walk in place is you only have to do one walk cycle, a left and right step for the entire walk, however long. This takes less work and time to do than a walk in space. The walk in place can be a more mechanical or a less natural walk. It works well for stylized animation like that done by the UPA studios in the 1950s and 1960s. The mechanics of a walk in place is like how a mime walks against the wind or a comic's walk in a vaudeville routine. The walk in place is done in two situations.

Where the character remains in the same place on the screen and a background pan moves in the opposite direction below. The character will appear to be walking on the sidewalk moving past a row of stores. In a live-action film, this is where the filming is done from a car moving at the same speed and direction as the actor.

Where the character, walking in place, is moving across the screen on 2F or 3F panning a cel over a held or moving background. Some animators feel that this type of walk should be done on 1's to prevent the pivot foot from appearing to slide since the pan is on 1's. Computer animation is often done with walks in place since they can be composited with a sliding background or as on a moving cel.

Using the same procedure for a walk in space, a process of doing a walk in place would be:

- Design the character. Same.
- Decide on the speed of the walk by frames per step. Same.
- Draw the first step.

The distance between the contact points is the length of the walk, same as in space. Draw the feet positions for contact points and mark it on the ground line. Then draw the key inbetween, the leg-crossing position. Mark the center of this foot position. This will be the center mark for the sliding of the contact foot. Mark off the inbetweens of the other foot positions, keeping them roughly even. Generally, you do not want to have the sliding plant foot flat for over two drawings as it may appear to be slipping, so have the heel or toe curve up away from the flat surface.

If you want a squash and stretch to do the walk, move the character straight up and down in its set position at the normal places for this movement in the walk. Going up and down with an object over a moving background will give the illusion of an object moving on a curved path.

Using the guide of the foot positions, do the individual drawings of one step. You can do the inbetweening in the same order as the walking in space (or do it straight ahead if you want to do more work for a slightly different feel). Make sure the body does not change position drastically.

Put the character model under each drawing so as to hold character. This character model can be on a smaller piece of paper. Number the drawings. Flip, pencil test and redraw, if necessary.

Draw the Second Step

Using the same pegs, trace the leg and body positions but change to the other arm and leg doing the crossover. You have done the entire walk.

Check. Same.

Pencil Test. Same.

Finish the Rest of the Walk. Plan the pan if needed.

Put on Model, Add Additional Actions and Clean Up. Same.

Illustrations for WALK IN PLACE:

Cartoon male character. One step, 12x/6 drawing, of a 24x/12 drawing cycle (fig. 7-17).

Cartoon female character. One step, 12x/6 drawing, of a 24x/12 drawing cycle. With exaggerated hip, bust and hand motion (fig. 7-18).

One difference of a walk in space or a walk in place is that a walk in space implies that the camera is locked down in one place so that the audience is more passive in its viewing. A walk in place implies a moving camera where the audience is moving and following the character, and the audience is a more active participant in observing the action. It is the difference between camera movement and camera non-movement.

A Really Easy Way to Do a Walk Cycle

The easiest way of doing a walk cycle is to do a silhouette of the legs so only one leg cycle is needed. It eliminates the left/right leg drawings. A 12x march time walk in place needs only six drawings. A drawback is that the arm swing cannot be done.

Illustration: Cartoon character. A 24x/6 drawing walk (fig. 7-19).

WALKS NOT BASED ON THE HUMAN OR CARTOON MOTION

You can also animate walk concepts by abstracting the walk principle for your purpose. Examples would be a paddle wheel, a spring, a sack walking, etc.

Illustrations:

Paddle wheel with an up-and-down head. A 6x/3 drawing walk cycle in space or place (fig. 14-5).

A cartoon with springs for legs. A 24x/7 drawing walk cycle in place. Filmed in this order, 1,2,3,4,5,6,7,6,5,4,3,2,1 and repeat. Can be done on 1's or 2's or without springs with the feet only going up and down (fig. 7-20).

WALKS IN PERSPECTIVE

A walk in perspective, either coming or going, straight-on or at an angle, can be done in place or in space.

In Space

First, do a perspective guide for the amount of distance moved in perspective by either method described. Movement in Perspective in the Asterisk exercise. I find using the positions of the guide for each step and to do the extremes very helpful. Next, do the main inbetween and then the rest of the inbetweens, keeping the pivot foot firmly in place. A six-drawing step cycle will not have normal inbetweens after the main inbetween, just animated straight ahead always keeping the fact that the character will move faster (more distance between drawings) as it gets closer. The background will not move, as only the character is moving forward or backward.

A walk in perspective is hard to do in traditional animation. In computer animation and stop motion, it is simpler. For a cartoon walk, swinging the crossing foot wide to emphasize it coming forward, exaggerating the size of the foot's sole or heel, having the arm swing partially over the body, a hip and perhaps a shoulder swing, and amplifying the up-and-down motion can help the action. Use the vanishing point to keep the feet in line and the body proportions to hold character. Putting the character in a perspective box can also help proportions.

In Place

Done in the same manner as a horizontal walk. Do the extremes first, 1 and 7 (if it is straight-on 1 can be flipped and copied for 7, as can the second step). A vanishing point can help keep the feet in their proper path. Next do the main inbetween, drawing 4, and then the rest of the inbetweens. The size of the foot will change as it moves back and forth will help create the illusion of depth (fig. 7-21).

To complete the illusion, animate the background, moving in perspective in the opposite direction. This movement can be done with as little as a three-drawing cycle of trees or telephone poles. To complete this illusion in place works better when the action is straight-on.

Illustrations

A cartoon forward walk in place, one step, 12x/6 drawings. With a 3 drawing telephone pole cycle. Same cartoon as a forward walk in space, 12x/6 drawings (fig. 7-21).

RUN

The rules for a run are:

- A run is done on 1's. They can be done on 2's if you want a loping effect.
- One to three different positions have both feet off the ground. In a normal walk one foot is always on the ground. Women, usually depending on the type of shoe they are wearing, sometimes do not have both feet off the floor. The woman in Muybridge, for instance, always has both feet on the floor. For argument's sake you could call this a fast walk.
- A run will be from three (fast) to eight (jog) frames per step.
- Characters usually are leaning forward, especially for a fast run. The character can appear to be off-balance to give logic to the running.
- The head should not go too high on the up position.
- A strong push off gives more energy to the run.
- Do not keep the same silhouette if there are only a few drawings.

For a run in space, with both feet off the ground and the front contact point problematic, gauging how far forward the character is moved for each position can be difficult. One solution is to measure the distance between the previous inbetweens and use that measurement for the forward distance when the character is off the ground.

Illustration Run

Cartoon character, 4x/4 drawing step for a run in place, and two drawings with both feet off the ground (fig. 7-22).

Human character, 6x/6 drawing step for a run in space. This can be shot on 2's for a slow run or lope (fig. 7-23).

Arms

Arms are very important in a walk. A slower walk or short step usually has less arm swing and a run has more extreme arm swing. Having the arm arc in an unnatural way–breaking the joint in the middle of the swing as the arm moves forward (back to front swing)–can be very effective. Do not make the arm movement too wild for the character, as that can overpower the rest of the animation. Finger action, as in snapping them, can add to the walk.

Hips and Rest of Body

The hips can rotate a little or a lot, depending on humor and culture. The hip bearing the weight is the highest, as well as the shoulder on that side. On a slow or heavy walk, you can put a lot of emphasis on the hips and shoulders.

The head acts as needed. If based on a normal human walk, the head, chest area and hip area do not expand or contract; only the neck and middle of the body (spinal cord) can do that.

Gravity

Factors in a walk are: gravity, attitude, weight, build, age, sex, health, dress of the character and the environment. Gravity is the most important physical law in doing a believable walk, as the weight of the body is always fighting the gravitational pull of the Earth to keep in balance. Gravity makes walking an act of falling; babies are always falling when they are learning to walk, till they learn to put one foot out after the other to keep their balance and move forward. If you don't consider gravity when animating a walk, the character will seem to be floating instead of walking. Animating the effect of gravity is hard, that is why computer animation is often about flying, toys, fishes, cars, etc., so that the need to animate gravity is minimal.

Exaggeration and Personality

Now you may well ask, "When I see people walking they are not going up and down as much as an animated walk cycle." True, people keep their feet pretty flat when crossing over (to conserve energy) and get very little up-and-down motion. But animation, to paraphrase Pablo Picasso's quote, is that "Art is a lie that tells you the truth,"[9] and a little extra squash and stretch will make an animated walk a lie that tells you the truth. Try animating the same walk twice, first with no up-or-down motion, then with an up-and-down motion. You should see the difference immediately. Animators have to exaggerate a very slight motion to get the true feel of the motion. This is why on a walk an animator will distort the foot swing, dropping the toe, instead of keeping it flat.

A walk reveals the personality of the character. A tired, old, sad or glum character will have a slow, dragging or bent walk. A happy, cheerful, merry character will have a bouncy, high-spirited walk. Animators, like actors, as the first step in developing the character's personality, develop the character's walk. Make your character walk is distinctive, walking with attitude. For a cartoon walk, exaggerate or caricature the walk or parts of the walk: an extra-high

9. "We all know that Art is not truth. Art is a lie that makes us realize the truth, at least the truth that is given to us to understand." "Pablo Picasso." BrainyQuote.com. Xplore Inc., 2016. 1 December 2016.

bounce or double bounce, which has two ups, one at the normal position and one at the crossover. Often done to a musical beat, it is a happy walk and did much to establish Mickey Mouse's personality. Also an exaggerated roll of the hips, the up and down of the stomach, breasts or buttocks, or an extreme shoulder action can be done. If pose of the walk is to be emphasized, slow the action up to and away from it by drawing the inbetweens closer together. If you want to avoid a rubbery walk on a cartoon walk have one position with both legs straight. Study comic walks: Monty Python's silly walks, Groucho Marx's, Chaplin's, etc.

Fat characters will have more squash and stretch and tend to walk side-to-side or waddling. You can get a comedy effect by having a large mass (a large beer gut) lag several frames behind the rest of the body's up-and-down motion. It could be going down as the rest of the body is going up, as Stromboli does in *Pinocchio (1940)*.

Generally the action and length of the step will determine the speed of the walk. A very aggressive character with a long stride could move quite a distance very fast for each step, or a woman in high heels (walking on their toes) and a short skirt or a child with short legs moves a very short distance very fast to keep up with other people. But more often, a short step is slow and sideways as in the case of an old man. If the body is leaning forward, it tells the viewer the character is moving forward. In a run, the character will appear to be going faster with an exaggerated forward lean.

Technical Considerations

On walks there are times when inbetweening is difficult. An example is march time, 12x or six drawings steps there is no true inbetween between 1 and 4 and between 4 and 7, so you have to inbetween by thirds or by animating straight ahead (1 2 3 4 5 6 7).

Normal proportions. The feet are roughly the same size as the head and a hand is about two-thirds of the head. When animating the shoe or foot on a walk, try putting a little squash and stretch in the shoe or foot that matches the up-and-down of the body to emphasize gravity.

An old cartoon formula was that a normal male walk was 12x each step (six drawings at 2x each). A normal female walk was 8x per step. If the walk is too fast, you can shoot a pencil test on 3's or 4's to see how many inbetweens you need. If a walk is too slow, you can shoot it on 1's or take out drawings.

Secondary animation of inanimate objects. Clothing, extra weight, hair or props (bats, handbags, a stack of animation paper) will generally move in the opposite up-and-down direction to that of the body. Cover the bottom half of the walk cycle on a pencil test to see if the upper body really moves like it is walking. For variation draw the walk from the feet up.

If you want to animate a walk straight ahead, decide the length of a step. At a normal brisk walk a person would cover roughly his or her height in a single walk cycle. Then either animate straight ahead or do the contact point and animate straight ahead for the rest of the cycle. Dividing up distance for the number of drawings can give control of the forward movement. Doing the positions of the leg as a series of stick-leg roughs can give an idea of the walk.

Do Yourself

One of the best ways to learn to animate character walks is to do your own walk. Walk around, analyze your walk: Are you in balance? What are your arms, hips, shoulders and knees doing? When you show it to other people they should recognize you.

These are just the basic principles for animating a walk. There are many types of walks: sneaking, tiptoeing, strutting, shuffling, fingers walking, walking with a crutch, etc. There are more than enough types for an entire book on walks.

How to Avoid Doing a Walk

Since walks are difficult, animators have come up with ways to avoid doing them. Some of the more popular ploys are:

Put the character behind bushes, a low wall, a table, anything to cut off the legs so you only have to move a bouncing upper body.

Do the walk in a shot from the waist up. If you use a headshot, make sure there is a moving background so that the head has a moving reference.

Cut to the eyes of an observer who is following the character walking.

A few frames of someone walking to establish movement and then cut away. A point-of-view shot of the person walking.

An old black and white show from TV's *The Mighty Hercules: The Lexas Lagoon* (mid-1960s) has many fine examples of how to avoid doing a walk. Recently I saw a very well-received animated feature with only a minute or two of a full figure walk.

Animal Walks

Animal walks are different. They have four legs, their front and rear leg cycles are a half cycle off from each other, their skeletons are structurally different, most walk on their fingers and there are far more variations possible than in a two-legged walk. Animal walks, at the beginning, can seem difficult, but like any animation practice makes almost perfect.

To start, decide if the animation is realistic or cartoon. For natural animal walks, Muybridge's

Animal Locomotion, published in 1875, is an excellent resource. Observation, drawing in zoos, digital tapes you take, rotoscoping live action or other animation are also resources. For a cartoon walk, many of them are based on a human in an animal suit, and there are many cartoon characters that can be studied like Honest John in *Pinocchio* for upright walking on two legs. In animation, realistic or cartoon are two common ways to animate a four-legged animal. Also experimenting and coming up with your own ideas is fun as you have quite a bit of latitude. Animals can be funny.

If you decide on a realistic animation, then what kind of animal is it? There are three main types of animal walks.

- Dogs, lions, cats. They walk on their toes, with the heel always in the air. Family: Digiti-grades.
- Horses, cows, deer. They walk on their hoofs with toes that are solid. Family: Ungulates.
- Bears, monkeys, mice. They put their full foot on the ground. Family: Plantigrade.

When you first start, it can be confusing. Below is a simple procedure to follow until you have enough experience to do animal walks without worry:

- First design a four-medium-size-legged dog or horse as a model sheet.
- Then do a drawing of its body structure, especially the legs, where its break points are, relative length of bone, etc., for the type of animal.
- On the layout draw two ground lines to account for the width of the body.
- Do one set of legs first, the rear or front. Do the same as human walks: contact points, crossover, main inbetween, etc. Flip and test.
- Then do the other set of legs, flip and test.
- Then attach the two sets of legs to the body that is the model sheet on a drawing below.
- Attach them so they are one-half of a cycle off. When the front legs are at the contact point the rear legs are at the crossover and when the rear legs are at the contact point the front legs are at the crossover.
- Put an up-and-down motion on the body to mirror the legs' action. When the front legs are at the crossover the shoulder is at its highest and the rear is at its lowest. And when the rear is at the crossover the rear is at its highest and the shoulders is at its lowest.
- If you put in a head motion, the head goes up when the shoulder goes up.
- For speed of walk or how many inbetweens, use the human walk as a reference.
- Flip and test.

For walking in space

Do a model of a dog's body so can put on top sliding bars to move forward each drawing to hold character. Make sure that the plant foot does not slide.

General thoughts on animal walks:

- When the tail is down the rear is up.
- The head can move forward and tilt on axis after the head comes up.
- In a diagonal-view walk, the path of left and right legs varies slightly.
- Be careful not to distort the thickness of the legs.
- Decide on the personality of dog or whatever animal.
- Keep the distance the same between the front and rear legs so the animal does not accordion.
- Have a good eraser.
- Many animals walk on their toes, think of it like the foot being an extra lower limb and the toe is then the foot.
- A natural walk can also work with a cartoon animal character or caricature, but a cartoon work normally does not walk with a realistically drawn animal.

Horses have several gaits. They are:

Canter - a smooth easy pace, a moderate gallop. The front legs will be off the ground together and the rear legs will be off the ground together.

Trot - a gait, as of a horse, in which the front leg and the opposite rear leg are off the ground at the same time, a high stepping walk.

Gallop - the fastest gait of a horse or other animal, consisting of leaping strides and all four feet off at the same time. (The reason that Muybridge was hired to take pictures of animals in motion was to settle a bet that Leland Stanford had made. It is reported that he bet $10,000 that a galloping horse had all four legs off the ground together. He won the bet and helped animation and animators.)

ILLUSTRATION

- Cartoon dog walking in place, 8 drawings/16x fast walk cycle (fig. 7-24).
- Naturalist dog walk in space, 6 drawings/12x one step, 24x walk cycle (fig. 7-25).
- Horse in place, 9 drawings/18x one step, 36x walk cycle (fig. 7-26).

Birds

There are several patterns to bird flight. A larger bird's wings move slower or its may hold it wings outstretched and soar on the wind currents. A smaller bird moves its wings faster or, after completing its wing cycle, folds its wings and shoots through the air. For a fast flight or in limited animation, use the extremes. The feathers are closed when the wing is moving down and open when going up. A bird tends to go up when its wings go up. A motion blur effect can be helpful in giving the illusion of flight, especially with hummingbirds.

Illustrated is a side shot of a medium-size bird (fig. 7-27). There are four drawings for the down motion and six drawings for going up. The shooting sequence is 1, 2, 3, 4, 3, 5, 6, 7, 2, 1 and repeat. It can be shot on 2's, for a fast flight on 1's, or on 2's with some inbetweens dropped.

Illustrated is a front shot of a medium-size bird with an exposure sheet for timing (fig. 7-28).

Butterflies (fig. 7-29)

Walking Bird:When doing a walking bird, a chicken, move its head forward so that it will remain in balance.

Illustrated is a young sandpiper running back and forth in the sand just beyond the surf. A blurring motion could help here, as they move so fast (fig. 7-30).

Fish: Fish move by twisting their bodies and/or fins sideways or up and down through the water.

Others and an inchworm

For snakes, centipedes, ants, spiders and other assorted critters please research your own sources, observation, film, other animation, etc. An example of others is an inchworm movement A to B, then B up to B1 while A remains in place, then B1 is the anchor and A moves to A1. This walk is repeated for the length of the inchworm's forward motion (fig. 7-31).

Final Thought on Walks

Doing a walk is like building a house: one thing at a time until it is right, starting at the bottom, so it comes out solid at the end.

References for Walks

Other sources of reference for walks are: rotoscoping live action, either yourself or others, rotoscoping animation, motion capture (for computer animation) and books, including:

The Human Figure in Motion and *Animals in Motion* by Eadweard Muybridge. The first and still best photographic analyses of locomotion.

The Animator's Survival Kit by Richard Williams. This is very good for its many walk variations, but they are done on 1's.

Tezuka School of Animation, Vol. 2: Animals in Motion by Tezuka Productions.

Animation: Learn How to Draw Animated Cartoons by Preston Blair. While this is great for classical cartoon walks, watch out because the illustrations of the walk cycles are not complete and will not hook up.

"Walks always have become troublesome and complicated to animate."
Frank Thomas and Ollie Johnston[10]

10. As I cannot find this, I am going to assume it was a personal communication to the author.

EXPOSURE SHEET - Assignment #7 see also p. 350

This assignment is to do and hand in the rough exposure sheets for the final project. They should be checked, graded and returned to the student. Students needing them to continue working should turn in a copy.

The exposure sheets could be regular 96x sheets or the ones handed out in class. The minimal information would be the timing for the film in large blocks of time with a rough description of the action. A bonus would be the layout information, including field sizes and exact length of each shot or scene marked in frames. The ideal information would be the completely filled out sheets, with all your levels and cels and BG numbering and any pans, trucks or dissolves planned out (fig. 5-52).

Example exposure sheets and assignment handouts. Examples of exposure sheets are available and information on them is in Chapter 5, Layout (fig. 5-52).

End of exercises.

Extra exercises are in Chapter 14.

ANIMATING - THE PROCESS

Hand-drawn animation is used as the example for this section as it is still the best and most flexible way for teaching animation. To review:

- Use the model sheets to reference how the model is built and moves, particularly the face (fig. 5-3).
- Use thumbnails to plan out the animation, especially the main poses (slugging) (fig. 2-1).
- Use the rough timing for the animation from the animatic or sound track.
- Draw the main poses first and when they work do the breakdowns, then the inbetweens in blue pencil (fig. 7-13).
- Animate only the basic shapes and basic movement for the rough animation.
- Constantly flip the drawings to see if the movement works. Check the timing. Do rough exposure sheets.
- Pencil test. Redo until the animation works (fig. 7-79).
- Add the details, clean up (figs. 7-44, 7-46).
- Pencil test again (fig. 7-79).

Analyze your action, think of what you want to do and how to achieve it. Rethink and restage each action in several different ways until you find the best, as you make good animation with your brain not your hand. For instance, does a close-up that would bring the action closer to the audience work better than a medium shot? Act out the action and consider the transitions in and out of the action. A cel with the TV cutoff inked on it under the animation paper will keep the animation within the boundaries.

DRAWING

If you want to be a character animator, keep a sketchbook and draw all the time. Take life-drawing classes and do a lot of quick sketch and action drawings (fig. 7-33). Try drawing poses from a basketball game on TV. When drawing, do the basic shapes first as that is what you will be animating. Draw from life and/or your imagination, women, men, kids, animals, clouds, emotions, trees, monsters, fire, explosions, houses, gods, devils, etc. Disney would give his people, if they were between projects, the day off to go to the zoo and draw.

Marc Davis (fig. 7-34), one of the Nine Old Men of Disney who taught drawing at Chouinard would have us, for one exercise, draw from the feet up, not the head down. This way the person would always be in balance. He also used 20-second or one-minute poses.

Glenn Vilppu, considered today as the top teacher in drawing for animation, believes "that drawing as it's practiced in the animation industry today is closest to classical drawing in the tradition of Raphael, DaVinci, and other great draftsmen of the past."[11] Study Glenn Vilppu's *The Vilppu Drawing Manual* and his videos; how to get them is in the bibliography.

CHARACTER ANIMATION

Good character animation means that the audience believes in your character. For an audience to believe in your film, they must believe in your character. To do good character animation, you must know your character's personality so you can see it in your animation. All movement in character animation should have a reason behind it. Random movement is far worse than no movement at all. It is a sign of poor or untaught animation.

Ollie Johnston (figs. 2-53, 7-13) tells the story that during WWII he picked up a hitchhiking serviceman. They started talking and the serviceman noticed on the windshield of Ollie's car a sticker of Donald Duck. He asked about it and Ollie told him that he worked at the Disney studio. The serviceman paused a long time and asked, "Do you mind if I ask you a question?" Ollie said no. The serviceman, pointing to Donald, asked, "Is he a real duck?"[12] Maybe this is why Frank and Ollie subtitled their book ,"The Illusion of Life."

A Character Animator

In animation, a character animator is the equivalent of the live-action actor. A character animator is an actor with a pencil. To do character animation, act out your scenes with your

---

11. Glenn Vilppu. Vilppu Drawing Online. Chapter 1: Gesture. Located http://documents.mx/documents/drawing-glenn-vilppu-online-articles-compilation.html.

12. I suspect another personal communication to the author.

body and face, feeling it or seeing it in a mirror. Feel the action you want to animate with your body. Acting in a mirror for facial expressions is a common practice. Act not once but many times, be your character, get the basic motive, and then their secondary motives or actions. If you do not use yourself, use an actor or animated character on film or tape for reference by studying or rotoscoping them. If you are acting with normal people around, be sure to let them know what you are doing so they do not think you are crazy. It has happened to me several times.

For good character animation acting, the audience should know what the character is thinking. And what does the character want? Ideally, the audience should know both what the character is thinking and the intelligence of the character at all times. An example of animation first showing a character thinking is Pluto trying to unstick himself from a sheet of flypaper in *Playful Pluto*, Disney (1934). It is often cited as a first example of character thinking. This pantomime of a dog wanting to get rid of sheets of flypaper is a perfect example of animated character acting. Ask yourself, "What is the character doing now and what is the character thinking now, and how do you show what he or she is thinking" as you animate. What in your animation lets the audience know what the character is thinking besides the dialogue, and what if the character is supposed to be thinking opposite to what the character is speaking? This is important even if the characters are symbols or stereotypes. An example would be the traditional bulldog bad guy in *Bad Luck Blackie* (1949), who shows what he is thinking and a funny film gets funnier because of it.

Do one pose that will tell the complete personality of the character. Do a set of face and body poses to get more expression in your animation. Make sure the character is drawn in proper size to the background (fig. 5-12).

Animate characters so their attitude shows. If they are happy, show a big smile with open body language. If they are old and mean, show a face with a pinched look and the body bent over and tired. If they are a young and happy child, let their movement show them skipping and laughing. Though often having a difference between the body design and the animation can work very well, like a young child's happy animation in an old bent-over body or a fat big hippopotamus in a tutu dancing as gracefully as any star 100-pound ballerina. I heard a story that for the dancing hippopotamus in *Fantasia*, Disney had filmed a very fat lady dancing for rotoscope purposes (fig. 5-45), but when they got the footage back instead of being funny and awkward she was incredibly graceful, so they went with that rotoscoped animation in the film.[13]

Putting on model or holding character means making sure in each drawing the character is on model according to the model sheets (fig. 5-3). This can take more time than the actual animation. In computer 3D animation, clean up is not needed since the character is a full

---

13. Clearly a story that was in the author's brain. Who put it there? I don't know.

model to start and this time-consuming step is not needed.

Character animators should know acting. If you are a natural-born actor that is fine, but if not, acting classes, doing theater and stand-up comedy classes are good ways to learn the basics of acting. The knowledge you gain from acting classes is also an excellent guide when you are directing your voice talent. You will know what information a voice talent needs from you, as you wanted from the director or teacher from the acting class. Acting can also help presentation of boards or ideas. Books such as Stanislavski's *An Actor Prepares* are also useful as reference. Study pantomime. If animating speech, first pantomime the speech with the full body and face, then animate the lips.

If the film is character-driven, the animation and the attitude of the character is as important as the idea. In the case of a character series--*Bugs Bunny*, *The Simpson's*-- the character is the idea.

A character animator is an actor with a pencil.

A Traditional Way to Construct a Character for Animation

First draw a line of action for the general stance, pose or action of the character (fig. 7-35). Then over that line of action put the basic forms, circles (spheres, oblongs), rectangles (boxes), etc., which make up the basic construction of the figure (fig. 7-36). Now over that put a simple one-line skeleton structure, one line with the joints indicated with small circles. The arms, legs, feet and hands can be indicated in this drawing (fig. 7-37). Then, especially over the head circle, draw the guidelines for the angle of the head to the camera. This is the perspective or tilt of the head. This line will normally be a vertical circular line through the height of the head unit (fig. 7-38). Then the guidelines for the placement of the features, the eyes, mouth, and nose are done. This is a circular line at right angles to the vertical line (fig. 7-39). Now put in the features of the face, roughly at first (fig. 7-40). Connect the body and head units so that the body and head have the exterior shape(fig. 7-41). Replace the simple arms and legs skeleton by cylindrical shapes (fig. 7-42). The hands and the feet can be represented by wedge shaped rectangles (fig. 7-43). The two basic shapes, the hand pad and the fingers, can indicate the hands (fig. 7-44). Then do the character's costume by dressing it over the basic form (fig. 7-45). Finally, add all the details and clean up (fig. 7-46). A few sheets of paper will be needed for the drawing and redrawing.

The way to measure the height of the character is by how many heads tall the character is (fig. 7-47). The proportions of the character are measured in height in head units; please see the next section for some examples. A large stomach unit with a small chest unit and a normal head unit could be the basis for a fat person (fig. 7-48). A large chest unit with the other units being normal could be a physically strong character (fig. 7-49). Two long, thin body units are a skinny person (fig. 7-50). Cartoon and cute characters are often based on a baby's body proportions (fig. 7-51).

Any part of the head or body that is going to squash and stretch can be designed as two units (fig. 7-52). Cartoon hands traditionally have three fingers and wear gloves to simplify the animation and forgo the details such as fingernails (fig. 7-53). This traditional way to construct a character can be changed or adapted to a personal drawing style.

Whether a character can be animated well depends on its construction. The basic body shapes should be designed to be easy to follow in the animation. What follows is one way to construct the basic units of a character.

Elements Involved in Character Design

Body

Core body - the basic units (fig. 7-36).
Hands - hands can tell a complete emotion with a clean pose (fig. 7-54).
Limbs
Costume
Proportions - the standard Western proportions are: Normal = 7½ heads high - 2 heads wide (fig. 7-55).
Ideal = 8 heads high - 2⅓ heads wide.
Fashion = 8 ½ heads high – 2⅓ or 1½ heads wide, the ideal woman is not as wide.
Heroic = 9 heads high - 2⅔ heads wide.
Babies = A 1-year-old baby is 3-4 heads high with a large head unit with the eyes in the lower ⅓ not the normal half placement of adults (fig. 7-56).
Cartoon = often 2½ or 3 heads high - it is almost the same as babies' proportions (fig. 7-47).

Face/Head

Eyes - are usually drawn as the most predominant feature in the face, as it is the facial feature most used to convey emotion in the animation.
Nose
Mouth - is it designed for lip sync or not? Is the inside of the mouth shown?
Hair - keep it simple or its animation will be time-consuming.
Ear Shape
Proportions -
Adult (fig 7-58).

Babies. Babies heads are quite large and when a baby holds up his or her arms all the way the arms and the hands will go as high as the middle of the head. The large head of babies is due to the fact the brain does not grow much and as humans we grow from the head down, not up. Humans may be predisposed to like babies (fig. 7-59).

Silhouette - does the character read strong in silhouette (fig.7-67)? Mickey Mouse is an example.
> Head
> Body (fig. 7-68)
> Costume

Color
> Character
> Costume

Distinguishing Symbols in the
> Costume
> Physical nature

Distinguished Movement/Mannerism
> Face
> Hands
> Body
> Walk
> Poses-what are the typical poses (fig. 7-60)?

Name of the character, does it fit the look of the character?

Summation of all the important elements that make the character unique.

The animator must know the personality of the character. This was covered in Chapter 2, Storyboard Content. You must always be aware of the dramatic flow and logic, the place in the film of the animation you are working on. Use model sheets, voice characteristics, character analysis and your own sense. Analyze the anatomy of your character; consider his or her weight, shape (basic and external), dress, personality, sex, age, physical deficiencies or strengths, and his or her character and philosophy - i.e. his or her personality. Think up clever little stuff for character or action that fits the action and makes your animation stand out.

Particular attention should be given to the eyes, face and hands, as they are the main outlets for expression. It is often said that film acting is done with the eyes (fig. 7-61). Eye blinks help bring life to a face, especially on turning the head, when it dips on the turn or just before starting an action (fig. 7-11). Eyeballs should work together except for comedy effects. Mustaches as a rule are hooked on directly beneath the nose. Keep the hands crisp, get character and acting into them. Make them dramatic and strong; we often talk with our hands, though this can apply for all body language (fig. 7-62). Do not let hands get puffy and fat even though they are drawn that way. The palms of hands are usually parallel to the sides when walking. Make arm and hand (really all movements) movements mean something. Do not forget the rest of the body, whose animation is often the foundation for character animation.

PRINCIPLES OF CHARACTER MOVEMENT

Overlapping Action

Called hierarchical motion in computer programming, it means a body movement or action that happens in parts. Like an arm raising first the shoulder and then the upper arm start the movement by moving up, the forearm follows by moving up from the elbow joint in a broader arc, then the hand drags up with the fingers following in an appropriate manner, down for languid, up for emphasis.

When the arm stops the upper arm stops first, then the forearm, the hand and the fingers last with maybe an accent before their final stop. Everything does not happen at once; the movements overlap each other. Shown is an example of a body turning from three-quarter view to three-quarter view, not as a stiff statue on a revolving disc but as overlapping action with one part leading, either the hips, the eyes, head, the hand–there are many ways. Shown is an example of leading with the eyes: they look, the head turns, then the shoulders, lead foot swivels, head and shoulders continue to move, back foot swings around with hip and lead foot swivels on toe, head in final position, shoulders in final position, hips in final position, lead foot forward for balance and final position. Anticipation is part of overlapping action; when the eyes move and the head turns, they are anticipating the body turning (fig. 7-63).

Accent

Accent is to go beyond the end of the animation and then come back in your final position, especially in cartoon animation. This is somewhat like overlapping action except it is at the end of an action, and is used to accent the action or emotion to add snap to the animation. You never get there all at once. First one part stops, then another, each anticipating the full stop. Before you go into your final stop pose, you could animate a little past and then back into your hold; this will add to the final anticipation for the stop. An example would be a character coming to a sudden stop, with the feet stopping but the body keeps going, stops, then rocks back and forth before its final position.

Example of finger pointing going beyond before final stops, straight for extra emphasis or down for gentle emphasis (fig. 7-64). Illustrated both as stiff animation and as loose animation in the arm, wrist and finger (fig. 7-65).

Follow Through

Secondary animation (in this case, an inanimate object) that follows the primary or living animation and follow through when the primary action stops. Hair or a cape will keep moving forward when the body stops. Each is animated separately, but the secondary animation depends on the primary animation for its movement.

These three principles are usually applied to body movement but they can apply to any animation. For example, in a Rube Goldberg fantastic machine starting, first one wheel starts turning, then another, then a belt, then smoke starts coming out, and so on until the entire contraption is shaking and moving. And now to other important considerations in character animation.

Arcs

Human skeleton structure movement is based on ball and socket joints. The movement of the ball and socket is the arc. Human body movement is a series of arcs. If you have a realistic human character, its movement must be in arcs. Rubber ball animation disregards these limited arcs rules (fig. 7-81).

Gravity

Gravity has been cited repeatedly throughout this chapter, especially when doing realistic-based animation. Any realistic still weight should fall unless held up or counterweighted or properly balanced. When you move a character, shift the weight to the planted foot to enable the moving foot to have natural freedom of movement.

Display the Action

Any animated action must have clarity to be seen. To show the action profile, clear it of the body so that it is in clear view of the audience (fig. 7-66). Make sure there is not a busy BG behind that will make the animation hard to see. A blank area is the best. A cut in to a close-up on a particularly important action like the picking of a flower is most helpful for reading that action.

Silhouette

A good silhouette, especially in keys, is very important. Often you read a character, its meaning and attitude, in its silhouette.

I have used the same drawing for both displaying the action and silhouette (figs. 7-66, 7-67).

Secondary Animation

Decide what is the primary and secondary animation. Primary animation is the basic movement, expression and actions that are caused by a character or object that is alive. Secondary is usually considered to be a follow through of an inanimate object that results from the primary animation. This animation follows the laws of physics and gravity, otherwise they will have life and perhaps primary action. Some people consider secondary animation as an extra bit of acting business to the main acting. As in drumming the fingers or scratching the head while thinking, wiping a hand after shaking hands, hitting the chest after taking a strong drink.

Cluttering

Watch out for the cluttering of the action, the movement and the staging. An example of cluttering would be to have two or more actions going on at the same time in different places so that the audience is confused. Good animation has a pattern, even if it looks like it does not.

Line of Action

The line of action in the character (fig. 7-35). Make the line of action simple, forceful and dramatic (if this is what is called for). The principle of the sine curve is often used; the top of the wave moves out along the length of the wave (fig. 7-68). Sine curve is a wave motion or how a wave moves that is used in certain animation. It can be a line of action as in a curve in the body movement or a flag waving or a whip striking out. See the illustrations (fig. 7-69).

Holding Character

Or putting on model is holding character physically and physiologically throughout the entire film. The model sheet is the guide for the physical character. To keep the features of the face from floating around, use structure lines in the head to keep the eyes, nose, etc., to anchor them. Hold the same volume on shapes to keep the illusion of reality. Especially watch both eyes on the same side of the nose.

ROTOSCOPING

Rotoscoping live action as an aid for animation or visual effects is common (fig. 5-45). Rotoscoping can become a substitute for animation. Ralph Bakshi's features in traditional animation and today's computer motion capture are prime examples. The drawback of rotoscoping or copying live action slavishly is that it lacks the magic of animation. The Disney studio has done rotoscoping as an aid for animation for many years. Margie Bell, who later changed her name to Marge Champion, was the actress for the live-action film used for rotoscoping the main character in *Snow White*. However, Grim Natwick, the animator of the character, said, "We used only the first frame and the last frame of her" from the rotoscoped footage.[14] (If a studio, as Disney does, has a morgue of past animation drawings, that can also be used for reference or copying.) You can rotoscope live action from a projected image, a printed copy or a computer screen. To achieve normal animation movement, copy every other live-action frame and shoot the final drawings on 2's. Rotoscoping for computer animation is called motion capture. Rotoscoping good animation can help a student learn the principles of good animation.

LIP SYNC

Syncing dialogue to the lips is the most common form of syncing sound with picture. This is commonly referred to as "lip sync." In creating good lip sync and contrary to logic, the animation of the lips is not the most important element. A good rule is to do the animation of the body and hands first, then the eyes and head, and finally the lips. There is an old Disney rule to animate the lips last. Remember to use overlapping action, so that all the elements mentioned do not happen at the same time and thereby negate one another.

Other ways to help achieve better animation on lip syncing is to say the words and act the meaning and action as you watch yourself in a mirror (sometimes best done when no one is around). Try it several ways and use the best, especially the accents, for your lip sync animation. Under normal conditions the thought should lead to the words. First animate the thought, then as a result of that thought, the words. Exceptions here would be a double take and/or a strong reaction. The animation of the eyes is very important in showing an animated character thinking process. The short with Pluto and the flypaper is often cited as the first example of a character exhibiting independent thought.

The top teeth stay in place and the bottom ones move up and down as a unit for reality-based animation. This is the way the jaw is hinged. Animating the tongue is optional, usually for some unusual effect. The eyes should react with the words, especially hitting the high points. Closing the mouth between words, which is usually not done in real life, will make the lip sync cleaner. In English, you must put your lips together on certain letters. Try "b," "m," "p," "w." Check the mirror for other letters (fig. 7-70). The mouth shape should be designed for ease of speaking in the character design. The animator should phase the dialogue. If the film is in limited animation, the mouth/face area should be designed so there is no need to ani-

14. "An Interview with Grim Natwick." http://www.animationartist.com/InsideAnimation/DavidJohnson/InterviewNatwick3.htm.

mate the whole body. The difference between seeing and hearing, mentioned in the Timing chapter, can be used here with the lips moving a frame or two before the sound.

The easiest way to do lip sync is hiding the lips behind a newspaper, beard, etc., or having the character talk off screen. Next is just opening and closing the mouth on complete words or sentences or randomly cycling an open and closed mouth, sometimes called bird beak animation.

Animating the first vowel and consonants, this is from Art Babbitt. Use the mouth positions in Preston Blair's book, usually only the vowel lip positions are needed. Animate the entire word rather than each letter. There was a short-lived TV series, *Clutch Cargo* (1959), where a live mouth and lips were combined with an animated character. It was easily the worst and funniest lip-syncing ever done.

BASIS OF MOVEMENT

Movement in animation is based on either:

- How we move in the real world where gravity and the laws of physics apply. Reality character movement is based on the head, chest and hip units to give the animation the illusion of life. Usually associated with 3D animation or a style of pictorial reality. One of the two pioneers in animation, Winsor McCay, chose this path.
- Movement not of the real physical world, breaking all the laws of reality and physics and based on the animator's creativity. It is usually linear and 2D, but could include the abstract, the non-realistic, the world of imagination and fantasy. The other pioneer of animation, Émile Cohl, used this approach.
- A combination of the two. A reality-based human who can fly or shapeshift. Combinations can give the animation its spark. Don't be confused by style here, a character can look very unrealistic but move according to Newton, or the character could look very realistic but move to non-physical laws.

ABSTRACT ANIMATION

Though most of the information given in this chapter is based on character animation, the same information can be used for abstract animation. A line representing a figure moving could have the same movement as the line of action in a character figure and the same attitude. A good way to begin abstract animation is using a reality source as inspiration. George Dunning used a rotoscoped Fred Astaire and Ginger Rogers dance number as inspiration for the *Lucy in the Sky with Diamonds* number from *Yellow Submarine* (1968) (fig. 5-46). Norman McLaren and Oskar Fischinger's films are good examples of abstract or non-narrative animation. Please check the Storyboard chapter on experimental animation for more discussion on abstract animation.

EFFECTS ANIMATION

Natural events, rain, snow, explosions, water, fire, smoke, etc., are effects animation. Effects animators are considered a separate work and skill classification at major studios.

The basic principles of animation apply to effects animation. Though there is more reliance on the laws of physics and chemistry, as you are trying the illusion of inanimate action. For dramatic effects, there is also more use of camera techniques such as multi-exposures. Effects are done on 1's and 2's depending on the action and type of effect.

Start by studying the way the effect occurs in nature and then modifying it to fit the film. One time at the Disney studio they got tired of doing a falling snow effect in the same old way so they rotoscoped real snow, but when they looked at the rotoscoped footage they found the old way was far better.[15]

Some Effects

Rain is done on cycles. Two types of rain cycles are shown. First is a loose type that is cycled in a random manner. Second is a cycle of raindrops falling in a straight line. The raindrops should start at different points and by distance have different speeds. Best on 1's. A gray card or a filter behind the rain on the second pass can add atmosphere. Cycles can be done on different levels for depth and a multi-pass on all or some of the cycles can add realism (fig. 7-71).

Snow falls as a cycle in a curved line. Do not make the lines turn curvy nor have too many snowflakes together. Illustrated is one snow cycle with a snowflake pattern (fig. 7-72).

Smoke. The simplest smoke is this three-drawing cycle for cartoon smoke coming from a chimney. Dissipating smoke keeps breaking up until it disappears. Smoke is often part of the aftermath of an explosion (fig. 7-73).

Fire - the five things to consider in animating a fire are (fig. 7-74):

- Generation. How does it start? If a fire, is it started by a match? Lightning? A flame-thrower? Is the wood soaked with gasoline, or is it wet?
- Development. How it goes, where it goes and what it does?
- Dissipation, breakup and closure. Does the fire burn out, or is water thrown on it?
- Timing. Of each of the above and the total effect. Importance and relationship to the total film.
- Secondary effects. Shadows, flickering effects on other objects, smoke.

Illustrated is a cycle for basic fire and a candle-flame cycle.

Fire Flame - Draw the full flame, then draw the cycle for each part of the flame always moving

---

15. Another story I cannot verify.

up. Can change the size of the flame by compressing or lengthening the interior S curve. Tips of flame may break away. To avoid repetition, mix two or three different flame cycles (fig. 7-74).

Candle Flame - The base of the flame does not move too much, perhaps do a traceback of it for the animation. Flame will whip around with any type of breeze (fig. 7-74).

Cyclone - Moving three values or colors around a cylinder of your choice gives you a spinning effect (fig. 7-75).

Wind - You could show the wind by how strongly it affects the objects in the scene. Trees bending and leaves blowing off, a person holding his or her hat with his or her clothes blowing around him or her. You also could show Aeolus, the Greek master of the winds blowing.

Explosions - Ways to do explosions vary, but two are:

A created flash followed by smoke and perhaps flying debris with the smoke dissipating to end it. Illustrated is a ground explosion with breakdowns of smoke.

An effective way for a flash is to shoot white, black and red, one or two frames each in random order for a total of around eight frames, two frames white, one black, one red, white, red, black, white. The created explosion mentioned above could be started with four frames of this effect for more punch. All should be accommodated by a loud sound effect.

For an explosion or earthquake of the whole frame, do a camera shake. Pan the whole scene both left and right one after the other for one frame. First left at one extreme, the right at one extreme and coming back to the center in decreasing increments until the shaking stops.

Lightning

On a flash caused by lightning, the effect can be heightened by cutting to a reverse black-and-white of the shot and then doing a quick dissolve to the shot. Put the action before the sound.

Twinkling Stars

Punch small holes in a sheet of black paper, then bottom light them so light shines through. These are the stars. To make them twinkle between the paper and the light, pan a long cel with black paint randomly dribbled on it. The paint on the cel will block the light, causing it to twinkle.

Multiple Exposures

Exposing the same section of film more than once. Used in effects animation and when there are too many cel levels in traditional animation. Mattes (a black area which holds out a film emulsion exposed for another pass in that area) are used in the first pass, leaving an area for the second pass (fig. 10-3).

Examples Are:

Shadows are done with an animated black second shadow pass on a percentage exposure over the background. Since shadows can range from light to dark, the amount of exposure you give the black shadow will set its value. In the opening of Disney's *Snow White*, as a singing Snow White is coming down the steps, you see her shadow following her. This was done by the whole scene except for the shadow was shot at 50 percent for the first pass, then on the second pass the whole scene with the shadow area was shot at 50 percent so that the background from the first pass appears through the now gray shadow. The second pass was shot at 50 percent so the entire scene is 100 percent exposed. Phil Denslow, *The Prisoner* (fig. 7-76).[16]

Candy apple glows. On the first pass (the first exposure) the whole scene is shot. On the second pass, a glow is added around an object. This is done by bottom lighting a top and bottom matte with a sheet of frosted glass between them, causing a glow. The brightness of the glow is controlled by the f-stop on the lens and a color glow is achieved by adding a color gel.

Animating on Levels

Animation with many characters is done on different cel levels so only the character moving is animated and the non-moving characters do not have to be redrawn and colored for each drawing of the animated character. By doing a mouth movement on one level while the non-moving body is on a different level saves you the time and work to redraw the body for each mouth movement (fig. 5-1). You do not want to have more than five or six levels of cels over a background as the density of that many cels will darken the background (fig. 5-47). When Winsor McCay did *Gertie the Dinosaur* (1914), cels had not been invented so he had the teenager next door trace the same background over for each drawing. The young man never worked on another animated film.

Bottom or Top Pegs

Along the way, starting here is as good a time as any, decide what levels go on top pegs (fig. 7-77) and what levels go on bottom pegs (fig. 7-78). If you have moving pan background on one

---

16. In the author's manuscript at this point, there is a phrase that reads, "Phil Denslow story?" I emailed Phil this section and he responded with this story. The author was also teaching at ArtCenter at the time. Phil's recollection of the story is as follows: "I was shooting a seven-minute film with dissolves between drawings to indicate motion and with percentage shadows, which meant shooting all the dissolves and scenes twice. The camera at ArtCenter required a change in the film magazine take-up mechanism each time you changed from forward to reverse and vice versa, so every time you began or ended a dissolve and every time you began and ended a shadow pass you had to move these levers in and out of position. Forgetting to get the take-up levers right would likely cause the film to break. About halfway along during my week-long shoot, I lost confidence in whether I had gotten things right or not.

Luckily, Dan's class was in session at that time and I went up to the classroom, interrupted the session and told Dan that I might have ruined my film. I'm sure I looked shattered. Dan came back to the camera room with me and looked things over. This included turning out all the lights and opening the camera so he could feel inside to be sure the film was where it belonged. He reassured me that everything was OK. When he returned to the classroom, Dan just said to the students: 'Mid-shooting jitters.'"

level and a character walk cycle on another level which stays in one place, then one must be on top pegs and one on bottom pegs.

Animating Two or More Different Characters

When you are animating two or more characters, you have a choice to make. Do you animate them all together? Or each character separately? Both ways can work, with the slight nod going to doing each character separately so that you can concentrate on their individual personality.

Animation and the Background

Consider carefully and visualize the contours of the animated surfaces, fingers, feet, touching the ground, tables, doors, doorknobs, etc.

Line Quality

The line quality whether loose or tight should be consistent unless concept calls for a change. Clean up your drawings, getting them down to one clean line if you want that look. This must be done before the Xeroxing or computer scanning. If you are inking yourself, it can be done at that stage.

When to Do Your Best Animation in a Film

Do the best animation at the end of an action, a scene or the film as that is the most important part, then do the next best at the beginning to get the audience involved. To help achieve this, start doing the animation in the middle so you can make all your mistakes when it doesn't count and you will get to know your character for better animation later.

Testing Your Animation

The results of shooting the sequential drawings on film, tape or computer is called pencil tests (fig. 7-79). Using the tape or computer is best as the animation can be seen immediately. In the old days, those lucky enough to do pencil tests did them on film. Film takes time to process, so the animation tests would be seen several days later. This is analogous to playing the piano and hearing the sound several days later. Always shoot the pencil tests using exposure sheets so that a record is kept of the shoot that can be repeated or modified. If you try a little experimenting, note it on the exposure sheets. To change the numbering on your drawings if you need to add more, for example, from drawings 3 to 4 you have to add two inbetweens, just number them 3a and 3b so you do not have to renumber all the drawings after 4.

After viewing the pencil tests, corrections are made as needed. Get the timing right before you do any clean-ups. After you have the proper amount of animation (the key poses) and you decide it works, then do the breakdowns and inbetweens, add the detail and clean up. Beginning animators often animate the first time through a completely drawn and rendered character for the pencil test. This takes a long time and if you have to do them over, even more time and effort. Doing them rough the first time will save you time. After the animation is tested and completed, it is inked onto a cel or cleaned up for scanning into the computer.

BACKGROUNDS

The best board to do BGs on is one-ply thick, but almost any stiff board will do. If the board is too thick, it will raise the overlay cels so high on the pegs that they could be not registered properly. Usually white board is used so that you can paint over it, but consider using other material, colored paper, patterned paper, cloth, etc. Watercolor paints are normally used but it can be animation paint, which is helpful because then all your colors will come from the same source.

A common problem with BGs is that they are done in a painterly 3D style, with shading, etc. While the overlay animation is flat and 2D, which causes a negative visual conflict between the animation and the BG. A good way to avoid this is to do a black line tracing of your BG, from your cleaned up layout, on a cel. This BG cel is then placed over a painted BG board. The black line that then defines the details of the BG matches the normal black line around the overlay animation and ties in the visual quality of animation and the BGs. You must always consider what is animation and BG, especially where they come in contact. An animated hand on a cel trying to open a doorknob painted on a BG can look very awkward. In this case put the doorknob on a cel.

Backgrounds can be done in any art style (fig. 7-80). They should complement the animation style and should be decided when the animation style is decided. The sections in Layout that deal with composition, color, etc., are really the sections to read for backgrounds.

Background artists are often fine painters, and a strong style or experience in painting and design is essential for a background artist.

TITLES

The main titles are the first thing the viewer sees and set the tone of your film. They will subconsciously set up certain learned expectations. If you do your titles at the last minute as an afterthought or with poor hand-lettering, they could have a negative impact on your film. Think of film titles as the search for designs and animation that will become the elusive visual moving statement, which instantaneously communicates the film's intent while generating the viewer's interest (fig. 5-40). They can add a level of meaning or understanding to your film in a very short time, or they could be a counterpoint to the intent of your film. For instance, your title "A Flies Life" could be seen as an educational film on flies when in fact it is a satire on education. Watch the TV cut-off plus an extra safety title area so none of your titles are cut off.

Titles can be at either the opening of your film or the end. In the old days it was the norm to have all the titles at the opening, so that the film ended with the film's theme and not a list of names. It is common today to have them in both places. For a short animated film, the title of the film and the maker (should it be "Filmmaker?" "Directed by?" "Written, directed, animated by?", etc., it's up to you) are the minimal titles at the opening (fig. 5-49). James Whitney was the only person who did not put his name on his films, as far as I know. Then the rest of the titles are placed at the end. Titles at the end should be short. Long end titles can take people right out of your film. There should be at least an end title. The film's opening action under the title puts the audience right into the film.

For your lettering you can use press-on type, computer typefaces printed directly or as line negatives for underlight shooting. Normal type size is 24 point at a 12 field, and anything lower than 12 point at a 12F would be very hard to read. The typeface should mirror or counterpoint the mood of the film.

To estimate the time needed by the audience to read the titles, read the titles aloud slowly once as you count the seconds for the reading. Convert the seconds into frames for the exposure sheets. The old rule used to be read it aloud slowly twice, but audiences today, who are more experienced, read visually much, much faster than previous audiences. If you use fancy lettering or have complying action under your titles, you should give the audience more time to read the titles. Roll titles at the end of the film are panned at .02 or .03 at a rotated 8F. In terms of written material you can use title cards, balloon dialogue, etc., anyplace in your film.

EXPOSURE SHEETS

Often exposure sheets are done before the animation, at least the key frames and some if not all of inbetweening. Keep working on them as you animate until they are finished (fig. 5-52).

BOOKKEEPING

The system you use for the numbering of your animation is important. You need a filing system for more pieces of paper than many businesses. You can start everything at one: use an A-1, B-1, etc., system; or by scenes; or levels; or by what is on the cel, example M-1, M-2, etc., as for the character on the cel whose name is Maura (fig. 5-47). These numbers are on the right-hand bottom of the cel for bottom-pegged cels, outside of the field area (fig. 7-78). The numbers would be on the top right-hand side for top-pegged cels (fig. 7-77). You have to plan how many levels you need. Think of different ways you can reduce your number of levels by combining different events on the same cel (fig. 5-1). Decide what goes on top pegs and bottom pegs. Especially watch when you layout your pans. By putting your cels on the proper top and bottom pegs you can save a lot of time in the shooting.

Keep all the art, from pencil tests on in folders (fig. 5-48), breaking it down by scenes or characters. You can keep a list on the cover of your folders on what the steps of production are and what you have done. It is a good idea to have a master log of each scene in the film and what is done and what needs to be done. All this planning and organization can save you hours of work even in setting up your daily work.

RUBBER HOSE ANIMATION

Just as the name implies, it is animation done like a flexible rubber hose: There are no rules, no interior human body structure, no joints, no arcs, so you can bend anything anyway you want (fig. 7-81).

It was very popular in the 1920s and 1930s. Sometimes, rubber hose animation can lend itself to very free and inventive animation that goes beyond reality. The early Fleischer animation of *Snow-White* (1933) is a good example.

For animation in the 1920s and 1930s there is a story that early animators to hold proportions used a dime for the head and a quarter for the body and overlapped a series for oblongs for the arms and legs. All you needed was 35 cents to be an animator (fig. 7-82).

INK AND PAINT

The changing of the line drawings into a solid-colored drawing is done by hand-inking and painting or using a computer program (fig. 6-3).

ON TO FILM

In traditional hand animation when all the art is finished, inked and painted on cels, the backgrounds are done and the exposure sheets completely filled out, then the final check and the shooting onto film.

FINAL CHECK

The checking of all the materials before the filming, preferably by someone else. There also may be a checking stage done after the animation and before beginning ink and paint to make sure nothing is left out. In a studio situation you would have a "checker," a specific job description for either check. The final check makes sure that all the material is there and noted correctly on the exposure sheet. Items usually checked: Are the field sizes correct? Is the frame count on the exposure sheets correct? Are all the cels fully painted and the painting extends beyond the field size? Is anything missing? Do the BGs and the overlying cels match? Are all the pans and trucks noted properly? Is the numbering on the cels the same as on the exposure sheets? This check should be done early so there will be enough time to make the necessary changes before shooting. If the film is being shot by a professional camera service and there are any errors in the art or exposure sheets, you will have to pay for the time the camera service has to check out an obvious error or the reshoot if it is your mistake. If a check is not done, you could have delays and extra expenses in the shooting.

FILMING

This is where you expose all your visual elements onto film one frame at a time. You will need a camera that can shoot one frame at a time and some sort of rig for shooting. A normal animation crane has all the elements to do this (fig. 7-83). You begin shooting by placing the exposure sheets where you can see them, then set up the material to be shot for easy access. Then check the field size, the focus, the f-stop, whether the shutter is opened or closed, counter at the right number (usually to start it's 0), where is the camera field center (the N/S/E/W coordinates), what is the camera shooting direction (forward or reverse), are the pegs at center, are the lights on and in their proper position, are the room lights off. Now raise the platen (the piece of glass that presses the flat cels together so you have no shadows) and place the material to be shot in its proper order and on the top or bottom pegs. Lower the platen and shoot a frame. Keep doing this with pans, trucks, camera moves and long holds (where you shoot many frames at one time) until you are done. If you do not have a professional crane, you will have to rig up a simple one.

Filming is sometimes called "going to camera," the "shoot," or "shooting (fig. intro-2.2)." The art will be shot on the animation crane either on 16mm or 35mm film. 16mm is generally used for student work and is fine for video. 35mm would be used for theatrical releases. It could also be shot with a digital camera. If you are in a school situation and are shooting the film yourself, you can plan for a normally difficult film, without too many pans, dissolves and trucks, to take a full day of shooting to get a minute of finished film. A very difficult film can take a full day to shoot a few seconds.

Tips when shooting: take breaks every couple of hours; if you make a mistake, stop, don't try to shoot through it, take a break and figure out how to turn the error into a creative mistake. If you have an overexposed frame or two, maybe you could add a loud sound effect at that point to make it look like it was what you intended. If you left an arm or mouth cel off for a couple of frames, you could always double expose that cel over black and at least have something in that area. Usually a one-frame error will not be noticed. If you have an error that you cannot figure your way out of, you will have to reshoot. If you can, overexpose the area that you have to reshoot, perhaps inserting your hand or a card saying "cutback." This will tell the editor what part has to be cut out during editing. If you know you have made a mistake and it involves only one shot, you can reshoot immediately and then go on with shooting the rest of the film. If you cannot do that, you can shoot all your reshoots at the end of the shoot. In 16mm you cannot cut reshot footage into the middle of a shot or a series of shots that are held together by dissolves if you composite in film. If you cut there, your finished film will jump at that cut. You will need to begin and end your reshoots at a cut, a fade-out or fade-in--a large explosion, etc. This may mean you will have to reshoot not only the bad shot but also extra, good shots until you come to a place you can cut. Often this break for editing is planned in the layout stage and this is called zero-cut planning.

If shooting a 2D stop motion film or doing unusual shooting on the crane, it is best to shoot a wedge test, where one frame is shot at each consecutive f-stop. This will give the correct exposure for the final shoot.

It is an advantage to shoot the film yourself as a student as you will see the logic of and understand the animation process. Even if you only want to do character animation and not do an entire film, knowing the complete process will help in becoming a character animator.

The only film stock available for shooting 16mm color negative is Eastman Kodak. Call them to find out the type of film obtainable. An ASA 100 is preferred because of the slow speed in shooting single-frame in animation.

After the film is shot it is taken to a motion picture laboratory to be developed and a one-light color workprint is made from the developed film for viewing. When you get the film from the laboratory and view it you are now in Post-Production, the next chapter.

CREATING DIRECTLY ON FILM

You can create an animated film by working directly on the film. For this you will need:

16mm or 35mm or 65mm film which can either be clear, black, a solid color or with a previous image. For clear film you can apply any type of transparent color that will stick to the film. Examples would be markers, inks and dyes (both food and shoe). For black film you can scrape away the black emulsion, leaving a clear white image. You can add color later if you so desire (fig. 6-9). You can shoot color cards (fig. 7-84) and then scrape or etch in that color on the print (fig. 2-59). For films with previous images you can both scrape and color. For tools to work the film you can use markers, brushes, pens, stamps, sponges, spray paint and anything else that will stick to the film. You can also Mylar-tape materials to the film or punch holes into the film. Opaque coloring will come out as a black image.

Your images can either be abstract or representational. If you want registration, you will need some sort of projection setup to project the previous frame onto the one you are working.

When you project your work you can destroy part of it each time (always clean the projector afterward). To save your work, it is best to get a print as soon as possible. The best way is to film it frame by frame on an optical printer. Often the stuff on the film will gum up the workings of a laboratory, and they will probably not print it if you just send it to them without warning.

There is a group of animators who do this, or as some prefer to call it, "cameraless animation." Filmmakers of note in this area are Norman McLaren, Len Lye, Bob Swarthe and Caroline Leaf. You can also draw the sound directly on film. Norman McLaren did a film showing the process of creating sound directly on film.

THE THEORETICAL BASIS OF ANIMATION

The theoretical basis of animation comes from the phi phenomenon and the persistence of vision. The phi phenomenon is a perceptual process, how the brain and eye see objects at different speeds. The persistence of vision is the ability of the human eye to retain an image for a brief interval after the image is gone.

An extreme case of after-image would be that unpleasant experience of having a flashbulb go off in your face and the retention of the image of the flash for a period after the flash has gone.

There is the formal theory developed from the phi phenomena and the persistence of vision.

To illustrate the phi phenomenon, think of two lights on the same plane in a dark room. If they are, turn them on and off at different speeds you will experience different phenomenon. The flashes will be perceived as two separate flashes if there is more than one second or longer between each flash. The flashes will be seen as moving back and forth if the speed between the flashes is one-twelfth of a second. The lights will appear to be blinking together as a double light if the speed of the flashes is one-fifth of a second. In 130 A.D., Ptolemy the Egyptian philosopher and mathematician demonstrated the phi phenomenon on the sea walls surrounding Alexandria harbor. He placed covered fire pots on the walls, and then on command (drums were thought to be used) the lids on the fire pots were lifted in an alternate sequence, thus giving the appearance of fire and light moving around the walls. This same effect is used today with alternating light bulbs around an opening or frame to give the same appearance and attract attention. Ptolemy also developed a form of thaumatrope, with one side color and one side white, which produced a blinking color when spun.

In 1824 the English physician Peter Mark Roget, of the thesaurus fame, published an essay entitled "Persistence of Vision with Regard to Moving Objects." Going further with phi phenomenon and persistence of vision, he theorized that a series of sequential images will give the illusion of movement to the human eye if they are presented fast enough at a regular speed, if there is enough even illumination for good projection, and the spatial distance between the objects is controlled. He further stated that these variables are interdependent and if one is changed, then all have to be changed. His theory was the basis of the technology of motion pictures.

Based on these theories, we have a motion picture projector that projects film at 24 frames a second of sequential moving objects that give the illusion of movement. But it is a little bit more complex than that, as the shutter that rotates between the film and the light source and interrupts the light that reaches the screen does so at 48 or 72 times a second, depending on the number of blades in the shutter. Once when the frame is being pulled down and replaced by a new frame and once or twice when the frame is sitting in the projection gate. The term "flicker fusion" is sometimes used to describe this event. It has to be fast for the protein that twists in the eye in response to light that makes vision possible takes 200 femtoseconds to complete its reaction and send the message to the brain. A femtosecond is one-millionth of one-billionth of a second.

AN OLD TRICK

An old Disney animator's trick is to animate each scene completely at least three times. The first time through establishes the strong poses, the path of action, and the basic movement and acting. The second time they add the effects of gravity to make the animation believable. The third time is to animate the personality of the character. Then the final clean-up is done, the clothes and secondary animation. This achieves good animation, whether Disney or abstract.

THE BASIC PRINCIPLES (RULES) OF ANIMATION

As they apply to character animation and for any type of animation:

- Squash and stretch. The Bouncing Ball exercise, exercise #1, pp. 153-158.
- Timing, exercise #2, pp. 158-162.
- Anticipation. Please see the Anticipation exercise #4, p. 166.
- Character movement - Overlapping action - Accent and follow through, p.190.
- Gravity, p. 191.
- Arcs, p. 191.
- Display the action - Silhouette, p. 191.
- Animating in and out of holds, p. 160.
- Primary and secondary animation, p. 192.
- Line of action in character, p. 192.
- Believability - Holding character, p. 192.
- Staging of the action, p. 191
  - Avoid cluttering, p. 192
  - Not enough exaggeration and caricature
  - Most beginning animation is too timid (fig. 7-85).

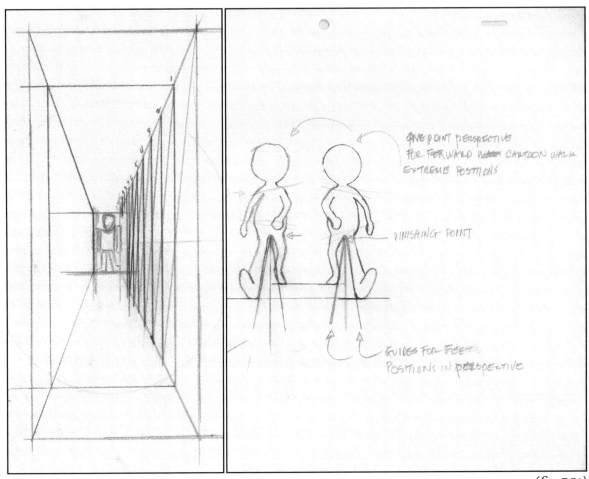

ONE POINT PERSPECTIVE
FOR FORWARD CARTOON WALK
EXTREME POSITIONS

VINISHING POINT

GUIDES FOR FEET
POSITIONS IN PERSPECTIVE

(fig. 7-21)

QUOTES

" 'Animator', is the special term applied to the creative worker in this new branch of artistic endeavor. Besides the essential qualification of bestowing life upon drawings, he must be a man of many accomplishments."

"He (the animator) must be an untiring and courageous worker."
E.G. Lutz, 1920[17]

"You have to do a thousand bad drawings before you do a good drawing."
Anonymous

"Good animation is done with the brain, not the hand."

"Don't be timid. All other things being equal, the animator who makes the most mistakes makes the best animation."

"If it were easy, everyone would be doing it."
The author

"It's hard to create the illusion of life when you wish you were dead."
Unknown animator

"The best you can do by next Tuesday is the best you can do by next Tuesday"
Charles Eames, designer 1907 - 1978[18]

Bill Shull's two rules: *"Pans are bad and Animators drink."*[19]

"It's what you learn after you know it all that counts."
John Wooden, basketball player and coach, b. 1910[20]

---

17. Google found these in a book called *Animated Cartoons: How They Are Made, Their Origin and Development* by E. G. Lutz (1926), pps. 58, 59. https://archive.org/stream/cu31924075701304/cu31924075701304_djvu.txt.

18. Since Google can't find and the author worked with Eames, I will saysay, "Personal communication with the author."

19. Bill Shull established the UCLA Animation Workshop and was the author's first teacher in animation. So again I'm gonna go with, "Personal communication with the author."

20. "John Wooden." BrainyQuote.com. Xplore Inc., 2016. 2 December 2016. Incidentally the author was a huge UCLA fan, both football and basketball. In his later years, his beer and Buster the dog never missed a game that had to be seen till the end, no matter what.

(fig. 7-48)

(fig. 7-52)

(fig. 7-50)

(fig. 7-49)

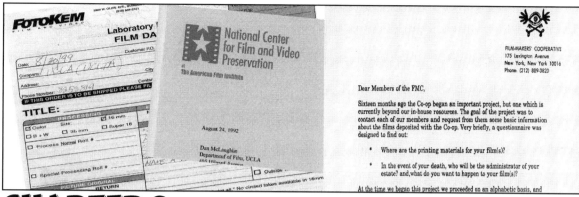

(fig. 8-2)

CHAPTER 8

POST-PRODUCTION[1]

The post-production phase of traditional animation starts after the film is shot and developed, and a workprint of the camera original is in hand. The following are the post-production stages for film.

- **Viewing** the silent workprint of the developed camera original film. The original film is never projected. On the emotional side, you will be viewing months and sometimes years of work. With all that time, dreams and work being compressed into minutes. However, usually you are too tired to appreciate the moment.

- **Editing** is splicing or joining the film footage together in the proper sequence. If the film was shot in sequence and there were no mistakes, the only editing required will be in the negative cutting. Otherwise you will have to physically edit your film to fit the exposure sheets.

- **Final sound mix.** If it has not been done, put all the sound elements together as one track. Today the final track has to be transferred to a magnetic track.

- **Interlock.** Viewing the workprint together, in sync, with the final mix sound track. This is the final check to make sure it all works. If not:

- **Reshoots** if needed and then redoing steps one through four.

- **Locking the film.** This means there are no more changes. The film is finished.

- **Negative cut.** Preparing the developed film for the final-composite print by having the negative edited to its final form for processing by the laboratory.

---

1. As mentioned in the Acknowledgements, the author completed the manuscript sometime around 2007 and the text has not been updated for accuracy. All statements reflect the belief of the author at the time of authorship and may, or may not, reflect current reality.

- **Optical track.** The magnetic sound track is processed by the laboratory into an optical track that is used for the sound answer print.
- **Answer print.** This is the first print of the finished film. The negative cut and the optical sound are combined in a laboratory for a composite print that has sound and picture on the same piece of film.
- **Screening** the composite answer print. A strange mixture of agony, triumph and fatigue that is experienced only by people who have done their own animated films.
- **Duplication.** To make copies of your film as film, video or a digital format such as DVD.
- **Distribution.** Seeing that the film gets to its intended audience.
- **Storage.** The art and materials of the film preserved for the future or for Christmas gifts.

A more detailed look at the 13 stages of post-production follows.

Viewing

You now view your filmed animation for the first time. It is best to do it in a projection room. If there is no screening room available, a flatbed or moviola will have to do. This is quite an experience. Usually all you want to see at this point is an image on the screen that is a properly exposed image without scratches, and you forget the rest of the film. One function of the viewing will be to check for mistakes or any major technical flaws, and deciding if reshoots can be done within your time and money limits. If reshoots cannot be done, then you will have to live with the mistakes. But try to look at the film objectively and not just look at the mistakes. See how the timing, editing and animation work. If you have to do reshoots, you can also change anything else that does not work or is questionable, especially sound. After you have looked at the silent footage, look at it with the sound as soon as possible. It will look quite different and as a rule will play better with sound. Sound not only will complete the film but it can change the timing of the visuals, making the slow parts faster and the fast parts slower.

Editing

The tools you need for editing are:
- The workprint and the sound on film, usually a magnetic track.
- Leader. Leader is film without an image. It can be black, clear or sort of a grey.
- Splicer. There are two kinds of splicers, a tape splicer for editing your workprint and magnetic track and a hot splicer for the negative cutting.
- Tape. Mylar tape is used for holding the cut film together. Mylar tape has precut sprocket holes so the edits can go through the projection systems.
- Film cement. Used for hot splicing.
- Equipment that will allow you to view as you are running film and hear your sound track

at the same time. This could be a flatbed, a moviola, an interlock projection system or a sync block with a sound pickup.

- An editing table with a light box and rewinds.
- Reels and cores. A special reel, called a split reel, allows you to keep your film on cores so that you don't need reels.
- Editing gloves (fig. 11-1), razor blade, regular white tape, Sharpie and a loupe (a handheld optical device that magnifies the frame) are some of the little extra stuff needed.

The mechanics of editing at this stage involve cutting and joining together with Mylar tape two pieces of film, using a film splicer on an editing table. This process is called splicing. A film needs to be edited when:

- The film was shot in sequence with no mistakes and the only editing to do is adding about 10 to 12 feet of heads and tails leader on both the picture and sound for threading up both of them for interlock viewing. That amount of leader footage is needed to allow the machines to come up to operating speed. The sync marks or punches are made on this leader. Enough extra film or magnetic track could serve as leader.
- The shots need to be assembled in the correct order. This happens when the film is shot out of sequence.
- The shots need to be changed, either shortened, repositioned or replaced. If you need to add footage for timing purposes, to sync up to sound or to give the time of shots to come, you can temporarily cut in blank or black leader.
- The film needs to edited like a live-action film. This is required when you did not pre-edit the film and therefore must post-edit it as in live action. This occurs in these forms of animation: 3D stop motion and computer animation. It also occurs in experimental animation when the result is unknown and post-editing becomes part of the experimental process. Examples of editing in experimental films are James Whitney's computer-assisted motion control films *Lapis* and *Yantra* released in the the 1950s and 1960s.
- The final cutting of the film is the negative cutting stage, discussed later in this chapter.

Editing is cutting and splicing (taping together) the actual film into the proper sequence. If there is a need to do extensive film editing, it may be faster to use one of the non-linear digital computing units but then the film has to be telecined to digital, which can be expensive. Non-linear editing is done in film and digital editing. Non-linear editing means that in the traditional film or the computer editing, individual shots (units) can be inserted and reinserted at will and the total length of the film will change accordingly. This process is very flexible and if done digitally it is very fast.

Linear editing is done on tape. The shots are not cut in but are recorded on the running tape. When you put in a new shot in the middle of a tape, you will record over existing images, losing that shot and changing the timing of the rest of the tape. There are technical ways, by doing some form of A & B editing, to achieve non-linear editing but it is not as flexible as film/digital. Tape and film editing is being replaced by the digital.

Reshoots are changes that are re-filmed for aesthetic or technical concerns. Always do your reshoots after you have looked at your film with the sound, as you may want to make some additional changes in the film based on the sound or change your sound. Reshoots can get expensive and take up critical time as you have to cut in the reshoots, check the sync and again look at the interlock. You may have to go with a flawed film if you have no time for corrections.

Final Sound

The range of sound work at this point can range from none to doing your complete sound. If you have all your sound mixed together on magnetic track, you can go directly to interlock. If you have to do some or all of your sound, then it must be completed before you can go to the interlock stage. This could delay the post-production process, though not necessarily. For instance, when inexpensive children's TV programming comes back from overseas, the editing in of generic music and effects tracks (M & E tracks) can take just a few hours, especially if there is a broadcasting deadline. The final stage of the final sound, also called the "final mix," is all the sound together on one track. Sometimes after viewing the sound track with the finished workprint you may decide to remix the track. A common reason for doing this is that the music or effects are too loud and the audience cannot hear the spoken words. Today the final sound needs to be on magnetic track for transfer to optical track. In the future, it should be possible to go from the digital to the optical without doing a magnetic track.

Interlock

This is when you see the complete film, picture and sound together, for the first time. After you have the leader on the heads and tails of the workprint and the magnetic track, you will need to sync up your workprint and magnetic track on an editing unit like a flatbed. A flatbed is a one-person viewing and editing system. There are others systems like a flatbed that are mentioned above, and any one will do. After you have run the picture and sound back and forth until they are in sync, you will need to punch a small hole or mark with a Sharpie the film and magnetic track leader at the same point about six to 10 feet before the first picture and sound. This will be your editor's or dead sync, and all you will need to do to run picture and sound together is to line up the holes or x mark in whatever machine. A side note here: "Printer's sync" is done by the labs for composite films, as the sound exciter lamp or sound pickup is located ahead of the picture projection system for composite projection. Therefore, the lab will take the sound and move it ahead of the picture for 26 frames in 16mm so the film will be in sync when projected.

It is important to always project the film in interlock in a mix room or with a regular screening projection system. Only by seeing it on a large screen with a good sound system can you see or hear any tiny glitches that you would not see or hear on a flatbed, and if your film goes to composite with them you will either have to live with them or get a new composite print after redoing part of your film.

Locking the Film

After the final viewing of the final workprint and magnetic sound, the OK is given to go to composite, the film in its final unchangeable form. This can be very scary, as what you have is the way it is always going to be. Sometimes this stage is called "locking the film," as the film will not be altered. Next is the laboratory process for the composite film or tape.

Negative Cut

This is the preparing of the developed negative film for the final composite print by having the negative edited or cut to conform to its final form that is needed for laboratory processing (fig. 8-1). In negative editing, the film is joined together using a hot splicer and glue so that you will not see the edges of the tapelines on the composite print. If you have no editing in your film, all the negative cutter will have to do is put on academy leader. If you have one cut, you will have to do A and B rolls. You can do the negative cutting yourself, but it usually takes knowledge of both splicing and, in 16mm, how to do A and B rolls. It is usually easier to take it to a person who does negative cutting. The academy leader is put on the negative so the laboratory can sync up the picture and sound tracks and the projectionists can sync up changeovers. The number 2 on the academy is the picture sync and is 48 frames before your first picture. This is synced up to a "pop" on your optical track. The pop is put on your magnetic track and transferred by the laboratory to the optical track. The negative cutter needs a synced (to the sound) workprint and the camera negative assembled or not.

Optical Sound Track

It is also necessary today to have an optical sound track made from your synced magnetic sound track. This is because film projectors can only play optical sound. You need to take the synced magnetic track to an optical sound house or a laboratory to have this done. Be sure to check with them if it is to be "A" or "B" wind (emulsion in or out). After the negative is cut and final optical sound made, they are taken to a laboratory to be turned into a finished film. You can take the materials or let the negative cutter and optical sound people do it for you.

The Finished Film

The laboratory will first make a composite first answer print. The first answer print is to be viewed by you and a color timer from the laboratory so that any color corrections can be made and the film will have a balanced color look. Working with a color timer for color corrections is normally needed for live-action films, but not always for animated films. If your film has been shot on an animation crane and the lighting did not change and the color on the workprint looked good, you can tell the laboratory just to use the timing numbers used for your workprint (or bring the workprint in) and avoid the time delay of getting a second answer print. If you shot a 3D object animated film, you should time it as you are doing live-action lighting. Some laboratories will offer to make you a low-contrast print; I have found them not necessary. After you have viewed and approved the first answer print at the laboratory, a master video copy should be made before the film is projected again. Anytime a print is projected there is a chance of scratching the film.

Screening the composite print. The viewing at the laboratory is one experience and the viewing with an audience is another. Both are a strange mixture of agony, triumph and fatigue that is experienced only by people who have done their own animated films. Hopefully you will laugh with delight or cry with joy, though I must confess that when I see a film of mine for the first time with an audience, I have the overwhelming desire to close my eyes until it's over. The other side of the coin is when you have viewed your film many times and looking at it has become pure torture (sometimes I think hell for filmmakers is being locked in a room and being forced to see your films and all their mistakes over and over again). The finished film will only be a percentage of what you imagined it to be when you started. Given the nature of the animated film-making process, you are lucky if you get 50 percent of your original vision on the screen. However, the important reality is that your film is now done. Fame, fortune and the true sense of artistic achievement shall now be yours. But alas, you still have three more things to do before you can let the film go. If the film is not going through the above process but coming out digitally as a composite in a digital format, you still must go through the last three steps.

Duplication

After you have approved the final answer print and you want more prints, you would order release prints that are much less expensive. If you plan to make more than one print, called release prints, you will need to make a copy, a printing master, of the camera original. This will protect your original film from being damaged or worn when making prints. It used to be that you could make about 50 release prints from a printing master. If you are going to duplicate your film on video or DVD, you will need to make a master tape of your film from which to make the duplicate tapes. In today's technology, it is best to have the film telecined (transferred) to a master digital. You need to find a laboratory that specializes in telecining film to tape. Once you have this, as many VHS or DVD copies can be made as needed.

Distribution

This will be covered in detail in the next chapter, especially festivals.

Storage

Storage and preservation of the negative film and optical sound track are essential if you want to make prints of your film in the future. They should be kept in a dry, temperature-controlled environment. The laboratory will store the printing materials as long as you are making prints, but when you stop ordering they will call and ask you to come by and pick up the materials. Try to find a professional film storage vault for the negative and track rather than the back of a closet. Storage of the art is a personal decision; the cels and other art may be packaged and safely stored and will last years until thrown away or become collector's items when you grow to be a legendary figure.[2] Today, motion picture film is the best preservation and storage format available (fig. 8-2). Digital and electronic formats are too temporal and fragile but if that is all you have, that is all you have. Sound can be stored digitally.

A way today of perhaps combining the best of the traditional and the digital for teaching, is to shoot the film on the animation crane or a camera for stop motion or experimental and transfer the film via a telecine to the digital. With the digital film in the computer, sync it to the sound and transfer the composite digital to a DVD or tape.

The post-production of the digital is discussed in Chapter 12.

The total cost of the above should be between $300 and $1,400, depending on where you live and the length of the film. Everyone who has foolishly tried to save a few dollars by not following this tried-and-true path has ended up spending hundreds more of the old greenbacks.

It will take between three days and three weeks to get numbers one to 13 done, depending on location and complications.

Fame, fortune and the true sense of artistic achievement shall be yours.
My hovercraft is full of eels.[3]
Dan- 8/05

---

2. Or write a book.

3. The case could be made that the author intended, "My hovercraft is full of cels." Much of the text of this book when I first got it existed only as written text and had to be OCRed, and in OCR 'cels' often gets scanned to 'eels.' Alas, the written text does not indicate that the author wrote 'My hovercraft is full of cels,' although I really wish the author had written that. However, knowing the author's style, I feel good about this choice.

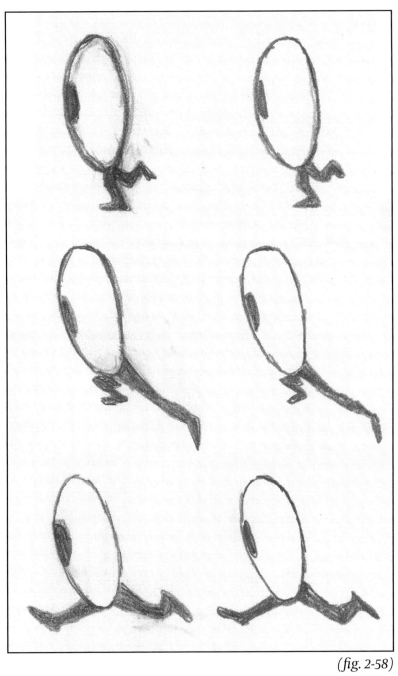

(fig. 2-58)

CHAPTER 9

(fig. 13-3)

DISTRIBUTION[1]

This is for your independent film -- not a series or features that you are pitching.

General

Your independent film is in composite, in the film can, done! Is it over? Not by a long shot if you believe in Shirley Clarke's philosophy that filmmaking is divided into three parts. The first part is the idea, funding and story (board) for the film. The second part is the making of the film. The third part is the distribution or getting your film in front of an audience. First, a list of rewards you will receive when making your own animated film:

- You will never lose the knowledge you have gained by making your own film.
- The personal satisfaction that you did an individual creative act. It can be quite a rush and a deep-seated sense of personal pride. And you own the film.
- Your film can be sent to festivals, and if accepted you will gain recognition, possibly money and free room and board at the festival, and knowledge that people are being affected by your vision on film.
- Distribution of your film by yourself or a distributing company, which can bring you recognition, money and the knowledge that the film is communicating your vision, sometimes to millions of people. With the advent of tape and digital film, distribution is minimal but still possible. Distribution on the web, on your own website where you can sell it or give it out free or on a service like YouTube where it will be free.

---

1. As mentioned in the Acknowledgements, the author completed the manuscript sometime around 2007 and the text has not been updated for accuracy. All statements reflect the belief of the author at the time of authorship and may, or may not, reflect current reality.

- It can be part of your portfolio, which can help you in a number of ways. A portfolio can generate support for your next film; help you get a contract to make a commissioned film (short, commercial, series, etc.); or help you to find employment.

Make sure the copyright is on the film before you start the distribution process. (fig. add. 1-1)

THE DISTRIBUTION PATHWAYS
Invited Screenings

The first distribution of your film will probably be a private or invited screening. Invited screenings can either be done on film, video or digital in a theater, or on video in an office or a home. The best-quality screening venue is a theatrical film showing on a large screen. The film will never look so good. If you made your film in a school, a screening should be part of your education and is an ideal way to get a large public screening at a low cost. Otherwise a theatrical screening can be quite expensive. To keep costs down, find out the different venues in your areas that project film and try to work out an inexpensive rental at an off-hour time. If you secure a location, invite all the people you can, be sure to mail the invitations early and watch that you don't conflict with an important date. A party before or after is a good way to get people to attend and/or leave them in a good mood. If your film's running time is too short to run by itself, try booking it with several other shorts and their filmmakers who could do a question and answer session afterward. Try to package it as a special event with a clever title. A screening for educational, medical or humorous films would give you a specific audience to invite.

Agents, Press Agents and Self-Promotion

Talent agents are a rather new phenomenon in the professional animation field. Up to about 12 years, ago animation was small and constant enough for most animators to know enough other animators to network with for getting jobs, find out who was hiring and what were the going salaries (the union rate sets the standards). Most people had friends or contacts and they would help each other. It still works that way to a large extent. For today's students, peers will often constitute their networks after graduation. But during the last 12 years with the expansion of animation through prime-time TV, features that could appeal to adults as well as children, expansion of animation to cable, computer animation and interactive anima-tion, the professional field is much larger and more fluid. The need for talent agents began to appear. A talent agent is a professional who will represent his/her client in employment and project placement (selling a TV series). They can act in the capacity of finding employ-ment for the client, but more often they will review the contracts and negotiate better terms for their client. For project placement (selling a series to a network) they will take an active role in seeking out interested producers or studios and doing the endless meetings, and if a sale is made they will review and negotiate the contract terms for their client. They will also write contracts for their clients. In contract reviews they will often work with lawyers, who are prohibited under California law from working as agents unless they are certified by the state as a talent agent. The rates will vary; for employment a talent agent receives a percentage up to 20 percent of the employment contract, possibly just for the first year. For projects, they will receive between 10 percent and 30 percent depending on the amount of work done. An example of a 10 perent commission would be if the creator has essentially sold the show and the agent's role is coming in at the end and wrapping things up. If the agents spend years working on selling the project they could get 30 percent. Agents are found in Los Angeles and perhaps New York. To have an agent represent you or your film depends on two things, do you want one and can you get one. If you are involved with goodly amounts of money and you are not a killer businessperson (most animators aren't), an agent can be an important person to have on your side. A talent agent's decision to represent you will be based on the agent's assessment of your marketability or potential. If you would like more information on talent agencies in California, you can write to the Department of Industrial Relations, Division of Labor Standards Enforcement, P.O. Box 420613, San Francisco, CA 94142 and ask for their pamphlets on "Law Relating to Talent Agencies" and the "Talent Agency License."[2]

Publicity is another consideration in distribution. If you have a heavy hit on your hands and know what you want to do as your next career move, hiring a public relations person may be beneficial in getting your name in the press and TV. Generally you will know when you need a press agent. If you feel a little extra publicity will help, you can do your own public relations work or self-promotion.

Self-promotion can range from putting your credits on your film to taking credit for someone else's film. It can extend from doing very little to doing anything that will promote your film or yourself, and I mean anything. There are well-known people today who I know whose partial claim to fame is based on self-promotion based on untruths about their pasts. To help you from believing these self-promotion myths, I would suggest that you believe only 50 percent of what is written about anyone in animation, and if they wrote it 20 percent. Some people do not have the personality to promote themselves but with others that is no problem. I know I always find it extremely embarrassing and feel it is not morally right to promote myself. I am mortified when people praise me. I can handle everything but praise, so I have been completely remiss in pushing myself. Other people do not have this concern. Which one is a personality defect? Which one are you? Animators tend to speak through their films and are reticent to aggressively push themselves and their egos. Their motto could be: I love to make them but hate to show them.

---

2. These items are available with these titles online as well.

Perhaps you can do some of the minor stuff, such as contacting the local news people and TV people to mention you or your film. Make a list of people to contact, and write promotional material on your film and send it out as e-mail. Develop a website and put a clip of your film on it along with any promotional material. See if you can get a human-interest story done on you by contacting the local papers. To move up to the next level, you should become aware if there are any events (parties, conferences) that can help you, and then muscle or sneak your way in. If you go to a festival, you will see all sorts of promotions going on. This is a spillover of the public relations and publicity that is associated with Hollywood and the entire entertainment field. Even in the independent film world where self-promotion can be justified by artistic principles, strong self-promotion exists. I remember back in the 1970s three moderately successful people in their fields, one in film, one in writing and one in painting, made a pact to mention each other's names whenever there was an interview, article or any type of exposure for one of them. They did and it worked, and within two years all three were abulously famous. Self-promotion is part of the American Dream. Or as Robert Benchley said, "Scrape off the tinsel of Hollywood and you will get to the real tinsel underneath."[3]

Festivals

Festivals are an excellent way to get your film before an audience and acquire exposure (fig. 9-1). Start entering them as soon as your film is finished (fig. 9-2). The downside to festivals is when your film is not accepted and your ego suffers. But you have to remember there are festivals with judges who do not recognize quality work. The upside is that it is very good for your ego if the judges are brilliant, know quality and accept your film (fig. 9-3). If they invite you to attend and you accept, it can be fun and a reward for all your hard work, with people telling you how much they love your film and how good you are. But always keep in mind the Thomas Mitchell story related elsewhere, "If you believe someone when they tell you you are good, you will have to believe them when they tell you you are bad."[4]

There are many types of festivals for all different kinds of films (fig. 9-4). Doing well on the festival circuit often depends on entering your film into a festival where your film will stand a chance to be selected. For a student or first animated film, these are the best kinds of festivals to enter: student film festivals with an animation category and animation festivals with student categories. The next best are any festivals that have an animation or a student category, which most do. Local or regional festivals are normally not as competitive as national or international. Regional festivals may favor that region and in-

---

3. Actually what I found was a similar quote attributed to Oscar Levant, "Strip away the phony tinsel of Hollywood and you will find the real tinsel underneath." "Oscar Levant Quotes." Quotes.net. STANDS4 LLC, 2016. Web. 12 OCT. 2016.

4. As I recall, Thomas Mitchell was the uncle to Dad's good friend Bob Mitchell, and Dad got this story from Bob.

ternational festivals may favor the host country or geographical area. Check to make sure that there are not restrictions on entering, gender being one. There are festivals that have a particular theme or subject area such as Peace or World Hunger. Other festivals have a slant toward a particular national, minority or sexual orientated group. Still other festivals are geared toward commercials; educational, industrial and medical films; or computer work. Make sure the film is in the right category. The choices usually are: animation (often meaning funny), experimental (but still done in animation) or documentary (again done in animation, but the subject is documentary or historical). Choose carefully. Information on festivals can be found in publications, especially animation publications, on the web, mailings from festivals you have entered and through animation organizations (ASIFA, SAS).[5] On the web, withoutabox.com[6] is an excellent source for festivals in general, including animation. You can build your own database as you enter different festivals. If you find out about a festival but it is too late to enter, put it in your database or file for next year. A two- or three-year cycle of entering festivals is about the limit as most festivals have a restriction that the film has to be made in the last two years to be eligible. This is why some filmmakers copyright their films for the next year if they finish late in the year. Once you get into a few festivals, they may start calling you and in some cases even guarantee a screening.

There are general expenses incurred in entering festivals. Most festivals charge an entry fee for students and first-time short filmmakers in the $15.00 to $30.00 range. There is also the cost of the VHS copies to be sent to the selection judges. If the festival doesn't return the tapes, it may not be worth the bother and cost of sending along the prepaid return mailing materials, as tapes can be very inexpensive. You should factor in a cost of one tape per festival. You will need to send a 16mm print, a Beta or a digital copy if your film is selected for the festival. The festival will inform you of their needs. The festival normally returns the film or the digital copy. However, there is a several month turn-around period, so you may need several 16mm or digital copies if you enter a number of festivals and your film does well. Digital copies seem to be becoming the preferred way of projection. I would not order extra 16 mm copies until your film is accepted into a couple of festivals. Most labs have a cost reduction if you order two or more release prints at one time. You have the cost of labeling the prints and tapes and their containers. The cost of mailing them out can rise if you have to do an overnight mailing, so mail early and look for special rates at the Post Office. There are film shipping agents for international festivals, but I have found the U. S. mail to be just fine and not as expensive. The cost of entering many festivals could run into the low hundreds of dollars. But you should know after submitting to a few select festivals whether your film is a festival-type film or not. If it is a festival film, it is money well spent. To me, a festival film is

---

5. For ASIFA http://www.animation-festivals.com/asifa-accredited/. SAS does not have this information on their website, and I emailed SAS directly and was told by Robert Musberger that they currently do not have that information. They did say some very nice things about my Dad, though.

6. This link currently works.

one that gets into roughly 40 percent of the festivals entered. If your film is not getting into any but a few small festivals, it may not be worthwhile to continue to enter festivals.

The cost in time breaks down this way: making film or digital prints, videotapes or DVDs; getting the shipping containers for tapes and films; filling out the addresses and entry forms; mailing; and keeping a record of the sending and receiving back of tapes and films. You should also keep lists of festivals entered and ones to enter, and keep track of your awards and put them in your vitae. When you fill out and send the forms, the festival will often ask for a picture of you and a reproduction of some art from the film. A brief biography and a synopsis of the film are also normal requests. You could be asked for a list of the festivals you have shown in, awards received and whether this is the debut screening. Festivals seem to love to have a world premiere of any film and sometimes grand prizewinners. On the other hand, some festival directors may feel if a film has been into a multitude of festivals it's not fresh or new and will not consider screening it.

Web festivals were another choice, but they disappeared along with web distribution for a while but now seem to be coming back as the technology improves (fig. 9-5). You should consider exhausting the film festival circuit before showing your film on the web to a general audience, as it could become overexposed and that may hurt your chances of getting into film festivals. There is also the concern of unauthorized tape copies being made from broadcasting on the web.

Occasionally someone may be playing loose with the word "festival." Be concerned if someone calls and invites you to enter their festival for a large amount of money ($300 to $600). The question here is: Is it a legitimate festival or rather a festival for profit (theirs)? I remember once back in the 1960s a festival was announced in Argentina with large cash prizes, free trip there and back, etc. Everyone sent his or her films. The deadline came and went and no communication was received from the festival and none ever was. It turned out one person just wanted a great collection of the best short films in the world for that year. He got them, as no one wanted to go to Argentina and try to get his or her film back. That also happened a couple of years later with a person in Boston. It's not too bad today with videotape, but those were two good 16mm prints that I lost.

If you want to make a film to get into festivals and win awards, here are some of the points you should consider: There are two basic types of festivals, one gives awards, the other one doesn't. In a festival (it could be called an exposition) that does not give awards, the award comes from the honor of having your film screened. This type of festival has only one jury, a selection jury. In a festival that gives awards, there are two separate juries that your film will have to pass to receive an award. The first jury is the selection jury, who reduces the entries down to a predetermined time or number that will constitute the final program and from which the final or awards jury will choose the winners. The selection jury will often have to look at hundreds of films, a very exhausting process. To save their eyes and brains, they will usually agree to stop a film if it looks like it has no chance of being selected. An example of this process is the Academy Awards' selection of films other than features, where the judges are given small flashlights. When a predetermined number of lights are turned on, the film is stopped and they go on to the next film. You should plan your film so that it will grab the audience's attention in the first minute; if you don't, it may not be around for the second minute. Keeping your film short means that it will have more chance to get in, as screening time in a festival is limited and the festival will often choose to screen three to four shorts instead of one long film of the same quality. Ditto for funny: Any festival director likes short funny films that will keep the audience awake. The standards of quality will vary from festival to festival. Sometimes there are guidelines given to the judges by the festival. If not, the jury will set the guiding principles for judging or leave it up to their individual standards. Personal prejudices (for abstract films and against narrative) and doing a favor for a friend every now and then will weigh into the judging process.

The final judging is regularly done during the festival itself and this also puts a time pressure on the judges (fig. 9-6). Frequently they will debate all through the night the day before presenting the winners. There may be a few films each year that are of such a high quality that they will win a majority of the awards. But generally there is a lot of discussion among the jurors. The one way that I have found to ease the tension is to let each judge pick his or her own winner after the established winning categories have been chosen. This whole process is not perfect but is usually fair. A practice that is becoming popular, especially in local festivals, is to have the audience choose one winner. Getting into festivals, and especially getting a prize, can really make you feel on top of the world.

The screening of your film, especially in festivals, can be an important part of your curriculum vitae for teaching animation, especially if there are any reviews or articles of the festival (fig. 9-7). There are academic associations, UFVA[7] being one, that at its yearly conference will screen your film and have a discussion afterward, much like presenting a paper at a conference.

Since the distribution of short animated films is in transition, festivals become an important way of getting your film before an audience and in finding a distributor. Perhaps festivals someday will form a distribution system for short animated films. But before we speculate on the future of distribution, let us examine the distribution of short animated films at the present time.

Distribution of the Short Animated Film

The distributing or putting your film out in the various markets available for the sales and

---

7. University Film and Video Association.

rental income is usually done by a distribution company (fig. 9-8). They will handle your film for a price (more on that later). You can distribute your film yourself, but it is a full-time job and the filmmakers I have known who tried to distribute their own films ended up becoming distributors. Unfortunately, today there are not that many distributors for short films as there were in the past. To understand why, we must examine the history of the short animated independent film, which has taken several distinct turns in the last 50 years. After the end of the Second World War, the use of 16mm film became widespread as a distribution form. Educational, industrial and short films could be shown wherever there was a 16mm projector. These were available at schools, businesses and small venues such as film societies. It was rare that a private home would have 16mm equipment. For home viewing there was the silent 8mm film. This period of 16mm distribution peaked in the 1970s and there were a number of 16mm distributors. Animated films for animation's sake could be sold and rented, and provided a small steady income and audience for the filmmaker. Several reasons brought this halcyon period to an end. The advent of video was the major factor; tapes were copied and passed around for free, tapes were less expensive, and had a smaller profit margin (you could buy a feature for $29.95 at the newly emerging video stores). Also lost was the revenue for the replacement cost of 16mm film breakage. At the same time there were limits set on property taxes, which led to cutbacks of the arts and film usage in schools. After Proposition 13, the reduction of property taxes passed in California (1971), the Los Angeles Unified School District, the largest district in buying 16mm films, dumped all their 16mm equipment and stopped buying films. Over the years other events contributed to the collapse, such as tape distribution. UHF TV and cable TV gave only minimal support to short film distribution. Videotape stores did distribute short animation, but limited distribution almost exclusively to Hollywood films. Also, the market became more competitive as increasing numbers of filmmakers appeared (thanks to film schools and technology). People increased their TV viewing and were less prone to see films, except for features, outside of their living rooms.

In the 1990s distribution on the web held great promise. Many animators signed on only to end up worse than they were before. They had signed a seven-year exclusive contract and now that the web distribution and screening (streaming) had gone belly up, the filmmakers ended up with a distributor who is out of business and a contract that does not allow them to take their film to any other distributor or distribute it themselves. To make matters worse, unless this is prohibited in the contract, the web distributors could also try to gain some profit by selling your film to a third party where you would have no rights.

Today there are several approaches you can take to distribution. To find out where the distributors are, check the web: http://www.videouniversity.com/distribs.html[8] has lists of distributors, mainly for specialty markets. You can also check websites to see if there are distributors

8. I think the author means this website https://www.videouniversity.com/directories/video-and-film-distributors/

224

handling your kind of film. There are theatrical distributors who will put together a series of short animated films and "four wall" them (renting the theater for the night and keeping all the money from admission). Their program is typically built around a theme in the vein of "The Best in World Animation" or for special audiences like the Spike and Mike's "Sick and Twisted" series. Video and record stores will usually only carry the major studios or a TV series tape as shelf space is at a premium. It is hard for a small distributor to get into a store, though there are exceptions and some are trying. If your film fits into the core curriculum that is taught in schools, whether you planned it or not, it could get a decent distribution. Check on this through a distributor or a website. If you are in the independent non-commercial, experimental film movement the two distributors are The NY Film-Makers' Coop in New York and the Canyon Cinema in San Francisco. Overseas distributors seem to be healthier; the only distributor making money for me today is in France (fig. 9-9).

For the future of short animated film distribution, about the best we can do now is hang in there until funding or new ways of distribution are found. Since film schools seem to be the major producers of short animated films, perhaps one day they can form a distribution circuit. If the technical concerns of the web can be solved and quality work can be transmitted at an affordable cost, perhaps we can distribute our own films and break the current monopoly that the media giants have on distribution. Short animated films will continue to be made as long as creative people need to put their visions on film. The current lack of major distribution will not last.

Below is a quick reference of the areas of distribution for the short animated film whether it is done in the traditional or computer animation technique. Any of these venues could work for the sale or rental of your film. Take into account the subject matter of your films as that can put you into one of these areas whether you planned it or not.

Theatrical: Festivals where a touring collection of short films is the most common approach. Screening a short with the feature is done in rare circumstances.

TV: Independent animation is often broadcast on programming that features new or short films. Public TV and cable are the best bets for this kind of programming.

Retail outlets, catalogues or websites: Cassettes/DVD: DVD is slowly replacing cassettes as the delivery system for the direct sale or rental of animation. Catalogues and emerging websites carry the bulk of this type of distribution.

Educational: Schools, museums and community organizations. The medical or health areas are a very important part of this distribution.

Special interest groups or hobbies: This is mostly a live-action area, surfing films, etc., but animated films are used occasionally.

Industrial/Corporate: As a motivation or training tool.

Religious: Religious organizations can have their own distributors and distribution system.

Websites: Whether streaming films or an interactive project, you can set up your own website for distribution. How to make money by doing this still has to be figured out. Did I mention that festivals are a good way to find a distributor?

Consider distributing your characters or film ideas in other forms such as children's books, coffee mugs, comic strips or panels. Or promote your short film as a genesis for a TV series, a feature and a TV special. A few years ago Hanna-Barbara sponsored the making of a number of short films and aired them. The ones that proved popular by the audience's reactions were made into TV series. They contacted me to see if any of my students were interested. One was, who had made a film, *Johnny Bravo*, in class. The people in development liked his film and hired him as a director to develop a series based on his film. Today it is a successful series. In return for the opportunity, the studio had the rights to the film and the series. If your film has a strong style (animating oil paintings) or a technical breakthrough (kinestasis), a sponsor or studio may want you to produce work in the same style or technique.

Contracts for Distribution

The best contract for you to get is a non-exclusive contract, which means that no one distributor controls the film. Any non-exclusive contract that is for a limited venue (theatrical, TV, web), a limited time of contract (a renewable two to three years) and designated countries or continents is a good contract for you. Only accept a written contract. Having more than one general distributor or different distributors for different venues, countries or different formats gives you more sources of revenue.

The best contract for a distributor is one that gives them the exclusive ownership of your film in perpetuity in all formats throughout the known universe. If you have to accept an exclusive contract, you must be concerned that your film just doesn't sit on a shelf through their lack of effort that can occur through change of ownership or financial insolvency. To prevent your film from forever being buried, you should put a best-efforts clause in your contract and always have a negative of your film in your possession. A best-efforts clause is a clause in the contract that returns the rights of your film to you if the distributor doesn't fulfill certain obligations, such as number of prints sold or rented per year or a certain level of income maintained, or if they go out of business. Be concerned if they can resell the rights to another company, or if they do, make sure you have approval of the sale and share in the profits or ask that that clause be removed. Remember that a contract is just the opening of negotiations. Read it very carefully, delete what you do not want and add what you do want. Send it back to them and start negotiating. The first contract you will receive is the opening contract offer that will ask for everything in the world. Of course, you are not expected to sign it unless you are a fool. Get your own lawyer, preferably one who knows contracts and animation, to help you. To illustrate, a student was ready to sign a contract recently, but when she consulted a lawyer she found that the contract gave the distributor the rights to all her films now and in the future. Another example, a student was just presented a contract that obliged him, out of his own pocket if necessary, to guarantee the distributor a $100 monthly income. Always check out the distributor. Are they honest? How much money can you realistically expect if you are taking a percentage? Ask for a list of their clients and customers and talk to them. If a distributor acts offended by contract negotiations or background checks, they are either just acting as part of the negotiations or upset because they are afraid that you will find out they are dishonest. Try not to negotiate a contract alone. An agent or a lawyer can be the best financial investment you can make.

Money and Distribution

How should you get paid for your film? You have three choices: the first is some variation of a one-time cash payment. Selling all rights for one sum, selling the rights to certain venues (theatrical, web, etc.) for one sum, selling or licensing for a certain number of play dates for varying sums (TV broadcast) are all possible. The second choice is to take a percentage of the revenue, through sales or rentals, generated by your film. The issues here are type of percentage and amount of percentage. The two kinds of percentage are gross and net. Gross is the total amount of money taken in before expenses. Net is the money left, if any, after the expenses have been deducted. Example of gross: If your contract calls for 20 percent of the gross and your film rents for $80, you would receive $16 from the distributor, who takes his expenses, including the film's costs, and profit out of the remaining 80 percent or $64. If your contract calls for net, the distributor can deduct all expenses he deems necessary and give you 20 percent of what is left. A percent of net can be a percent of nothing. You can always ask for an advance on the gross or net (if they won't do it on the net, watch out) and often that is the only money you will see. Always stipulate that you have access to the books and quarterly or yearly accounting statements. The third way is simple: You make the DVDs and sell them to the distributor for a profit and they double the price for their expenses and profit.

Taking a percentage of revenue or royalties gives you the best opportunity for making the most money, but also the most chance for no revenue whatsoever. A direct sale means that you will have at least some money in your pocket. Which choice to make for payment is up to you and your judgment of what your film is worth. You may have to make different choices if you have different distributors for different venues. Doing all this dealing can get very time-consuming and unpleasant, but it is very important because you are up against business people who deal in business and make money, not art. If you can't do all these business transactions, just don't give up and give your work away, but find someone you really trust or hire an attorney or agent to represent you.

One of the shocks to people selling their films is how little money the filmmakers get for the effort (fig. 9-10). Another shock is how many people make part of their living from the film-maker's work, ranging from the distributors to the network executives to the people who sell the popcorn. None of them would have that job if it weren't for the artist.

These are some typical methods for payment (revenue sharing) for different venues:

Broadcast TV/cable. You are paid by the broadcast. The licensing agreement will specify the number of times shown and the rate each time. The amount is usually less each time.

Web. A lump sum payment that only gives away the web rights is the best at present.

Theatrical film. In a theatrical release, your film will probably be part of a program of short films so the percentage has to be divided among several filmmakers. This can be done by length or the money is equally divided. I believe equal division is the fair way to go, and not because I make short films. Also in theatrical releases, if a theater owner or exhibitor is involved he or she normally takes 60 percentage of the box office gross, leaving the distributor with 40 percentage for himself and the filmmakers.

Educational/non-commercial screens. Rental payment for each screening or could be an outright purchase for a school or library.

Distributor. For a distributor who handles all venues for your work, your percentage will range from 50 percent with some cooperatives to 15 percent to 30 percent from most commercial distribution. Special distributors for special venues can have other arrangements. The percentages I refer to are percentages of gross. You can always bargain for better money.

When in doubt or if the people are too friendly, get a lawyer.

Your Reel

This is a collection of your films or clips of your films. It can be on tape or DVD, though most places that you will show it will only have cassette decks. Your reel is to show to prospective clients, employers, distributors, and financial or grant backers. It is a portfolio of your film work. A general rule for a reel or portfolio is to keep it short, as most people can usually tell if it's what they are looking for in a minute or two (they may be smart or just have the short attention spans that are current today). If you show too much for too long, you could be showing more of your lesser work and the basic rule in showing your work is "you are only as good as your worst piece." One way to keep it short is to have your best clips first, followed by your films if the viewers want to go on. I find that when you put anything in a viewing order, it is best to have your best last and your next best first and all the rest in between. Your reel should be directed toward the purpose of the viewing. If you are looking for character animation work, show full character animation, not beautiful layouts or background. You could have several reels specifically assembled for a particular purpose. Titles on your reel, with the essential information, can help place the viewer into your work immediately. This could be your name, the screening order, festivals won, etc.

Should you just drop off a tape of your reel or have them view it with you present? If at all possible, you should do the former and be there to answer questions and make an impression. Your presence will forestall any rude remarks people will make about your film, either deliberately (there will be politics in a studio that you will not know about) or because the person is a comedian. You can always tell them you have only one tape, and you need it the next day so you can't leave it. Only when you have no other options should you just drop off a tape.

A final word on distribution: ***Don't give up!***

(fig. 7-85)

229

(fig. 7-33)

CHAPTER 10

(fig. 6-6)

THE FOUR OTHER CATEGORIES OF ANIMATION[1]

This chapter is devoted to the first of the four other areas of animation. Two have been around since the beginning. They are:

- **3D Stop Motion Animation**
- **Animation as a Visual Effect in Live-Action Films**

The other two have arisen since the advent of the digital. They are:

- **Computer Animation**
- **Interactive Animation**

These four other areas of animation have as their foundation the basic principles of animation that have been presented in this book. Only the production processes of these other realms of animation differ when different materials and tools necessitate a change from the traditional process. Examples are: the addition of 3D lighting, to 3D stop motion, computer and interactive, and the differences in the development of idea and storyboard for interactive because the nature of interactivity involves a non-linear approach to the story rather than the normal linear structure. How the traditional production process has been adapted to the needs of these other forms of animation will be a subject of this chapter. There will be an overview of the different production processes with an in-depth analysis only when crucial, such as the use of 3D lighting in 3D and computer animation, or when the techniques

---

1. As mentioned in the Acknowledgements, the author completed the manuscript sometime around 2007 and the text has not been updated for accuracy. All statements reflect the belief of the author at the time of authorship and may, or may not, reflect current reality.

used to combine animation and live action in visual effects and the issues of non-linear communication in interactive animation are discussed.

The first area, 3D animation, has been intertwined with traditional 2D animation from the very creation of animation. It has the same relationship to traditional animation as sculpture does to drawing and painting in the plastic arts. The second subject, animation as a special effect in live-action film, has also been an animation genre since the start of film. Traditional and 3D animation are used in special effects. Today the predominance of animated special effects in live action is done with computer animation. The third section, computer animation, uses a new tool, the computer, to either assist in traditional animation or to do the greater part if not all of the animation. The fourth and last area, interactive, is animation that is used in the emerging interactive genre.

I. 3D STOP MOTION ANIMATION

3D animation is the filming of real 3D objects, typically a model of a character, in stop motion (single frame by single frame shooting). 3D stop motion animation is often called just stop motion animation (particularly in Hollywood) and is also referred to as model animation, table top animation, object animation and puppet animation. The variety of 3D animation is very broad. It can range from being the technique used to make a complete film, as in *The Nightmare Before Christmas* (1993), to having a limited role in a live-action film such as *King Kong* (1933). When it is used in a live-action film it is generally classified as a special or visual effect. This section will discuss what you need to know about 3D stop motion animation, whether it is a complete film or has a limited function in another genre of film.

3D stop motion animation has a multi-thousand-year-old history and tradition through its direct link to the puppet theater, whether hand, string or rod. This history and tradition continues through the 3D articulated puppet animation to today's 3D computer character animation, which is another form of 3D animation. When 3D computer animation first came out I thought it would supplant 3D animation, but instead of being relegated to history 3D animation is more popular than ever. Below is a review of current 3D animation.

The Major Categories of 3D Stop Motion Animation

- Articulated 3D puppets or models. They typically can be made out of plasticine (modeling clay), clay, cloth, rubber, paper or cast latex, and are usually supported by a movable skeleton of a metal ball and socket structure or wire, which is called an armature. Alternatively, they can be solid movable puppets made of wood, metal, or plastic. George Pal *Tubby the Tuba* (1947), Kihachiro Kawamoto *Oni* (1972), Nick Park *The Wrong Trousers* (1993), are examples of articulated 3D models. Another example is taken from the UCLA Falling Lizard Film *Pirates vs. Ninjas* (fig. 6-10).
- The animation of everyday objects or unusual items.

- Pixilation.
- Flat or semi-flat puppets or objects.

I will discuss the first category (articulated models) in detail and then the other categories briefly, as many items discussed in the 3D articulated model section also apply to their categories.

ARTICULATED MODELS

Articulated puppet models are the most popular form of 3D animation. The puppets are usually around 9 inches high. They can vary from 4 to 18inches in height if there is a need for a size contrast, such as having a huge monster and a little child in same shot. Puppets have been built from wood, metal, rubber, fabric, paper, leather, plastic, foam, latex, clay and plasticine (a modeling clay that doesn't harden). An articulated skeleton called an armature over which the outer material coating that forms the model is molded, sculpted or cast usually supports puppets. Another type is a solid model with articulated joints, like a theatrical puppet, articulated doll or toy soldier. Body movements, from basic to complex, are achieved with these articulated joints that mirror the living body. Movement not related to the joints, facial expressions for example, can be done in two ways, by shaping the covering material or by replacement. Clay or plasticine can be molded or sculpted to show animated facial emotions. Willie Hopkins' *Swat the Fly* (1916) is an early example of this clay manipulation. The other common way to animate features or action is by replacement. Replacement is simply replacing a new head, a new mouth or new eyes for the old one. George Pal's *Puppetoons* (1940s) are good examples of replacement puppet animation. Replacement is an example of adapting the tradition of the puppet theater to film. These two approaches, sculpturing and replacement, can be used together on the same model to create the animation. Other, less used, ways exist for animating expressions such as complex armatures with facial movements, such as eyelids opening and closing. Articulated animated models could be viewed as the next step in sculpting. It is also the basic model used for 3D computer character animation.

For puppets, the simplest armature is one made of wire. Thick, soft wire or several thin wires wrapped around them for strength are bent to the basic form or skeleton of the puppet. Wire armatures have a bad habit of breaking at a critical time. A more complex, reliable and flexible armature, credited with being first used by Willis O'Brien in *King Kong* (1933), is one based on metal ball and socket construction. The best armatures of this type would be made of light metal, with adjustable ball and socket units at the joints that can be loosened or tightened (Allen screws are good for this). These can either be made or purchased. They can be quite detailed and should always be adapted to fit the requirements of the character.

After the armature is built and working, it is covered with the material that will form the body of the puppet. When building the body, you will want to keep its weight down to prevent the model from being top-heavy, which will make it fall over and difficult to secure in place. To prevent this the covering can be of two or more levels. The first level would be the bulk of the body and very lightweight. A light resin or styrofoam could be used for this purpose. The basic lightweight body would then be covered with malleable material for the animating, like plasticine, for the top level. A simple example for a head would be a ping-pong ball covered with plasticine. Coloring, sculpting, molding, the adding of details such as eyes (white beads with a black dot for the pupil are always good) and clothing would then be done to the top level to complete the model. The covering could also be a full cast figure, perhaps cast in latex from a mold created by a wax or clay model. Latex is very flexible and can give you a good-looking surface, but it is difficult to cast properly. Some people have likened it to a religious ceremony. Other materials that can be used to cover the armature are: rubber, cloth, papier-mâché, etc.

For the second type, solid models, wood is the traditional material. Plastic or metal is also used. The joints, as well as the extremities, can be wire or the joints could be constructed as the joints are on movable dolls, toy soldiers or the wooden puppets used by artists. These manufactured movable puppets can also be used as an armature for building a new model, or resculptured and repainted into a new character puppet.

It is always a good idea to build two complete models of each puppet, so if one breaks while shooting you can keep on shooting. In the case of clay, more than one duplicate may be needed, as the models can get so dirty and beaten up that replacements are regularly needed.

There are also full-scale models that are controlled by technology and shot in real time. Whether it was a crane that raised the giant model fist of King Kong that held Fay Wray (she was terrified of falling off, as they were about 10 feet off the ground and King's thumb kept falling off, so her grabbing of his rubber covered rabbit fur wasn't acting but surviving)[2] to today's computer-controlled dragon's head, it is more often than not shot in real time to interact with live actors so that the entire scene can be shot in one take. One term used today for this approach is animatronics. Putting people into costumes to represent gorillas and monsters is a technique which we will not discuss as it is live action, which comes from the tradition of two actors who would don a donkey suit in vaudeville.

SETS

Indoor sets are usually built on a waist-high table at least 4x4 feet. The set should have enough space around it for you to move and animate the character as well as the lights and camera. The set, camera and lights should be secured solidly so that you will not bump into them and change their position during the production. Nails, gaffer's tape, glue or small sandbags are good for locking everything down that is not supposed to move.

The set is either built on the tabletop or on its own base, say a 4x4 feet piece of wood, which

---

2. I am unable to locate the source of this story.

rests on the tabletop (fig. 10-2). Having the set on its own base makes it portable and reusable. You may need access to the underside of the set if you are using magnets or nuts (a pegboard or a board with holes pre-drilled is needed for nut and bolt anchoring) to lock your models down into each of their positions as they move. The base could be made of corkboard if your character has pins in its feet or base to anchor it. A basic indoor set would have three walls and no top. Where the fourth wall would be is the space where you place your camera. The top is open for lighting, registration gear and access to characters for animating. If you are using different camera angles in the scene, you can have four removable walls so that you can have four walls to shoot against. For the props on your set, props are anything--chairs, lamps, etc.--on the set that does not move, be sure they are in scale to the set and characters unless they are distorted for a story point. Ready-made props can be found in toy, doll, party, model and model train stores. If you are building the props yourself, try to use materials like balsa wood or styrofoam that are easy to find and use. You always should secure your props to the set.

Sets of the outdoors are usually bigger and you will need some sort of cyclorama, a large screen that is used as a background for a stage setting. The most commonly used cycloramas are either neutral, black, shades of gray or a sky cyclorama, and if you have different camera angles they must curve around the set to some degree. The props may come from the same sources as indoor sets or they can be built. Hills and curved land can be made of chicken wire covered with papier-mâché or out of styrofoam. Some sets are so large that they will be built in sections so that you can walk through them. The simplest set is just a flat, neutral surface with a neutral cyclorama.

When building models and sets remember that anything can work, look in unusual places for finding solutions in kinds of materials and types of constructions. Look at the films of Jan Svankmajer and the Brothers Quay to see the possibilities of different approaches. Audiences love seeing animation done in new and different styles. One of the first 3D animated films was one of the most unusual, which used embalmed beetles and insects. That was *Camera-man's Revenge,* (1912) by Ladislaw Starewicz (later he changed it to Ladislas Starevich).

ANIMATING THE 3D MODEL

For animating or moving your model you can shoot on 1's or 2's. 1's are smoother but take twice the time, and if you are not careful it can cause too much activity in the animation. For most movements you can shoot on 2's and get away with it. Though shooting on 1's or 2's is maybe a matter of personal taste, so shoot some tests on 1's and then on 2's and see what you like best. The principles of animated movement that apply to 2D animation also apply to 3D animation. The principles of squash and stretch, anticipation, caricature and exaggeration, overlapping action, follow through, accents, arcs, etc., are all relevant. However, some methods of 2D animation cannot be used as you have a physical character. In 3D you cannot animate from key pose to key pose; do the two key poses and then the drawings inbetween as you do in 2D. Even with the technological advances mentioned below, where you can see or test your next move, you still have to animate straight ahead, and not knowing exactly where you will end up can add a sense of challenge or adventure to the process. You will still end up in key poses at some point, more than likely holds for accent and acting.

In 2D drawn animation you often end up moving the character parallel to the film plane, chiefly on pans, as it is time-consuming to animate in perspective. In 3D animation you can avoid this mechanical look as you have the ability to move the model in any angle to the film plane. You should make the most of this ability to move in perspective because it is a key difference between 2D and 3D animation. Of course it is more live-action like, and you may not want to move too far in that direction.

Beginning 3D animators often get bored and frustrated with the time it takes to animate a 3D character and shoot fewer positions to get the scene over with quickly. This is a common mistake that can make the action move too fast and perchance jerky, especially if you do not put in any holds or holds on key poses. Patience is a great gift for an animator.

For the changes in expression, or acting, we have discussed hand movements and the techniques of sculpting or replacement. For facial expressions the sculpting and replacement techniques are frequently combined. An example would be replacing a mouth position and sculpting it to match the rest of the face. Eye positions, or rather the positions of the pupils, can be done by replacement or rotating an eye model in its socket. You can be quite creative in finding solutions to animating expressions. Doug Chiang in his film *Mental Block (1985)* took color 35mm still pictures of his face expressing different emotions. Since he had planned the size of his head in the still to be the same size as the head of his clay puppet, all he had to do was cut out his head from the photo and slap it on the front of the clay head of his model when he needed a change in expression. It also allowed him to be the star in his 3D animated film.

For replacement 3D animation acting, George Pal would first do drawn pencil tests for the timing and expression before doing the models (fig. 5-52). From this pencil test he could then put down on his exposure sheets how many poses or movements, and how many and what replacements he needed for the shot. This would reduce the time and cost of building the replacement units and reshooting changes in the animation.

For the timing of 3D animation, you could do pencil tests (fig. 7-79) to do your exposure sheets or they could be based on your sound track and the animatic. On the exposure sheets, since you do not have numbered cels to refer to, you will just block in how many frames the action will be and just make sure that you do not end up at the final position with 100 frames to spare. You can just write in the frames for key movements in the action to help avoid this. When you have dialogue, you can write down the frame by frame instructions on the exposure sheets for the lip sync and then block in the basic movements by showing how many frames are needed for an action; i.e., a frown, a double take or a look of anger. You should always use this exposure sheet when you shoot. One thing you will need to consider when you shoot is how to register your model in space.

The registration of the 3D model in space, or keeping the model in place vertically from frame to frame so that it didn't wobble all over the place (unless you do a drunk as was done in *Closed Mondays*), used to be quite difficult. Keeping the model in space vertically refers to keeping the distance between the camera and the vertical centerline running through the model constant when you cannot see it while shooting. How do you tell if the top of the model is closer to the camera for one frame and then farther away on the next frame? In the old days, a combined vertical and horizontal pointing device could be swung into position to show the previous position and that would allow you to register the new position. Then the device would be adjusted to show the axis of the new position. Today you can use a digital camera and a computer with its playback capabilities to achieve the same result. This is achieved by capturing each shot in the computer as it is filmed. This will give you a registration system as you film. You can move to your next position on the computer and register it to the previous image showing on the monitor. Then you can shoot it and play it back to see if it works. This can be particularly helpful for the positions of Slo out Slo in. If you do not have a computer for this purpose, you can use a pencil test unit that will do single frame video. You can mark the last position of the model on the monitor screen (with a wipe-off marker) to register your new position. The use of computer or single frame video to record along as you shoot on film allows you to play back the completed shot to see if it needs to be reshot. When you had film only and had any doubts, you had to reshoot. This instant playback can save days in production time and worry.

The next concern in 3D animation is how do you keep your character from falling over all the time. Especially if the character is walking and has to have one foot off the ground at some point and you have to show the legs and therefore can't cheat and just compose the shot from the waist up. The first thing you do is to make the top (usually the head) as light as you can and then you make the legs and feet as big and as heavy as you can without looking too ugly. After you have your model as light and balanced as possible, you have to figure out how to anchor your character's feet to the base in some clever way (this is a problem sculptors have in supporting their statues). These are some of the ways that have been used in past films: using something sticky, like clay or Velcro to hold the bottom of the foot to the floor; using something that attaches the foot to the floor, like a bolt in the ankle and foot of the character that protrudes out and goes through a preset hole in the floor and is then secured by screwing on a nut with a washer; using a pin protruding from the foot to stick into a floor made of cork; using a magnet under the floor to secure the foot that has metal in it. Whatever the method used, you must set your camera angles so you do not show the anchoring device or the holes in the floor. For bolt and nut anchoring, this can mean constantly redoing the surface of the floor.

One way to get over the problem of anchoring is to shoot on angled glass with a background behind the glass. The glass is set on an angle like a drafting table at about 30 to 45 degrees with a painted or photographic background behind it. The camera is set up over the glass so that the film plane is parallel to the glass. The animator can sit between the glass and the camera to move the characters. Lighting can be a little tricky but it can be done. The models used for this style of animation are flattish, maybea half-inch to one inch thick, sort of a 2½D. These models do not need complex armature. The can fly or jump around without wires or hidden rods. Like 3D they can be animated by replacement, movable armature or sculpting techniques. This form of 3D is like traditional 2D animation as the plane of the film is parallel to the plane of the art. A variation of the use of glass would be to have a sheet of glass placed in a normal 3D set in such a manner so that you could fly objects like a bird or a rocket ship by sticking it to the glass.

A style of clay animation was developed by Bob Gardiner and Will Vinton in their film *Closed Mondays* (1974). In their clay animation, it is called claymation; the acting was achieved by rotoscoping. First they would film the live actor acting out the emotion, then the film of that actor's face would be projected onto the clay and the clay sculptured to conform to the photographic image. The projector was then turned off and the lights were turned on and a frame or two of film is shot. Then the lights were turned off, the projector was turned on to project the next frame and the whole process repeated itself. This is the normal rotoscope technique except it is done in 3D.

CAMERA

A 16mm film camera like the Bolex, that takes one frame at a time, is a good camera to start with in shooting 3D animation. A 35mm camera would be needed for 3D films intended for theatrical release. Regular video cameras are not used, as you cannot do single frame with standard video equipment. Video cameras can be used to imput your images into the computer. You can use inexpensive computer cameras for digital capture. When you have recorded all of your animation digitally you can do any editing, sound or effects necessary using the computer programs and then, when the film is done, output it to digital, video or film. The advantages of using the computer as your camera and production tool are:

- You have instant playback to see if you need to reshoot.
- As mentioned previously, you can check your movements frame by frame for proper registration.
- You can erase a movement you do not like and reshoot it.
- You have access to the different computer programs for further manipulation.
- The digital to video or DVD route is less expensive and faster than the film route.

The advantages of using film are:
- Film is of better quality, at least today.
- The digital output cannot be currently distributed to major theaters for economic reasons. Today the digital files would have to be output to film to be shown in theatrical release.
- If you want to preserve your animation for the future, film is the way to do it.

As mentioned before, you can utilize two different recording tools, the film camera and a digital camera, to do your shooting, using the film for its quality and the computer as an instant playback and as a registration device. If you do not have access to a computer or digital camera for the playback and registration capabilities, a video pencil test machine will work. When you set up the video or the digital, it should be as close to as possible and in parallax to the film camera.

An electric camera motor that will shoot single frames is the best way to run the camera during filming. A control box for the camera motor, that allows you to shoot forward or reverse with single frame or continuous shooting switches, is very useful. If you do not have a camera motor and have a camera with a wind-up spring motor, be sure not to wind it up during the middle of a shot as you can easily move something slightly and thereby cause a jerk or bump in the shooting. It is a good practice to wind the camera before each shot. For a spring-wound camera, you usually have to push the single frame release control button by hand. Be very careful you do not jiggle the camera when you do this, as it will cause the shot film to jiggle also. Instead of pushing the button by hand, get a release cable that will attach to the release button and allow you to shoot by just pushing the button in the release cable. This means you can be several feet away from the camera when you shoot and thereby lessen the chances of accidental bumps. A student once told me that to prevent getting tired when you are shooting, to not keep holding your breath when you click the release button.

To support your camera, try to use a tripod with a geared camera head. This type of head will allow you to pan (rotate on a horizontal axis, move over or across a background or landscape, an x axis) or tilt (pan up or down, the y axis) in a smooth manner if done properly. To anchor your tripod, put the tripod legs in a base, which is called triangle, and put sandbags on the triangle to hold the camera steady. This is also a good idea for the lights stands. If your camera is on a high hat, which is a gear head mounted solidly on a flat piece of heavy wood, you can clamp or gaffer tape the wooden base to the table. When you have to move your camera for a different shot, you may be able to move the set (an example would be to have it on a turn-table, like a Lazy Susan, that would allow you to rotate it to a new position and lock it down) so you can leave the camera setup alone, and save the time and effort of moving the camera and adjusting the lights.

For moving shots with a locked-down camera with a geared camera head, you can either:
- Shoot single frame movement (move, shoot a frame, move, shoot a frame) as you would

in filming pans or trucks in 2D animation. This type of shooting has to be done when you are coordinating a moving shot with animation and can be done for a moving shot without animation. For moving shots, I would always advise to shoot on 1's never on 2's. You will need to mark down the position of the geared camera head for each frame, usually a marked piece of tape will do. Be sure to watch your focus and depth of field so that you do not go out of focus.

- Shoot at normal camera speed (24 frames a second), or at high speed (more than 24 frames per second) for a moving shot if there is no animation going on. If you pan the camera over the scene shooting at 24 frames a second, you are liable to get bumps and jerks as the geared camera heads are not designed to do the smooth movement required in shooting miniature sets. To get smoother movement, try panning while shooting in slow motion at 48 or more frames per second. Since you are shooting at twice the normal speed or more, you must move the gear head twice or more as fast.

When the footage is projected at the normal rate (24 frames per second), the fast panning will eliminate many of the bumps and jerks resulting in a smoother movement. Another trick is to start the panning move before the start mark, so that you are moving smoothly when you reach the start and do the same at the end, going past the end mark. The wasted footage can later be thrown away. To help make a smooth pan, you can practice the move several times to find the final position of your body and shoulders. Then when you are ready to shoot, set your body and shoulders in the final position and turn your head to the start position and just move your head while panning and shooting.

For moving shots with a moving camera:
- Move the entire camera rig on a moving platform. This type of platform is called a dolly in live action. A dolly is a three- or four-wheeled platform that can be pushed around as needed to which the camera and a geared head is securely mounted. If you do not have access to a professional dolly you could try building one from available units. I once saw an excellent dolly made from a sports car frame. You could build something a bit smaller by using anything that will move well and support the camera. A small tricycle, a skateboard, roller skates or large model train for instance (a train will have its own tracks) could fill the bill. For shooting with a dolly, you can either do single frame or shoot at speed following the notes above. A track can be laid down that will guide the wheels of the dolly and then guide marks can be placed on the track for shooting each frame. A track can be a simple as two secure parallel pieces of wood that will guide the wheels of the dolly. The term "tracking shot" refers to a shot where the camera follows a character, often walking. Dollies and tracks can be used for pan shots mentioned above, but probably their most important use is for moving in or out on a scene. This is a zoom shot, a trucking shot in 2D animation, and is often referred to as a dolly shot in live action,

as to dolly in or dolly out on the action. This also can be done by a zoom lens, which is discussed in the next section. Dolly shots can be quite complex. Like an overhead dolly shot with fiber optics tubing for moving down a model street at street level around and around and in and out of buildings.

For professional shooting the top of the line is a motion control dolly. A motion control dolly is a robotic dolly with a movable-shooting arm with both controlled by a computer. It can be programmed for any type of complex moving shot. It is also used in special effects to match animated and live-action shots.

For moving shots with a moving set:

- Have the set on a movable surface. We have already mentioned a rotating base, but anything can be used that is fairly stable and strong: carts, toy wagons, a mover's dolly, a sliding window placed flat with its glass replaced with wood and secured down, a Lazy Susan. You can shoot this unit at speed, high speed or frame by frame.

LENS

Regular Lens. Two or three good prime lenses, perhaps two normal focal lengths, say a 25mm and a 50mm, and one telephoto or long focal length, say 150mm, should be all that you need. Try to get lenses that can focus at least within 18 inches as you could need to be close to your subject.

When you shoot so close you could have a very shallow depth of field, which means that the areas that will be in focus may be only two or three inches wide. If your model moves out of this zone, it will go out of focus or your background could be out of focus. One solution to this problem is to stop down the lens, say to f-16 or 22, which will increase your depth of field. To stop down the f-stop, you can use high-speed films and increase the light. Having a viewfinder handy to help you decide the lens you want to use is helpful. There are two kinds of lenses, the prime lens and the zoom lens. The prime lens is a focal length that is fixed, meaning that you can't make the object look bigger or smaller by adjusting the lens itself. The advantage of a prime lens is:

- They can focus within a few inches.
- Some cinematographers believe they are of higher quality. Others believe a very good prime lens and a very good zoom lens are roughly the same in terms of quality.

The disadvantage of a prime lens is: You have to move to change the size of the shot.

Zoom Lens. A zoom lens is a lens that reduces or enlarges the picture through its optics, thereby giving the impression that you are moving in or out on the subject. The advantages of a zoom lens are:

- You can change the size of the shot immediately.
- You can try using them for doing a zoom or trucking shot, which usually does not work well, as the optical elements in the lens are not fine enough to handle subtle moves. If you are going to try this, you can either shoot at speed or high speed or frame by frame. If you shoot frame by frame, you will need to mark on the lens or build a device with a pointer on which to mark your frames.

The disadvantage of a zoom lens is: A zoom lens can only focus within three to five feet.

LIGHT METERS

A light meter will tell you, given the speed of your film, what your f-stop should be. Light meters can either be reflective or objective. Reflective meters are placed in front of the camera, and when pointed at the subject, will give you the read of the reflected light that reaches the camera. Incident meters read the light source(s) at the subject as the meter faces the camera. Both will work but I prefer the incident, as you know your subject at least will be properly exposed. When you use the incident use the flat disc, unless you are very experienced. Whatever meter you use I would strongly advise that you shoot wedge tests, as that is the only "meter" that is 100 percent accurate. If you are shooting with a Bolex, you will need to change the shutter speed to 1/25 for single frame from the normal 1/50 for 24 fps.

A SPECIAL CONCERN IN 3D STOP MOTION ANIMATION

There is a problem when you want to move a character fast. When you shoot a fast moving stop motion character frame by frame, the character is always sharp and clear. But when you shoot a fast-moving character in live action, there is on some frames a normal streaking or blurring of the character caused by the camera speed being too slow to capture the fast movement. We may not see this distinctly in a live-action film, but we know it's there. And if it isn't seen in 3D animation, some people may be disturbed as they have gotten used to this inaccuracy in live-action photography and feel it is normal. This need to match the normal streaking or blurring in live action is more of a concern when 3D model animation is used in special effects. One way to streak or blur a held image, a painting or a 3D object is that you move the character with the shutter open. This is a variation of streak photography and will be discussed more under motion control in the special effects section. For streaking a 3D character, you could mount the character on a moving platform and with the shutter open move it slightly. This will give you a long exposure, leaving the shutter open for one to three seconds per frame and can change your f-stop. You will have to shoot tests to see what works for the effect you want. Or you could put the footage into the computer and add the blurs at that time. All this effort spent to duplicate a mistake of the live-action camera.

EFFECTS IN 3D STOP MOTION ANIMATION

The most commonly used special effect in 3D animation is the blue screen. Though properly speaking, it is in 3D special effects situations that its use is most common. In straight 3D it is used for putting in a complex background. The compositing of the foreground and background elements in the blue screen process would be done digitally. Other effects such as wind, rain, snow, explosions, flying (try using a sheet of glass mentioned earlier to help do these effects), etc., are done in various ways with much too much detail to go into here. Please consult books or articles in the area for the effect you want to do.

USING THE COMPUTER AS A CAMERA FOR 3D STOP MOTION ANIMATION

I will keep this section simple as the tools change constantly. Essentially you are replacing the film in the camera with the hard drive in the computer. You will need an optical system to input the image into the computer. Today that could be a digital still or digital video camera. The computer should be as fast as you can get, and the bigger the hard drive the better. You will need gigs of storage. The computer will need a program that grabs the frame when you hit the key. To keep up with the latest in the field, check out a website that is devoted to digital stop motion animation. The digital cameras being developed will record professional-quality images and should be able to be used for 3D stop motion animation. They may be the basic tools used in the future.

LIGHTING 3D STOP MOTION ANIMATION

A major difference in the production process between traditional 2D animation and 3D animation is in the use of lighting. It is also a major aesthetic difference. The physical lightning in traditional 2D animation are the two sidelights, and occasionally a bottom light, used to illuminate the flat artwork on the animation crane. Any shadows or lighting effect in the finished film must be done in the art or during the multiple exposure of the art. 3D lighting is reserved for 3D stop motion (using real lights) or 3D computer animation (faking real lights), and both normally follow the rules for lighting that come from and are usually the same as live-action films. What follows is a summary of these rules as they apply to 3D animation, whether real or simulated.

LIGHTS

The lights themselves can be the smaller lights used in live action. The type of light that you should use is a Fresnel lens light. This type of light will give you an adjustable beam so that can go from a focused key light to a broad fill light. Your bulbs should be in the 250 to 650 watt range and must be tungsten (lights with these bulbs will be smaller). A lighting kit from Mole-Richardson that contains three midget solar spots with the stands, and the scrims, screens and barn doors, is all you will need for a basic light setup. These professional lights will have flanges for holding the accessions that give you further control over lighting. These are the filters (used to change the light), gels (to change the colors), scrims and silks (to diffuse the light), barn doors and snoots (to direct the light), etc., for live-action shooting can be used on these lights. What follows is a short description of some of the principles of this type of lighting.

PRINCIPLES OF LIGHTING

Many of the principles of lighting of motion pictures came from a study of use of the light in real life or as it had been interpreted in paintings. Lighting is a good area for study, especially in mood lighting. Light has come from the sun and the human face has evolved to give us recessed eyes and eyebrows to act as sunshades. Shadows are created on the underside of the planes of the face, the eyes, and the bottom of the nose, lips and chin. Likewise with trees, rocks and elements of nature. Human's first artificial light came from fire that caused light to come from below (the flames of hell), or the cave fire, or later from the side when candles and oil lamps were developed. When the electric light arrived around the same time as motion pictures, we designed our lighting sources as either from the sun or from candles. The point of all of this is that normal lighting is lighting from above, and so most of the lighting for motion pictures is done from above. There are also the psychological aspects of light to consider. Soft, romantic, sensuous mood lighting can with a few lighting alterations turn into a dark, moody, depressing scene. The bright, terrifying glare of the police interrogation light can with the placement of a few more bright lights turn into a bright, happy birthday party.

The two basic methods in lighting are:

- Using the available natural lighting, basically the sun. This would be natural lighting on a sunny day. For obvious reasons, this is not usually done in stop motion animation.
- Controlling artificial light sources for varying degrees of realism, naturalism, atmosphere, clarity, abstraction or mood. This can range from a normally lit interior to an expressionistic scene of strong unnatural shadows and colors. In lighting, one should decide how much a style or control of the lighting would add to your film or its emotional content.

The two basic elements in artificial lighting for 3D stop motion are control and placement. Light is controlled in these five different ways:

Direction or source of the light

Motivated: like outside with sun coming from above. A tip here is the best place to put your sun source is from behind.

Unmotivated: for mood. An example would be the evil shadows created when a face is lit from below.

Color

Normal color in lighting can be either natural (sun) or artificial (electric/tungsten). Film is color-balanced for either one. Indoor film for artificial light has a color temperature (balance) of 3200 Kelvin, which is strong in the orange-red hue but looks white to the eye. Daylight film is 5500 K. If it is used with tungsten lights, a Wratten 85 filter must be utilized to achieve proper color temperature. Correction filters may also be needed if the light sources are mixed.

Artistic color in lighting is to change or intensify the color through theatrical gels or other means.

Diffusion

Diffusion is a scattering of light rays, the dispersion and softening of light. It is used in this case to describe the two types of light that can hit the character and the set.

No diffusion will give you a hard-direct light that will produce strong shadows. The stark light and dark   shadows of a desert under a cloudless summer sun is an excellent example of no diffusion.

Soft diffusion is achieved by using diffusion materials, scrims, filters, etc., over the lights or using bounce light, which causes the light to lose its intensity. This can bring out the details in the shadows or give you little or no shadow. As a cityscape would look on an overcast day when the clouds diffuse the light and there are no shadows. A note here, live-action films must have shadows according to the laws of physics. Shadows are rarely used in traditional 2D animation. That there is normally no lighting or shadows in traditional animation causes animation to break the laws of physics. So animation is not bound to reality--this is one of the strengths of animation. Lighting and shadows in stop motion animation can make it more believable, but the animation is still with non-living characters. This unique position of 3D stop motion animation, halfway between 2D animation and live action, gives 3D stop motion an exclusive charm.

Intensity of the lighting

Is the brightness of the light how you want the scene? The intensity is caused by the amount of incident light that falls on the surface. It begs the question, how much light do you want?

Shape or composition of the lighting

This is the design of the whole shot as a composition of lights and darks and the shapes of those lights and darks. This is a result of your choice of where the light falls and where it does not fall.

PLACEMENT OF THE LIGHTS

The traditional lighting placement or setup is called three-point lighting. The formula for fundamental three-point lighting is:

Key light. This is your basic light. It is the main source of illumination for the scene. The key light defines the character(s) and the set and can also set the mood. It is the key to your lighting plan. Often apes natural light, the sun from above or the light from a lamp. It is used to set your exposure. Typically the key light is set to one side of the camera and higher than the camera, with the best location usually considered the three-quarter front angle.

Fill light or diffusion is used to bring out detail in the shadows and to lessen the contrast. Multiple shadows can be a problem with a fill light. To help solve this problem, you can remove some of the lighter shadows by using a diffused fill light (some sort of diffusion filter over a light source) or by using bounced fill light that will create a soft light. They are often placed at a 45-degree direction from your key light.

Backlight is used to separate an object from the background and to add depth to the setup. Typically this light is set high above the object facing the camera, making sure there is no light flare into the camera. Some people prefer to use a kick light for this effect. A kick light is a light that strikes the subject from the direct opposite angle of the key light. It outlines the shadow side of the subject from behind. These lights are smaller and less intense than the key light.

TWO COMMON PROCEDURES USED IN LIGHTING

High key or low key lighting. The ratio of fill light to key light will determine whether the lighting is high key, which means there will be a great amount of light (detail) in the shadows, or low key, where the contrast is great between the light and shadow areas. A standard ratio for high key is that the intensity of the key light is twice that of the fill light or 2:1. This would be measured in foot-candles, say 100 foot-candles for the key and 50 for the fill. This 2:1 ratio would give you a nice, normal color scene. A 6:1 ratio would be low key. Essentially, in high key lighting you are using the amount of fill light in ratio to the key light to control the density of the shadows in the shot. You do not need to change the f-stop because of the fill light, as the f-stop reading off your key light is the only important one.

Lighting the set. This section has been mainly concerned with lighting the characters or objects, but the first things you normally light are the walls of the set. There should be enough light to see the set and it should be subdued enough so that your character(s) will stand out. Controlled random or casual lighting of the important elements of the set can help set the mood and the make the set interesting. For realism in the shadows and to avoid multiple shadows, this lighting should come from the direction of the key light (the light source). Watch out for shiny or reflective objects. If you are shooting a cyclorama, see if you can set up some type of a small skypan, which is a flat light unit made up simple light globes mounted in a row with a white or reflective backing and mounted below or above the backdrop. This will give an even lighting to the scenic backing.

CLOSURE ON LIGHTING

Changing the lighting approach during the course of the film, from scene to scene if possible within the concept of the film, can add quite a bit to the production quality of the film. Variety in the lighting can minimize the dullness that results from using the same lighting throughout the film. A well thought-out overall lighting pattern can make a positive contribution to the total effect of the film.

When you have your basic lights in place, either three-point lighting or your own, set up some different lighting combinations. To practice lighting, do lighting setups for the different times of the day, morning, noon and evening. Try lighting different moods from very dark to very bright. By experimenting you will gain flexibility in your lighting. Lighting concerns should be considered from the very beginning of the film, and it should be part of the planning in your storyboard.

To test how your lighting will look on film, you can shoot the complete lighting setup with a Polaroid film camera or a digital camera. This will give you an immediate visual feedback that will allow you not only to see if you like it but you can do another lighting setup, shoot another still and compare it with the first. You can repeat this procedure until you get the lighting that you want.

You should always shoot test footage of the set, the characters, the lighting, any tricky effects (like a blue gel for an undersea shot) and your wedge tests. This is very important. I could tell you hundreds of horror stories of people who did not shoot tests and had a fatal flaw in some piece of equipment that caused them to lose their whole shoot and the time it took to shoot it. Last but not least, always be sure and pay the electricity bill so the power is not shut off in the middle of your shooting.

Please see the section on Computer Animation for some thoughts on lighting 3D computer animation.

THE OTHER CATEGORIES OF 3D STOP MOTION ANIMATION

Everyday objects or unusual items. Anything that is 3D and that can be moved is a potential star. Household furniture in *Le Garde-meuble automatique* (*The Automatic Moving Company*) (1912) by Bosetti, pumpkins, *Pappa Oh Mama* (1974) by Jon Woluluk, and cut-up vegetables and a wide variety of items in *Dimensions of Dialogue* (1982) by Jan Svankmajer are all example of this type of film. In this form of animation, the only limit to finding objects to animate is your imagination.

Pixilation is shooting a live human figure one frame at a time in sequential poses. The human figure becomes a 3D stop motion animated character. Norman McLaren's *Neighbours* (1952) and *A Chairy Tale* (1957), Mike Jittlov's *The Wizard of Speed and Time* (1979)(fig. 6-16)[3] and Paul de Nooijer's *Transformation* (1976)[4], are fine examples of pixilation. In pixilation you can animate a live person zipping around the world in a minute, riding a bicycle that does not exist or flying around the room. It is easy to do and lots of fun. It can be combined with object animation as McLaren did in *Chairy Tale*. Shooting live action at less than 24 frames a second will give a pixie-like effect, but is not pixilation. This is seen in silent films, which were shot at 16 fps and are now projected at 24 fps (today's projectors cannot project at the old silent speed), causing the sporadic comical movement. This speeding up of the action (done by shooting at less than 24 fps) can be used in live-action films for a comedic effect. Though not properly pixilation it has much of the same effect as pixilation, that of causing the audience to laugh. Why, I do not know.

Flat or semi-flat puppets or objects. This could be the 2½D models or sculpting on angled glass already discussed, or it could be flat, a bas-relief (sculpture in which the figures are carved in a flat surface so that they project only a little from the background) of objects or clay. Jan Svankmajer in parts of his *Dimensions of Dialogue* animates 3D objects (food, nuts, bolts, etc.) loose on a flat surface. Joan Gratz used a palette knife to manipulate oil and clay on a flat surface. She painted with clay to make her Academy Award-winning film *Mona Lisa Descending a Staircase* (1992).

Summation

3D stop motion animation, whether film or computer is today enjoying a renaissance in the motion picture world. It has never been so popular nor has so much been produced. Even though many predicted that 3D computer character animation spelled the death of 3D stop motion. There is just something about that old puppet tradition.

---

3. Wikipedia gives two years for this film. 1979 for a short, and 1989 for a feature.

4. Most of the rest of the internet says this film is called *Transformation by Holding Time* and credits the year 1976 for it.

II. VISUAL EFFECTS ANIMATION IN A LIVE-ACTION FILM

An animated visual effect is any visual element that is added to a live-action film after the original shooting. There are two forms of effects in live-action film. The first, called a "special effect," is an effect done on the set as the scene is being filmed. For example, fog created by fog machines and blown by fans. The second, called a "visual effect," is an effect where any or all of the effect is added after the scene is filmed. A "time warp speed" insert of streaking colors outside of the spaceship's windows. Another reason the two different terms are used is because of the budgetary and scheduling needs of planning a production. All would be part of the total budget. Special effects would be budgeted and scheduled during production and visual effects during post-production or an effect could be budgeted in both areas if it is a combined effect.

There is a subset of animation that uses visual effects techniques to make a complete film and creates a form of animation all its own. This area will be discussed at the end of this subchapter.

Before we get into visual effects, just a few words about special effects. Special effects are done with physical or chemical materials normally operated mechanically. A special effect could be wind (large fans), smoke (smoke pots), rain (sprinklers), snow (in the 1930s snow was painted white cereal corn flakes dropped from a big shifter: I once got sick eating them on a set because they were covered with lead paint),[5] bullets striking a wall (puffs of smoke from small explosive charges in the wall set off during the action), blood gushing out of a person (blood bags concealed under the clothing), limbs chopped off with even more blood (fake arms or legs), artillery shells exploding (small explosions in the ground), flak bursts (flashbulbs). Special effects are often combined with stunt work, bullets hitting, shells bursting and blood squirting. The sources of supplies for special effects can be quite specialized. A neighbor's family where I once lived made the finest movie blood. The ingredients were a family secret but they had to cook it for a long time, so whenever you were visiting there was always a pot of blood bubbling away on the stove. Real-time rear-screen projection and miniatures that give an impression of outdoors or great distances are used so that you do not have to leave a sound stage. Historically these film special effects are related to the traditional special effects used in theater productions.

The two forms of effects are often combined for the total effect. An actor flying is a common example. The actual flying would be done on a set with the actor in a harness suspended by moving wires, a special effect. It would probably be filmed with the added special effects of

---

5. To listen to the author talk about his time as a love-action extra in Hollywood during the 1930s and early 1940s please see http://danmclaughlin.info/talk.html.

cape and hair blowing in the wind, which is done with fans. The flying actor would be shot in front of a blue or green screen so that the background, like a large cityscape, could be added later. The actor could be filmed on a set so part of the final background is in the scene; a balcony on a tall building where the actor flies in and lands is an example. The shot footage would now go to the post-production visual effects stage with the wires digitally removed frame by frame and a background added. Other visual effects could be added such as laser beams seeking to destroy our hero. The combination of special effects and visual effects is very common in contemporary filmmaking.

A visual effect, the other type of effect, is animation that is combined with the live-action footage after the live action has been shot. This is done in the post-production stage of production that is commonly referred to as "post." Today post-production is done digitally after the film has been transferred into the digital format if it is not shot in digital. The animation is digitized or is created digitally in the computer. After the animation has achieved the desired effect, the digital elements, both animation and live action, are combined or composited together in the computer. Color correction and whatever else is needed is done and then it goes back to film, video or digital for the public viewing. Visual effects, by its practical nature, means that you are combining several different elements, created at different times, into one piece of film. The shorthand for visual effect is VFX.

Today, whether good or bad, visual effects in some films are becoming more a part of production, equal to live action. This new hybrid film form will be discussed as part of this section.

TYPES OF VISUAL EFFECTS

The animation in a visual effect could either be a recognizable something, a dinosaur in the park, a landscape of Mars, or it could be an effect not possible in reality, eyes glowing, holes in the actress, a space warp fly-through, etc. The animation done for a visual effect often uses the principles of animation taught in this book but has the added responsibility of fulfilling its role in live-action sequence. Simulation or mimicking reality will depart from some of the principles of animation, for example squash and stretch and anticipation. Visual effects will more follow the principles of physics. Below is a list of the more common types of animated visual effects.

- Combining a live-action character and an animated character. *Alice in Cartoonland* (1925), Gene Kelly and Tom and Jerry in *Anchors Away* (1945) and *Who Framed Roger Rabbit* (1988) are examples of combinations done in the non digital film format.
- Combining live action with a created monster. *King Kong*, (1933) is another example of a non-digital film format.
- Combining live action and a realistic animated effect such as lighting.
- Changing the live action by combining two live action shots. *Forrest Gump*, done digitally.

- Combining live action with a created background that could be painted, a model, or digital.
- Combining live action with a computer generated object. The digital "space warp" or "a crazy force field" effect.
- Creating a complete shot. The making of very realistic waters that is an entire shot.
- Enhancing a live shot. The making of glass shattering really well after it has been filmed.
- Getting rid of unwanted elements in an existing shot. Wire removal for flying people, mistakes such as a telephone pole in a 16th-century shot. The common response (or an excuse) to a mistake in filming is, "We can fix it in post."

VISUAL EFFECTS BEFORE THE COMPUTER AND AFTER

The first effects were done on film. The early introduction of the optical printer allowed great control over the visual elements and improved quality. The optical printer held sway over the visual effects world until the introduction of the digital at the end of the 20th century improved the control and quality to the next level. This next section is a brief description of the visual techniques used before the introduction of the digital tools. Knowledge of these visual effects done in film is helpful when using the digital to achieve them, as the digital has generally taken the same effects and converted them to the new tool.

The term multi-pass refers to exposure of the same frame more than once. You can do as many passes as you need, I have done as many as 33.[6] Film (or at least color reversal film, but the principle is the same for all color films) is composed of three levels of emulsion (C, Y, M, cyan, yellow, magenta) on an acetate base. When exposed to light, the levels of emulsion record the images in the exposed color. When developed, they become permanently fixed on the film with the base becoming clear except where the emulsion has not been exposed, which becomes black. When the film has been exposed to white or a very bright light, there will be no emulsion left and the film will be developed clear. A projected white image occurs when the projector light reflects off of a white screen. Black on the screen indicates the absence of light. You can avoid burning off all the emulsion by adjusting the exposure by "stopping down" or closing down the aperture (each stop is 50 percent less light sensitive). In terms of f-stops the rule is as follows: Each stop over the correct stop loses half of the light. So if f-8 is 100 percent, then f-11 is 50 percent, f-16 is 25 percent, etc. Going the other way, each change up doubles the light: f- 5.6 would be 200 percent, etc. Lighter values in your art will burn off the emulsion faster than darker values. Preparing for multi-passes by "stopping down" your f-stop or using dark colors is a way of saving emulsion for other passes.

An alternative way of keeping the emulsion intact is to put black, called a matte, over areas

---

6. That would be in the *Gymnastics* film, later titled *Shapes of Movement* (fig. 7-78). I got to shoot some of that movie. Thirty-three passes is a lot. Honestly, I really haven't cared very much for that film, then or now.

of your art pass so that it is not exposed to light. Since the emulsion remains unexposed to light, it can be used again on future passes. If the emulsion is burnt off, you can "put it back" on by using the optical printer. Please see section below for optical printing.

Two examples of multi-pass done in camera would be: black and white photos can be double-exposed with color cards (fig. 7-84) on the animation crane to create color images instead of black images, or shadows can be added to the images on your film by double- and triple-exposing black mattes of your images over a second pass of the scene at a percentage exposure (fig. 10-3). The first pass of the scene without the matte would also be shot at a percentage exposure.

As you do different passes on film it involves generations of film so that the quality of the final film will suffer. It was always a battle to keep the generations as close to the original as possible. In the digital world, the multi-exposures are handled as different levels and their digital combination is done quickly and without loss of quality.

Some of the film visual effects techniques are:

Optical Printing: Not only can you combine different elements, you can also freeze frames, take out frames to speed up the action or shoot the same frames several times to slow down the action, or create staggered effects. Combined with mattes (fig. 10-3) (usually used in conjunction with bipacking, which is two different clips of film, one over the other, on the same spool so that both are projected or filmed together; often one of these films is a matte), you can add new information such as titles over a live-action scene. An optical printer is essentially a camera pointed at a projector.

Front and/or Rear Screen: In this technique, a model is combined with existing live-action footage. In front screen the live-action footage, with actor(s) included, is projected by way of a beam splitter onto a screen. The model is placed on a small set in front of the screen and the projected image and the model are filmed together one frame at a time. In rear screen the image is projected onto the screen from behind.

Matte Shots: A matte shot means using black to cover the part of the frame that is to be re-exposed on a multiple pass. An area of the frame is "matted out" so that it will have full emulsion for reshooting (fig. 10-3).

Glass Shots: A glass shot is a matte shot achieved by placing a glass in front of a locked-down camera. The parts of the glass to be matted, looking through the camera, are covered with opaque material.

Aerial Image: This is when live action is projected from underneath an animation crane so that it is projected as a backlight image, and is then combined cleverly with animation on top of this image. The top animated image becomes its own matte. For reference, see Gene Kelly dancing with Tom and Jerry.

Blue Screen or Green Screen: This is a technique whereby first an actor or an object is shot in live action against a blue screen, and the film is then processed in the lab so that the blue turns to black. With the negative turning black, it makes a perfect matte for combining a live-action shot with another shot. Sodium screen is an older form of blue screen. A blue or green screen is used because it is a rare color in a human. Today, digital matting has almost completely replaced film matting. A green screen is normally used for digital matting except when blue is used for colors in a human that are close to the green, blond hair for example.

Rotoscoping: Frames of live-action footage are projected onto a working surface with peg bars so that it can be traced onto paper or cels (fig. 5-45). Rotoscoping can be used to:

- Register the live action so that a later-animated effect will be in its proper place. In the movie *Dune* (1984), the live-action characters' eyes had to be rotoscoped so that they could be replaced with an animated piercing blue (the spice).
- As mentioned elsewhere rotoscoping, or as it is now called motion capture, when it is used in digital animation to: **1.)** To copy live action in animation so that the live action becomes the animation, **2.)** To learn animation by copying animation or live action.
- In computers, rotoscoping or "roto" means essentially cutting masks manually for added effects. To put something behind a live-action character that was not shot on a green screen, the live actor would have to be cut out, often frame by frame, to make masks or mattes for the later compositing.

MOTION CONTROL

A computer controls a crane and camera shooting the artwork or model. For example, the use of a computer for the Star Gate sequence (art) and spacecraft (models) in *2001: A Space Odyssey* (1968). Used to record in the digital compositing complex movement, usually of the live-action, so that the move can be repeated for multiple passes of added effects. For example, a miniature scene with a camera move could have multiple passes that include a shadow pass and several lighting passes. Using the same camera move for each pass gives more control in the compositing stage.

Motion control can be used to create a "clean plate." This is when a complex moving scene with an actor is shot twice. The actor is only shot once and is not in the scene on the second pass. This allows the actor to be removed to put effects behind him or to replace him with an animated character so that the other actors in the scene have someone to act and react to. Gollum in *The Lord of the Rings* (2001, 2003) was done using this technique. Clean plates can also be done in post-production. Motion control is used today in many music videos and commercials.

Production Pathway Today for Visual Effects: Today, the digital has taken over as the main production tool for animated visual effects in live-action films. The advantage of the digital, with its seamless combining of animation and live-action without a loss in film quality, has increased the role of animation to such a degree that few live-action films do not have some amount of digital animation. It can range from fixing a mistake in shooting, or as Con Pederson calls it "digital plastic surgery," to its planned use as an integral part of the film in films such as *Forrest Gump* or the *Star Wars* epics. A production pipeline for a VFX house for normal post-production visual effects, not an effect-driven film, could look like this:

Pre-production: They receive the script and discuss the scope of VFX. The basic question is: Is it a bare-bones or a knock-our-socks-off approach. This is usually determined by the budget and type of project; blockbuster, indie, TV movie, or TV shows. In other words, "How big is the boat?"

Breakdown: Calls out each effect described in the script. Some things in the script may not appear to be effects (mountains in BG that need to be put in or taken out), while others are obvious (the character liquefies, reaching out a metallic tentacle toward our hero).

Methodology: Deciding what methods will be used to achieve the effect. Many times there will be more than one way to achieve a similar effect. Cost, time and quality are the factors.

Production: Doing the effects, getting approval, compositing final form, color correction and delivery.

We are seeing today where visual post-production effects in many cases are turning into being a normal part of the production. When the visual effects are such a large part of the production that they become part of production. One major studio recently reorganized its studio departments to reflect this reality. In the recent film *Sky Captain and the World of Tomorrow* (2004), since the sets were done on the computer and the actors were shot in front of a blue screen, the visual effects were everything on the screen except the actors and props and so were a large part of production. The detailed stages of production for an effect-driven film could look like this:

The usual script breakdown, planning, budget, scheduling, bidding of shots and subcontracting are done. But let's go into a little more detail on the steps:

- ***Previsualization (pre-viz):*** A tool used by most complex effects-driven movies. It is in essence a digital animatic. Rough animation is created with camera moves to simulate how the sequences will be animated and paced. It is not unusual for all the computer sequences to be previsualized and edited with the live-action sequences together with a temporary soundtrack. Next is:
- ***Modeling:*** Modeling involves creating free-form 3D objects. This could be a character or a digital set.
- ***Rigging:*** Rigging involves setting up the computer model to be able to be controlled and animated. For example, setting up control of the mouth, eyes and forehead, creating a skeleton or bone structure through inverse kinematics. These tools when made properly make the animator's job much easier.

- **Animation:** The animator uses the model and rigging to bring life to the character and fit the animation into the overall scope of the scene and the entire project.
- **Texturing/Shaders:** Creating textures and shades defines surfaces and materials and how they react to light and color. It is used to increase detail without adding 3D geometry. These can be based on photographs or drawings or Photoshop renderings can be used, or programmers can write them as code.
- **Lighting:** The lighter is essentially a digital cinematographer, creating mood, adjusting surface properties and matching on-set lighting. Often reference materials are available to the lighter such as photographs of the set and stand-in characters with the additional help of photographs of on-set chrome and diffuse balls to match angles and intensity. In some houses the lighter will also be the compositor, particularly in animation with no live action.
- **Compositing:** Compositing involves meshing multiple elements to look proper as a whole. This involves color, contrast, tracking, matching, adding grain, matching blurs and depth of field, and adding additional 2D elements. Usually many elements are involved: live-action plates, blue and green screen footage, still photography, matte paintings, effects plates, stock footage and 2D and 3D multiple-pass animation.
- **Output to film or video:** What looks good on a computer screen might look very different in TV or film. These three mediums have inherently different color spaces with different luminance and chrominance fall-offs. This final step is critical. Often the pipeline of a house will make sure things will look proper in final form, wedges or tests, with match frames and calibrated monitors being the most critical steps to ensure proper results.

Additional Notes

3D Tracking
3D tracking software programs help facilitate the creation of a digital camera to mimic the movement of the on-set camera, often recorded in motion capture. This digital camera data can then be brought into a 3D program or a compositing package to match the real camera with its lens, focal distance, movement and depth of field. It is invaluable for the animator.

Technical Directors
A vital link in the production process in helping the various fields reach their objectives. This is a problem-solving person who knows how to get things done technically and artistically. However, each studio uses different nomenclature for their specific departments and respective titles.

Big Houses vs. Smaller Houses
Generally specialization is more prominent in larger houses, while a smaller house will be filled with more generalists. In a smaller house often a 3D artist will model, rig, animate and light his or her own shot while in a larger house this might pass through four different departments.

Summation

The first Academy Award for the effect categories was given in 1939. It was called Special Effects until 1964, when the name for the category was changed to Visual Effects.

An alternate title for this subchapter could be "Live Action as an Effect in an Animated Film." As I have noted there are more and more films of this nature, even though some are disguised as live action. If you are going to do an animated film with live-action sections or combinations, make sure the live action is done well and you have plenty of money.

VISUAL EFFECTS TECHNIQUES AS A COMPLETE FILM

The techniques of visual effects can be used in an artistic or experimental manner to create a complete film. Norman McLaren's *Pas de deux* (1967) is one example; Pat O'Neill and Tony Venezia are two filmmakers currently working in this format. Sometimes called "painting with film" it is an art form in its own right.

Another technique used for making a complete film is the technique of changing camera speed. This is done by either:

- Time-lapse photography, which condenses time by shooting one frame with a period of time between each frame. A flower growing by shooting one frame a day, beach changing over a 10-year period by shooting one frame a day for 10 years, clouds flying across the sky by shooting a frame every five minutes or the Earth turning by holding the shooting stars every five minutes with a time exposure (this was done by a student of mine, Bill Mitchell; it was a wonderful film).[7] As an effect, it can show a long period of time passing very quickly as in the speeding up of the changing of seasons.
- High speed photography that gives slow motion. This is shooting at higher speeds than 24 fames a second. Can go as high as thousands of frames per second with a rotating prism. Often used as an effect in sports or fighting. I shot the titles for the feature *Where's Pappa?* (1970) at 800 frames per second (fig. 10-4).

Norman McLaren's *Canon* (1964) is a dictionary of different approaches to 3D animation and VFX animation and an excellent film to study.

---

7. Phil Denslow says this film was Zebu which won the 1987 Student Academya Award in the experimental area. he also adds that, "I remember that William Mitchell shot his film by hand. Meaning he put a 35mm Mitchell camera on a tripod and used the hand-crank instead of a motor. When the camera was stopped it was in the open-shutter position making an exposure. Then every minute or so he would turn the crank around once to advance to the next open-shutter exposure. (You could change the crank from being 12 frames per rev to 1 frame per rev.) I'm sure his biggest technical issues were staying awake all night and remembering to advance the film at regular intervals."

III. COMPUTER ANIMATION

Overview: The Computer Animation Production Process Today

Currently there are three major ways that computers are used in the production of animation. In the first, the computer assists or does the full production of 2D (drawn) animation. An example of this type of animation (assisted) is the Disney animated feature, *The Lion King* (1994) or Jay Shipman *One Final Encore* (2016) (fig. 6-12). In the second, the computer is the primary production tool for 3D model character computer animation. An example of this type of film would be DreamWorks *Shrek 2* (2004). The third is 2D computer animation that is 2D motion graphics. In 2D motion graphics, art, archival art, film and effects are used to create moving graphics. Examples of this type are inexpensive TV commercials. The computer is also used in 3D stop motion, visual effects and interactive animation to fit the special technical needs of those fields, which is discussed in those sections. Since the specific use of the digital is constantly changing, I will describe in only very general terms the major elements of the production process for computer animation. At the end there will be a list of the computer tools used at the present time, which should be good for about two years.

For all computer animation production, you will follow and not need to re-evaluate or change the principles of animation, especially those contained in the chapters dealing with idea, storyboard, timing and sound. For the computer motion graphics film, you may be tempted to create as you put the images into the computer without going through the pre-production phase. This working through the process and creating as you go along without planning is what some painters prefer as it gives them the freedom of spontaneity. In animation, because of the complexity of the process, this method of production can lead to a long production time and early frustration.

One general statement that would apply to all computer work is to constantly back up, or save your files. One professional computer animator I know backs up her files every 20 minutes. She has saved much production time due to loss that way. We will now discuss briefly each of these three paths that the computer can take you down to a finished film.

COMPUTER-ASSISTED TRADITIONAL DRAWN ANIMATION

For the first way, computer-assisted traditional 2D animation, you will either follow the traditional production process of drawn animation through animation paper and pencil stage until you get to the ink and paint step, and then you go into the computer for the rest of the production. Specifically you will input each drawing into a computer where the ink and paint process will be done as well as the "shooting" (compositing). You will digitally apply the color to the drawing either individually or in batches. If wanted, the shading, highlights, shadows, etc., can be added at this time. The different levels of the animation are now combined or composited together. The final complete background, which has either been digitally captured into the computer, created within the computer or some combination of the two, is now composited with the animation. Make sure the background and the animation work together. Then arrange the animation and the background files in the proper sequence for playback viewing. Use the computer equivalent of exposure sheets with your animatic, pencil tests and sound track as your timing guide. A movie file (a digital motion picture) is then, made and the sound files from your sound program are imported and synced to the movie files for a composite digital movie. If you have the time you can bring a new or added stage to the animation production process at this point, after the film has been in a sense completed, by making digital adjustments while looking at the total film in the timing, color (color balancing and correction is a common change) and sound. The last stage in the creative process is to look at the movie files as a work in progress for the last time, take a deep breath and declare the film finished.

Or you would go right to the computer with your 2D storyboard, either scanned or drawn using the computer. Then you would do all the timing, the layout, the drawn animation, the backgrounds, the final timing and the compositing digitally. You will need to find out what programs are available to you at the time you are ready to start. In either case, the sound would be done on the computer.

To get your movie files out of the computer and into a distribution format, you will have to output it either to digital tape or DVD, magnetic tape, or 16mm or 35 mm film. If you are going to the digital (tape or DVD) or magnetic tape, the sound and picture will be output together to that format. If you are going to film, you will film the visual digital image and then take that film through the traditional film laboratory process. Transferring digital to film can be expensive to get good quality. The sound will then be added in the laboratory in the usual manner to make the composite film print.

The type of distribution will determine the final viewing format. Today, if you plan to go into theatrical release and preserve your film for years to come, you will need to go to film. For the preservation of your work on digital files, the problem is that it is a hardware-dependent medium where the hardware keeps changing. That means the format your files are now in can only play on certain pieces of hardware that probably will be kaput in five to 20 years. Then you are stuck with materials you cannot view. For a professional, this can mean that just updating your reel can become a major headache. If you want to preserve your work for the future, going to film is the only real option today and an important reason for going to film for your final format.

Some of the present concerns of the computer-assisted traditional animation process are: If you have a break in the line of your drawing, the color that you paint in digitally will leak out and fill the screen. You will need to clean up your drawings, making sure the line is solid, before or after you input them into the computer. This clean-up stage can be quite time-consuming. You should consider using the options of highlights or shadows on a character carefully before doing them, as they can add days to your production time. If you have not made your color choices before going into the computer, doing it in the computer can drive you crazy, as you can choose from a million different color variations in the computer palette. Make the color decisions for the complete scene, animation and background together. If you do them separately, the values and chromes of background color can easily become much too vivid, bright and warm, which can overpower the colors of the animation. Computer programs in this area can give you many wonderful options of enhancing your art, but you must be aware when you are really adding to the work or just playing around. Never confuse activity with accomplishment. Always consider the entire film when you make any decision, as it is easy not to see the forest because of the trees.

2D computer animation is replacing the traditional pencil, paper, cels, ink and paint, camera and film in the animation process. Traditional ink and paint and camera are still used because of the low cost of overseas production and teaching animation. The traditional way is still the best way to teach animation today. One production path for teaching could be to hand-ink-and-paint and shoot the film on the animation crane so the student gets that experience then transfer (telecine) to digital for the final steps. This can save time and money.

3D COMPUTER CHARACTER ANIMATION

3D computer character animation is 3D stop motion animation with a computer. In the pathway for production, start with your idea as always and do a rough storyboard. Then do your animatic. It may be best to keep the models simple in the animatic until you have your idea, editing and timing decided. Alternatively, come back and do a complete animatic after you have your model built. You can always use pencil sketches for the first animatic. You need to build an articulated (rigged) 3D character before you can begin the animation stage, which can be the most time-consuming part of the animation. In layout you will do rough character models, rough layouts and rough backgrounds in the computer. In the animation phase you can use more of the live-action techniques, as you are moving in a 3D world with full 3D camera movement, lighting and shadows. Traditional 3D stop motion animation is a very good training ground for computer 3D model animation. The production process discussed next will follow the steps in a high-end computer program, Maya for example. The high-end programs will give you the best 3D computer animation offered today.

There are five major steps of computer character animation. First is the construction of the model. The model can start as a skeleton, which is then normally followed by a wire frame model of its final form over the skeleton. Or it can begin as a wire frame model. The second stage is setting up the articulation, making the model ready for the animation and setting the range for the type of movement and your control of it. This is called the set-up, stringing (from the puppet theater?) or rigging stage. For the rigging, first do the joints of the skeleton that will be moving, then the inverse kinematics or hierarchical movement (IK) describes what happens to the rest of your arm if you move your shoulder. How the upper arm, the elbow, the lower arm, the wrist, the hand, the fingers (each joint) will all move as separate units reacting to how the shoulder moves. This involves muscular attributes, weight, gravity, clothing, etc. Then you put in the facial controls, next the secondary animation, and the last thing you do is tweak the whole kit and caboodle. The rigging or making the model ready for animation can range from complex realism, subtle facial muscular ticks, to simple animation such as a head turning. The rigging gives you the controls you will need to animate. You should plan what needs to move so that you do not spend time setting up part of the model that is not going to move, or find out later in the animation phase that the movement you need is not set up. The next two elements to decide on are the covering of the model, sometimes referred to as texture and bump mapping, and the selection of the colors of the mapping for the model. Some of the sample questions you will have to ask yourself at this time are: Is the model covered with flesh, hair or steel? Is it smooth, rough or shiny? Are the surface elements scanned in or created in the computer? Is it a combination of different texture and bump maps or just one? Do the colors work with the action? Does the combination of colors direct your eye to the salient features? Do the background and model colors work together? These two steps are analogous to the painting step in traditional animation. The last major element in model building is the lighting, the basic principles of which are discussed in the 3D Animation section. Once you understand the principles of lighting, you need to ask yourself these questions: How many light sources are there and where are they? Is it light and bright with few light shadows, or dark and moody with many dark shadows? Does it endeavor to look realistic or does it go beyond reality into animation?

If you have trouble with any decisions as you go through the production process, please remember you should find the answer to any question by going back to and reviewing your basic concept. If you do not find an answer in your concept, you may have a major problem in the original idea.

After you have your model(s) built and functioning and the handles for the animation in place, you can start your animation. You can animate from pose to pose or straight ahead. Normally the basic movements, walks, body actions, etc., are done, for speed of operation, with the wire frame model. You may need the model covered with a default surface and color or give it its final surface to check the finer movements of the timing and acting. The basic information for the timing, of course, will come from the animatic and the sound to be synced. The mapping and the lighting can be done before, during or after the animation. As far as the animation goes, you could follow the traditional three-step process for character animation, animating the basic movement, adding the gravity and finally the acting. The unique elements of personality that make that character distinct (normally the animating of the facial handles) and the secondary animation, especially on the clothing. At what stage in the animation you do the final lighting and the texture mapping is tricky. You do not want to get too much into detailed texture mapping or lighting at the beginning, which can be fun, and forget the animation. Sometimes the lighting, color and texture mapping are an integral part of the animation, so you will need to do them in concert with the animation. Whenever you do them, give them the attention they need as bad lighting, color and mapping can distract from the animation.

LIGHTING IN 3D COMPUTER ANIMATION

Please read the lighting section in Chapter 5 for the basic principles of lighting (p. 118). Also see Emud Mokhberi's article, "Lighting in Animation," in Issue 14 of *Animatrix*.[8] In his excellent article, Emud points out several differences in computer animation lighting. One is that the lighting is often not done on a set with the 3D characters but rather at a later stage in the production, thereby not allowing the interaction of the character with the set and the lighting. Planning the lighting when planning all animation and the backgrounds helps unify all the elements. Backlighting and bounced lighting has been a problem for technical considerations, but can be worked around.

Another thing for lighting in 3D computer animation is that you are not lighting a dark set as in the other ways of lighting but a white screen with objects in it. Instead of carving out of the black you are putting the darks and blacks in. Much like some water colorists who first paint their dark areas. Maybe darkening the scene before you start lighting it could give the feeling of carving out the action. On a short film or mood piece, lighting can be as important as any other element.

BACKGROUNDS IN 3D COMPUTER ANIMATION

The basic design of the background, the environment, the stage, however you want to think of it, for the animation should be in your storyboard, probably in pencil. For the animatic stage, you may need to build a wire frame or limited texture model of the background. In the layout, you can choose to build the background to the requirements of the path of action or staging of your animation. If the background is not an integral part of your concept, you can leave it until the animation is finished and then do the finished lighting and texture on the background. If the background and the animation need to be in sync technically and aesthetically, you may need to do full lighting and texture coating on the background model

---

8. "Lighting in Animation." Mokhberi,Emud, *Animatrix: A Journal of the UCLA Animation Workshop.* 2006, Issue 14, p.17.

at this stage to make sure that the background and animation work together.

You could also choose to use the near-finished 3D background during the decision-making in the layout stage. You would go "on location" in the 3D computer set and plan the shots, compositions and camera moves by moving the camera around as you would on a live-action set to figure out how you are going to shoot the scenes before you set about animating.

The Two Aesthetic Controversies in 3D Computer Animation

There are two major aesthetic controversies in computer 3D model animation. The first is: Should the major thrust of computer character animation be toward achieving an undetectable simulation of reality in human characters? If so, we could reach a point someday where animated computer generated synthetic actors would replace live actors completely. The director of the Artificial Intelligence Laboratory at MIT believes there will be no clear distinction between real and virtual reality by the year 2030.

Should 3D character animation continue to work in the areas of fantasy and magic that have been so successful in the past? As Aldous Huxley, in paying tribute to the 1920s *Felix the Cat* shorts, wrote in his essay "Where are the Movies Moving:" "What cinema can do better than literature or the spoken drama is to be fantastic. On the screen, miracles are easily performed, the most incongruous ideas can be arbitrarily associated, and the limitation of time and space can be largely ignored."[9] Are we too familiar with our world to be fooled by artificial reality over a period of time? In live action, the more realistic you are the more believable you become. In animation, the opposite is true as animation is based on art, not reality. You are doing an animated film, not trying to reproduce reality. You should never want your audience to think you are trying to make a live-action film with what would inevitably be pallid imitations of humans. Rather your goal should be an animated film with fully realized animated characters. The drive toward simulation or realism is essentially a technological challenge, one that is easier to undertake than an artistic challenge. A material goal that synthetic actors would be less expensive than live actors is a possibility that might make some producers very happy. If someday motion pictures are cast with simulated actors directed by artificial intelligence, perhaps we could also have synthetic audiences with or without AI. This could free us from the necessity of going to the movies.

The second aesthetic debate in 3D animation is whether the actual movement of the 3D computer characters is done by using the principles of animation or by rotoscoping. Rotoscoping, or the copying of live-action movement from film, has been used in animation since 1915 and

---

9. "Where are the Movies Moving? The Brilliant Success of the Cinema in Portraying the Fantastic and Preposterous." Huxley, Aldous, *Vanity Fair* July, 1926, p. 39. Accessed http://www.docfoc.com/where-are-the-movies-moving-aldous-huxley.

is normally used in traditional animation to provide information, or reference footage, on live-action movement for adaptation by the individual animator. Today, rotoscoping is called motion capture in the computer 3D world. It is achieved by recording, by various sensors, the movements of human action. The recording of these data is then fed into the computer and becomes the animation for the 3D computer model. The 3D computer model is replicating the movements of the live actor. All the animators I know hate motion capture that is only motion capture.

As you can see, these two debates do overlap; the pro simulation group will usually take the motion capture viewpoint. Some motion capture advocates (usually the people making the motion capture equipment) support the use of motion capture. These different viewpoints, especially simulation, have been an arena of discussion since the advent of computer character animation.

The path of human simulation and motion capture in 3D character computer animation has led to some interesting legal questions. One such question is: Can a computer-animated image of John Wayne be used in a new film or can a computer avatar of Jim Morrison be used in a new musical video of The Doors as copyright-free material? To forestall this Marlon Brando has allegedly done a motion capture computer animation of his likeness so it can be copyrighted by his heirs. But the main fear, that 3D computer character animation replaces human actors, will never come to pass, as the uniqueness of the individual creative force can never be replaced or programmed.

Additional Concerns of 3D Computer Character Animation

One trap, when you are learning to create 3D character animation, is that you can forget the pre-production, storyboard, sound and timing and jump immediately into character model building. This can lead to a bad film and wasted character animation. Knowing the limitations of the program you are using and working within them can save you time and result in better animation. One of the limitations of computer animation that exists today is the lack of programming that can mimic gravity (Maya can simulate gravitational pull to an adjustable degree for animated particles). Often a veteran animator has to massage or tweak the software to fool it into creating movement affected by gravity. This is one reason computer animation is better used for flying in the air or water, where the effects of gravity are less noticed. Experienced animators also complain that the interpretation of inbetween motion is solely mathematical. While one can adjust ease-in and ease-out with splines and such, unless a person has a real sense of the personality of the character's movement they will be sucked into the computer's interpretations that can kill the believability of their character.

COMPUTER 2D MOTION GRAPHICS ANIMATION

Motion graphics is a form of computer animation where mostly 2D archival art, photos or live action film is input into the computer and the movement, editing, effects, and compositing of the art into a film is done by controlling the programs in the computer. It can also be referred to variously as collage, digital or limited motion computer animation and can be quite varied in its style and approach. This type of computer animation has its roots in traditional limited animation that has no or little character animation, and then later the various tools are used in TV to do motion graphics, effects and titles. A danger in this type of computer animation is that you introduce the art elements into the computer too early, before the storyboard, and then spend a great deal of time looking at the options in the different programs without a definite goal in mind, waiting for a miracle to give you a good film.

Some interesting work is being done these days in low-end motion graphics. One example is in telling a first-person narrative story. This has been done in secondary schools with excellent results. As part of the teaching, the student is asked to do a computer motion graphics film about some part of his or her life with his or her voice-over. It is another way to write one's story. Carroll Blue of the University of Central Florida is a leading pioneer in this field.[10] Other possibilities are abundant, for the computer has opened up filmmaking for people who never before had the opportunity to make their own films.

Basic Computer Equipment Needed Today

The equipment needed today for computer animation break down into three categories. First the hardware, the computer; then the software, the programs that run on the computer: and last the peripheral tools needed to fill in the holes in the production process. Given the marketing and changing technological aspects of the computer industry, there will always be different variations of these tools.

Computers for Animation[11]

Even what used to be known as low-end computers, today are powerful enough to run most of the programs. The low-end computers are used for less powerful 3D programs and/or the

---

10. I think he is talking about this: The University of Central Florida, College of Education and Human Performance, http://education.ucf.edu/.

11. As I hope you have noted before, the author finished various sections of this book between 2002 and 2007. Needless to say, this section is not to be relied on in any technical sense, but is included to show the author's general sense of the field.

programs used in 2D computer-assisted traditional animation and 2D motion graphics. The high-end computers are used for high-quality 3D computer character animation. These give you the speed and power to run the more sophisticated 3D character programs and can also run any of the other programs. Some of the differences today between these two classifications of computers is how many processors they have. The high-end computers have four. Also whether the system is 32 bit, low-end, or 64 bit, high-end, and the space on the hard drive, RAM, higher-end graphics card, etc. In addition, perhaps, what kind operating system (OS) is used? Knowing what type of program you will be using is important in selecting a computer. We have found Macs are the best for student work at UCLA.

Programs

To purchase the programs, you will need to know the type of computer animation that you will be doing. In the computer animation field today, there are certain programs that are essential to any complete computer animation program. These programs are: Premiere, which is used for editing, exposure sheets and occasionally sound; After Effects, which is used for compositing images and producing effects; Photoshop, which is used for painting and image enhancement and manipulation; and a sound program (SoundEdit 16 works well with the programs listed above) friendly with your other programs and the computer.

For computer-assisted traditional drawn animation you can use the programs mentioned above in concert. You can also purchase dedicated ink and paint systems.

Programs exclusively for 3D computer character animation divide into two categories. For the best theatrical quality 3D character animation, the Maya program seems to be one. Maya is a very complex program, may have a yearly service charge, and can take several years to learn completely. For Jess complex animation, TV and games for example, today there are easier programs like 3D Studio Max, Softimage, XSI, etc.

Both 2D character and motion graphics animation can also be done on most of the programs listed above. *South Park* was done in Maya. There are also low-cost programs available for 2D character animation. One very popular 2D program today is Aash, which will be discussed in the Interactive section. For motion graphics, Premiere and Photoshop would allow you to do the basic production process and you could expand to other programs as needed.

Peripherals

There will be more other computer-related things required than you thought possible. First you will need something to input the drawings and art into the computer. This could either be a scanner, a video camera or a sketchpad (today, the Wacom tablet for example). To input moving images, either video or digital, you will need the proper serial ports and hardware in your computer. Storage devices and backup devices are a must. They can be individual units, such as an external drive or a central storage device or server (a central server is more of a concept, as often it can be several machines in various locations networked together, but for the animator it seems to be one unit). For an individual or for individual students, separate storage units work the best. In a school situation there are fewer problems if the students are responsible for their work, and the purchasing, staffing and maintenance of a central server can be quite costly. For a production company centralized storage is the best, as the data will be needed to network to different people in the production. You will need programs to help maintain your computer, including anti-virus programs. A hookup to the web is always good. If you need networking, or computers talking to each other, you could need extra hardware and software. If the final output will be to film, you will need a film recorder of some type or you will have to take your computer files to a production house that converts the files to film, and then you will have to go through the composite film route in a film laboratory. At UCLA we, in the past, have simply filmed off a monitor one frame at a time. If your final output is to tape, you will need a machine such as Final Cut Pro or a ProMax system connected to a tape deck or take your files to a professional transfer studio. You will need a desk or table and a decent chair; this is a very important consideration, as animators will spend hundreds of hours sitting at their computers. Workplace health issues, or ergonomics, have to be addressed in any computer animation production. You will always need more cables and connections.

Costs

The total cost of a high-end complete computer setup (NT and Maya)–the computer, the programs and peripherals, and without a film recording unit and central server–will run about $25,000. Maya also has a yearly cost running into the thousands. A low-end unit, especially for 2D computer or computer-assisted animation, can run under $10,000, again without a film recording unit and a central server. You will also need personnel to install and maintain this equipment, perhaps on a yearly salary. For any equipment or program, always verify the manufacturer's claims to performance and especially its reliability. Be skeptical of all sales pitches. Check everything out with people you know and trust in the field. Ask the salespeople for names and addresses of people who use their product so you can call them. Give the product a trial period. Computers are buggy and crash-prone so you need to have the most reliable one.

Remember, on any cost or budget estimate that the machines and programs are good only for a few years. Understand that you will be buying new machines and programs approximately every two to five years. This pace of technology development is expressed in Moore's law. Intel co-founder Gordon Moore predicted in 1965 that the number of transistors, or electronic switches on a chip, would double every 18 months, thereby increasing the speed and the need for updated software until the year 2011. It is also an expression of the economics of the computer marketplace.

JOBS

Following are some of the positions in the computer animation field today that arise out of the computer production process. These areas may change as the technology changes.

Modeling – the person who builds the 3D model.

Set-Up – the hard worker who makes the model ready for animation, and strings the movement.

Lighting – the person who designs the lighting for the 3D model and the entire scene, including the background.

Animation – the animator who gives life to the 3D model.

Background – the individual who builds and texture maps the 3D background.

Scanning – the human being who inputs the art into the computer.

Compositing – the person who puts together all the different levels/files onto one level/file.

Technical Director or TD – the person who coordinates the computer production between the art and the technology concerns.

Programmer – is the person who creates the programs. I have not talked about the role of the programmer, as that is not within the scope of this book. An animator need not be a programmer to do computer animation, but a programmer should know animation to write animation programs. It does not hurt if an animator knows programming.

Support – the various people who do the maintenance, often daily, that keeps all the systems up and running.

In the digital computer area, visual effects, computer animation and interactive, there is an ebbs and flow in the needs of the industry and this affects the job market. There may be a need for motion capture for two to three years and quite a bit of work, and then no need and no work. Knowing animation and the different areas and what you want to do will always stand you in good stead regardless of what is the current flavor of the month or year. Today, change is the name of the game in the digital.

DIFFERENT APPROACHES TO TEACHING COMPUTER PROGRAMS

- **Lectures and Laboratory.** In this method, the teacher gives the lecture and demonstration for a particular computer exercise or tutorial where only the instructor has a computer and the students take notes. The students then will do the same exercise or tutorial as an assignment on individual computers during laboratory time. This pattern is repeated until the course is finished.

Concerns: Some students may not follow, lecture and become frustrated in the laboratory session when they try to do the assignment. A teaching assistant could be helpful in this situation.

There is no feedback on performance. This would be the instructor looking at and commenting on the finished assignment.

- **Lectures, Laboratory and Discussion.** Same as lecture and laboratory, but a teacher's discussion of the individual performances of the assignment at next meeting is added before going on to next lecture.

Concern: Same as above. Written material to supplement the lecture or suggested third party books can be very helpful.

- **Multiple Computers.** All the students would have a computer during the lecture so that they are doing the lecture/demo along with the instructor. This is the classic way typing is taught. Laboratory assignments and discussion of performance are optional, but probably necessary.

Concern: Classes can be slow-moving as the learning curve is tied to the slowest student unless you can find an approach so this does not occur. This approach is also very expensive, with large space and equipment concerns. You will need technical support. This is very important.

General Notes on Computer Animation

The computer has expanded the scope and importance of the animation field by adding two new genres of animation, 3D computer animation and interactive animation, and by increasing the role of animation as a special effect in live-action film. In the last 10 to 15 years these attributes of the computer, coupled with the advent of cable TV and the acceptance by adults of animation as a viable entertainment form, has raised the animation industry to new levels of employment and production. The use of the computer in animation has offered more employment opportunities to animators who are skilled in both computer and traditional animation. This is especially true when there is a slowdown in one area of production (traditional) and there is usually work in the other areas (computer, interactive), allowing an animator educated in both traditional and computer animation to keep out of unemployment lines for long periods of time.

The current built-in obsolescence of computers and their programs makes it difficult to leave a project for a period of time, as the changes in technology during the delay can make your project impossible to finish or very expensive to update. I hope that we can return someday to a level playing field of technical consistency so that we do not have to spend an inordinate amount of time and money buying and learning the latest wrinkles of computer animation.

This constant need to buy new computers and programs makes computer animation very expensive.

Beware of all the hype surrounding computer animation. I remember back in 1971 a salesman for a new computer company claimed, nay promised, that within two months their computer would only need 30 days to produce an animated feature of *Snow White* quality. He was only 25 years off on the first animated feature (and it took more than 30 days); the quality promise is still an open date. Spokespeople for different computer products are still making similar promises today with the same lack of results.

A Thought on the Current Situation
Between the Tool Maker and the Tool User

The relationship of the tool maker, the computer hardware and software people, and the tool user, the animator, is a very interesting one. Perhaps it is even a new type of relationship for the two groups. Historically the tool maker--the piano maker, the pencil maker, the camera maker--built a tool that the user plied along with the discipline of his or her art. Now, because some of the functions of the animator are built (programmed) into the computer, is the tool now also the user? Or at least a partial user? Does this make the tool maker the tool user? I was once at a computer conference where they refused to use any traditional animation terminology, declaring it old, worthless and outdated so they tried to invent a new and different language for the technology of animation. We see this trend in any computer programming today. This is just one of the minor areas that reflect the lack of communication or understanding between the tool user and the tool maker. At the same conference a revered guru of AI declared Western art dead, that it had only been repeating itself for the last 2,000 years, and that now his computer disciplines were going to take over and reinvent a better art. The audience of computer students broke into wild applause. That programmers are superior is an underlying attitude that still prevails in computer programming today. This is a curious reverse of the tradition of the artist making his or her own tools; the artist and the tool maker were the same. Now the tool maker becomes the artist or feels that the artists are just their tools. The artist, on the other hand, feels, just give me the tool and go away and let me work. Besides, we all know that animators are superior.

It is easy to see why this lack of understanding between the tool maker and the tool user can happen, as today we have a new and perhaps "super tool" in the computer, one that by its very nature moves into the realm of the user. There will have to be better understanding and cooperation, and less of an attitude, between the tool maker and tool user before the computer can reach its full potential in animation.

Learning Animation First vs. Learning the Computer First

Learning to operate a computer and its programs takes a great deal of time and energy. It has a very steep learning curve. If you learn the computer and all its programs before you learn animation, you will be too tired and burnt out to learn animation. A common error in early computer animation programming was that many of the programmers who wrote the programs did not know animation and could not give animators the tools that they needed, making computer animation programs very user-unfriendly and inflexible. The computer programs of today still have these limitations, which stifles learning animation. The people who want you to buy their computers and programs have fostered the myth that the computer does the animation, and that if you buy a computer and some programs and learn how to use them you will know animation. What you will learn is the computer operating system and temporal programs relating to animation. You will learn how to move objects around on the screen but you will not learn animation.

We ask that you use your hand and brain to learn animation. The hand because it is the most simple, flexible, complex and direct tool we have to physically express ourselves and it is directly connected to the brain. The brain because it is the most powerful tool we posses for generating ideas. The computer is an impressive tool, but a limited tool. At times it can be a block between our body and mind and a hindrance to our work. Computer programs and technology are in constant flux, forcing you to spend an inordinate amount of time constantly relearning computers. The Murphy's law of computers is that they will always break down at crucial moments. The discipline you will learn from this book will never change nor break down.

IV. INTERACTIVE ANIMATION

Interactive media is when the audience makes decisions on the course of the action within the recorded experience. The audience is not a spectator but a participant, a player. More formally, interactive digital media is a digital machine-based system that combines events in text, sound, graphics, live action and animation, designed so that the human user(s) is part of the decision-making process of flow or interaction of the events. Interactive animation is a new form, not only because of its digital production but also because the audience's relationship to the work is a complete break from the past. In the past, a passive audience simply watched a recorded event with varying degrees of interest.

Static or Dynamic

This new form can be divided into two spheres, static and dynamic. In the static sphere the interactive recorded data is controlled completely by the audience. The machine's interactive programming is passive or static. This could be a database for a library or a search engine on the web.

The dynamic interactive sphere is created when the computer is programmed to independently respond so that the user is not always in control. The program in the computer is active and has as much a role as the audience in choosing the flow of information. The machine can present you options that will have responses beyond your control; it may or may not obey you, answers can change and you may have to think to have control. A dynamic interactive audience responds to "smart" content, or digitally smart content created by other people. Example: games. Games, in their long history, were usually immediate events between people, not machines. Pinball machines, one-arm bandits and their ilk have been the only human/machine games available. Film and video technology could not be a player in the game world, they could only stand outside and record the events. Now that has changed today, interactive digital allows recorded games in immediate time. These games are popular, and the economic reality of interactive today is that games are the dominant player. "Drive them or shoot them" is often the quote used to describe the content of these games.

Animation is the core of the visual content of interactive digital media. An interactive animator does not have to know programming or scripting–more on that later--but knowing at least one interactive program does help enormously, especially if you want to be a director/designer. Animation in interactive tends to be units of linear animation in themselves while the entire interactive structure is non-linear. To be an animator in the game industry you should know 3D computer animation, today these are: 3D Studio Max, Maya, Softimage, XSI, etc. Knowing a program will help the animator figure out ways to get around lack of memory, or power in the computer, and also help to do the complex animation asked for by the art director or director but within the impossible technical limits set by someone else in the studio.

Animation in the gaming world could concentrate on:

- Action-based animation, raw action. Do four-seconds exercises, as in jumping off a cliff or a sword fight.
- Character acting, short bits of acting.

These can be done with a simple pre-rigged model.

The four working positions usually include:

Events and actions. The basic concept is a video game example. If the events can change the branches and links, it is dynamic interaction. Through this change, a possible number of events can happen. An example would be when you move a character over a goodie (a hidden trigger), you cause an event. An example would be when a character reaches a trigger near the door, an event is triggered to a column of enemy characters to rush to the spot. Action is what happens from the event, as in a score going up or down. Events precede action. Events and their storyboard are needed in a dynamic interaction games presentation.

States of behavior. Events and their actions lead into states of behavior, which is how the object reacts to the various events and actions.

Animated transitions. Similar to branching but animated. Example, a running character is an animated state of behavior, the character falls and animates into another state of behavior. Animated transitions can exist in either static or dynamic interactivity.

Procedural animation. Computer-generated game animation that the player has no control over. Examples would include: when grenades explode, characters are thrown through window via the game procedurally, using game physics. Or when many game enemies point their weapons at the player interactively, it is because the computer does this procedurally.

In a flow diagram for the planning of an interactive work, the static flow diagram is similar to a storyboard for a regular animated film. Whereas the dynamic flow diagram is complex because of the many things you have to deal with. Each state of behavior is presented as a little storyboard. Often the dynamic flow diagram will combine static and dynamic interaction. The static is only static.

The Programming Aspects of Interactive Needed by an Animator

How much programming do game animator need for scripting, as they are almost always dabbling with some sort of scripting? Today they need, depending on the culture of the studio, something as simple as writing MEL scripts, Maya's programming language, to enhance their personal workflow, to do complex behavior and performance modifying scripts. They could also tweak Artificial Intelligence code on almost a daily basis. These will be changed by the time this book is out, but it shows being able to modify existing codes helps an animator. Some people feel that at least one semester of C++ and a working knowledge of a good scripting system, such as Lingo or Flash, are helpful.

Games and Other Forms of Interactive Animation

The reason games took off and became the major entertainment venue of interactive is because games are non-linear, the events are constantly changing and the outcome is unknown. They could not become a recorded media for this reason, as were theater, dance, music and the new art form of animation, until the interactive digital media made it possible. Games could be thought of as the last major entertainment giant of the 20th century, as it was the last one left. (Please see History of Interactive for more details.) Games are now the big money gorilla. In arcades, at home, and on the web they generate more money yearly than the first run of feature films. Animators and their animation give the visual creative form to these games as well as other interactive media. It is a major area of work for animators. There are other areas in interactive animation, though none as close to generating the cash flow of games. In the 1990s there was quite a bit of activity in these areas and quite a bit of money invested, but by the late 1990s the bubble had burst and only games were the real moneymaker. The other areas are still around and are generating work on a small scale. Some of them and their uses are:

- Character animator.
- Character modeling, with the rigging and texture.
- Backgrounds, the lighting, modeling and texture. This could be a separate department.

A typical animation-intensive game generally has an animation director (sometimes called an Animation Lead) working on the project. Time, experience and opportunity in the field are what make an animator into an animation director. A good animation director is a person with a solid understanding of motion, acting, the technicalities of game engines and game production, while also being able to lead and motivate the troops.

A Game Director, Designer, Game Lead, Lead Designer, or even a Level Lead if referring to a designer directing an individual level of the game, is one who starts off the design process, works with various departments such as engineering, animation and backgrounds to implement the elements of the game, and puts it all together and sees it finished. A good designer is very imaginative, technically savvy of the game engine and various game systems, is excellent at the art of collaboration, recognizes and approves quality, and is a leader. Time, experience and opportunity are what make a game director. One way an animator makes a move into the game design aspects of the industry is by taking the initiative, showing enthusiasm, seeking opportunity, accepting bits of design work as they come and growing into the position.

The delivery systems for these games are:

- The consoles, such as PlayStation 3, Xbox, and GameCube
- Computers
- Arcades
- Web on-line games. These can be 2D, especially Flash animation.

Flash is one program today that deserves its own category. This software is for animation and website creation. A person can create an interactive animated sequence and post it on his or her own website, which many animators are doing. Flash can also be used for linear animation creation and has a timeline setup similar to After Effects. The difference is that the animation is created with vector graphics, not raster graphics as in 3D computer animation.

Vector allows the creation of line drawings that can be blown up or shrunk down without losing line quality. The computer does this by calculating the distance between two or more points and connecting them with lines much like a game of connect the dots. Raster uses small squares called pixels to create lines so that when their size changes, the image distorts because the pixels, which are little squares, enlarge or shrink and the line they create can start to look like a bunch of little boxes or stair-steps, an effect called the jaggies. However, raster graphics also uses anti-aliasing to smooth out and blend the line with the rest of the image, making it appear to be part of and not something floating on the image. With Flash, one can create an animated website, everything that needs to be drawn, animated, edited and output are in this program. Because the vector graphics allow one to create movies with very small file size, whole projects can fit easily on one floppy disk and they can be enlarged to output to film or video. In Flash, the animator can do the scripting.

The Interactive Storyboard

For the interactive storyboard there are several high-level concepts you should need to know. I will not go into the details of code and syntax, as it will be obsolete by the time this goes into print. Some people think knowing C++ can be helpful. The few high-level concepts that are important to know are:

- **Animated branches and links** - This is the basic structure of all interactive, the simple branching or links of the elements or events. For the static interactive it is a conditional branch, a fixed branch that is not going to change.

- **Medical** - Training as in anatomy and explaining medical and dental procedures. There are many uses that are being explored. One being the use of virtual reality as a control for severe pain. Virtual reality is where you enter a computer-generated space with goggles and gloves and can have limited mobility and choice.

- **Architecture** - Designing by walking through a virtual reality of the building.
- **Communications** - The phone company has explored the use of virtual reality in phone messages. Virtual reality still has not reached its potential.
- **Informational** - Libraries of today and tomorrow. We are in the first stage of large storage and delivery systems of information. The web is one such system.
- **Engineering and Manufacturing** - CAD/CAM (computer-aided design and computer-aided manufacturing) can use interactive tools to aid in designing and visualizations.
- **Science** - Visualization a research tool.
- **Military** - This was the principle source of funding for interactive for many years. Pilot training and flight simulation was the first large-scale development and use of interactive animation. It was the granddaddy of them all. Still used.
- **Legal** - A personal example would be my early AIA (Animation Interactive Analysis) system,

an interactive laser-based system for analyzing animation. One reason I had for developing that system to use in court by me as an expert witness for Fox in case Disney sued over Fox's *Peter Pan & the Pirates* TV series.

- **Business** - Direct sales, marketing and training for their employees. Advertising.
- **Religion** - A few years ago, The Church of Jesus Christ of Latter-day Saints began using interactive video kiosks to spread its message. Located at 17 different sites around the country, each kiosk allows users to explore the topics of Jesus Christ, Purpose of Life, Families and Church Beliefs, and ways for users to leave their name and phone number for future contact.
- **Publishing** - Nonfiction and children's books are leading the way in the field of electronic publishing, mostly on DVD. Does not seem yet to be a major venue.
- **Education** - Its main impact now seems to be in the home, business and on the web, in areas other than in the traditional education establishment. Its use in classrooms is controversial; for now it seems that it will become an alternative to traditional methodology. In history, Spielberg's Survivors of the Shoah Visual History Archive is an educational endeavor that planned to be the first major archival database using interactive media. Funded with $16 million of seed money from his funds and studio contributions, it is expected to cost between $50 and $60 million. It was started several years ago and I do not know its present status.[12]
- **Entertainment** - As usual in a new media, the erotic has made a large impact on the interactive market. By generating controversies about pornography and censorship and boosting the sales of DVDs, it has affected the multimedia sector in much the same way that video pornography influenced the videocassette industry in the early 1980s. The first big interactive erotica hit was *Virtual Valerie II*, with total sales of about 100,000 units.
- **Gambling** - Online poker and digital poker machine.
- **Art** - A slowly developing area. The main venues seem to be in gallery situations as an extension of the plastic arts. As an art form, it has not found its Cèzanne or Beethoven. Slowly developing on the web, as in my poetry site.[13] Interactive animation aesthetic principles are gradually evolving and it could be an emerging art form.
- **Web design** for any of the above. Of course, you always have the interactive computer screen.

A former student, Sunil Thankamushy, an animator in the gaming field and part owner of a gaming company, wrote me recently in answer to my question about jobs for animators in gaming.[14] This is his reply:

---

12. Currently exists as the USC Shoah Foundation, https://sfi.usc.edu/.

13. I don't think this exists anymore.

14. I think the author meant Spark Unlimited, but the Internet now has him as CEO of DEEPBLUE Worlds Inc.

"Actually, the job possibilities in the game industry for animators, I think, is enormous (and I hope I don't sound biased). In the U.S. alone, there are about 400 game studios. I would guess the average number of animators per studio to be at eight. So in the U.S. alone, there would be 3,200 game animators. Worldwide, my sources tell me there are about 1,300 studios. So the number of animators in games worldwide in my estimation is about 10,400. In a typical game team (each studio can have anywhere from one to three teams typically), the ratio of animators to other groups are:

Animators	5
Designers	7
Environment artists	6
Programmers	5

The outlook for game studios continues to grow. Each year, new ones keep popping up. Whole countries seem to enter into the market each year. For instance, there were less than three good game studios in India just under five years ago. Today, the number is almost 10."

That, in the last four subchapters briefly, is the rest of the field of animation.

Quite a field, isn't it?

Dan McLaughlin 7/07

(fig. 15-1)

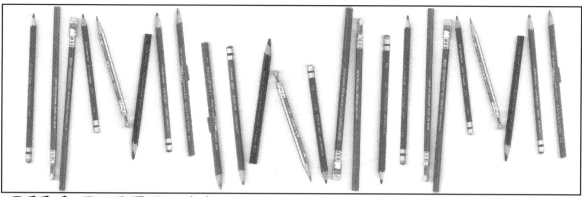

(fig. 11-2)

CHAPTER 11

MATERIALS, TECHNOLOGY AND EQUIPMENT[1]

Traditional Animation Materials

Background board (BG board) - Any thin (one-ply) illustration board will do when cut and punched to proper size.

Brushes - Any good round point (do not use a flat) will work; size will depend on the area needed to be covered. A #3 brush would cover most needs. Remember, you puddle your paint on a cel. Always get a good brush; a cheap one will give too many problems.

Cels - Are made of acetate and are usually .005 mil thick.   A 1 field cel = 10½"x12½", 2 field = 10½"x25", and a 3 field = 10½"x37". Cels have a density to them and you should not stack more than five high or deep to avoid a degeneration of the color and image (fig 7-77).

Exposure sheets - Different studios will print their own or they can be purchased at an animation supply house. They are always done in pencil (fig. 5-52).

Field charts - A 12 field chart or guide that is printed on a cel with all the standard field sizes on it. The standard fields go from a 12 field (12" across) to a 4 field (4" across) (fig. 5-36).

Folders - Just a regular-size folder will do for keeping your scenes or different animation for a scene in an organized manner. This is most important as you can waste too much time searching for stuff (fig. 5-48).

Gloves - White editing gloves. Used when you ink and paint cels to keep them clean. Of-

1. As mentioned in the acknowledgements, the author completed the manuscript sometime around 2007 and the text has not been updated for accuracy. All statements reflect the belief of the author at the time of authorship and may, or may not, reflect current reality.

ten you cut the tips of the gloves off the thumb and the first two fingers to give you a more tangible feeling when working (fig. 11-1).

Ink - Animation ink is any ink that will adhere to a plastic surface.

Lettering - If you don't hand-letter your titles or subtitles, and it is not a good idea to hand-letter unless you know how to do it, one of the press-on lettering sheets or computer print-out type put on a cel by a printer should work to give a good look to your letters (fig. 5-49).

Markers - For the inking process or as color. Sharpies and Staedtler Lumocolor are both good choices.

Paint - Animation paint is a paint that will adhere to cels. The best is a vinyl acrylic copolymer paint. Should come in let downs. Let downs are colors that are designed to match the same color even though separated by several cel layers.

Paper - Usually 16 lb. bond cut to a 10 1/2" x 12 1/2" size, or in various lengths for pans (fig. 7-1).

Peg systems - A three peg registration unit. The center peg is round and the two side pegs are rectangular. There are eight inches from center (peg) to center (peg) on long peg bars or pan cels. Pegs are based on either an Acme or Oxberry system; punched paper on one system will work on the other system.

Pencils - Blackwing 602, Eagle Draughting 314 and any No. 2 for graphite. Blue color pencils are used for rough animation and layouts. Sometimes a red pencil line is used to show animation and a blue pencil line to show background elements in layout (fig. 11-2).

Pens - Regular pen points (can give a thick and thin line). Drafting (automatic) pens will give an even line and have the advantage of not needing to be dipped into the inkwell all the time, but clog constantly.

Plastic peg bars - If you want to work at home cheaply.

SUPPLIERS

Cartoon Colour, at 9024 Lindblade St., Culver City, CA 90232 has been a complete supplier of animation materials for many years. Most brushes, pen, pencils, etc. can be purchased at an art supply store. If you are going to use a large amount of paper a paper company may cut animation paper to size for you. Regular 8½by11 paper can be used, but you will be forced to work on a smaller field.

TRADITIONAL TECHNICAL DATA
Cranes and Cameras
An animation crane is the piece of equipment on which the camera is mounted that films your art. The two most common commercial cranes and cameras in the industry in the U. S. were the Oxberry and the Acme. Since the introduction of the computer they have not

been made, and have been pretty much phased out of the production process except in schools, overseas and independent production (fig. 7-83). If you need a crane today, they can be found used or you could build a simple one. An animation camera is a camera that can shoot, forward or reverse, one frame at a time. The Oxberry and Acme animation cameras are excellent cameras as they have a fixed-peg registration that will give you a steadier image. Of the non-animation cameras that are inexpensive, the 16mm Bolex camera that takes one frame at a time is probably your best choice. Normally a 35mm camera is used for theatrical work and a 16mm camera for teaching. For camera needs, lenses, film stocks, exposure meters, etc., for 3D shooting, stop motion filming and the use of the computer in filming, please look in Chapter 10.

Film

Motion picture film comes in two professional sizes. 35mm film is 35mm wide. A millimeter is 1/25th of an inch so 35mm film is almost an inch and a half wide, and is normally used for theatrical films as its size generates better image quality. 16mm film (a 16mm wide frame) is used in schools, television, experimental and documentary films. It is about half the cost of 35mm. All sound films, whether 16mm or 35mm, have a projection speed of 24 frames or individual pictures per second, which translates to 1,440 frames a minute. Silent projection speed varies from 16 to 24 frames a second, with a common range of 16 or 18 frames per second. In animation the symbol for a frame is "x". Twenty-four frames would be written 24x. Film is not only measured in time but also in physical length. In 35mm 16xs equals one foot (in the silent days 16xs also equaled one second) and 90 feet equals a minute. In 16mm 40xs equals one foot and 36 feet equals one minute. Footage is used as a way to package film. 16mm film is usually sold in 100-, 200- and 400-foot lengths. Laboratory costs are normally governed by footage; 21 cents a foot for developing color 16mm film would be the average cost today. Freelance animation is often paid by the foot, and at the studios quotes for the week are often set by the foot. In the 1960s the quota for animators at Disney (feature) was 12 feet a week and at Hanna-Barbera (for television) it was 65 feet a week (fig. 11-3). These film standards are worldwide and are a major reason for the international popularity of film.

Film stock comes in color negative and reversal, and black and white negative and reversal. Film for color is balanced for either indoor or outdoor shooting. Indoor color negative film balanced at 3200 Kelvin is the normal film used in animation (see Lighting under Layout for more information). Raw stock is the term for film that is unshot and undeveloped. A film in a film can must always be labeled "Raw Stock" or "Exposed" if the can has been opened, especially after downloading when finished shooting. This same rule applies to video and digital tape.

Videotape

In videotape several different international standards exist. In North America and Japan, a

NTSC (National Television System Committee) standard is used with 30 video frames (59.94 fields - a field is 1/2 the lines of a frame - 60 cycles) equaling one second and a line resolution of 525 lines per frame. In England and parts of Europe, a PAL (Phase Alternating Line) standard is used with 25 frames a second (50 fields a second and 50 cycles) and a better line resolution of 625 lines a frame. France and Russia use the SECAM (Sequential Color with Memory) system also with 50 fields per second and 625 lines a frame. Brazil has its very own PAL standard called PAL-M. Videotape is not commonly used for animation filming, as it is quite difficult to shoot a single frame.

Digital Tape/Computer
Not 24 frames per second yet and not single frame yet, but it is getting there. Now its main use is to shoot digital live action that can be downloaded into the computer as files to be manipulated or combined with live action. The computer can also be used to record animation. By using a video camera as a feed, the computer with the proper program and the storage unit, you can shoot puppet or flat animation.

Screen Ratios
Screen ratios are rectangular on a horizontal axis. They approximate the horizontaliy of human vision and are much like the landscape ratios used in painting. Screen ratios are expressed in numbers with the first number the width of the screen and the second number the height. In TV and 16mm the ratio is 1:33 to 1, with the coming high-definition TV ratio being 1.78 to 1 (fig. 2-2). For the theatrical wide screen, a 1:66 to 1 ratio is common to European films and a 1:85 to 1 ratio is common to United States films. These ratios are achieved by using an aperture plate to mask 1:33 to 1 film to this different ratio and a wider lens to project the film larger. Anamorphic lenses are also used that will give you a 2.39 to 1 ratio and better projection quality than the 1:66 or the 1:85. There are also venue-based special wide-screen formats such as Omix[2] and Imax, which use 70mm film.

Sound
Today sound is recorded on magnetic tape or digital tape. It can be edited on magnetic 16mm film track or as digital files. If in 16mm and in digital, it must be transferred from 16mm mag track for transfer to 16mm optic picture track that is needed to make a composite film print with the standard optical area track. If your composites are on tape you will not need to go to film at any stage, just stay in the digital and mag worlds.

Editing Equipment
Editing is the stage of production where the already shot film is put in its final form. Since

2. I am really not sure what the author is referring to here.

animation does this before the film is shot very little editing is needed except in 3D stop motion animation and to correct technical errors and changes of mind. For film the traditional live action editing equipment is used. This equipment normally consists of an: editing table, rewinds, splicing block and editing tape, leader, reels, cores, split reels, a loupe, a hot splicer for negative cutting, regular tape and a Sharpie. The equipment for digital editing is discussed in Chapter 10.

Projection Equipment

Various systems are used: 35mm projection or larger-format projectors are used in theatrical situations. Digital projection is just a matter of time. As soon as the theaters are equipped with digital projection, the cost of making prints will be history. Satellite or digital files or tape will be the distribution format, not film. You can see this in 16mm, which is being used less and less for educational films and small venues. Video projectors and digital projectors have replaced 16mm.

Distribution Formats

Most films for non-theatrical viewing are distributed in the different international VHS formats. But that is changing and DVD, the digital format, looks like the next major distribution format. Digital theatrical projection and therefore distribution are slowly happening, but the expensive theater conversion costs are holding it up as the theater owners and the film producers argue over who is going to pay for the conversion. Streaming film over the web has had very limited success, as it reaches only personal computers and not the living room stereos and TV sets that are used for entertainment.

Theoretical Basis for the Technical Development

Two of the theories that led to the technical development of motion picture technology are:
- In 130 AD Ptolemy, the Egyptian philosopher and mathematician, demonstrated the Psi theory on the sea walls surrounding Alexandria harbor. He placed covered fire pots on the walls, and then on command (drums were thought to be used) the lids on the fire pots were lifted in an alternating sequence, thus giving the appearance of fire and light moving around the walls. This same effect is used today with alternating light bulbs around an opening or frame to give the same appearance and attract attention. Ptolemy also developed a form of thaumatrope, with one side color and one side white.
- In 1824 the English physician, Peter Mark Roget, of the thesaurus fame, published an essay entitled "Persistence of Vision with Regard to Moving Objects." In this work he theorizes that a series of sequential images will give the illusion of movement to the human eye if: 1) they are presented fast enough, 2) there is enough illumination for good projection and 3) this process is interrupted regularly. His theory was the basis of the technology of motion pictures.

An example of number 3 would be the shutter used in motion picture projection, which rotates between the film and the light source and interrupts the light that reaches the screen 48 or 72 times a second, depending on the number of blades in the shutter. Once when the frame is being pulled down and replaced by a new frame, and once or twice when the frame is sitting in the projection gate. The term "flicker fusion" is sometimes used to describe this event. It has to be fast, for the protein that twists in the eye in response to light that makes vision possible takes 200 femtoseconds to complete its reaction and send the message to the brain. A femtosecond is one millionth of one billionth of a second.

What Does the Future Hold for the Use of Film in Animation?

Film has been the recording medium of animation. It is being replaced by the digital. The factors today governing the choice between film and digital is: Is the final production to be shown in tape, digital or film? If it is tape or digital and you have the proper equipment, the production should be done in digital. If the final output is on film and it is not 3D computer animation and you have the proper equipment, at least the original should be on film, though the computer will be a large part of the process. As mentioned before, animation never used videotape as a major recording medium, only as a distribution medium.

Animation has moved directly from film to digital. Some of the factors that explain this are:

- Digital has the faster turnaround time, immediate editing and effects that can result in lower costs. The costs of the computer equipment and programs can offset these savings.
- Quality. Film has the better quality at present, but digital is getting better. Except for features and some experimental work, animation does not need the quality required in the subtle color palette of the live action film. Even though in theory you do not lose quality in digital editing, the equipment does introduce errors that can cause time and quality to be lost. As long as film is needed for theatrical projection, film will be used as a recording medium.
- Converting a film animation crane to a digital animation crane by mounting a digital camera is possible, but as mentioned before the digital cameras do not yet have distribution-quality images.
- Animation has already made a major move into the digital with the advent of computer and interactive animation.
- Today, film animation is still the best way to teach the principles of animation as you deal directly with the basics of animation and there is not a machine between you and your animation.

Summation

Motion pictures and sound are involved in three technical domains, the chemical, electronic and digital. Today motion picture (animation) production is a flexible hybrid of all three, and is in a constant and tiring state of technical change. You should know all three to properly use animation to its fullest extent. Digital will be the main production and distribution media of the future. The visual aesthetic difference between film and tape will be discussed in another chapter.

(fig. 12-1)

CHAPTER 12

MAKING A LIVING IN ANIMATION[1]

*"You know, the only way I've found to make these pictures is with animators --
you can't seem to do it with accountants and bookkeepers."*

Walt Disney[2]

"I used to be Snow White, but I drifted."

Mae West[3]

Overview

There are two kinds of jobs:

- One is when you bathe after the job.
- One is when you bathe before the job. Animation is a #2 job if you bathe.

There are three kinds of working conditions:

- You work for yourself, or as an independent filmmaker, or as a freelancer with your own studio or business.
- You work for someone else.
- You do both of the above. You work at a job (teaching, your own studio) for a living so that you will have the time and/or the money to do your own film.

There are three options for film ownership:

- You own the film and control its content and distribution. This is normally called independent filmmaking.

1. As mentioned in the Acknowledgements, the author completed the manuscript sometime around 2007 and the text has not been updated for accuracy. All statements reflect the belief of the author at the time of authorship and may, or may not, reflect current reality.
2. Frank Thomas and Ollie Johnson. *Disney Animation: The Illusion of Life.* Abbeville Press, 1981. p. 159.
3. "Mae West." BrainyQuote. Explore, 2016. 17 October 2016.

- You own or control the company that owns the film. Your company has to make money to keep itself in business, therefore others influence the content. In effect you own the film but the company and your paying public are your partners. Walt Disney, the original, is an example of this type of ownership.
- You do not own the film. You have no control over content. You control to some extent your contribution to the film. Nevertheless, you do the film the way the owner wants unless you can convince him or her to do it a better way, your way. If you are doing a film freelance, having the owner of the film disregard your advice can be frustrating. You are hired as an expert but you are not allowed to use that expertise. Examples of this option range from freelancing to working in a studio.

WORKING FOR FREE

Quite often, students or beginning filmmakers in animation are asked to work for free as "a wonderful way to learn," or for "a credit on a sure-to-be-award-winning film" or "on speculation" (meaning if it sells you will be forgotten). The simple answer is no. Another way to say no, if it is an associate producer calling, is to ask them if they are getting paid, and if they are why not you. Or ask them for an equal amount of free work in return. Or if "no" is too harsh simply ask for an hourly wage. This will stop them and they will have respect for you. If you work for free in Hollywood, you will not be respected.

WORKING FOR FREE, ALMOST

Sometimes a producer or a company will announce a contest with a cash prize for the best student or independent film. This is fine, but there is one type of contest that is an attempt to get a film for next to nothing. As an example: A recently announced contest was for a music video done to a song by a singer under contract to a major recording company. The prize was $2,000 and the finished film belongs entirely to the recording company, costing them $2,000. The student gets $2,000 for all costs and time and some exposure, with no guarantee of on-the-air credit. The school provides a free studio and equipment. Production studios and animators who make a living doing music videos will be out at least one job. These professionals could be very angry toward the school and the student. Several years ago MTV tried this low-cost approach to acquiring music videos, but Karl Cohen, a teacher at San Francisco State University, and I were able to stop it by mobilizing school and student opinion.

MAKING YOUR OWN FILMS

It is exciting and personally rewarding being an independent animated filmmaker and doing your films your own way, but it is difficult, especially in the United States. As Shirley Clarke used to say: "The best way to be an independent filmmaker is either to be born rich or marry rich, preferably both." She did both. But for the rest of us the need for money, both to do the film and to live, is the single major drawback to doing our own work. There are only a few grants for animation in the United States, most of them on the East Coast, but not enough to support more than a few people at any one time. In many other countries subsidized film-making exists. Today the National Film Board in Canada and Channel Four in England subsidize animation, and most European countries have some form of grants and support for animation. The subsidized animated films produced under the Communist governments in Eastern Europe and Russia before the Berlin Wall came down were world famous. Without government support these are some strategies, in combination or singly, for making your own films and staying alive.

Shirley Clarke's solution is mentioned above.

Work. Make a lot of money, then use that money to live on when doing your own film. Faith and John Hubley would do commercials nine or 10 months and then do their own work during the rest of the year.[4] Barrie Nelson would take out a second mortgage on his house, make a film and then go back to freelancing to pay off the second. Another animator would get up at 3 a.m. and work on his film until it was time to go to his day job. I believe he collapsed from exhaustion before he finished the film.

Grants. Most federal, state, local and private grants categorize animation under the "non-commercial arts; music, opera, ballet, painting, etc" category. Animators can still get them but it takes a lot of work and the competition is fierce, especially in the United States.

Distribution moneys. This is the income from the rental, sales, film, TV, DVD and web rights of your films. Bill Plympton does it by observing his three rules: make it: funny, short, and cheap.[5]

Using your own company. Subsidize an independent film through your own company's cash flow. Bill Melendez Productions and Jim Keeshen Productions are companies that have done this.

Outside funding, whether from individuals or companies. For companies, you will usually need a business plan and guaranteed distribution.

Teaching. This is a good way if you can find the time. Usually a college or university will expect you to do your own films as part of the research requirement for promotion. You will have access to equipment and the summers off to do your research.

---

4. According to Emily Hubley, this is not entirely accurate. In her words, "They stopped doing commercials in the early 70's when CTW started making *Sesame Street* and later *Electric Company,* at which point they supplemented their income by making educational segments (including the "Letterman" series with Zero Mostel and Gene Wilder). When that dried up, they never went back to making commercials, although some of their films were commissioned."

5. According to "Master Class: Bill Plympton's Guide to Telling Animated Stories," Fastcocreate.com by Joe Berkowitz, the fuller quote is, "There are three rules to success when making a short film. Make your film short: five minutes or less. Make it cheap: a thousand dollars a minute or less. And make it funny. Being a talented artist is good, it's nice, but it's not the most important thing. I think being a good storyteller, having a good idea, a good gag, is probably more important than being a great artist."

Students. Do as many films as long as you can as a student.

Just do it because you have to do it. Faith Hubley made an animated film each year for the past 20 years (fig. 2-34). She raised money by a combination of grants, donations, income from previous films and sheer guts.

HAVING YOUR OWN BUSINESS
Owning the Film

Though there were other independent animation studios that owned their films before Walt Disney Studios, Disney is the major model of a studio making, owning and distributing its own films. Even as the major success story as a producing studio, Disney found the going extremely difficult. Though Disney started in the 1920s they did not show a profit till the 1950s as they had to put any profit back into production. For the last 40 years, most independent studios existed by making it in children's TV series: Jay Ward Productions, Hanna-Barbera, Phil Roman and Klasky Csupo. There is also the occasional independent feature. Interactive animation companies are flourishing. Today web based companies, if they can find a way to generate income and when their distribution is accessible, could be a way to start an animation company. I just talked to a former student who is in partnership in the first pay-for animated greeting card company on the web. They are showing a profit after six months. To start your own studio you will need to follow proven business procedures: have a good business plan, a good lawyer, good management, sufficient capital and a balanced team. Outside of doing good films, the biggest problem that my former students find when they have started their own companies is greedy or incompetent partners or management. Be sure to build in legal protections for yourself against this in any company documents. If you own a studio, the ideal situation is that you own the films you produce so that you reap any profit. If you do not want to do this or do not have the capital to invest, then you will do films under a contractual arrangement where the paying party is the owner.

Working Under Contract

Animation companies of this nature do everything from features to commercials, from the digital to traditional, they may specialize in one area, form or technique, or mix and match as the client dictates. This section will cover companies such as Rhythm & Hues, who do digital animation and employ a number of people who are working on several projects at once to a single animator doing one film at a time. One person working alone could be called a freelancer. When you are working under contract you do not own the film.

In setting up for this type of production follow prudent business practices, for the contracts get a good lawyer and budget the production correctly. I know of one animation house that budgeted for the effects in a major live-action feature film. They made just one little error: They forgot to include the cost of film and processing and would have lost money on the project if the studio had not let them go for other reasons.

The two issues in budgeting are: One, how do you make your money, through wages or company profit or both? If it is just the wages, you can put yourself down as director and/or producer for a handsome salary in a line item budget. If your money is to be the profit in the budget, include a percentage of the carefully worked out budget as your profit. How to figure a profit is difficult, and you can make or lose money depending on how accurate your budget is. A good rule of thumb is to add 20 percent of your final budget to make your total budget to take care of the unexpected. I remember many years ago *Sesame Street* was paying $4,500 a minute for the animation (prorated if it was under a minute) (figs. 6-15, 13-3, 2-52), so you would have to budget everything, including music, voice, and up and including a release print for under $4,500 and still have enough left over for you. A former student recently called and was going to contract to do five one-minute flash animations. He was to receive $2,000 for each minute and he budgeted one week for each minute, probably a 70- to 80-hour week, so excluding his space overhead and computer costs, he would make $25 an hour. Since this was his first time I advised him to work out the method of payment in a written contract. A payment schedule that works well is a third, a third, and a third. This means that he would get a third of the $2,000 when the storyboard is approved or the contract signed, another third at the sound or pencil test approval, and the last third at the delivery of the finished work. The first two-thirds should cover the production costs so that he would never have to put any of his money up front. This is a cardinal rule; Never put your money into production. The last third should be all profit. There are other ways to be paid; one is a weekly accounting, billing and payment, with all monies to be paid within five days. Never let them stiff you. Some other issues that can be discussed in the money area could include: a participation in distribution profit, say a 5 percent of the net profits. The catch here is whether it's net, which can show a profit, or adjusted gross receipts, which can never show a profit. If you are involved in a percentage deal (sometimes called "points") and you want to see any money, it should always be a percentage of the simple gross before any deductions. But any special deal for payment should be on top of your regular pay, otherwise you will be working for free.

The second issue is clarifying in the contract the redoing of the work or making changes. If the client cannot approve the board, character design, etc., or trust in the animator's expertise and insists on change after change, then you have to avoid doing a lot of work for free. One solution is to have in the contract that they get one change for free and after that you go on an hourly rate, but be sure to get some money up front and let the changes roll. If they change their mind after final approval has been given, then the budget will have to be adjusted upward and the completion date pushed back. They have to know if they want changes it is going to cost them. Even working in-house this can be a major problem. You just have to let your supervisor know if they want a late change, the finished work will be late also. Put it in writing if you do not trust your supervisor.

Another concern in the contract is the client's lateness in making decisions on storyboards, character design and sound, especially voice talent, so the film is not finished on time and goes over budget; or overtime is needed to finish in time and the film goes over budget; or it is finished quick and dirty but it makes the deadline and is on budget but it is of poor quality and your reputation suffers. To avoid this, a date must be set for client's final approvals in the contract. If the client does not make that date, a solution is that for each day past the date a day is added to the production schedule with the completion date moved back accordingly. Or that the agreed-upon time of production starts only after the clients have given their final approval. If the completion date cannot be moved back, then extra money needs to be in the contract to hire extra production people. The inability of top management to make decisions is one of the largest needless expenses in animation production. It can add millions of wasted dollars to a project. There are many stories about whole production crews spending weeks playing volleyball at the beach, drawing full salary, while a producer was trying to make up his mind. This results in working 80- to 100-hour weeks to finish, going over budget, a bad film, and in some cases the collapse of a company. I remember once, when I was animation director at the Eames studio, it was 10 o'clock at night and Opticam in Santa Monica was standing by to shoot the last scene in an animated sequence for a film that had to be back east the next day. The color lab at MGM was staying open all night, for a huge sum of money, to develop and print the film after Opticam shot it. The commercial flight that was going to take it to Philadelphia left at 7:00 in the morning. Rae Eames had spent the better part of two days trying to decide the background color for the shot. At 10:14 I had to tell Rae, "Unless you tell me the color in one minute, I will have to tell the driver outside to go home, call Opticam, MGM and the airlines, and you will have to call the people back east to cancel the whole operation, because in one minute we run out of time." She chose a light brown.

When you look over the contract, check these issues. Is the contract clear on what you have to deliver? Do you have to supply the sound and the rights? In what final form, composite print or digital files, does film have to be delivered? If you develop original characters or plot lines, do you own them or do you share in any future right or revenue? If any merchandising is done, do you have a percentage?

Regardless of what is in the contract there is often a major problem of how to get your money, especially the last payment. If you have not worked with them before, check out if they have a history of late payments or no pay. Get all your money up front if their history is poor. If it looks like there could be a problem, you can always hold delivery of the final materials, the negative or digital files, making sure the check will not bounce before delivery of the film. Do not spend too much time working on a project without seeing the money. Leo Salkin once told me about working with two young fellows who were the nicest and most sincere people that you would ever want to meet. After working several weeks kicking around their idea for a series, Leo told them he would have to be paid. "No problem, we love you, Leo," they said. Leo told them he would need a cashier's check the next day. "Hey, don't worry, first thing in the morning, we really want to work with you, we love you and it will be a great series, trust us." He never saw or heard from them again.

In Hollywood they say the three elements of filmmaking are: money, time and quality. Money is staying within an adequate budget. Time is being finished by the completion date. And quality is making a good film. They also say in Hollywood if you get one you are blessed, but there is no way you will get all three.

FREELANCING

Is freelancing owning your own business? Yes, but in an another mode. Freelancing is a specific employee/employer relationship in animation. The animator usually contracts only for a specific piece of animation or for work on a specific film. He or she is not part of a studio (except his/her own) and is normally paid by the 35mm foot or for an agreed-upon amount with limited changes to be done in the animation. The term "freelance" is generally thought to come from the name given to medieval mercenaries whose free lance or weapon was for sale for use to the highest bidder.

Historically, the freelance animator did not become a major force in animation in the United States until the widespread use of commercials in television in the 1950s. Until that time freelancing was mostly animation done for education or industrial use, and heaven help the animator who was not in a studio. Freelancing as an alternative to working for the major studios has had its economical ups and downs since the 1950s but has remained a significant economic and artistic force in animation in the United States. Today, with the lack of stability in the major studios in Hollywood and given the technological changes and expanding markets, permanent employment in animation is the exception not the rule. Most of the animators of the future will be freelancers at least once in their careers if not for long stretches of their careers.

This factor of freelancing in the economics of animation is important in that it can cause chaos in the marketplace -- specifically in wages paid to animators, which is a major factor in the cost of animation. When animators are in high demand, the higher wages paid to the freelancer can drive up the wages paid to the studio animators. Traditionally the highest animation wages have been paid to the best freelancers. Conversely, when many animators are out of work and almost by definition become freelancers, it can drive the wages down as they compete for work.

There seem to be two types of freelance animators. One is hired for a drawing style or technique of animation, such as animating directly under the camera with sand or someone like Chris Cassidy who does lightning better than anyone else. The other type of freelancer is one who can do quality animation of just about anything, one who does not have a particular style of animation and is mostly interested in doing quality movement or animation.

This implies that for the freelancer of this type, the emphasis is more the ability to animate above all other considerations. This type of freelancer should have the ability to animate anything from 2D flat to 3D character, from cartoon to painterly, from human to animal, from abstract to realistic, from Disney to TV. Perhaps an animator who does a more pure animation in movement. This type of animator is not tied down for long periods of time to one studio repeating one style over and over, but is continually honing his or her skills on new and different animation challenges. Because of this there may be another aesthetic benefit of freelancing, that a freelancer can develop (either consciously or subconsciously) a particular strength or direction in animation that would not be possible under the constraints of studio production.

How do freelancers charge for their work? For animation it is traditionally by the foot, there are 16 frames in a 35mm foot. Currently it seems to go from $250 to $400 a foot for theatrical feature character animation or commercials. The rate per foot will depend on how many characters are in the shot, how complex is the action and what is the final venue. Per foot for TV children's series can go very low. Freelancers could also charge an hourly or weekly rate or give a set figure for the entire job. On storyboards they may work by the page. Today the minimum per page for a storyboard for a theatrical feature is $350. Freelancers should be aware of the concerns of payments on time, charging for extra work, due dates delays caused by the producer, rights issues and other concerns discussed elsewhere in this chapter.

The ownership of characters or other art that you develop when you work under contract for someone else belongs to them under the "work for hire" law, unless you have a specific contract that gives you the right to the character or to use the character in your work. If you have developed art that is or was yours you should make such a clause, giving you the rights as part of the total contract.

The federal law's definition of a work for hire is:

- A work prepared by an employee within the scope of his or her employment; or
- A work specially ordered or commissioned for use as a contribution to a collective work, as part of a **motion picture** or other **audiovisual work**, as a translation, as a supplementary work, as a compilation, as an instructional text, as a test, as answer material for a test or as an atlas, if the parties expressly agree in a written instrument signed by them that the work shall be considered a work made for hire. For the purpose of the foregoing sentence, a "supplementary work" is a work prepared for publication as a secondary adjunct to a work by another author for the purpose of introducing, concluding, illustrating, explaining, revising, commenting upon or assisting in the use of the tables, editorial notes, musical arrangements, answer material for tests, bibliographies, appendixes and indexes, and an "instructional text" is a literary, pictorial or graphic work prepared for publication and with the purpose of use in systematic instructional activities.[6]

---

6. This is a more or less accurate transcription of USPTO Circular 9 "Works Made for Hire."

WORKING FOR OTHERS
Jobs and Wages

To give you an idea of the jobs and the weekly wages in the animation field, here is a sampling of the Animation Guild Local 838 IATSE classifications, the current media going rates and the union minimum in 2001. These are union rates and also include the usual benefits: vacation, health and retirement that raise the employer's costs.[7]

Classification	Current Median Average Rate	Union Minumum, 2002
Assistant Director	1,725	1,134.16
Timer	1,500	1,134.16
Staff Story Editor	3,150	N/A
Stroy Sketch	2,570	1,082.41
Character Layout	1,465	1,391.09
Background Layout	1,890	1,391.09
Ass't Backgound Layout	1,225	1,028.72
Charactor Animator	2,120	1,391.09
Effects Animator	2,025	1,391.09
Inbetweener	900	862.84
Background Paintors	2,000	1,391.09
Ass't Background Paintors	1,200	1,028.72
Inkers	875	853.72
CGI Animator	1,938	1,209.64
Texture Map Painter	2,200	N/A
Digital Painter	900	847.16

These rates are between the union and the studios that have a union contract. These are the "journeymen" rates. There are also unit rates for story development and storyboards. DiC Entertainment paid $50 a page for storyboards. This would be the low end of the pay scale.

---

7. For more current data, please take a look at http://animationguild.org/contracts-wages/

Teaching

Part-time teaching currently ranges from $40 to $200 per hour. Tenure-track positions will start in the 30s and tenured positions in the 40s or higher.

UNIONS

The main union in Hollywood is:

The Animation Guild, Local 839 IATSE
(International Alliance of Theatrical Stage Employees)
1105 N. Hollywood Way
Burbank, CA 91505
https://animationguild.org/
Phone (818) 845-7500
Fax (818) 843-0300

In talking to Tom Sito, the past president of 839, he notes that they do a survey of animators, asking what they want from their union when they first start working. At first they do not want any rules restricting them into categories, they want to do what they desire. A few years later, in answer to the same question, they want to make sure they get credit for their work and their just share of the money. Years later, their quality of life is the main issue. They just want to go home on Friday and meet the family and not have to work 80-hour weeks.[8] With the rise of the digital, all Hollywood unions face jurisdiction concerns which producers can exploit to avoid union rules.

Often your first job in the industry is of an exploitative nature. In Hollywood it's called "paying your dues." It is done to gain the experience, get a credit and most important "get your foot in the door," so you can make the necessary contacts for future employment. As a recent example, several students worked on a non-union theatrical feature as animators for $900 to $1,200 for a 72-hour week before they were paid overtime. Six 12-hour days and then Sunday on overtime. They did it, got the credit and hopefully move on. What they do not want to do is repeat the same experiences. However, this condition is not only limited to the first job; a reccurring story at one major animation studio is, "if you can't come into work on Saturday, forget about coming in on Sunday."

Unemployment in the Animation Industry

"The lifetime-staff work of the old studios has disappeared with the old studios, to be an artist of filmmaking means having to hustle until you die or retire. If you do not want the lifestyle then you are in the wrong profession. That's also why we have a union," says Tom Sito, animator

---

8. This is a story I am not able to verify.

and director and president of the Hollywood Animators Union Local 839 (MPSC 839). [9]

That is the basic employment situation today. But it is not as bad as it has been. In the early 1970s, there was only 20 percent union employment, and animation was mainly dependent on TV programming and the unemployment office. Nine months of work, if you were lucky, and then three months of unemployment checks. Today animation has the digital and interactive media, the new distribution systems of cable and the web that must be fed and increased feature production of both animated and hybrids of live action and animation. Also, in the United States there is a renewed awareness that animation is not only for kids, so now you have more of an adult market. On the downside for animators in Hollywood is the fact that most of the animation production is done overseas and the increasing competition from other countries often fueled by government subsidy. But, even though it is far better today, layoffs still occur and are occurring.

To avoid long layoffs or have semi-permanent work, you should be very, very good at what you do and make sure what you do is in demand. You should be the type of person who gets along with people, whom others like. You could do a very good job, but if you have a negative personality you may be the first to go. Being able to work in different classifications – layout, character design, story, animation – is a big plus. Or that you can work in either of the two technical areas, traditional and digital. If you are doing character animation, the better you can draw is a good form of job security. If you are only in digital, constantly upgrading to the newest digital will help. Or if you are only in one technical area, learn the other. These are things you can do on the job or after you get laid off. When you get laid off, make sure that you have kept your portfolio and resume up to date. Have the latest examples of your work in your portfolio. When you are laid off it may be hard to get these examples. Be sure to know where the closest unemployment office is, and go there. Keep up your contacts in the field, do lunches, network. Your contacts will often be the source of information for your next job. Be nice to people, because the person who you just upset could be the person not hiring you for your next job. Try out different jobs; sometimes you have to move laterally to move up. A former student was a technical director at a commercial studio but wanted to be a computer animator. However, he was too valuable as a TD for them to move him to an animator, so he had to quit to get a job at another studio to become an animator. Check the publications in field, *Animation Magazine,*[10] SIGGRAPH News Letter,[11] the web, especially Ron Diamond's.[12] Check the Hollywood dailies to see who is in production and call friends there or just do a cold call. But most important, don't let a layoff get you down; it's not personal, no matter how hard you work. If there is no work there is no work. It has happened to the best. Try a little vacation before you go back and start looking. You probably need it.

9. Another quote I have no proof of.

10. Both a print version and a web site, it seems http://www.animationmagazine.net/

11. Apparently now its just a website. http://www.siggraph.org/

12. I am not sure what sites the author had in mind, but googling Ron Diamond and animation brings up several interesting sites.

Usually what happens is after months of looking you get two or three job offers on the same day and then you have a harder decision, which one to take. Especially if you took the first offer without thinking about it overnight and allowing the other offers to come in.

AREAS OF WORK

This is a breakdown of the forms of animated production, with a note or two about each. Any of these areas can be in the traditional or digital format or a hybrid of the two. And any can be distributed as film, video, laserdisk, DVD,or on the web.

Theatrical Features. There is usually a year or two of work. Feature production will go through cycles, as one or two features are big hits and then everyone jumps in expecting easy money. Usually bad management drives up the cost and makes poor films and money is lost, or not made, so feature production is cut back. Features can be a good investment as merchandising can make more money than the film. Animators get no "points" or percentages of the proceeds, as do actors. In the feature market Disney is the one constantly producing studio, with an extensive and aggressive marketing policy. In character animation, Disney feature animation is considered the top of the line for money and talent.

Titles for Theatrical Live-Action Features and TV Shows. This is steady work for a few people. The search for the right title design is the search for the elusive visual statement that should instantaneously communicate the film's intent while generating audience interest. They can range from graphics and animation as in *The Pink Panther*, the traditional title cards of *Meet Me In St. Louis* (1944), the graphics and live action as the gun motif in various James Bond titles, to live action with print titles superimposed. Titles are always needed. In TV, a graphic designer who should know animation may do them.

Visual Effects for Live Action Features and TV Shows. It is a small industry in itself. All the composition is done digitally, while the actual models and effects can be either real or digital. Fairly steady work and several people can win an Academy Award at the same time. The budgets for TV are lower.

Theatrical Shorts. The classical theatrical short died and was buried in the 1950s. An occasional short is shown but the most active form is a series of shorts, usually of the festival or perverted quality. The *Animation Celebration* or *Spike & Mike's Sick & Twisted* releases are current examples.

Educational, Industrial, Corporate and Medical Shorts. Not too glamorous but there is always some work. A place to start, especially a small business in a non-Hollywood location (figs. 2-52, 6-15, 13-3).

Direct to DVD. Ranging from features to shorter formats. Mostly for the children's audience, but educational and religious films are also produced. A larger market than most people realize.

TV Features/Specials. Most all of the holidays have been done. Occasionally a show based on a comic strip or children's stories, like a *Charlie Brown* or a *Grinch* special, is done.

TV Children's Series. With the advent of cable, this area is much expanded. Often the work is cyclic, with layoffs each year between where the old TV season ends and the new one begins. Today production is international as story, storyboards, voice recording, timing, some layouts and M&E (music and effects) are done in Hollywood, but the animation, backgrounds, ink and paint, camera and processing are done overseas because of the much lower cost. Japan, Korea, Taiwan and Australia are just some of the countries where that work is done. Sometimes an entire series will be done overseas but still produced in the United States. Called phone booth animation, as the producer only needs a phone booth to get a film done. The rising use of the digital, which could lower costs especially in ink and paint, may change this arrangement. In some countries, thegovernment is heavily subsidizing animation done for the U. S. market to undercut U. S. animation.

TV Prime Time Series. *The Simpsons* gave rise to a new wave of prime-time animation series that adults watch. It appears that prime-time animation series are here to stay.

TV Commercials. Animated commercials are always done, but it is cyclic with some years animated commercials being hot and some years they are not. Usually done by small production houses. Storyboards are often done at the advertising agencies (figs. 2-48, 6-14, 12-2).

Web Shorts. Right now technical and financial limitations restrict their growth. But it is an area for start-up animation studios to explore. It has the potential for being a new and comparatively open distribution system for animation once they can get into the living room. It may be able someday to bypass the capricious nature of film and video distribution and still be profitable for the filmmaker.

Web Commercials. New, following the TV commercial pattern.

Interactive. Another new area where animators are needed. Games are the only large market at present and distribution can be through machines, storage units/discs or the web. Lack of demand keeps educational, artistic and entertainment interactive production low.

Teaching. This area has grown from two to three schools 50 years ago to over 100 today. Ranging from middle schools, high schools, junior colleges professional schools to colleges and universities, animation is being taught from one course to a complete degree track. Teaching positions can range from full-time tenure to part time one night a week. If you are interested in teaching and since students are eager for animation courses, propose a course for you to teach at a local JC or college. See the chapter on Teaching for more information (fig. 13-5).

Documentary. A documentary made of still photos, animation or stills in a live-action film.

Religious. An often overlooked area. Many are films for children.

Peripheral venues include: an animated screen saver, animation for amusement rides, laser animation for large-scale projection (legal issues has limited laser animation) and animation for the legal profession are a few of the many smaller venues.

Notes

When working on a project, you can get notes from the producer or anyone who thinks they

are in charge. Notes (or emails) can be the bane of a project as they are often confusing and/
or wrong. They usually will never say directly what is wrong with the area under discussion
and can give a poor solution if they do. But you will get them as it justifies their jobs and
protects their asses. A friend of mine did freelance work mixing for Disney TV. He had been
doing it for years until one day a new executive took over at Disney. When he showed her the
latest mix, she wrote a note. "Make it better." He asked her what she objected to, was it too
loud, too low, etc.? She replied, "I don't know just make it better." So he quit and never went
back.

When you get a note like that you can either forget it or do something a little different so she
can say "my leadership made it better." And then resubmit it. Other options are to talk face to
face with the person and try to work it out. Come up with something clever. Quit.

PORTFOLIOS

Your portfolio should be tailored to the studio (Disney, TV series) or position (layout, animator), that you are applying to or for. Call the studio to find out what they want in a portfolio
or what they are looking for at that particular moment. Know what you want to do and what
you can do for them. Do not go in saying, "I will do anything, push a broom, please give me
a chance." Say, "This is what I can do for you: I can make you money, etc." Do not emphasize
what you (the employer) do for me (the applicant). Walk in as a solution, not a problem. But
do not be arrogant.

You may have more than one portfolio reflecting different positions and studios. The
classical drawing portfolio will have life drawings to show that you can draw, and it will have
some action, quick sketch and gesture drawings that catch the expression, the moment or
the movement. Animators do not do drawings that move, they do movement that is drawn.
Try gesture drawing a basketball game and a ballet. Marc Davis (fig. 7-34), in his drawing for
animation classes, would have us do 20-second poses one after another for hours. Do not
copy well-known animated characters. Have a drawing of two of some common object, perhaps from different angles. Have some drawings that show perspective. If you are pushing
layout, you should have a lot of perspective and extreme perspective layouts. If you have a
sketchbook or two, bring it along and you can show it if you have time. Background artists
should have examples of their work, perhaps showing different styles. Keep the use of color
simple unless you are strong in it. Essentially any drawings that compare well with Rembrandt or Michelangelo will do. Some studios will give you a test to do -- layout, animating,
inbetweening or storyboard to do at home and bring back.

A good or award-wining film or films is the best thing to show. Your grasp of concept, story,
animation thinking, layout, timing, backgrounds and animating will be immediately apparent. I have had students who have never submitted a portfolio, their films and awards did it
all. One studio's guidelines for submitting reels are:

- The reel should not be longer than four minutes
- Include a résumé and a shot list
- Be brief, to the point and accurate
- Be specific about the position for which you are applying
- Put the best work first
- Show recent work
- Edit the reel very carefully
- Label everything
- Prepare an organized presentation
- Do not become discouraged.

Do not pack everything into your portfolio. Putting everything they have and hoping the reviewer will find something they like is a common mistake that people starting out often make. This is wrong for three reasons. 1) The person looking will have a pretty clear picture if the portfolio is any good or not by the first three pieces and may not even look at more because, 2) They probably do not have a lot of time and even less time for looking at poor stuff and 3) Your portfolio is only as good as your worst drawing. Less is more and when in doubt throw it out. A few, five to 10, life and gesture drawings (figs. 7-33, 7-62) and one or two object drawings, and a sketchbook or two, a film or two and if you have them, is just fine. Also have a resumé and maybe some Xeroxes of your work to leave for their files. Your portfolio, unless you can draw as good as da Vinci, should look as professional as possible. Go to an art store and purchase a good portfolio case. Mount your art well and with flair.

Get your teeth cleaned if they are too yellow. Being a good person and easy to get along with can be the deciding factor in getting employment. If you are a negative person and hard to work with, you must have an extreme amount of talent to get work, as there are a lot of nice, ethical, fun people with a lot of talent. An employer is often looking for a person with good communication skills, a willingness to accept direction, who takes pride in quality work, shows them something that they haven't seen before, has the technical skills, demonstrates how he or she can make the company money and has a good sense of humor. Good luck, fella.

Research the field you want to work in and then research any company where you go for an interview. Research through word of mouth, the trades, the Internet. Some people will read the trades, including the Internet, every day to keep up with what is current. Join organizations, a union, ASIFA and SIGGRAPPH and get known. One of my former students always made it a point to have several stuffed small birds in her fluffed-up hair. Within a month, everyone in animation knew who she was. Especially after she attended an ASIFA awards banquet where she was the center of attention.

Be persistent. If there is no work where you are applying, there is no job there to be had so do not take any rejection personally, it is not. Keep trying everything changes. Mel Blanc, the voice of the Warner Bros. characters, persisted for a year and a half before he was hired. The story goes that when he first applied Treg Brown, the sound person at the studio, said, "I'm sorry but we have someone and we will probably use him until he dies." Mel didn't give up and every day went to Warner Bros. to see if there was any work. Finally, one day, he knocked. Treg opened the door and said, "He died, come on in."

The best portfolio is a good film.

ETHICS - A SYSTEM OF MORAL STANDARDS OR VALUES

Ethics is potentially the most painful issue you will have to deal with in animation, both your own ethics and the ethics or the lack of ethics of those around you, and then how you act on them. The majority of questions I receive from graduated students deal not with animation production but with ethics. Doing the job is easy, the fun part. The politics is the hard part; it will kill you, literally. I have had good friends who are dead now because of Hollywood. How do you avoid a physical but more than likely a psychological or living death?

In ethical considerations, first you should know and be committed to your own personal ethics and values. Second consider how you will act when other people's ethics or lack there-of come in conflict with yours. Third know your aesthetic ethics. You should start thinking about your ethics before they are put to a test. You ought to be prepared, as these tests will come up at any time and without warning.

Hollywood and Ethics

People working in Hollywood often describe Hollywood as having no ethics. That Hollywood is only about making money (or if you want the big four: money, sex, success, power). If it is true that Hollywood has no ethics, then does that mean the people who work in Hollywood can have no ethics? Does this mean if you go to work in Hollywood and if you have ethics, you must lose them or lose period? Can you keep any of your ethics when you go to work in Hollywood?

Much of Hollywood is a business, and if you act professionally you will at least get respected as a professional and probably a get fair deal. Acting professionally means that you only enter into any business situation with a lawyer, an agent or a hard-nosed attitude. If your attitude says, "I trust you to do the right thing," you will probably suffer a lot.

Practical Ethics in Hollywood and Animation

Personal. Your ethics, your moral standards or values, including aesthetics. The first and most important principle is to know your ethics so that you will know what to do or not do in any ethical decision making situations and how to respond to those who treat you unethically. Stay with your ethics is the second principle. If you lose your ethics you may lose an essential part of your being. For examples of the first principle, I will list some of the more common concerns that my students encounter.

Receiving credit for your work. This could be a fellow worker or your boss taking credit for something you did. Do not allow someone else to take credit for what you have done. To make sure you receive credit for your work you have to remain proactive, ever alert, sign everything, leave a paper trail, without being overbearing let everyone know what you have done, don't let someone else represent you, keep updating samples of your work, get copyrights when necessary and legally don't give your rights away. Practice what you will say or do in a meeting when someone tries to steal your idea. Do you say nothing and let it be done? Do you say nothing and try to remedy it later? Do you make a simple statement, "That is my idea." Do you make a joke about it? Do you attack verbally, "Joe, are you stealing my ideas again, you told me you would stop," or do you attack physically? Deciding your response before the meeting can make you happier after the meeting.

Getting paid for your work. This was discussed earlier but to review. Get some money up front, a retainer. Have a tight payment schedule and stop work if they don't pay you on time. Don't worry about them getting upset, they will respect you for standing up for your rights. If you accept getting less than what is owed you, they will have no respect for you. If they have no money, too bad. Barter something – their car. If they owe you, go to small claims court, get a lawyer, keep the film or art or figure out ways to get your money. One sound studio did a remix of a foreign animated feature into English. They were paid $25,000 for the job, but when they took the check to the bank, it bounced. The checking account was active; there was just no money in it. So the person with the mixing studio called every day and asked if there was any money in the account, and the answer was always no. Finally after three months, there was money in the account, so he got right over to the bank and cashed his check. About two hours later the producer called him, madder than heck, as he had just been transferring money from one account to another and accused our sound friend of being a terrible person to take his money, even though he owed it to him.

Another story: Mike Jittlov (fig. 6-16), a young filmmaker, had his film accepted into a prestigious film festival. He had signed a release giving them permission to show it after they had made verbal commitments of free passes to the entire festival. After delivery of the films, Mike went to pick up his tickets. Sorry, they said, the rules have changed and even though we promised you the tickets, it's like the story of the three eggs, two bad. We have the print and you can't stop us from showing it. Mike left, but about a week later called the projection booth where the films were and told them he was bringing up a new print that was balanced for Xenon projection. He brought it up and they looked at the first few feet, and it had the right titles so they gave him back his first print and he left the new one. Mike went home and wrote a letter in which he informed them that they now had in their possession, after the titles of Mike's film, not his film but 12 minutes of outtake footage of NASA launchings. By this time the film was listed in the program and people were coming to see it, and Mike had said that he would stand up in front of the audience to explain why they were paying their money to see public domain footage and not his film. He got an immediate letter back with his tickets and asking him to please return his film so that they could show it.

Lying. People will lie to you, sometimes deliberately, sometimes because they want to impress you, or any number of reasons. One way to handle lying is to take everything with a proverbial grain of salt. One experienced editor once remarked that the lower scale of lying is OK in Hollywood. "Darling, I JUST loved your film, acting, writing, or whatever you did; I GOT a directing job coming up; yours is the FUNNIEST animation I have ever seen," are some of the everyday lies. The one lie you should never ever believe is: "TRUST ME." Hollywood is the land of the little white lies; sometimes people will lie just to tell a lie. Bear in mind Hollywood is the land of make-believe or as Robert Benchley once said about Hollywood, "When you scrape all false tinsel off you get to the real tinsel underneath."[13] These lies shouldn't hurt you unless you believe them. The lies that hurt are the ones that are deliberately done to blame or damage you. Like when your boss will tell you to do one thing a certain way, you do it and it comes out badly, and then your boss lies and says that she never told you to do it that way, which leaves you hanging and taking the blame. The answer with this type of lie is to be careful and to get everything in writing. Sending an email back to the person saying, "To clarify the main points of our discussion yesterday you asked me to..." should do the trick. Being deliberately misquoted, being lied about, being given the blame for something you did not do, are other types of lies. Always be careful how you answer a tricky question like "Don't you think so and so is no good?" You may be getting set up.

Stealing. People will steal ideas, films, work you did, anything of value. One time back in the 1960s I heard that *The Dick Clark Show* was using one of my films without ever contacting me. I called and it was true. An associate producer had stolen it and it was already taped in the show. I told them not to show it, as they did not have my permission. The associate producer told me about the honor of being on *The Dick Clark Show* for free. I still said no. He called back and offered a small amount of money. I said no again. He called back and offered a large amount of money. This time I spelled out no and sent a letter to the head of the network legal department saying I would sue if they showed it. They did not show it. Later, the associate producer called and cursed me up one side and down the other for getting him into trouble for stealing my film. I was a bad person for not letting him steal my film, and it was my fault that he has gotten into misfortune for theft.

This is an attitude not uncommon to producers. In the 1970s my friend Bob Mitchell (fig. 12-1) had his own studio doing commercials and one day an animator came in looking for work.

---

13. As noted above, actually what I found was a similar quote attributed to Oscar Levant, "Strip away the phony tinsel of Hollywood and you will find the real tinsel underneath." "Oscar Levant Quotes." Quotes.net. STANDS4 LLC, 2016. Web. 12 OCT. 2016.

He showed Bob a reel of seven commercials he said he had done. Bob immediately knew that wasn't true because six of the seven he had done himself, and he knew the person who had done the seventh. This practice continues today. A recent graduate of the UCLA Animation Workshop was just hired as a computer animator on a feature, and one of the first topics of conversation he encountered at his new job was about an animator who had just sent in a reel of "his" work. Unfortunately when it was shown to a group of the animators working there, there was a chorus of "That's my work," "I did that," "Sam did that." The Bob Mitchell mentioned above, to start his own company had to quit a commercial house where he was the top director (fig. 12-2). Later, when clients would call and not knowing that Bob had left, would ask for him to direct their commercials, they would be told that Bob had died but they had another director who was just as good. The production house stole his clients.

One time *The Smothers Brothers Summer Show* showed my film *God Is Dog Spelled Backwards* under the title *Classical Gas*. It was a major success. I was up in the Rocky Mountains when the film was aired, and when I came back I was not able to get through to them, nor did they call me. The reason became apparent a few weeks later when they aired a copy of my technique, which was now called kinestasis. This film using this technique was also a great hit. I heard later that they had decided to take my technique and hired someone to do it for their future shows. When people called and wanted to get in touch with me about hiring me, they told people I was a Canadian professor and had gone back to Canada and that there was no way to get in touch with me. What I should have done to prevent this is to have been in town when the show came out and schmoozzed everyone like crazy, hired a public relations person, etc. (everything I cannot do).

What about being asked to take part in stealing? Your answer will depend on whether you steal things or not. If you steal there is not a problem, but you really cannot complain when someone steals from you. But if you don't steal, what do you do when asked to do something that isn't right? For example, one time I was doing titles for a feature and the animation camera service charged $20 an hour, but they said they would charge the production company $25 an hour and kick back the $5 to me if I would give them the job. What would you do?

Taking Care of Yourself
How do you defend yourself from the above? We have discussed some strategies but if someone really takes you–steals an idea, lies to or about you, cheats you out of your money–it is best to operate by this rule: The first time don't blame yourself, blame them. Analyze what happened, how could you prevent it from happening again, learn and make a negative a positive. Don't let it happen again. If it does, then you are to blame. You should have learned. First time shame on you, second time shame on me. Be responsible for yourself. Be ever vigilant and protect your spirit from being crushed, as you are an artist in a multibillion dollar entertainment industry that has little compassion.

Don't get greedy, this is how any deception works. They appeal to your need for fame or fortune, you get greedy and don't take the usual precautions and agree to a bad deal too quickly. Some producers make their living telling people how wonderful they are so they won't realize how they are being taken. Be aware.

Most people's ethics kick in at a certain point. You should know what you won't go beyond or what you will accept from others. How would you rate your ethics on a scale of one to 10 with one being no ethics whatsoever and 10 being a saint? Know this. If you go too far past the point where you would lose your ethics forever, you may lose yourself. Some people, to cope with their ethics, have one set of ethics at home and another set at work. If you do this, leave your work ethics and what they do to you at work. Never, ever, take them home.

As I said at the start of this section, always act like a professional.

ETHICS AND FILM OR CINETHICS
Your Ethic and Morals
If you are working on a film, do you agree ethically with the content? Does it matter? Would you work on a film whose content is against your moral standard? When cigarette ads were legal, some animators would not work on them because of the content. Will you do any type of film? I knew of one old-timer who quit the business entirely because at that time many of the children's TV programs were controlled by toy manufactures who used that control to make the series one long commercial for their toys. He finally got so sick of it he could no longer do this. Luckily he could afford it, but sometimes one may have to go against his or her own Cinethics for economical reasons.

Film Content and Society
Are you in any way responsible for the effect the film you are working on will have on society? Or is it just a job and you have no responsibility? This is an ongoing debate within our society and each person will have to answer for him or herself. We know that films can influence people. That's what commercials and advertising are all about. That's not the issue. The issue is whether you will take responsibility for your films, and if you do what kind of films do you want to make. Remember there are three ways you can leave the world when you die: 1) the world is a better place because you caused harm and the world is better off, 2) the world is a worse place because you did good and will be missed, and 3) the world will be neither better nor worse because you didn't do anything while you were alive.

The Film and Your Aesthetics
Your artistic ethics or standards: What are they? Will you lower them for economic reasons? Do a quick and dirty job if the money is little? (Producers, take note: You get what you pay for.) How low will you go? This is what makes ethics in animation different from other areas, because your art is part of the package. I heard of one old-time painter who quit animation

after she had painted 1,132 blue eyeballs for the rotoscoped blue eyes in *Dune* (1984).

- Some producers or directors can exploit an artist's insecurity about his or her art; all artists are insecure at one time or another. But for those who are always insecure, certain producers will use this to keep them in line by using such techniques as controlling them through constant criticism, keeping their pay low, their hours long and taking the credit for their work.
- Another way some producers can use your artistic standards to manipulate you is to tell you how great your art is, how wonderful you are, they will praise you to the skies and you don't need to read the contract, just sign it, just "Trust me," they say. In Hollywood when you hear someone say, "Trust me," put your hand on your wallet and get out the door. If you trust them, trust them to have you working 80 hours a week for minimum wage and no credit.

Your Film and Compromise

When you receive an offer to have your film publicly shown but some changes will have to be made to the film, do you let them change your film or do you stand by your aesthetic principles and perhaps lose a public venue? Your decision, and it can be a tough one. The best way for me to illustrate the complexities is with a couple of stories. *The Perry Como Show* wanted my film *God is Dog Spelled Backwards* (figs. 1-3, 2-32, 2-54, 6-7) to be on the show as a background for his singing. I said no, it would have to be treated as a film and shown by itself. Later that year on *The Smothers Brothers Summer Show* starring Glen Campbell, Mason Williams, a writer on the show, proposed that they would present my film as a film, but they wanted to use, Mason Williams', music, *Classical Gas*, as the sound track instead of *Beethoven's 5th*. I said yes as long as they used the original title. Well, they showed it as a film but retitled it *Classical Gas*, which caused the record to go to the top of the charts the next week. I understand that on the feature *Yellow Submarine* that George Dunning, the director, put at least $60,000 of his own money so the film could become a quality work.

Freedom of Expression

In the United States there is quite a bit of freedom of expression, at least in the making of a work of art. However, censorship exists in the distribution chain of getting it shown. It could be economical, cultural, religious or political correctness. Culturally, violence is OK in the United States but sex is not, and in Europe sex is OK but violence is not. Political or social differences are rarely expressed in animation in the United States, but that is changing somewhat with cable and the web.

Industry - General Thoughts

- Theater, music, dance and art (as in animation). Because now they can be recorded and distributed widely and cheaply through film, records and all their current formats have become a multibillion dollar global industry and business for the first time in history. No longer is art done by a few for a few. No longer can the artist just worry about his or her art and not have to worry about making other people rich. How are you, the artist, responding to these changes, with traditional standards meeting new standards or no standards? It is something that is just now being worked out with your blood and tears. How to operate ethically and artistically in an art that is now a business, a business where the owner may decide its the only purpose is making money and its only driving value is greed? These are concerns that you will have to address; it is a new game for artists. Do you adapt to the ethics of business or the aesthetics of art? Are there new standards for this new situation? Can the creative spirit exist in the entertainment industry? Can you exist in the entertainment industry? Can you exist as an independent artist?

- Hollywood. Are there any ethics to adapt to? Are there any rules in Hollywood? Or is the only rule to do whatever you have to do to get ahead? Or, do unto others before they do unto you? Though there are two other rules I have often heard repeated about Hollywood. One is that money, power, success and sex are the basic value standards of Hollywood. The other is that you are never a success in Hollywood until your best friend is a failure.

- Stupidity and envy. How do you deal with it, from the one producer who hates animation, to the other producer who does not know animation, to the third producer who hates talent? All these producers are drawn from real living people. To answer the question, do a good job and don't let them take all the credit, even though they may threaten your life. I remember, about 30 years ago, telling a new student who was rushing straight into Hollywood to be aware that many producers were envious of talent and would do their best to grind it down to make talent a prisoner of their non-talent. He laughed at this, said it couldn't be true. Two weeks later he said it was the truth.

- Stupidity, envy and greed. The worst possible combination, also one of the most common. Remember, some producers are not animators or know animation, and because of this they will cause many problems in production.

- As mentioned earlier, before you enter any serious business relationship, check on the reputations of people. Know whom you are going to deal with so you can prepare yourself. Run if it is a bad reputation.

- When producers, who are part of a larger company, is asked to greenlight a production they face this quandary. If they say no, they have no problem, they can go play golf, go home and get drunk and forget about the kids, no worries. However, if they say yes, they have to go to work. They may lose their jobs, no more golf or getting drunk.

The Rest of Society
Many of the major issues in our society are cast in terms of ethics. How do the ethics in your

film relate to ethics in other areas of American and world culture? Should we factor this into our filmmaking? It is really the same as responsibility mentioned earlier.

Does your ethics have a price? What is it? A cynic could say if you have a price be sure and make it a worthwhile one.

Most ethical systems come from religion, "The Ten Commandments," "The Golden Rule," Moslem, Hindu, etc. Some of the major, non-religious ethical systems of Western society are:

- Hedonism, the doctrine that pleasure, variously conceived of in terms of happiness of the individual or of society, is the principal good and proper aim of action. A late example is in the Declaration of Independence's "Life, Liberty, and the Pursuit of Happiness" (Happiness was originally Property).
- Categorical Imperative, that your behavior should be governed by principles which would have you govern the behavior of all people, a universal law. From the German philosopher Immanuel Kant, 1724-1804.
- Utilitarianism, always do whatever seems likely to produce the greatest good for the greatest number. Championed by John Stuart Mill, 1806-73, an English philosopher.
- Stoicism, all is governed by unvarying natural laws and the wise man will follow virtue through reason alone and remain indifferent to passion or emotion. From Zeno, c. 308 B.C., a Greek philosopher.
- Existentialism, you are totally free but totally responsible for your acts. Started with Kierkegaard, a Swedish philosopher.
- Situation Ethics, that moral rules are not absolutely binding but may be modified in the light of specific situations. Many students seem to favor this ethic.

Example of a contemporary ethical system: Feminist ethics arose from a controversy between Carol Gilligan vs. Larry Kohlberg in 1977. He, in writing on the stages of moral development from self-interest to the ideal in humans, claimed that men could only reach the highest stage, the ideal. Women cannot reach the highest stage, as women were deficient in moral reasoning. Her point in rebuttal, he used men only in his study and women use a different set of values, not justice (a manly value) but the values of responsibility and caring as their most important value. Do women not do well in Hollywood because they have a different value system? Do women find it harder to face rejection as in being turned down for a job than men? Is this because male ethics rule in Hollywood? These are issues women face when they seek employment in animation and should come to their own conclusion of how to deal with it.

To add to the complexity of ethics, is that different societies or cultures have different ethics and what is right for one group is wrong for another. Your ethics or your culture's ethics can undergo severe pressure when they come in contact with what I will call Hollywood ethics.

For some, the word Hollywood and the word ethics are mutually exclusive. And perhaps they are, so if you want to not call them ethics but rules for survival in Hollywood that's fine. I will address only the ethics or non-ethics of Hollywood, as that is all I know along with academia (which probably is more vicious). Since I was born and raised in Hollywood and worked there from the age of 4 months, many of my views were arrived at before I was 10 years old. Of course, my view is biased because of this but that does not mean it is not true.

Conclusion
I don't want to paint too negative a picture, animation is a wonderful field, just be aware and you won't get too bummed or burnt out.

Employment Trends in Animation
Animation production was mainly centered in New York City until the 1930s when the Disney Studios lead the shift of animation production to Hollywood, which was hastened by Fleischer's move to Florida after the strike against the studio in the mid 1940s. In the 30s and 40s, except for Disney, animation was part of the studio system and produced shorts to accompany the studios' features. Employment was mainly in those studios, but there was steady work in educational and industrial production. Special effects were part of the studios' operations. Through no fault of its own, the end of the Second World War, like the end of the First, left the United States as the dominant filmmaker and distributor in the world. With the demise of Hollywood animated shorts and the rise of TV animation in the 1950s employment moved to TV series, specials and commercials. The education area was hurt by the advent of videotape and smaller educational budgets, but is still active. Animation limped along in the 60s. At one point Disney was going to drop feature animation, but the returns on *Robin Hood* (1973) luckily changed their minds. In the 1970s digital animation and its first cousin, interactive animation, opened up two new areas of employment for animators, which was sorely needed as employment was low. The digital process also allowed digital or digital controlled special effects companies, helped by the success of *2001: A Space Odyssey* (1968), to move outside the studios and form their own companies. In the 1980s the animated feature became the Hollywood musical, and feature film production increased and made some obscene amounts of money. In the late 80s *The Simpsons* opened up prime-time TV again for animation, *Who Framed Roger Rabbit* made watching feature animation acceptable for mature people, and cable increased the need for animation production and diversified content. All this made for a boom time in animation employment in the mid 1990s. As we moved into the next century this high peak of animation employment has leveled off. With work going overseas and the failure of some prime-time shows and features, animation has yet to reach the heights of the 90s. Though with the new fields of computer and interactive animation and possible new distribution via the web animation employment should remain good, albeit with cycles in the foreseeable future. One area to

watch will be the emerging hybrid animation/live-action form.

You can see that employment in animation ebbs and flows, but if you have a clear idea of what you want to do you can ride the currents or better yet direct them. You need to map out the future of animation and where and what you want to be doing in that future.

Preparing for the Employment Trends of the Future

With constantly changing technology and new and updated delivery systems keeping the production of animation in turmoil, stability in animation employment is not part of the present landscape in animation. Not only at a studio but also in the broader area of animation is this true. However, when one area has low employment, another area is hot. Layoffs can be rampant in traditional animation, but they are hiring like crazy in computer animation or interactive games. To prepare for this you should learn the three legs of animation: traditional, computer and interactive, as the students do at UCLA. This way you can move into any area that is hiring. Also keep your portfolio up to date (try to get copies of your work before you get fired), keep up the contacts, save your money and know where the unemployment office is located. This advice also applies to "Freelancing" that is discussed earlier in this chapter.

The effects of changing technology and delivery systems also can affect a small (or large) animation studio. The overhead of digital equipment and the cost of research can close up a shop very quickly. It is critical for a studio to be flexible and move fast into new areas and drop obsolete systems. A great help here is to have a reliable source of financing. Always keep the plan 10 years ahead.

HISTORICAL NOTES

"We trained hard, but it seemed that every time we were beginning to form into teams, we would be reorganized. I was to learn later in life that we tend to meet any new situation by reorganization, and what a wonderful method it can be for creating the illusion of progress while producing confusion, inefficiency and demoralization." Petronius Arbiter, Greek Navy, 210 B.C.[14]

The Six Stages of a Professional Animation Production

- Wild Enthusiasm
- Total Confusion
- Utter Despair
- Search for the Guilty
- Persecution of the Innocent
- Promotion of the Incompetent

---

14. "Petronius." In Wikipedia. Retrieved October 24, 2016.

In a discussion, make any statement a question. It will help put you in the driver's seat and prevent the other person from asking you a question.

The Story of the Two Arabs

Once upon a time there were two Arabs who set out on their camels to cross a desert. They arrived at an oasis as the sun set. The first Arab dismounted and took a rope from his pack and tied his camel to a date tree. The second Arab dismounted and found he had forgotten his rope. He said, "Brother, I have forgotten my rope and I see you have an extra rope, could I borrow it so I can tie my camel to a tree." The first Arab said, "I am sorry brother, but I cannot lend you my rope as I need it to tie my water jugs together." Then the second Arab said, "But brother, you do not understand, if I do not tie my camel to a tree, it will run away in the night, and you do not need your rope to tie your water jugs together." To which the first Arab replied, "No brother, you do not understand, when you don't want to do something, one excuse is as good as another." As told to me by Bill Scott c. 1980.

The Story of the Frog and the Scorpion

Once upon a time there was a scorpion that needed to cross a river. He saw a frog sitting on the bank of the river. He approached the frog and asked, "Mr. Frog, I need to cross the river and since I cannot swim, would you be a good fellow and let me ride on your back to the other side." Mr. Frog looked surprised and said, "No, Mr. Scorpion, for if I let you on my back, you will sting me and I will die." "Oh no, Mr. Generous and Handsome Frog, for if I did that I would drown and we would both die." Mr. Scorpion pleaded and flattered until Mr. Frog finally said yes. So Mr. Scorpion got on Mr. Frog's back and they started across the river. Halfway to the other bank, Mr. Scorpion flipped his tail down and stung Mr. Frog. Mr. Frog's last words were, "Why did you do that? I will die and you will drown." "I couldn't help it, it's my nature," were Mr. Scorpion's last words.[15]

QUOTES

"There is never enough time to do it right, but there is always time to do it over."
Overheard at every production house in Hollywood

"Dan, to be an artist you must be a little bit of a crook."
As told to me by George Antheil,
a 20th-century American composer, when I was 10.

---

15. This seems to be the author's version of this story.

CHAPTER 13

(fig. 13-4)

TEACHING ANIMATION[1]

This chapter will contain the syllabi for the three basic courses in traditional animation: a beginning course, a storyboard course and a two-quarter or semester production course. At the finish of these three courses the student will have completed an animated film. If you are an individual using this book to learn animation, you should use the approach, structure and assignments in this chapter and other chapters as a guide to making your animated film and learning the principles of animation. The concept behind these three courses is that the best way to learn animation is to learn by doing.

These courses are based on a ten-week quarter system and can be easily adapted to a 15-week semester system by allowing more time for either extra assignments and/or more time for the final. An example of a 15-week course structure is given for each course at the end. Since two out of the three courses are production courses, a certain amount of equipment and material is necessary. The exercises for the beginning course are in Chapter 14.

Equipment and Materials

The equipment needed by a school for the assignments in these courses are: animation discs and desks (12 would be excellent), an animation punch, work tables, shelves, comfortable chairs (people will spend many hours in them), a sink with running water, a pencil sharpener, a tack board, a writing board, a video pencil test unit, an animation camera and crane (16mm is best) (fig. 7-83), and computers and software (we found Macs the best). For sound, you will need access to recording equipment, preferably digital, and a computer with the

---

1. As mentioned in the Acknowledgements, the author completed the manuscript sometime around 2007 and the text has not been updated for accuracy. All statements reflect the belief of the author at the time of authorship and may, or may not, reflect current reality.

correct program for transferring and mixing the sound is necessary.

Traditional magnetic track mixing equipment will work fine if you have it. Using the computer for sound does not detract from learning the principles of animation; in fact, it gives you better quality and speeds up the sound process considerably. A video pencil test unit is used for the pencil tests for the beginning class, perhaps for storyboards for the storyboard class, and animatics and pencil tests for the production class. The animation camera and crane would be used for shooting the final in the beginning class and the production class. If you do not have access to film equipment, the best alternative is to scan the animation art into a computer and finish digitally. A 16mm film projector, a VCR with monitor or a computer will allow the viewing of the work. If you were an individual following this program, having an animation disc and desk and a video or digital testing unit would be ideal. Access to a digital tape recorder and a computer with sound mixing software would be a big help. Equipment may possibly be rented or found at animation production houses. You may have to be a little creative in getting the equipment, but it can be done and once you have it, you have it. The above is assuming you will have the space for the equipment and the teaching. If you do not you will have to adapt.

Materials needed by the student would include: pencils (graphite and color) (fig. 11-2), animation paper (punched if you don't have an animation punch) (fig. 7-4), markers, paint, cels (if needed) (fig. 7-78), field charts (fig. 5-36), exposure sheets (fig. 5-52), BG boards, etc. A scheduled and committed amount of time is also required. As one of my former animation students Seth, who had an MS in computer science, once said, "Animation is sure labor intense."[2]

If you do not have any or all of this equipment, but have the time, the desire and this book, you can use the basic tools that are readily available. First you will need something to make your mark with; any yellow No. 2 pencil is fine. Next, something to mark on that terrifyingly blank sheet of paper, any 8½by11 bond paper will do. Then you will need a way to register the paper so that the drawings will be sequential. Two 90-degree corners made out of wood or cardboard placed at the top of a drawing board will work. Or, if you have a two-hole paper punch and some wood doweling the same diameter as the punch, you can rig up a peg registrar system. To make a light table, cut a rectangular hole in your drawing board or table a little larger than the paper you are using and secure a thick sheet of plastic or glass in the hole. If you have pegs, you can attach them to the glass or plastic. Prop up the board and fix a light below it, preferably neon, as that is cooler than incandescent. If you can't find a field chart to copy on a cel or paper, you can make one. Exposure sheets can be hand-drawn and Xeroxed, the same with storyboard panels or bar sheets. If you have no cels and want color on paper, remember most paints will cause paper to wrinkle so color markers or colored pencils can be used for color. Plan to shoot on a small field when using colored pencils so as to cut down on the rendering time. If you want to use cels, best order them and the animation paints from one of the few animation supply houses in the world. While any la-

2. I have no idea who Seth is, but I thank him.

tex paint can be used, the best kinds, unless you want an effect, are the paints that flow. For shooting, a 16mm Bolex camera is more than adequate. Unfortunately film and processing is expensive, but working with film should be part of your education. If using film is out of the question, you can scan your art into the computer and finish there. If you are shooting stop motion animation you will need a camera or a computer with a video feed, proper light, and a puppet with a complex or simple armature. To understand the traditional production process, the student will shoot his/her final project on film on an animation crane. David Silverman (fig. 13-1), a former student and now a famous director, was helped on his first job *The Tracy Ullman Show*, where *The Simpsons* first appeared, by the fact that the animation crane they were using in Korea to shoot the series was very similar to the one David had used at UCLA (fig. 7-83) to shoot his films, allowing him to achieve quality animation at less expense.

After you have learned or understand the principles of animation as taught in these three basic courses you may want to explore nontraditional or experimental animation. See Chapter 6 for any number of different approaches. In the experimental realm any and all material is fair game. Look around where you are: How many things are there that you can animate or can give you ideas for animation? The paper clips, the patterns in your rug, the smoke from your cigar, the reflections from the water are all potential sources. Len Lye said he was attracted to animation because of the changing cloud patterns over his native New Zealand.[3] This type of approach can be very successful as it can be new and unexpected, letting people see everyday things in a different light. Two of my students have won Student Academy Awards with their excellent films by using only a bucket of sand and the necessary feathers and sticks to manipulate under the camera.[4] To shoot all the great art in the world at two frames each, as I did in my film *God Is Dog Spelled Backwards,* all I needed was a camera, two lights and a library card (fig. 1-3).

It does help when you are learning animation to use the standard animation tools, because they have been proven to be the most efficient for industry production. Also you will be familiar with them if you want to work in the animation industry. But that said, it should be noted that it is not the tools that make a good film, as the same tools are used to make a bad film. Don't fall into the trap, "If only I had the right tools I could make a great animated film." The only tools worth anything are a good idea, great (good) timing and brilliant (good) movement.

PENCIL TEST ASSIGNMENTS

In the first course these exercises are given each week with the lectures and readings. The lectures will cover, in their normal order, the animation production process and the pencil test assign-

---

3. That statement can reasonably be extracted from Ray Thorburn, "Len Lye at the Govett-Brewster." Art New Zealand April/May 1977. Accessed through http://www.art-newzealand.com/Issues1to40/lye05rt.htm

4. The first film mentioned, the bucket of sand film, was *Sand Dance* by Richard Quade, which won a student Academy Award in 1989. Celia Mercer says the other film is *Unborn Baby Blues* (1997) by Mark Dale Levine. It won the Gold Medal Award, Animation Category, in the 1998 Student Academy Awards.

ments illustrate the principles of animation. Repetition of information will occur between the pencil tests and the lectures as the lecture and the tests are not parallel in content. When the animation lectures are reached, the student will have several weeks of practical experience in animation. This double learning helps the student understand the complexity and interdependency of all the elements of animation.

The basic exercises are in the Animation chapter (Chapter 7). They can be printed and handed out for each week's assignment.

At UCLA, a Teaching Assistant will shoot the finished pencil tests on one tape for ease of viewing (fig. 7-3). The students can shoot tests on a pencil test unit as they work on the exercise. They can see their animation immediately. In the old days your pencil tests were shot and developed on film before you saw them, a delay of a few days to a week. This was somewhat like hitting the keys on a piano and hearing the notes three days later.

Extra Exercises
To Improve Your Animation is under the Teaching chapter
The first set of exercises could be the redoing each of the basic exercises from the 181A class several times. The timing and length for each exercise would be up to you.

Extra Bouncing Ball Exercises (figs. 7-5, 7-6, 14-1)
Squash and stretch or bounce different objects: rocks, glass balls, putty, hardballs, softballs, odd shaped balls, pogo sticks, faces, people or animal's bodies (check out Preston Blair) are just a few of the many things you could bounce or squash and stretch. You can bounce any of these on smooth, uneven or different surfaces and at different angles. Do them in perspective, with shadows, with rotation and changes in the object. I was just talking to Con Pederson, and he was talking about just doing an exercise of a bouncing ball that was dripping water. Con started animating at Disney in the late 1950s. I am sure you can easily come up with many more exercises; how about the squash and stretch in anything taking off, like a fat person or a basketball player?

Extra Asterisk
This is a timing and external movement exercise. See how many ways you can time the movement of an asterisk with the same movement. See how many movements or paths of action you can achieve with an asterisk. Take a risk with the risk in asterisk. Remember, the animator who takes the most risks does the best animation. Substitute different objects for the asterisk: a spaceship, a person moving, etc. Take any scene from your previous films and see how many ways you can time or animate it. How many ways can you move an asterisk in space?

Extra Anticipation
Do variations of the teakettle (fig. 14-4) and the egg to start. Do action that starts a movement,

especially variations of scenes from your film. Do anticipation in a character as an acting exercise, as in thinking then action. Consider the follow through at the end of an action as anticipation.

Extra Walking (figs. 7-14 through 7-21, 7-24 through 7-26, 14-5)
Most books on how to animate have many walk examples in them, so check them out. You can also study Muybridge, live-action films, other animated films or watching yourself walk. Walk all sorts of different people, from all different angles, over all different surfaces. Try walking animals, birds, pillows, fingers, matchsticks, objects without legs (sacks). Can you tell the character of the person from your walk? You should be able to.

Extra Facial Expressions (figs. 7-10 through 7-13)
Grasp a mirror or a book on drawing expressions, cartoon or realistic–your choice–and go to town. Do big, do small, do old people, do kids, do animals, turtles, birds, rocks, urinals, fish cats. Do pages and pages of drawings before you start to animate. If you have a character, then do hundreds of facial expressions of that character in every possible emotional situation before you start to animate the character. As you animate a character, always ask yourself what is he or she thinking at this particular moment? Does the audience know what he or she ia thinking? Check out Pluto with the flypaper *Playful Pluto* (1934). Study actors both live and animated. What makes an expression work? You will need to be able to judge and analyze good animation before you can do good animation.

Miscellaneous Exercises (figs. 7-68, 7-69)
Variations of sign curve animation, water, flag waving, cape, etc., is a good exercise. Variations of the primary curve or sine curve in a character as it moves that will show happiness, sadness, stealth, etc., is another one. Do the exercises as moving shots, pans and trucks. Add your own exercises.

Other Pencil Test Assignments, especially for a 15 week semester.
- An animatic of the storyboard.
- Sound. Everyone animates to one passage of music. This is very hard to do because of the syncing problems. One way to make students aware of musical beats/rhythms is to give the frame count of a simple beat --The opening of a TV show, Beethoven's 5th, etc. – and have everyone put their images to that frame count and play them all back to back without the sound. It can be quite illuminating to see how musical beats appear at visual timing.
- Panning one to three levels. Do on paper and shoot backlight. For three levels plan try sliding blocks that hit one another (figs. 7-39, 7-40).
- Do a dissolve.

- Animate a metamorphosis, which is the changing of one shape into another.
- Animate an action. In one that has been used, a character is sitting at a table, the doorbell rings, the character goes to the door, receives a letter, reads it and you know by his or her expression what was in the letter. Unfortunately, this would take longer than three seconds. For squash and stretch try, a complete leap of a lion or a human.
- Analyze a piece of animation, and describe what makes it good or bad in your opinion.
- Animate the conductor leading an orchestra to music of your choice. Do it to different types of music. *The Band Concert* with Mickey (1935) is a great example of leading a band during a cyclone.
- Animate a monkey swinging from one branch to another.
- Do any of the exercises so that they involve editing. For editing exercises you could do each animation 20 different ways: as a master shot, using different size shots and angles. Say start out with long and medium shots only and three cuts, then MLS, M, ME and five cuts, each shot a different size and 15 cuts, etc., all one type of shot such as close-ups, or all one angle, AU in perspective or all point of view shots. Try to do these exercises with different timing.
- Do the exercises with different animation (full Disney, very limited, very aesthetic) or go to "Diversity of Animation" (Chapter 6) and try out different techniques. A series of short, 15 seconds or so of drawing or painting under the camera, animating sand, cutouts, photos, matchsticks, etc., etc.
- Perhaps you and a fellow student or two can work on these exercises together for feedback and discussion. If you do not spend time learning animation, you never will.

You need to do quite a bit of animation before the principles of animation are second nature.

THE CORE COURSES

A Syllabus and Course Outline for a Beginning Course
This is based on the course taught at UCLA for the last 54 years. (fig. 13-4) First the usual stuff:
Professor:
Office:
Office Hours:
Phone:
Lecture: Three hours per week
Laboratory: Six to nine hours per week
Location: Preferably an animation room
Units:
TA: If possible
Technical Support: If possible

Course Requirements:
- Regular attendance
- Weekly assignments
- Midterm: A board presentation of your proposed final project
- Final: A good 15-second silent animated film (15 seconds works well in the 10-week quarter; other lengths can be tried, but do not make it too long).
- Additional assignments as required.

Prerequisites: None except a desire to learn animation and to make a good animated film. Ability to draw is not required. Timing is considered more important than drawing for animation.

Purpose: An introduction to the principles, practices and philosophy of animation.

Content: Each student will learn the animation process by making a 15-second silent animated film. Also taught and discussed, in both a practical and aesthetic context, will be the history, ethics, current practices and future directions in animation.

Texts: Animation Rules **Recommended:** Preston Blair's *Animation.* Animation tapes and books should be available.

Average cost per student: $25 to $75 for materials not provided.
Average time per student: One to eight hours per pencil test, 20 to 200 hours for the final project
Grading:
- Class attendance/participation   10%
- Midterm   10%
- Pencil tests   15%
- Exposure sheet assignment   5%
- Final – the completion of a good animated film   60%

FINAL PROJECT

Required: A good animated film.
Length: 15 seconds/360x (frames). Titles are included in the 360x. No more than 360x will be shot.
Content, viewpoint, style, concept and form are entirely the choice of the filmmaker. Exposure sheets and all material must be checked before you shoot. You must shoot at your scheduled time to avoid an F. You will shoot the silent film in a scheduled two-hour period on an animation crane with color film. Each student will receive: (this is open – film/processing

and exposure sheets are good to supply). The student must provide all other materials. The final, a screening of your film, is on _____.

10-Week Course Schedule

WEEK DATE	ASSIGNMENT*	LECTURE	CHAPTER**
1	Bouncing Ball	Introduction	Intro, 6, 12
2	Asterisk	Idea, Storyboards	1, 2, 3
3	Board for Final	Boards	1, 2, 14
4	Anticipation, Crane Video boards?	Board presentation to the entire class	5
5	Facial Expression or Animatic of Final selection of shooting dates	Layout, Techniques	5
6	Walk	Layout, Animation	5, 7
7	Final Production Exposure Sheets	Animation	7
8	Final Production	Animation	7
9	Final Production Shooting	Sound, Distribution	4, 8, 9
10	Final Production Shooting	Digital, The Future	10, 12, 13

For screenings, please see Chapter 15.

This schedule may change at any time for any number of reasons.
The final is on _____.

The assignment is given on the day indicated and in the case of a pencil test, it is done by the students and shot during the week before the next class, where the project is viewed and reviewed by the class and the teacher with the appropriate comments. The same goes for the storyboard assignment.

** *The chapters listed relate to the lecture given. The individual pencil test assignments can be copied from the Exercise Chapter (14) and given to the students or they can be assigned the pages to read for the assignment. The students should of course read the entire book, preferably in the first three weeks.*

A typical three-hour session would go like this:

1:00-1:10	Special announcements.
1:10-1:30	Viewing the pencil test assignment with discussion.
1:30-2:30	Lecture.
2:30-2:45	Break.
2:45-3:15	Assign the new pencil test or lecture or screening.
3:15-4:00	Screen animation films/tapes and discuss.

A typical weekly schedule would look like this:

Monday	Lecture class	1 - 4 p.m.
Wednesday	Lab for doing pencil tests	1 - 4 p.m. TA present to assist the students.
Thursday	Lab for doing pencil tests	1 - 4 p.m. TA present to assist the students.
Friday	Pencil tests are shot by the TA for viewing during the upcoming Monday class. They are shot by the TA for class viewing so they will all be on one reel and no time will be lost in showing them (fig. 13-1).	

We have found that Monday works well for the class meeting. This gives the students the middle of the week to do the assignment, which are shot on Friday. A second day for additional lecture and or screenings could also be scheduled.

Introduction Lecture at the First Class

These are two ingredients I have found successful as part of the introduction at the first class meeting. The first, is an overview of the complete animation process helps anchor the students in the weeks to come. For example, I have taken one of my *Sesame Street* spots *(Bus)* (fig. 13-3) and mounted examples of work from each stage of the process on large boards: from the five different ideas proposed to the storyboard, bar sheets, layout, animation, ink and paint, exposure sheets and finally to a piece of the finished film. These boards are easy to attach to the tack board and the whole lecture/presentation takes about 45 minutes depending on questions. At the end of the verbal overview, I show the film. The second ingredient is that for the animation screening I show student films from the previous production courses. This is the best way to show the students the purposes of these three courses.

Films

Films recommended for screening are listed in Chapter 15. They have been selected to give both a historical and international reference within a broad range of approaches and techniques. Though most of these films have been selected for their quality, I find it also valuable to show films that are on the other side of the spectrum. *The Mighty Hercules* (1963-1966) or a similar very limited TV animation is a good example of the use of cost-cutting measures that lower the quality of animation. Features and current films that the students can watch are not shown given the time restraints of the class. But it is important for students to see the difference between feature animation and short animation, so showing clips from two to three features can serve that purpose. Screening feature and current films, and for an in-depth discussion of all films, one would need an extra class session or an animation history/seminar class. Animation students should always be learning by analyzing animation, so a library of tapes, films and DVDs is necessary for the students to view outside of class. With this library you should also have the means for viewing. A cart with a monitor and players for this purpose is a valuable asset in any animation class or program. Also devise a good check-in and-out system to prevent "loss."

Pencil Test Assignments

These assignments are intended to teach the basic principles of animation. For much of the course, they are given with the lectures and reading on the different stages of animation. Each week the student will be learning both a stage of animation, such as layout, in lecture and a principle of animation by doing a pencil test. When, in the schedule, the animation lectures are reached, the student will have several weeks of practical experience in animation behind them. Therefore, some repetition of information will occur between these assignments and other chapters, especially animation. Repetition in learning animation is the nature of the beast. This double learning will help the student understand the complexity and interdependency of all of the elements of animation. Lecture and learn, do and learn.

Back in the arena of practical matter, when the student comes into the animation room for his or her laboratory session, the animation paper, if supplied, should be available by the animation punch. The TA should be there to answer questions. In the shooting of the assignments and the final, I have found the best way is to have the TA shoot the video or digital pencil tests. This allows the student to concentrate on the animation and puts all the tests on one tape for viewing.

If you do not have a TA, let each student shoot his or her own pencil test, but you will have to set up a strict shooting schedule to prevent the students from coming in at the last minute to shoot, and it will take more time to view as students never cue up their tapes. For the final, it is best for the student to shoot his or her own project on the animation crane, for this is the only way he or she can fully understand the production process of animation. Giving the student a set time to shoot his or her film, two hours, and meaning it will mean the shooting will end on time and the students will learn a professional lesson.

CONCLUSION

At the end of the beginning course, the students should have a fairly complete working knowledge of the animation production process (excluding sound), by doing a number of basic exercises in animation and completing a 15-second animated film that is all theirs. This information will give them the knowledge to make a good animated film in the production course. In addition, they will just know a hell of a lot about animation.

Syllabus and Course Outline for a Storyboard Course
(Can be given concurrently with the beginning course.)

Professor:
Office:
Office Hours:
Phone:
Lecture:
Location:
Units:
Course Requirements:

- Regular attendance.
- Completion of four production boards with assigned topics.
- Presentation of each board twice, or once a week for eight weeks.
- Additional assignments as required.

Prerequisites:

- Beginning Animation -- can be taken concurrently.
- Consent of instructor.

Content: Research and practice in the creation of the visual and verbal content of animation (story) boards. The primary purpose of this course is for the students to create and develop boards that they can turn into films. It is a class for ideas and animation thinking. How to do storyboards is part of the process of coming up with a good idea or content in a concept, and that is a basic objective of the class. An alternative class title could be "Creative Storyboards."

Form: Each student learns "animation thinking" by doing four animation boards that express his or her ideas/vision. Traditional narrative, animation narrative and experimental approaches are all valid.

Texts: The first five chapters from the *Animation Rules*. Books, films, videos and DVDs are available for reference.

Budget:	Average cost per student:	$25 to $50
	Average time per student:	Eight to 18 hours per week

Grading:	Class participation/discussion	36%
	Completion of assignments on time	64%

Suggested Topics:

Board One: Adaptation of published material with verbal content.
The purpose of this assignment is twofold. One is to take the selected published material and to turn it into a board that has your viewpoint and content. It has to go beyond merely illustrating the text. Two is to deal with the verbal, either spoken or visualized. Poetry, songs, short stories, jokes, epigrams, the label from a dog food bag can be possible sources. The

selection of the right material is a very important part of the process.

Board Two: International -- The board communicates visually and is language-free.

The purpose of this assignment is a board, either original or adapted, that communicates visually without the benefit of language. Grunts and groans, laughter and crying, music and sound effects are fine, but no spoken or written language are permitted. With these conditions the film can be shown anywhere in the world, hence the topic title.

Board Three: A public service announcement or a board with a verbal supplied by the maker. If it is a PSA, the final will be a video/animatic board.

The purpose of this assignment is: to do a board for a film that is limited in time, one minute or less, and has a specific goal that is a public service: i.e., curing cancer, saving the seals, etc. If a specific organization is involved, the student should contact that organization for information and possible sponsorship. Alternatively, the assignment could be a board, any length, with a verbal supplied by the maker. If you have not done one, this may be a good time to do an all experimental or abstract board.

Board Four: The student's choice. It cannot be a redo of boards one through three. Any of these boards could be for the film in the production course.

You will choose between a narrative, an animation narrative or an experimental approach for any or all of the topics. Any genre is welcome and is your choice: comedy, drama, documentary, poetic, farce, absurd or abstract. The same goes for style. Outside of board three, which is a minute or less, the boards should be for films one to 10 minutes long. Two to five minutes is fine, since the boards are intended for films the student may make. Boards for longer films will take longer to do and present. They also have different concerns in structure. If a person wanted to do a longer board, a feature or a half-hour TV special, they could take the class a second time and concentrate on a longer form with its particular concerns. A student once worked on a board based on Milton's *Paradise Lost* that was six hours long and incorporated Indonesian shadow puppets. He never made the film, but turned the project into a very long poem that was published. Students will be asked to make written comments (be positive) on their peers' first presentation of each board. The boards will be turned in to the teacher after the second presentation. They can be turned in as a board on paper, disc, or tape. They will be returned during the final. You may be taped presenting your board so that you can see how the presentation looks to others. Any board could be your beginning or production animation project. Create.

The Final is on:_____.

WEEKLY ASSIGNMENTS - STORYBOARD COURSE

Week	Session	
1	1	Introduction – Three Chapters assignment[5] – Critiques
	2	Lecture/Discussion
2	1	Hand in assignment/discussion/lecture/assign first board
	2	Lecture/Discussion
3	1	Original presentation of first board
	2	Original presentation of first board
4	1	Second presentation of first board – Hand in
	2	Second presentation of first board – Hand in
5	1	Original presentation of second board
	2	Original presentation of second board
6	1	Second presentation of second board – Hand in
	2	Second presentation of second board – Hand in
7	1	Original presentation of third board
	2	Original presentation of third board
8	1	Second presentation of third board – Hand in
	2	Second presentation of third board – Hand in
9	1	Original presentation of fourth board
	2	Original presentation of fourth board
10	1	Second presentation of fourth board – Hand in
	2	Second presentation of fourth board – Hand in

The final is given during the 11th week and will be a critique of your complete body of work done primarily by the instructor. Or a presentation of the board you intend to turn into a film, with the appropriate changes.

The first class meeting assignment is an opening assignment given to get the juices flowing. In this case, it is to read the three chapters and give a one- to three-page critique of them. These would then form the basis of a discussion. Other assignments could include: Do a storyboard for the very first animated film c. 1905.[6] Or analyze the content, story, and characters in a short film, *The Hill Farm* by Mark Baker for example.

A Typical 3 Hour Session would go like this

1-1:15	Announcements
1:15-2:30	Presentation of the boards by the students with comments and discussion

---

5. See the second paragraph below. I THINK what the author means is that the students should read the introduction and first two chapters of THIS book, and provide a critique of them.

6. I THINK what the author means is that students should imagine it is 1905 and they are going to do the first storyboard for the first animated film. Celia Mercer thinks another alternative is to storyboard early animated films such as *Fantasmagorie* (1907) or *Little Nemo* (1911 but first a newspaper cartoon in 1905).

| 2:30-2:45 | Break |
| 2:45-4:00 | Presentation of boards continues |

Method of Presentation of Boards

Ask for volunteers to put up their boards first. Some people may have to leave early, or like to present first to get it over with or to allow more time for their redo. If 15 minutes is allotted for each board and discussion, that would mean a top of 20 students for the course with 10 presentations per class. The boards should be pushed-pinned up on a corkboard, a corkboard is standard for an animation studio or classroom. If the pin-up process takes too long, the students can mount their panels on larger boards, six to nine panels to a larger board, and they just need to pin up the larger boards. Paper for the students to write their comments on should be passed out beforehand. These comments will be given to the students when they are done. During the discussion after the presentation, the students can also make verbal comments but the verbal comments will essentially be the teacher's role. Encourage the presenter to ask questions of the group and teacher.

There are five basic questions that can be asked for any board after it is pinned up and before the presentation. The answers to these questions will help the teacher and the students in forming their comments on the board. As a teacher I would write down the answers as part of the permanent record of the class. The questions are: 1. Title of the film, 2. Proposed length of the film, 3. Purpose of the film, 4. Proposed audience for the film, 5. The sound planned for the film, which breaks down into three areas, verbal, music and effects. Numbers 3 and 4 need only be answered if they have a bearing on the discussion of the board. The purpose of the last two questions is to allow the class to focus the discussion to the particular purpose and audience for the projected film and not go off on a tangent. After the second presentation, the boards will be handed in to the teacher and returned during the final.

The storyboard class can be very creative, inspirational, fun and fulfilling. The only negative comment would be the teacher saying, "If it can be done in live action do it in live action, and your board can be done in live action. This is an animation course."

Syllabus and Course Outline for a Production Course, Two Quarters

Professor:
Office:
Office Hours:
Phone:
Lecture: T, TH. 10-1
Laboratory: TBA 20-40 hours per week
Location:

Units:

TA: Two of the TA's primary concerns will be: Sound-transfer and editing/mixing, and the final check of your film before shooting.

Technical support:

Course Requirements:
- Regular attendance at lecture, laboratory and scheduled individual meetings.
- A storyboard at the first class meeting.
- A good traditional animated film, normally a two-quarter project. You can complete your film in one quarter. The required schedule is:

1st Quarter:
- Midterm: Animatic or video board of the final layout with exposure sheets. At least a rough mixed track if not a finished one.
- Final: 1st quarter: A finished sound track and finished pencil test or its equivalent (according to your content/style).

2nd Quarter:
- Midterm: Finished ink and paint (real ink/paint).
- Final: A finished film in composite, film or tape.
- If you have a work in progress, an individual schedule will be arranged.
- Reading the text *Animation Rules*, the informational basis for this course.

Prerequisites:
- Beginning Animation, Storyboard course is not required, but recommended.
- Consent of instructor.

Purpose: Organization and integration of the various creative arts used in traditional animation to form a complete quality study of a selected topic - your own film.

Content: Each student will learn the principles of animation by making their own traditional animated film. The computer will only be used for sound and animatics as the computer blocks learning. Computer animation can be learned only after you know the principles and practices of animation.

Texts: *Animation Rules.* Tapes, DVDs and books are available.

Average cost per student: $300 to $1,200.

Average time per student: 400 to 800+ hours per quarter. 40-80 hrs. per week.

Grading:		
Class Participation	12%	
Laboratory	18%	
Completion of scheduled goals on time	70%	

ANIMATION PRODUCTION SCHEDULE FOR TWO QUARTERS

This is not a class or lecture schedule, but a production schedule you must keep to finish your film the end of two quarters. This production schedule is flexible and can be adapted to different techniques and puppet animation as long as the weekly schedule is kept.

WEEK/CLASS *(Each week as two classes)*

1   1 – Storyboard presentation. Fine-tune storyboard outside of class. Begin the talent search. (Usually the voice(s) and music.)

       2 – Continue with the storyboard presentation and fine-tuning the storyboard. Lecture on sound. Talent search continues.

2   1 – Storyboard re-presentation. Selection of style and color. Talent selection continues. Start bar sheets.

       2 – Storyboard re-presentation. Selection of style and color. Talent selection made. Work on bar sheets.

3   1 – Shoot the storyboard for timing. Set up talent for recording. Begin the key layouts. Rethink style.

       2 – Shoot the storyboard for timing. Set up talent for recording. Begin the key layouts. Rethink style.

4   1 – Recording of talent. Time recording for rough exposure sheets. Finish key layouts and test shoot. Set style.

       2 – Recording of talent. Time recording for rough exposure sheets. Finish key layouts and test shoot. Set style.

5   1 – MIDTERM – animatic or video board (with exposure sheets handed in) of the final layout with a sound track.

       2 – MIDTERM continues.

6   1 – Finish all the layouts and x sheets. Start the animation. Do the final sound recording if necessary.

       2 – Finish all the layouts and x sheets. Start the animation. Do the final sound recording if necessary.

7   1 – Animation doing the key poses first. Mix the sound if necessary.

       2 – Animation doing the key poses first. Mix the sound if necessary.

8   1 – Animation. Read the sound and transfer to x sheets.

       2 – Animation. Read the sound and transfer to x sheets.

9   1 – Finish the animation and x sheets.

       2 – Finish the animation and x sheets.

10   1 – Shoot a pencil test from the timing and x sheets.

       2 – Shoot a pencil test from the timing and x sheets.

FINAL A finished sound track and finished pencil tests or the equivalent (according to your content or style).

During the break, you can catch up or go ahead. Don't waste it.

11 1 – Ink and paint. Backgrounds.

    2 – Ink and paint. Backgrounds.

12 1 – Ink and paint.

    2 – Ink and paint.

13 1 – Ink and paint. Final x sheets. Backgrounds completed.

    2 – Ink and paint. Final x sheets. Backgrounds completed.

14 1 – Ink and paint.

    2 – Ink and paint.

15 1 – MIDTERM Finished ink and paint.

16 1 – Prepare for shooting/check material with TA.

    2 – Prepare for shooting/check material with TA.

17 1 – Shoot.

    2 – Shoot.

18 1 – Film to the laboratory for developing and workprint. Make sound adjustments.

    2 – Film to the laboratory for developing and workprint. Make final sound adjustments.

19 1 – The negative cut is done and the sound is made into an optical track. Then both go to a laboratory for a composite print.

    2 – The negative cut is done and the sound is made into an optical track. Then both go to a laboratory for a composite print.

20 1 – The laboratory makes the composite print. A videotape copy is made from the composite.

    2 – The laboratory makes the composite print. A videotape copy is made from the composite.

FINAL – Screening of composite print, the finished film. If possible an invited screening should be held, as it will give the filmmaker a sense of a public reaction, which is part of his or her education.

Typical Class Sessions

First two weeks. As required, the students will bring a storyboard to the first class meeting. The boards will be presented in the same manner as the board class, with written notes from the peer students. If the board is approved for production both by the instructor and the student, the student will begin the production process immediately. If the concept or board needs more work, the board will be presented again in the second week. It should be ready to go after that presentation. If time is available for lectures, a lecture on sound is advisable, as the students will be finding their sound during these first few weeks.

The third and fourth weeks. Finish up any stragglers with board concerns. If they have trouble with an original board, they can do an adaptation. If they do not have a board by the fourth week, they should either drop the course or start the production process with a less than adequate board; the film may not come out too well but at least they will know the process. Some students will block at this stage, either with fear of failure or they are natural-born talkers and not doers. They can be separated out at this stage. When boards are not being presented, lecture on any areas deemed important. Teach any of the sound tools or other tools if necessary.

Then the midterm. This should be a time of heavy discussion and encouragement.

In the next five weeks they will follow the above schedule. The student should hand in his or her weekly work schedule for the film, which is how he or she plans to spend his or her 40-plus hours per week. It is best if he or she schedules 8 to 12-hour uninterrupted workdays. Trying to work an hour or two just won't cut it because you will need that time just to set up and get organized. If more brush-up lectures are not necessary, set up a schedule of individual sessions as soon as possible. Each student will meet with the teacher at least once a week. The number of students will determine the time of the individual sessions. At these sessions the student will show the teacher the work he or she has done, and the teacher will know if he or she is on schedule. The student will also bring his or her questions to the sessions and the teacher will teach according to the individual needs of the student and his or her film.

Final. If a student is not done with their animation or its equivalent or even close, planning should start on ways to shorten his or her film or finding quicker technical means to finish his or her film. But be positive.

Second Quarter
The first class meeting should be taken up with the students showing the work they have done over the break. During this week lectures on post-production, distribution and any areas that look weak are given.

The next four weeks will be spent in individual sessions and keeping the students on the schedule.

Midterm. It is important here to make sure the films can be finished on time. Improvise if needed. The last five weeks will be individual sessions and finishing the films.

Final. The finished film with fame, fortune and the satisfaction of having done something.

SETTING UP A COMPLETE PROGRAM IN ANIMATION
Above are the three core courses in an animation program. Besides these three courses, five other courses are key for a complete four-year program in animation. They are:
Computer animation. Two courses (very expensive)
Interactive animation. One to two courses (ditto)
History of Animation. Seminar in animation, one to two courses
A Senior Project. If a four year undergraduate program or a thesis if a graduate program

Drawing for Animation. Every quarter/semester if possible. It could be taught concurrently from the beginning course on. The total program:

- Beginning Animation - Traditional - one semester.
- Storyboard - At least one semester.
- History - At least one semester.
- Advanced Animation - Traditional - two semesters - completed film.
- Computer Animation - Two semesters - completed film.
- Interactive Animation - One to two semesters- completed project (web, DVD).
- Senior Project in one of the three areas - Student's choice - one year.
- Drawing - What you can - every semester if possible.
- Live Action - At least one course is very helpful.

A very fundamental curriculum structure could be:

First year:	Fall - History
	Spring - Beginning animation
	Storyboard
Second year:	Fall - Advanced animation
	Spring - Advanced animation
Third year:	Fall - Computer animation
	Spring - Computer animation
	Interactive animation
Fourth year:	Senior project in one of the three areas - Student's choice
	All semesters, if possible- Drawing
	Additional courses as desired

Assuming one course only for each subject, the total courses taught for each semester for the above would be:

Fall: History, Advanced Animation, Computer Animation, Drawing, Senior Project= 5 courses

Spring: Beginning Animation, Storyboard, Advanced Animation, Computer Animation, Interactive Animation, Drawing, Senior Thesis= 7 courses

OTHER COURSES

Other possible animation courses that teach an aspect of the animation process can be added to the program after the key courses have been scheduled. These courses could include:

- Timing
- Practical storyboarding
- Character animation
- Assistant animation and inbetweening

- Layout
- Special effects in animation
- Script writing for animation
- Background painting
- Experimental animation
- Puppet animation
- Acting for animation
- Directing animation
- Producing animation
- The economics of animation
- The theories of animation
- Under computer - modeling, lighting, programming, learning the latest animation programs (these are constantly changing), 2D, 3D
- Under interactive- recorded interactive as web-based interactive and DVDs.

These courses could come from the Art arena:
- Painting, Drawing
- Composition/Design
- Perspective
- Color
- History
- Sculpture

From the Film arena:
- Camera/lighting (this is very important for puppet and computer)
- Sound
- Acting
- Writing
- Live Action Production, both film and TV. This is important as live action and animation are blending more and more together.
- Editing, also very important as the structure of film language
- History

COST OF THE PROGRAM

The bad news is that film programs, next to medical and dental programs, are the most expensive in education. The good news is that animation is the least expensive of the production film programs to teach. The greatest yearly cost, outside of salaries, is in computers. For a fundamental four-year undergraduate program as outlined above, the data and cost, based on the program discussed, is:
- *Data:* 12 courses per year
- *Average Class size*: 15-20

- **Total students in program:** 60. 20 enter per year, but an average drop rate of 75 percent would lower the total number. Factor in transfer students as appropriate.
- **Instructors needed:** Two, or to start one full time w/ part time help.
- **Staff needed:** Two or one full time to start, w/ part time
- **TA's needed:** 4
- **Relation to other programs:** Should be open to all, but the budget then would increase by roughly a factor of two as you would need to double up on most courses. Avoid becoming a service course at all costs. Animation is a legitimate major.

Cost:		
	Start-up equipment=	$50,000- $100,000
	Faculty (2) =	$100,000
	Staff (2) =	$80,000
	Yearly maintenance and equipment budget =	$35,000
	Total yearly budget	$225,000
	Space:	3,000 to 4,000 sq. feet to start
	University overhead:	?
	First year. Less space and overhead =	$335,000
Income:		60 students x $15,000 per student = Endowments/donations =$900,000 gross
Endowments/donations =		$?

For a graduate program, the costs are roughly the same, but the number of students is smaller. As animation is here to stay, in a big way, starting an animation program early will pay off in the future. Now some conversions to a 15-week semester schedule.

15 -Week Schedule
For the Beginning Course

WEEK	ASSIGNMENT	LECTURE
1	Bouncing Ball	Introduction
2	Asterisk	Idea
3	Anticipation	Storyboards
4	Facial Expression	Layout, Techniques
5	Walk	Layout
6	Board for Final	Layout
7	Animatic	Midterm-Board presentation to entire class
8	Exposure Sheets or Extra Pencil Tests Animatic is presented to the class	
9	Crane/Exposure Sheets/Final Production	Animation
10	Final Production	Animation
11	Final Production	Post-Production/Distribution

12	Final Production	Sound
13	Final Production	Digital/Computer Animation
14	Final Production	Interactive
15	Shooting	The Future

Final:_____.

Other Pencil Test Assignments are in Chapter 14, "Exercises."

Options for a 15-week schedule for the Storyboard Course

These are some options for a 15 week schedule. Add an extra topic or two. Spend more time in lecture and discussion. Take an extra week or two to record (tape or animatic) all the boards for a final presentation. Do a group storyboard. Do a board under time pressure. If we have a free class, I will divide up the class into groups (always make it uneven like three, five or seven so that any activity will not end in a tie or an argument) and give a topic (a board about the tooth fairy) at the beginning of class, then send them out of the room to come up a team board within the next hour and a half. When they return, each group will present its board to the others with great fun and learning had by all.

Options for a 30-week schedule for the production course

In a 30 week (semester) program more time could be added in the storyboard, layout and animation stages. They will need it. The important thing is to keep everyone on schedule.

TEACHING AT A COLLEGE OR UNIVERSITY

Ah, teaching - yes - the four easy steps to a successful teaching career:

- Step one: Have high standards and principles for your profession – teaching.
- Step Two: First get the job. No job is perfect at the start. It should ideally be tenure or a tenure track position. Be diplomatic about Step One if you run into opposition.
- Step three: Continue to be diplomatic and get tenure. Make sure what is needed for tenure: this means good teaching and lots of research, both professionally and academic (more below).
- Step four: After you have tenure, let animation rule.

To get tenure you will probably have to pass through the academic battlefield. This means the battle between the type one teacher and the type two teachers. A type one teacher is one who (1) is an academic with an academic degree (Ph.D.), (2) his or her field (if not in the sciences) exists mainly in the academic arena and (3) His or her students can only find work in the academic field. A type two teacher is one who (1) has much more experience in their field than the academic field (an MFA is the preferred degree), (2) his or her field exists mainly outside of academia and (3) his or her students work mainly outside of academia. The battlefield is fought on the academic's home ground, academia, where the type one teacher is fighting for the control of the hiring process and the direction of higher education, as that means security and power for him or her and jobs for his or her students. It can be a tough battle; you can be the enemy through no fault of your own. But don't blame them; it is part of their nature, like the story of the frog and the scorpion. One way to put some odds in your favor is to do papers for presentations at the SAS or UFV A and get them published.

Deans and Chairs can be incompetent and therefore a problem. This is a quote from a book I am reading: "There was in his manner a nervous intensity which contained the odd mixture of aggression and defensiveness which rodents have, and those who engage in university politics."[7] But you will win: deans and chairs come and go but the faculty always remains.

No job at the beginning is going to be perfect. My job was not perfect. It took many years of hard work to achieve what the UCLA Animation Workshop has become, but after you get tenure it can be done (fig. 13-5). There is no perfect job. You will make the job perfect. Patience.

CONCLUSION

Whatever the student expects, the above program should provide. It should be flexible enough for the students who want a rigid curriculum, and rigid enough for students who want an open curriculum. It should leave plenty of room for their own creativity or vision. It can lead to the workplace or the studio, perhaps to a lifetime in animation. For as a teaching philosophy, Kant once said (slightly paraphrased): There are three classes of students, the very smart, who you provide support for and stay out of their way, the large middle, who you teach, and the others who only want attention and so you do not waste too much time on them.[8]

If the three levels of education are Information, Knowledge and Wisdom, these basic animation courses will more than provide the first level, Information, give the foundation and a strong leg up for the second level, Knowledge, and a direction and encouragement for the third level, Wisdom.

Many years ago a friend was teaching at a local state university. One day a student approached him after class and said, "In lecture today you said the purpose of education is to teach you how to think. Another of my professors said the same thing. Is this a new policy of the school?" All Peter could think of was to find out the other professor's name so he could talk to him.[9]

Cheating is hard to do in animation courses but some students will try. One young woman student, who I had not seen for several weeks, brought in a 10-inch stack of animation paper, saying it was her work for the quarter. When I started to flip through the stack I found that the only drawing was the one on top.

---

7. Sorry, I have no idea where this came from. Kristi Haar, the diligent proof-reader, suggests Robert Barnard, English crime writer, or the book, *Hypocrisy: Don't Leave Home Without It* (2002).
8. While I am unable to find the source of this quote, it does sound like something that the author would say.
9. Again, I have no idea who Peter is.

"It is hard to teach a young dog old tricks."
The Author

"If you remain a pupil, you serve your teacher badly."
Nietzsche[10]

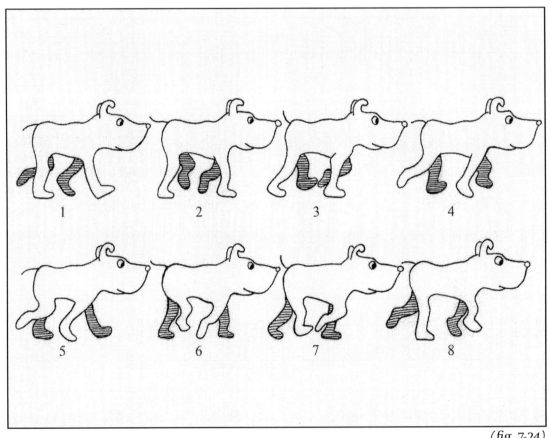

(fig. 7-24)

---

10. Goodreads has this as, "One repays a teacher badly if one remains nothing but a student." goodreads.com/quotes/279256-one-repays-a-teacher-badly-if-one-always-remains-nothing

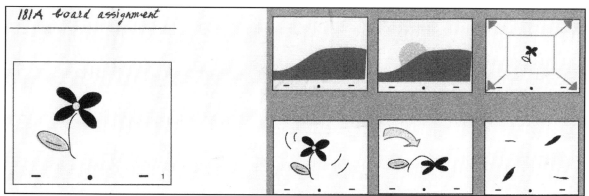

(fig. 2-11)

CHAPTER 14 EXERCISES

PENCIL TEST ASSIGNMENTS[1]

These assignments are intended to teach the basic principles of animation. For much of the course, they are given in parallel with the lectures and reading on the different stages of animation. Each week the student will be learning both a stage of animation--layout, for instance--in lecture and a principle of animation by doing a pencil test. When, in the schedule, the animation lectures are reached, the student will have several weeks of practical experience in animation behind him or her. Therefore some repetition of informtion will occur between these assignments and other chapters, especially Animation. Repetition in learning animation is the nature of the beast. This double learning will help the student understand the complexity and interdependency of all of the elements ofanimation. Lecture and learn, do and learn.

Back in the arena of practical matter, when the student comes into the animation room for his or her laboratory session, the animation paper, if supplied, should be available by the animation punch. The TA should be there to answer questions. In the shooting of the assignments and the final, I have found the best way is to have the TA shoot the video or digital pencil tests (fig. 7-3). This allows the student to concentrate on the animation and puts all the tests on one tape for viewing. If you do not have a TA, let each student shoot his or her own pencil test, but you will have to set up a strict shooting schedule to prevent the students from coming in at the last minute to shoot, and it will take more time to view as students never cue up their tapes. For the final, it is best for the student to shoot his or her own project on

---

1. As mentioned in the Acknowledgements, the author completed the manuscript sometime around 2007 and the text has not been updated for accuracy. All statements reflect the belief of the author at the time of authorship and may, or may not, reflect current reality.

the animation crane, for this is the only way he or she can fully understand the production process of animation. Giving the student a set time of two hours to shoot his or her film, and meaning it, will mean the shooting will end on time and the student will learn a professional lesson. One of my students, now a famous director, was helped immensely because on his first job, *The Simpson's* segment of *The Tracy Ullman Show*, the animation crane (fig. 7-83) they were using in Korea to shoot the series was very similar to the one David[2] had used at UCLA to shoot his films. Understanding the crane allowed him to achieve better-quality animation at less expense.

BOUNCING BALL - Assignment #1 see also pp. 153-158

The origins of bouncing ball exercise, probably the first exercise in animation, are lost in the dark and murky beginnings of animation. The term "ball" is somewhat misleading as you will be really drawing a rough and changing circle (figs. 14-1, 7-5, 7-6). Your animation will make this circle appear as a ball by the way you time, move and change it. If you wanted to make it a baseball and a crate of apples (a rectangle was added to this exercise about 40 years ago), you would add the details of the baseball and the crate later after the animation is completed on the basic shapes. This is the way animation is normally approached: First get the movement of the basic shape(s) down, then add the details.

Your tools are a Blackwing 602 pencil (fig. 11-2) or a No. 2 yellow pencil (your standard pencil) and a Sharpie. Your materials are at least 30 sheets of punched animation paper (fig. 7-4). The equipment needed will be an animation disc and desk. The assignment a circle (ball) falls into the screen from screen left (entering from screen left is somewhat arbitrary, but is based on the fact that European languages read from left to right). It hits and when it hits immediately changes into a rectangle, bounces once as a rectangle, hits a second time and immediately changes back into a circle and bounces off the paper (be sure to draw it all the way to the edge). You will do this in 24 sequential drawings (fig. 7-5). However, the first actual drawing will be of your layout, which in this case will consist of a path of action: of the ball/rectangle bouncing and hitting. For this you first mark the two impact or hit points toward the bottom third of the paper, but not too close to the bottom because of the TV cut-off, and each one about a quarter in from the side. The path of action can follow a normal circular arc, though a high or low arc can be done for different effects.

If you have a field chart (fig. 5-36), it is helpful to place that on your animation disc so that you can see the edges of a 12 field. Everything should be inside the 12 field center (12FC), roughly one-quarter inch on the top and the sides and one and half inch on the bottom. And speaking of the bottom, this is where the punch holes should be so that you can register the paper on

---

2. Silverman. David Silverman is the student in question (fig. 13-3).

the bottom pegs of the animation disc. In the old days (the 1920s and 1930s) animators on the East Coast used top pegs to register their paper and animators on the West Coast used bottom pegs because they claimed it made it easier to flip their drawings when they checked them. The West Coast position won for no particular reason and today we use bottom pegs as the basic pegs.

Now on a sheet of paper mark off 24 positions on your path of action for the 24 positions of your art (fig. 7-6). They can be numbered if you like. You will vary the distance between these marks to make the animated object go slower or faster (the greater the distance the faster, the smaller the distance the slower the image will move). This is to mimic the effect of gravity, which pulls us down--the Earth sucks--and will slow the bouncing object at the top of its arc and move it faster as it goes down and bounces up. So the spaces will be farther apart going up and coming down and closer together at the top of the arc. Now draw the circle or rectangle on the path of action, roughly centering it on the position marks. The shape of the circle and rectangle will be constantly changing to reflect the pull of gravity and the squash and stretch of the impacts. They will stretch when going up or down and squash, hitting with a flat bottom and a bulge on the top and sides, at the impact point. It could be that the only normal circle or rectangle will be the drawings at the top of the arc.

You now have a master layout sheet with all the drawings on it. The next step is to copy each drawing to its own individual sheet, using a pencil or Sharpie. Do not use ballpoint pen as it will be too light and hard to see when it is filmed or taped. Keep your drawings loose; they will have more "life" that way and you won't go insane trying to make each one perfect. But if you are a perfectionist, at least use the lid of a jar for the circle, not a compass. As you copy each drawing, always number each piece of paper in the lower right-hand corner of the paper. When done, you should have 24 sheets of paper in order, each one with a drawing of a circle or rectangle on it. It should only take a couple of hours to do this exercise. You will not need exposure sheets for this assignment as the bouncing balls will be shot three times. Once at one frame shot for each drawing, once at two frames shot for each drawing and last at three frames shot per drawing. This is called shooting on 1's, 2's or 3's. The reason it is shot at these three rates is to illustrate the three basic film shooting speeds that give smooth, continuous motion.

This also shows if an action has the required amount of time needed to make its action believable. When the 24 drawings are shot on 1's, the action will last one second on screen (24 frames = one second). When shot on 2's, the bouncing ball will be on the screen for two seconds or 48 frames. On 3's it will be on for 3 seconds or 72xs. Which timing looks correct for a bouncing ball to cross the screen? Or do all three look acceptable and is it an aesthetic choice that the object is moving either faster or slower? This is one of the basic questions animators ask themselves on each bit of animation they do.

As mentioned before, a good way to get a sense of the time needed for an action is to move your finger or an object over the path of action and count seconds to yourself until you find the proper time needed for the action. Then, you take that time and convert it from seconds to frames (at 24x's per second) and divide that number by 2, assuming you are shooting on 2's and discounting holds. The resulting number will tell you how many drawings you need. This assignment will be on the screen for six seconds or 144x's.

In a classroom situation each student should do a name sheet to be shot for 12 frames at the beginning of his or her exercise. Twelve frames of blank paper should be shot between each student's work and between each 1's, 2's or 3's. Twelve frames are used so the students can get used to how long is a ½ a second, a march time beat in music, and is usually considered the minimal time needed to read an image. Twenty-four sequential drawings in order, preferably on punched animation paper, with the student's name sheet on top and held together with a paper clip will be turned in to be shot. The punched holes should be on the bottom and each sheet must be properly numbered in the lower right-hand corner. When the numbered drawings are in order starting from the top, this is called a cameraman's stack, as they will just put the whole stack on the pegs of the animation crane and remove them one at a time, shooting them as they do so. An animator's stack is with the numbers on the bottom of the stack so that it is easier to flip them when checking the animation.

And you can start flipping your animation to see if it works with this exercise. Check the squash and stretch when the circle/ball object hits. The type or the material of the object is defined by the way it reacts when it hits. If it is a glass ball it will shatter and break, a ball of wet dough will sort of go "splot" and not bounce too well, a shot put will hit, bounce very little and roll away, and a tennis ball will react as a tennis ball in this assignment. You will not need a ground line (unless you want to put a dent in it when the shot put hits), because when an object hits and bounces, the ground line is defined in the viewer's mind. You can put in speed lines, cartoon-like lines behind the object to give the impression of speed. But do not put in too many or for too long, or else they will become part of the object. A moving ground shadow is OK to do, but remember to keep your light source constant. Keep the circle and rectangle 2D for this assignment. Make sure the volume remains roughly the same or you may be getting into 3D movement (by changing the size, you can give the impression that the object is coming toward you or away from you) or character animation (by changing the size in a random manner, you may imply that the object has life and is not a secondary or inert object that obeys the laws of physics). Do not rotate the objects (too hard to control at this stage) nor put faces on them (maybe interpreted as a cheap gag used to hide the fact you cannot do the work) in this exercise. This assignment is to learn the principles of moving a simple image through space. We call this exterior animation. Interior animation, movement within the object, will be in future assignments. Moving it through space is hard enough. Even though everyone will be doing the exact same exercise, each bouncing ball will be different, and this difference is one of the powers of animation.

Later you can use this exercise for different learning experiences. Bouncing a realistic object, a 3D baseball, a pogo stick, a human or an animal jumping, leaping, or bouncing. You can bounce in 3D, either advancing or receding. Osamu Tezuka made a very good film based on these principles *Jumping* (1984).

With the Bouncing Ball exercise, you have completed the most basic and oldest animation pencil test. Even the first computer animation was a bouncing ball done at MIT in 1950 by a chap named Saxenian. In this traditional beginning exercise you have been introduced to:

- The principle of squash and stretch.
- The process of doing the layout, with the timing and movement planned, before starting your animation.
- The controlling of the speed of movement by changing the distance between drawings.
- The logic for the changes in speed of movement, in this case gravity.
- The changes in speed or time on the screen between shooting on 1's, 2's or 3's and seeing which of these works better for making the animation believable as relating to the time the action is needed to be on the screen. This will help you later to visualize time and movement on the screen when you plan your animation.
- The audience's acceptance of an immediate change in character, an instantaneous metamorphosis, justified by an action, the hit.
- The audience's acceptance of the nature of the bouncing ball, like a tennis ball, and of a ground line by the way the circle and rectangle react.
- Seeing the relationship between sequential drawings on paper that turn into your first (for most) animation on a screen.

A cautionary note, this assignment is done as straight-ahead animation, which is unlike the process of most animation where you first do the key poses and then the drawings in between.

Handouts and display: Written assignment. An example of the entire assignment is tacked to the board, including the 24 sequential drawings, numbered and in order, and the layout drawings, so they can refer to it during the laboratory session. Though these can be copied, most students will want to do their own and do it better. If someone copies them, then you will know what kind of student he ot he or she is. Even though there is one master template, I promise you they will all look different.

A review of some basic principles of controlling speed in animation. If you have read this in the Animation chapter, skip over it if you like. If not, read on.

There are only four basic changes in speed that animators use:

Even speed. The distance between each drawing is the same and it is all shot at the same rate. The speed of this movement is constant and unchanging. It is a mechanical movement, such as a pan or truck or how a mechanical robot would move. Usually even speed will lack life, unless something else is going on. It is not to be used if you want your moving image to live as in character animation. Keeping everything at an even speed is often a concern for beginning animators in cycles, and in computer animation programs as it can make the animation dull and boring.

Slow to fast. The distance between drawings is close at the start and farther apart as the movement speeds up. It is used to change speed. In character animation it is used to go from a slow take to a fast reaction. Often it is used for starting a movement that is unprovoked, or when a ball is starting to fall.

Fast to slow. The distance between the drawings is farther apart at the start and closer together when the movement slows down. It is also used to change speed as would happen when a character puts his or her hand on a hot stove. It can also be used in stopping a movement. A very experienced animator once said she always used either slow to fast or fast to slow to go into or out of a hold, and usually it didn't matter which, but that the change of speed moving out or into hold was absolutely essential.

Any combination of 1, 2 and 3, slow, fast, even, slow, even, fast, slow, fast. When all three of the above are used in combination, you can get a skillful rhythm and flow to your movement.

The principle of controlling speed is: The shooting on 1's, 2's and 3's and the distance between each drawing are the ways you control the timing (speed) of movement. The other aspect of movement, which is non-movement or holds, will be covered in the second assignment – the asterisk.

ASTERISK - Assignment #2 see also pp. 158-162

For this assignment you will animate a simple shape anyone can draw – one asterisk (*). The purpose of the asterisk assignment is to introduce you to the creation and the control of time in movement by animating a movement with holds and using exposure sheets as an integral part of the process. You will be controlling the time of both movement and non-movement. Non-movement is very important. Sometimes, if timed correctly, it is more important than movement, as it defines, accents and anticipates the movement. Holds interrupt the movement and therefore have a different impact than continuous movement, and this exercise is to begin to show the student this difference. Think of a hold as a pause. Observe how often we pause in speech, in movement, in thinking and in music. Life is a series of stop and go, pause and movement. Holds, done in a pattern, can add beats or a rhythm to your animation. A common beginning mistake of a student who wants to learn full character animation is that he or she gets drunk with full movement and never pauses to consider if the animation is really working.

For this assignment the type of movement is up to you. Sequential, random, poetic, staccato, flowing, jerky, a path, an action (a pause, then a fall and bounce), an abstract movement or an abstract mimic of character movement. Paul Klee once said "a line is just a dot taking a walk."[3] In your movement at least one 12-frame hold (a hold is the same drawing shot for any number of frames over four) is required. You can use more holds of varying lengths if you want. But please do not do one hold for the entire assignment–that is a still picture. This assignment is 72x's long (three seconds) and when, in that 72x's, the 12x hold occurs will be shown on the exposure sheet. Outside of the holds, the animation should be done on 2's. Shooting on 1's for any length of time can take up too much shooting time. The information of how long each drawing is to be shot is on the exposure sheet (fig. 5-52). Even if you are shooting the animation yourself, you must do an exposure sheet. Why? Exposure sheets are a very necessary part of the timing and are integral to the animation process. They are a record of what you have shot, and believe me you will forget the timing of what you have shot 10 minutes after you have shot it, unless you have written it down. Putting the number of frames to be shot on the bottom of the paper is far less effective than exposure sheets, as you do not see the entire timing sequence as you do on exposure sheets. Exposure sheets are in common use the world over. I had a student once who went to work at a studio in Paris. He didn't speak French, but found it no problem in his work, because exposure sheets were a universal language, even in Paris. In the world of animation, if you know exposure sheets, you rule. From now on you will use exposure sheets for all your animation. The recommended length for this test is 72x's or three seconds. Keeping it short and controlled will make the student understand the value of one frame and start to give him or her one frame acuity. Knowing what one frame is and what can be done with one frame is a mark of a good animator. To paraphrase Godard, "animation is truth 24 times a second."[4]

On the asterisk, please retain the basic shape and animate only one. The purpose of this test is to control a singular unchanging object in time and space. If you animate what is happening within that object (its character), you will miss the purpose of this assignment and also show that you can't do the assignment. So please, no funny faces or cute little spiders. There will be plenty of time for that later on. This will be a good time to start using a blue pencil for your rough layout, at least the path of action, and your animation, at least the main poses (fig. extra 2. punch). Remember to vary the speed of the movement if you want your animation to "live." Be sure to consider how to animate in and out of the hold; generally you ease in and out of a hold unless you want a jarring effect. Start to practice flipping your animation to see if it works. Many animators feel that this is when your animation first comes alive, and it can give you a rush that will never be duplicated.

You can use cycles. Cycling is a form of animation where the animation is repeated to create

---

3. "Paul Klee." BrainyQuote.com. Xplore Inc., 2016. 9 November 2016.

4. "Photography is truth. The cinema is truth twenty-four times a second." "Jean-Luc Godard." BrainyQuote.com. Xplore Inc., 2016. 9 November 2016.

the action. If you animate your * moving in a circular pattern for five drawings (for discussion's sake let's say they are shot for 2x's each) and those drawings were numbered as 1, 2, 3, 4 and 5 and you repeated those numbers on your exposure sheet the cameraperson would shoot them again and the action on the screen would be the * moving in a circle twice. By shooting the complete cycle five times the * would move around a circular path five times. The exposure sheet would look thus: 1, 2, 3, 4, 5, 1, 2, 3, 4, 5, 1, 2, 3, 4, 5, 1, 2, 3, 4, 5, 1, 2, 3, 4, 5. If you went 1, 2, 3, 4, 5 (hold 12 x's), 4, 3, 2, 1, then the * would move around one way, stop and then move around in the opposite direction. A walk cycle is one of the most popular cycles used in animation, as a walk is normally a cycle (fig. 7-16). The use of cycles can save time and money and can be overused. Cycling is as old as animation. Forty-three percent of the animation in *Gertie The Dinosaur* (1914) are cycles, especially in the moving holds that keep Gertie alive. This shows that Winsor McCay, while pioneering animation itself with Gertie, was also pioneering ways to cut the drudgery out of animation. McCay also developed the key-pose method of animation, which he called the "McCay Split System." And out of respect for Winsor, you should try key-pose animation for this exercise. Do the key drawings first. Then flip them to make sure they work, and then change them if necessary. When they work, do the inbetweens. You do not have to remain 2D for this exercise, you can also move the * in 3D. But you have to be aware of the law of movement in perspective. Briefly, the law is that the closer the object is to the viewer the faster it moves, and the farther away from the viewer the slower it moves. The two examples of telephone pole perspective in the illustrations will show you how to graph out the positions of a 3D move so that it will appear to be natural.[5] You can also put the whole screen on hold by making the hold a blank screen, by having the * animate off the screen or pop off, and shooting a blank piece of paper for two frames (a blink of a blank screen) or for more frames to give a hold on a blank screen. This in the action will become anticipation (see the next assignment) of the *'s re-entry. This is similar to an empty stage in the theater or an empty room in live action.

Final notes. Part of the lecture for this assignment will have to involve the basics of exposure sheets. If you have a pencil test video unit available, the students can start using it for their tests. Any pencil test exercise, including this one, can incorporate animation that will be in the final project. This exercise can take more than two hours to do if done properly and with thought. Any of these exercises can be faked and done in a short amount of time and are very easy to spot, as they look terrible. But some students will try anything. Once, one young lady brought me a ten-inch stack of animation paper, saying it was her work for the quarter. When I started to flip through the stack, I found that the only drawing was the one on top.

Conclusion: This is your first timing exercise and it is very important, as timing can make or

---

5. Honestly, I couldn't find this illustration in his effects, but I think he illustrates what he is saying here with a fence in illustrations 7-21. As a side note, this might serve as a reminder that if you wish to leave behind a magnum opus, please make it clear where you have squirreled stuff away to Those Who May Follow.

break your animation. For this assignment you will be introduced to:

- The creation of time and how to do the timing of animation.
- Exposure sheets.
- Pose or key Animation -- hopefully.
- Flipping.
- Perhaps movement in perspective.
- Whole screen control.

Handout and exhibits: Written assignment and exposure sheets with different configurations of holds tacked on the board.

STORYBOARD FOR THE FINAL PROJECT - Assignment #3 see also pp. 163-165

The storyboard assignment for the final is given early on so the student can rethink, redo or completely change his or her idea and still have time to finish the film. The assignment is to do the storyboard for his or her 15-second film (fig. 2-11). Depending on the concept, eight to 15 storyboard panels should suffice (fig. 2-4). If color is important, then the storyboard should be in color, otherwise marker or pencil will work at this stage. If the film is to be character driven, character model sheets should accompany the board (fig. 5-3). By doing his or her board panel on 12 field animation paper, a student can save time later in the layout process (fig. 2-5).

To start to time his or her film the student will do a vertical bar sheet, - a timing guide that will help fit the film into the required 15 seconds (fig. 2-62). This is done by marking off 15 seconds on a vertical line a few spaces apart. Then students can visualize the action(s) and count off seconds and put the results next to the marked seconds. It can quickly be seen if there is enough time for the action. If there is not enough time, rethink the action, cut, overlap titles and action, cut again, and then retime it starting with your last scene or action. Working from the end and timing it back to the beginning will tell you where you will have to start your film. The board will be presented by its maker to the class at the next meeting. During the presentation, it is very helpful to have the other students write down their comments and give them to the presenter at the end of the pitch.

It would be a good idea to go over the points below when the board assignment is given. This is just a partial list; please add to it from your experience.

- Reread the first three chapters of this book, especially Ideas.
- This is the chance to express your own vision, perhaps something humorous, artistic, creative, political (fig. 7-9)or ?
- Take some time and put in some effort to come up with the idea. Disney would give the

day off to someone who had just received a new scene so that he or she could give it his or her unencumbered thought.

- Make sure the timing is not too quick. Do you want your audience seeing and understanding the film or saying "what?" First do the bar sheets (fig. 2-62) and then the exposure sheets (fig. 5-52).
- Emphasize the area of animation you are interested in. Content, movement, character animation, humor, background painting, story, directing, experimental, color, and on and on.
- A story is not required, the film can be purely visual.
- Seek inspiration from the other arts. Example, from writing, what visuals can you add when animating the word "therapist," splitting it into two words "the rapist."
- Try to make a strong style statement.
- Stress quality, but don't make quality a stress issue and that becomes a block.
- Have the students think how long it is going to take, then double it and that will just be half the time necessary. It cannot be done overnight.

WHAT TO DO AFTER YOUR BOARD PRESENTATION

Presenting your board to a group can give you a new insight, which you can then use to enhance your film. Take notes during the verbal comments. Immediately after the presentation, write down your thoughts and how you see the reaction of others. Read the written comments. Which ones would help your film? Which ones have nothing to do with your film? Is there a general misunderstanding about any part of your idea? Focus on what you want to say and eliminate confusion. Consult with the teacher or the TA. Redo your board if needed, or perhaps do a new and better board.

Now onto production, start as soon as possible. First, tape or animatic your board using a bar sheet or timing guide. Retape until the timing is correct, then rough-in your exposure sheets with the main blocks of time. This is the final editing stage in animation. The tape may be presented to the class as an assignment or shown only to the teacher or TA.

You now have the idea, the board and the basic timing for the best-ever 15-second animated film. The next stage of the process is the layout.

Layout includes:

- In pencil (fig. 11-2), do all the art in their final field sizes including the rough and then the final composition with the staging of the visual elements and animation (fig. 14-3). This will include your key animation poses (fig. 2-43).
- Decide what types of transitions are to be used: cuts, dissolves, animated, metamorphosis, etc.
- Make the technical camera movement decisions with pencil layouts of trucks (figs. 2-15, 5-38) and pans (figs. 5-39, 5-40).

- Try different art, techniques, and styles (fig. 7-80). Then do some final art to set the visual look (fig 2-33).
- Do the color and character model sheets (figs. 2-4, 2-5).
- If you have not done so, do the final background layouts in pencil (fig. 5-1).
- Budget (fig. 5-50) and schedule your time (fig. 5-51) for the production.
- Work on all the little technical details.
- Start the exposure sheets. You can even finish them (fig. 5-52).
- The layout stage must be done before you start to animate or the chances are that you will have to do your animation over.

Now, finally, the animation. Remember, you animate with your mind, not your hand. You are doing movement that is drawn, not drawings that move. What happens between the frames is more important that what is on the frame. Timing makes the animation work. Do the key poses first, rough (fig. 7-10) and in blue pencil (fig. 2-10). Check by flipping, restage the action if necessary. Re-animate, adding character and gravity (if you want gravity) while still keeping the animation rough. Do the inbetweens if the key poses work. Remember to use the eyes for acting (fig. 7-61). If a character, try adding some movement or gesture the audience can relate to. Pencil test and pencil test (fig. 7-79) again if needed, always using exposure sheets. Then clean up in graphite pencil, adding all the details of figure and clothes, and doing more inbetweens if needed. Pencil test. Redo until it has the quality of movement and timing you desire (fig. 2-66). Fine-tune your exposure sheets as you go along. If you are not doing drawn animation but are using some other form such as photos or cutout collage, adapt the above process to your technique (fig. 2-64).

Final art: Ink and paint on cels, or color on paper with pencil, markers, etc. (fig. 6-3) (work within a small field here to save on time), or some combination of possible techniques. This is a very time-intense stage. Do the final backgrounds to match your overlays. Clean up all the material and get ready for the final check. Do a final pencil test tape.

Schedule a final check of all the materials and exposure sheets with the TA a day or two before you shoot. If you are not checked by the TA, it will count against your grade. If you do not shoot at your scheduled time, you could receive an F. The TA or Technical Supervisor will guide you during your shoot. A tape copy of your film, if possible, will be available to you.

The FINAL is on:

SHOWING THE CRANE

During a laboratory session, the students should be introduced to the crane (Hello Mr. Crane, how are you?) to give them some idea of the filming process (fig. 7-83). By showing each part of the crane and camera and how pans, trucks dissolves are filmed will not only help them when it comes their time to shoot, but will also help them understand the practical reasons behind the process. It should be emphasized that they are not expected to learn all about the crane from this viewing, it is to only give them a taste. It should also be mentioned that they will shoot under technical supervision.

SELECTING A TIME FOR SHOOTING

During a class period (fifth week?), a drawing should be done to select the shooting times for the final. For a 15-second film, a two-hour shooting period should suffice. Mark off on the board the days and times available. Then put the students' names in a hat and draw them out until all the times have been filled. A very professional attitude must be held for the shooting. The films must be ready and checked on time. If they run over the two hours, turn off the camera. If they are not ready for their two-hour period, too bad, the curtain goes up at 8:30. Do not reschedule them. This is the only way the course can be run. At the start of the two-hour period, have the technical support person or a TA there to help set them up and show them the equipment again. If there is panning, trucking or dissolving in the film, take them through it step by step. Shooting a film on the animation crane can seem quite overwhelming at first, but if your exposure sheets are filled out completely, all the materials are in the proper order and it is checked, it is mostly repetitious. In fact, the main problem can be just staying awake.

ANTICIPATION - Assignment #4 see also p.166

Anticipate: to look forward to; expect (*Webster's New World College Dictionary*).[6] In animation, the anticipation of an action will make that action more effective. This is both as a strong action itself and as an action that moves the film forward. Proper anticipation will make sure the audience sees the action by directing them to it before it happens. Without anticipation, an action could be weak or confusing or it may happen too fast for the audience to see or understand. Anticipation may be as simple as a long or short hold in the animation before the action. Anticipation can also be starting an action with a movement counter to the final movement. A counter movement may be slight or exaggerated depending on the style of animation. An exaggerated anticipation would be a baseball pitcher drawing way, way back and cocking his arm and really winding up before he throws his pitch. Or when a Tex Avery character needs to leave the scene at a great speed, he or she first jumps into the air with an extreme lean counter to his or her exit, spins his or her legs until they blur, and then is off the

---

6. Because the author used a 1996 *Webster's New College Dictionary*, (3rd edition. revised) in an earlier footnote, I am assuming that dictionary is the source of this quote as well. Unfortunately I have been unable to locate a copy of this dictionary to verify this wording.

screen in from zero to three frames, leaving only speed lines. In both cases, 90 percent of the time of the final action was spent in anticipation. What you are doing is controlling the view of the audience, setting up the event before it happens so they will see it when it happens. In a group scene, if all is still, the audience will look at the first character that moves and follow his or her action. The hold of the whole group anticipates the movement of the individual. You will need to allow a few frames for the audience to react to the first move. Conversely, in a group action scene, if all are moving and one suddenly holds the audience will focus on that character. The movement or non-movement anticipates the movement. With two characters, you need to have them act and react separately. If two characters who are acting and reacting to each other are animated at the same time, their action can be confusing and lost on the audience. All of their action and reaction animation should contain the anticipation animation for the other's response.

Anticipation is frequently needed to start a movement. For example, going in the opposite direction as in a weight shift, a coil and strike, and the good old squash and stretch are times when anticipation is demonstrated. Overlapping action, an animation principle in its own right, can be an important part of anticipation. You don't start a movement all at once. If a character is turning, the head may start the action, followed in a few frames by the shoulders, then the torso and finally the legs. The first movement, the head turn, anticipates the following movements (fig. 7-63). The same rule also applies to the finish of an action--you never get there all at once. First one part stops, then another, each anticipating the full stop. And before you go into your final stop pose, you could animate a little past and then back into your hold (fig. 7-64). This will add to the final anticipation for the stop.

For this assignment animate any anticipation of an action. An example is a teakettle boiling over (fig. 14-4). The exposure sheet example for the teakettle will include the use of a forward and reverse cycle for building tension. These exposure sheets illustrate how different timings of the same drawings can achieve different types of anticipation (fig. 14-4). Another example would be to anticipate the hatching of an egg (with a surprise inside?). It would be a very good idea to animate any anticipation action that will be in your final project. The start of a movement or of action would be a good choice.

You should observe the principles of key pose animation before you do your inbetweens. Practice your flipping. The assignment is 72x's long on 12FC. Exposure and name sheets are required.

Handouts and display: Assignment handout, and exposure sheets and teakettle examples tacked on the board (fig. 14-3).

In this exercise you will use the movement and timing experience from the previous exercises to animate a specific action: anticipation.

FACE - Assignment #5 see also pp. 167-169

The purpose of this pencil test is to animate a change of emotion or an action of a character through a change of expression on the face of a character. A change of expression could be considered going from one self-evident pose to another (fig. 7-13). This will be animation within the character, interior animation, not of the movement of the character through space, exterior animation, as in the *. If you have character(s) in your final project, please use them in this assignment.

Now to the process.

Think of what you want, do some roughs, decide (fig. 7-10). Act it out in a mirror (this is why we should have mirrors on the desks). Think about the possible ways a face can express a thought or an action without being based entirely on live action, but based more on your imagination. Rough out the timing on exposure sheets, remembering to consider the timing of the pauses. Then do a character model sheet of facial expressions. Consider how many of the features (eyes, nose, mouth, etc.) do you need--all of them or just the ones needed for the action? Do your layout, getting the face in the proper place and the right size on the screen. Start the animation, using the key pose approach (blue pencil is optional), and doing your inbetweens after the keys past the flipping test. Animate the thought first, then the resulting action, and if called for, a reaction. Understanding the action will allow you to get the essence of the movements down for your animation. Keep the drawing rough to get the basic movement. Animate only the basic forms at first. For example, just do the head and the eyes. Remember, the eyes are the windows to the soul. The eyes, hands and face are the most important elements used to convey expression. This is why animated characters have big eyes, and it is easier to act with the eyes when they are the prominent feature (fig. 7-61). Eye blinks will add life to your character (fig. 7-11). For example, when turning the head from side to side, it is good to dip the head and blink the eyes in the middle of the arc (fig. 7-63). Bear in mind overlapping action, the principle that everything does not happen all at once. The eyes and head can anticipate the mouth's smile. You should know your character so that the action is true. Check the character section in Storyboard chapter (pp. 48-50). When you design a character you need to build your character so that it will be easy to animate, usually with the basic shapes: balls, cubes or rectangles (fig. 2-46). The same principle applies to the face, in that you decide the basic shape and the essential features (fig. 7-40). You animate these basic shapes first to get the essential movement down. In terms of the face, this means you can draw a face based on reality. Where the eyes are located halfway down the face (in an adult (fig. 7-58); in a baby, the eyes are a third of the way from the bottom (fig. 7-59), the bottom of the nose halfway between the eyes and the tip of the chin, and the mouth is halfway between the bottom of the nose and the tip of the chin. The eyes are one eye apart, and the middle of the pupil when in the middle of the eye projects straight down to show the end of the lips. Also, the tops of your ears usually go from your eyebrows to the bottom of your nose. You can use these simple proportions to keep the features in the right place if there is head movement--or as it is called, "holding character." Animation for this type of reality character is usually based on simulated movement and gravity. The expressions are based on reality or exaggerations of that reality.

If you are not using a reality character, you can design any style of face you like, big nose, big ears, whatever works for you and your character. The animation for this type of character need fit only your imagination. Don't be timid. If your face is based on cartoon standards, you can use established cartoon expressions. Since this is an exercise, check out different styles of art or drawing. Change your art if you find something better.

When you get the key poses down, first do the inbetweens and then the final drawings (cleanup). Check drawing with the exposure sheets on the pencil test unit if possible. This assignment is 72x's long on a 12FC. Exposure and name sheets are required. This animation can be part of your final.

Handouts and display: This assignment and various examples of cartoon features.

In this exercise, your animation will bring an emotion to life.

WALK - Assignment #6 see also pp. 169-176

Do a walk; it could be a character from your final project. Even if your character does not walk, animating him or her walking will help you understand the character. If you do not have a character in your film, walk anything you like: a realistic character, a cartoon character, an animal (four legs are hard), fingers, blobs, stick people, centipedes, whatever. The walk animation normally takes far more time than any of the other pencil test assignments. First I will explain how to animate a walk in space and then a walk in place.

A Walk in Space

A walk through space is animating how we normally walk. Each drawing of the character will be in a different place on the paper as the character is drawn a little forward each time. A walk in space is used in animation when the walk is not parallel to the screen. In other words, walking in space is walking in 3D or not in a straight line (fig. 7-21).

Basic to all walks is the repeating cycle of the leg movement. This is the first movement that is drawn, the legs in their different positions, the walk cycle. Keep it simple, a stick figure or just the rough legs are fine here. You don't need to do both the left and right legs at this stage. One leg will serve as the model for both. Analyze the positions of a moving leg: your own walk in slow motion is an excellent choice, checking how each part of the leg moves as it moves up, across and down. Rough-in the leg positions for one leg. Now time out the walk you want. How long does it take for one step? If it is half a second, that would be six drawings if you are shooting on 2's, if it is two-thirds of a second or 16x's for one step, which would be a pleasant walk speed, you would need eight drawings for each leg, and if one step takes a second you would need 12 drawings. A fast walk uses less drawings, a slow walk more. Rough-in the positions for the leg to equal the number of drawings you need for the time required. With one leg's position roughed in, the second leg's position can be traced. Now that you have your leg positions, you can consider space or place.

If you walk in space or how we really walk, the plant foot stays in one place as the body pivoting on it moves forward along with the non-pivot leg. This means you have to redraw the body moving forward in each drawing. How far forward each time depends on the types of movement, a run, an old or fat person walking, etc. A rule of thumb would be that for a normal walk cycle, the left and right legs, would travel the distance of the height of the character. Measure off the height of the character on the ground line and mark off 12 (if you have six drawings for the left foot and six drawings for the right foot) roughly even marks. This will tell you how far forward to draw your character each time. I usually use a point in the middle of the top of the head as a consistent reference. This rough path of action will be your guide that you will put under your individual sheets of paper as you trace on them your different leg positions from your master walk cycle sheet. A common mistake is to move your planted foot as you move the body forward. This will cause your character to do a strange skipping movement.

A Walk in Place

A walk in place is a cycle that will end up as part of a pan, either as single-field cel over a panning BG (this will look like a character walking down the street with the camera following the character) or as a character on a panning cel over a BG (this will look like a character moving across the screen, as with a locked down camera in live action) (fig. 7-4 through 7-20). A walk in place has a less number of drawings to do and the example shown is the easiest of the easy. Just six drawings to be shot on 2's (fig. 7-19). You don't have to do 12 drawings as it would normally be done, needing six drawings for the left leg and six drawings for the right leg, because in the examples the legs are solid black so that you can't tell the left from the right. Also you don't have to do a drawing for every two frames, you just repeat your cycle drawings and the panning movement will move the character through space.

Why are 12 drawings called for in this complete walk cycle? Because that is march time. When walking to march time, one foot hits every 12x's or half a second, 24x's or one second for a complete cycle. Walk around to a march tune. Hut, two, three, four, Hut, two, etc. You will find that this is a good brisk walk.

If you are going to do a walk in place, you have to fake a real walk with the body moving forward. You do this by sliding the plant foot back. This tells the viewers that the body is moving forward. You draw the body in the same place for each drawing and the illusion of forward motion is achieved by drawing the moving foot swinging forward as you are drawing the plant foot sliding back. With the pan going on, the change in the relationship of the body to the background will complete the illusion of walking. A note here: You generally don't want to have the sliding plant foot flat for over two drawings as it may appear to be slipping, so have the heel or toe break, or curve up away from the flat surface. After you have done these drawings and they work, check by flipping or a pencil test. Now do the drawings for both the left and right foot (unless you did my trick of having only a silhouette). To check if the left and right leg positions match, lay out the left leg drawings in order on a table and then lay out the right leg drawings directly below them. They should match. If they don't, fix it by redrawing the positions to match. Pencil test.

After You Decide

After the walk cycle is set, and in place or space has been decided, what is the anatomy behind the walk? Is it based on human/animal anatomy or a walk based on a concept? If based on real anatomy, we have to understand how we walk and why we move in a particular manner. The controlling force is gravity. Gravity is always pulling us and our anatomy down. We spend our whole lives fighting gravity. Disney animators typically animate a character three different times after they have decided on the staging and personality of the animation. First they do the basic movement, which can be done with stick figures to work out the rough cycle. Second, they add the effects of gravity and clean up the character. Third, they put in the personality for that particular character and the secondary animation (clothes swing, etc.).

Gravity makes walking an act of falling. Babies are always falling when they are learning to walk until they learn to put one foot out after the other to keep their balance. One foot goes down and plants itself, and then the other foot crosses over and becomes the balance or plant foot. The hips can rotate a little or a lot, depending on humor and culture. The arms swing opposite to the legs for balance. The head acts as needed. The whole body often has a bounce to it, a hit, squash and up movement, that you can plot by a curved up-and-down line at the top of the head. Remember, this is based on a normal human walk so the head, chest area and hip area do not expand or contract, only the neck and middle of the body (spinal cord) can do that. You can get a comedy effect by having a large mass, such as a large front or a rear, bouncing two to four frames behind the rest of the body's bounce (as in the film *Walking*).[7] Your animation should express the attitude and personality of the character through his or her walk.

---

7. I think the author is thinking of the film *Walking* by Ryan Larkin (Canada, 1968.)

An old cartoon formula was that a normal male walk was 12x each step (six drawings at 2x's each). A normal female walk was 8x's per step (fig. 7-14). In high heels, one has to take shorter, faster steps, so the type of shoes can be a factor. A run would be 4x to 6x per step (fig 7-23). Specialty walks such as "trucking" or a goose step where exaggeration is used for a particular effect are best acted out and timed first. Study comic walks such as Monty Python, Groucho Marx, Chaplin, etc. You can also animate walk concepts by stylizing or abstracting the walk principle outlined above for your purpose. This is usually done when the character is stylized or abstracted, as in a 2D character. Examples would be a three-drawing scissors cycle, a pinwheel cycle (fig. 14-5), a piston cycle, a spring cycle (fig. 7-20), etc. If you want to animate in perspective, remember the rules of telephone pole perspective. The character moves faster the closer they get. For this assignment, you do not need to animate a walk of a defined character, anything will do: a blob, just legs, stick figures, your fingers. If you have trouble deciding what to walk, you can copy a well-known character from the comics. In animating a walk with a character, you are animating a character both moving through space and within itself.

Factors in a walk cycle are: attitude, weight, build, age, sex, health, dress of the character and the weather. On a slow or heavy walk, you can put a lot of emphasis on the hips and shoulders.

The exercise is 72 frames long and exposure and name sheets are required. This will be the last pencil test assignment; you must have all your pencil test assignments done by now. Next weeks' assignment will be to turn in your exposure sheets for the final.

Handouts and display: This assignment handed out and examples of walks with their exposure sheets displayed.

In this exercise you, will do a difficult and complex piece of animation.

EXPOSURE SHEET - Assignment # see also pp. 183-184

This assignment is to do and hand in the exposure sheets for the final project. They should be checked, graded and returned to the student. If the student needs them to continue working, he or she should turn in a copy.

The exposure sheets should be regular 96x sheets that are available from Cartoon Colour. The minimal information on the exposure sheet would be the final timing and layout information, including field sizes and exact length of each shot or scene in frames. The ideal information would be completely filled out exposure sheets with all your levels and cels and BG numbering and any pans, trucks or dissolves completely planned out (fig. 7-32).

Handouts and display: This assignment and the display of exposure sheet examples (fig. 5-52).

EXTRA EXERCISES TO IMPROVE YOUR ANIMATION

The first set of exercises could be the redoing of each of the basic exercises from the 181A class several times. The timing and length for each exercise would be up to you.

Extra Bouncing Ball

Squash and stretch or bounce different objects: rocks, glass balls, putty, hardballs, softballs, odd shaped balls, pogo sticks, faces, people or animals' bodies (check out Preston Blair) are just a few of the many things you could bounce or squash and stretch. You can bounce any of these on smooth, uneven or different surfaces and at different angles. Do them in perspective, with shadows, with rotation and changes in the object. I was just talking to Con Pederson and he was talking about just doing an exercise of a bouncing ball that was dripping water. Con started animating at Disney in the late 1950s. I am sure you can easily come up with many more exercises – how about the squash and stretch in anything taking off.

Extra Asterisk

This is a timing and external movement exercise. See how many ways you can time the movement of an asterisk with the same movement. See how many movements or paths of action you can achieve with an asterisk. Take a risk with the "risk" in asterisk. Remember, the animator who takes the most risks does the best animation. Substitute different objects for the asterisk: a spaceship, a person moving, etc. Take any scene from your previous films and see how many ways you can time or animate it. How many ways can you move an asterisk in space?

Extra Anticipation

Do variations of the teakettle and the egg to start. Do action that starts a movement, especially variations of scenes from your film. Do anticipation in a character as an acting exercise, as in thinking then action. Consider the follow through at the end of an action as anticipation.

Extra Walking

Most books on how to animate have many walk examples in them, so check them out. You can also study Muybridge, live-action films, other animated films or watching yourself walk. Walk all sorts of different people, from all different angles, over all different surfaces. Try walking animals, birds, pillows, fingers, matchsticks and objects without legs (sacks). Can you tell the character of the person from your walk? You should be able to.

Extra Facial Expressions

Grasp a mirror or a book on drawing expressions, cartoon or realistic – your choice – and go to town. Do big, do small, do old people, do kids, do animals, turtles, birds, rocks, urinals, fish and cats. Do pages and pages of drawings before you start to animate. If you have a character then do hundreds of facial expressions of that character in every possible emotional situation, then start to animate the character. As you animate a character, always ask yourself: what is he or she thinking at this particular moment? Does the audience know what they are thinking? Check out Pluto with the flypaper. Study actors both live and animated. What makes an expression work? You will need to be able to judge and analyze good animation before you can do good animation.

MISCELLANEOUS EXERCISES

Variations of sine curve animation (fig. 7-68), water, flag waving (fig. 7-69), cape, etc., is a good exercise. Variations of the primary curve or sine curve in a character as it moves so that it will show happiness, sadness, stealth, etc., is another one. Do the exercises as moving shots, pans and trucks. Add your own exercises.

Other Pencil Test Assignments, especially for a 15-week semester

An animatic of the storyboard.

Sound. Everyone animates to one passage of music. This is very hard to do because of the syncing problems. One way to make students aware of musical beats/rhythms is to give the frame count of a simple beat. Use the opening of a TV show, Beethoven's 5th for example, and have everyone put their images to that frame count and then play them all back to back without the sound. It can be quite illuminating to see how musical beats appear at visual timing.

Panning one to three levels. Do on paper and shoot backlight. For three levels, try sliding blocks that hit one another.

Do a dissolve.

Animate a metamorphosis, the changing of one shape into another.

Animate an action. In one that has been mentioned before, a character is sitting at a table, the doorbell rings, the character goes to the door, receives a letter, reads it and you know by his or her expression what was in the letter. Unfortunately, this would take longer than three seconds. A shorter example is the squash and stretch and a complete leap of a lion or a human.

Analyze a piece of animation, and describe what makes it good or bad in your opinion.

Animate the conductor leading an orchestra to music of your choice. Do it to different types of music. *The Band Concert* with Mickey (1935) is a great example of leading a band during a cyclone.

Animate a monkey swinging from one branch to another.

Do any of the exercises so that they involve editing. For editing exercises you could do each animation 20 different ways:

- As a master shot
- Using different size shots and angles, say start out with long and medium shots only and three cuts, then MLS, M, ME and five cuts, each shot a different size and 15 cuts, etc.
- All one type of shot such as close-ups
- All one angle such as low
- All in perspective
- All point of view shots
- Do these exercises with different timing

Do the exercises with different animation (full Disney, very limited, very aesthetic) or go to the "Diversity of Animation" chapter (Chapter 6) and try out different techniques. A series of short, 15 seconds or so of drawing or painting under the camera, animating sand, cutouts, photos, matchsticks, etc., etc.

Perhaps you and a fellow student or two can work on these exercises together for feedback and discussion. If you do not spend time learning animation, you never will.

You need to do quite a bit of animation before the principles of animation are second nature.

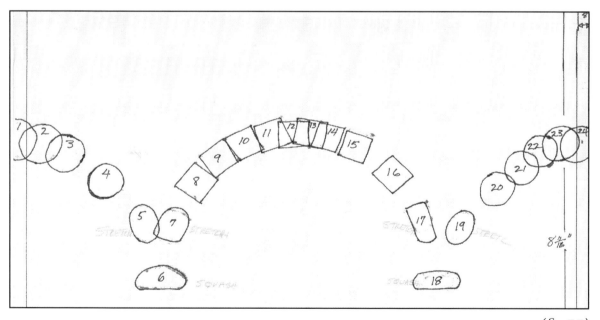

(fig. 7-5)

UCLA
animation
workshop

http://animation.filmtv.ucla.edu/

The UCLA Animation Workshop, as part of the School of Theater, Film, and Television, was founded in 1947 by William Shull. Since that time it has become the leading workshop of its kind in the world. The philosophy of the workshop -- one person, one film (one person does the completed film) --

one person,

was introduced from the very beginning. This philosophy allows each filmmaker complete control over their film, its content, idea, viewpoint, style, purpose, audience, form, process, and value. The filmmaker learns the complete animation process by doing it. The Workshop has a complete animation studio which includes: 16mm and 35mm animation cranes, video pencil-test system, two computer labs (Macintosh and SGI) with 2D and 3D graphics programs; 16mm optical printer and complete sound, editing and viewing facilities. Internships with high-tech houses in Hollywood keep students abreast of the latest developments in interactive media, computers, and other new areas of animation. The animation collection in the UCLA Film and Television Archives provides students with a strong resource for research. Each student is asked to consider ethics, history, society, concepts, aesthetics, structure, style, process, content, viewpoint, philosophy, conviction and ideas. But each student sets their own direction. Therefore films range from conceptual to cartoon, from object animation to computer, from entertainment to experimental, and from traditional animation to new animation. Students who have gone through the Workshop enjoy a high degree of success. Some own their own production houses and many are leading animators.

Some teach at colleges and universities and others are renowned independent filmmakers. Animation is viewed as an art communication form that has only two limitations: one's imagination and exhaustion. The Workshop prepares the student not for the first position they will have but for the last. In addition to completing three animated projects, students in the MFA program are required to take live action and television production courses as well as graduate seminars. Instruction is intensive and begins on either the undergraduate or graduate level. The UCLA Animation Workshop is committed to excellence in defining, expanding, and creating a new art form -- animation.

Professor Dan McLaughlin
Assistant Professor Celia Mercer
UCLA Animation Workshop 310/825-5829

Graduate Admissions:
Applications are available beginning in August.
For information, contact:
Student Services
UCLA School of Theater, Film and Television
Box 951622
Los Angeles, CA 90095-1622
310/206-8441

one film

(fig. 13-5)

CHAPTER 15

(fig. 2-33)

BIBLIOGRAPHY[1]

BOOKS/PUBLICATIONS - some of the best are:

All of Glenn Vilppu's work on the web.

Animated Cartoons: How They Are Made: Their Origin and Development. E. G. Lutz. Bedford, MA: Applewood Books, 1998.

Animation: Learn Wow to Draw Animated Cartoons. Preston Blair. Laguna Beach, CA: Walter T. Foster, 1949.

The Animator's Survival Kit. Richard Williams. London: Faber and Faber, 2001.

Chuck Amuck: The Life and Times of an Animated Cartoonist. Chuck Jones. New York: Farrar, Straus, and Giroux, 1989, 1999.

The Courage to Create. Rollo May. New York: Bantam Books, 1975.

Creating 3D Animation. Peter Lord and Brian Sibley. New York: Harry N. Abrams, 2004.

Drawing the Head and Figure. Jack Hamm. New York: Perigee, 1983.

The Illusion of Life: Disney Animation. Frank Thomas and Ollie Johnston. New York: Abbeville Press, 1981.

Pedagogical Sketchbook. Paul Klee. New York: Frederick A. Praeger, 1977.

Scriptwriting for Animation. Stan Hayward. New York: Focal Press, 1977.

---

1. As mentioned in the acknowledgements, the author completed the manuscript sometime around 2007 and the text has not been updated for accuracy. All statements reflect the belief of the author at the time of authorship and may, or may not, reflect current reality.

ORGANIZATIONS

ASIFA. Association Internationale du Film d'Animation was founded in 1957 in France, and chartered under UNESCO in 1960 as the only membership organization in the world devoted to the encouragement and dissemination of filmed animation as an art and communication form. In its 40-year existence, ASIFA International has grown to more than 1,700 members in 55 countries.

The Hollywood Chapter is the largest in the world. Its headquarters are in Burbank.

Iota. A Los Angeles based organization for abstract film www.iotacenter.org.

SAS. Society for Animation Studies. They have a yearly conference where scholarly papers are presented.

SIGGRAPH. For computer animation.

University of Film and Television Association – UFVA. Promotes interest in the making and teaching of film and video.

Women in Animation. A Los Angeles based group.

MAGAZINES

Animation Magazine. A monthly magazine from Hollywood.
ASIFA AND SAS NEWSLEITERS

WEB SITES

Animation World Network. www.awn.com specializes in resources for animators, with an extensive website offering news, articles and links for professional animators and animation fans.

Big Cartoon Database. www.bcdb.com says it is the world's largest collection of animated films, episode guides and classic cartoon information.

Jerry Beck's Cartoon Research. www.cartoonresearch.com Cartoon research is Jerry Beck's personal website and blog devoted to animation history – past, present and future.

Films, Episode Guides and Classic Cartoon Information

ANIMATED FILMS YOU SHOULD SEE

An animator should study the short animated films on this list. They have been chosen for: historical significance, quality, variety, and international overview. Unfortunately many good films have been left out so please supplement this list with your own favorite or least favorite films.

This is how they are listed: title, director, (producer), date, length, and country of birth and or production. Notes and any awards. We hope that you have seen the important features, as they are not listed at the present. This list is in rough chronological order and goes through the mid 1990's.

Fantasmagorie, Emile Cohl, 1908, 2 min., France. Fantasmagorie is arguably the first drawn animation done as a complete work.

The Cameraman's Revenge, Ladislaw Starewicz, 1912, 13 min. Russia. An entomologist makes an animated film using real stuffed bugs. Apparently, he tried live bugs but they proved to be bad actors.

Gertie the Dinosaur, Winsor McCay, 1914, 9 min., USA. First animated character. Appeared as a multi-media event with McCay live on stage interacting with Gertie on the screen. [2]

Felix in Hollywood, Otto Messmer and Pat Sullivan, 1923, 8 min. USA. Felix was the first popular animated character.

Symphonie Diagonale, Viking Eggeling, 1924, (3 min. excerpt), Germany/Sweden. Very abstract, Eggeling died six days after its premier of deprivation.[3]

Lost World, Willis O'Brien, 1925, 90 min., USA. Very early special effects with prehistoric creatures in live action film. Willis later did King Kong (1933). [4]

Prince Achmed, Lotte Reiniger, 1926, 60 min., Germany. Silhouette animation.[5]

Steamboat Willie, Ub Iwerks and Walt Disney, 1928, 8 min., USA. First everything.

Skeleton Dance, Ub Iwerks and Walt Disney, 1929, 5 min., USA. First Silly Symphonie.

Flowers and Trees, Walt Disney, 1932, 8 min., USA. First three strip Technicolor animated film, First A.A. Winner.

Betty Boop in Snow White, Dave Fleischer and Max Fleischer, 1933, 7 min., USA. Done by Grim

---

2. Various online resources give the running time as 12 or 13 minutes.

3. Wikipedia says 16 days and the total running time was 7 minutes.

4. Wikipedia gives the original running time of 106 minutes and 93 minutes for the 2000 version.

5. Wikipedia suggests 65 minutes.

Natwick and partly based on the singer Helen Kane, Betty was first designed as a dog. She later changed into quite an independent young woman and became the first female animated star. (fig. 15-1)

Carmen, Lotte Reiniger, 1933, 9 min., Germany. Silhouette animation.

Three Little Pigs, Burt Gillett and Walt Disney, 1933, 8 min., USA. A.A. winner.

Night on Bald Mountain, Alexander Alexeieff and Claire Parker, 1933, 8 min. Russia, USA, France. Pinscreen.

Rainbow Dance, Len Lye, 1936, 4 min., New Zealand/England. Special effects techniques used to make a complete film. A theatrical commercial for the General Post Office Film Unit in Great Britain.

Allegretto, Oskar Fischinger, 1936, 3 min., Germany. Abstract, Oskar called his animation 'absolute animation'.

Popeye meets Ali Baba and His Forty Thieves, Fleischer Studios, 1937, 17 min., USA.

Porky's Duck Hunt, Tex Avery, Warner Bros., 1937, 8 min., USA. Daffy Duck is introduced to the world.

Peace on Earth, Hugh Hannan, MGM, 1939, 9 min., USA. A pacifist film, perhaps intended to keep us out of WW II, A. A. Nominee.

Wild Hare, Tex Avery, Warner Bros., 1940, 8 min., USA. First Official Bugs. A.A. Nominee.

Knock, Knock, Walter Lantz, 1940, 7 min., USA. First Woody Woodpecker (with Andy Panda).

Dover Boys, Chuck Jones, Warner Bros., 1942, 9 min., USA. Done in a flat, 2D Style.

Hen Hop, Norman McLaren, NFB Canada, 1942, 4 min., Canada Drawn image and sound on film.

Hell Bent for Election, Chuck Jones and John Hubley, 1944, 13 min., USA. UPA embryo.[6]

Anchors Aweigh, The Tom and Jerry, and Gene Kelly scene, MGM, 1945, 4 min., USA. This early combination of live action and animation is a classic.

Bad Luck Blackie, Tex Avery, MGM, 1949, 7 min., USA.

Song of the Prairie, Jiri Trnka, 1949, 21 min., Czechoslovakia.

Begone Dull Care, Norman McLaren, NFB Canada, 1949, 8 min., Canada. Painting, etc. Painted directly on film.

Gerald McBoing Boing, Robert Cannon, UPA, 1950, 7 min., USA. Based on Dr. Seuss (Ted Geisel). A. A. winner.

---

6. According to Emily Hubley, her father worked on the storyboard, but not the final film. She also indicated that *"Hellbent"* was one word instead of two. Wikipedia put a hyphen between the two words *"Hell-Bent."*

Rabbit Fire, Chuck Jones, Warner Bros., 1951, 7 min., USA.

Two Mouseketeers, William Hanna and Joseph Barbera, MGM, 1952, 7 min., USA. A food fight with Tom and Jerry with Tom getting it in the neck, A. A. Winner.

Neighbors, Norman McLaren, NFB of Canada, 1952, 9 min., Canada.Pixillation, A. A. Winner. (Best Documentary, Best One Reel Short).

Duck Amuck, Chuck Jones, Warner Bros., 1953, 7 min., USA. Self-Reflective.

One Froggy Evening, Chuck Jones, Warner Bros., 1955, 7 min., USA.

City of Gold, Wolf Koenig, NFB of Canada, 23 min., Canada. One of the first films to use still photos as the primary visuals.

La Jette, Chris Marker, 1962, 28 min., France. A brilliant film on many levels. Done by freezing the crucial frame in each shot and letting that frame become the shot. Question: is this an animated film? Answer: yes.

The Adventures of an *, John and Faith Hubley, 1956, 10 min., USA (fig. 2-36).

Chairy Tale, Norman McLaren, NFB of Canada, 1957, 10 min., Canada. Pixillation of a man and a chair.

What's Opera Doc, Chuck Jones, Warner Bros., 1957, 7 min., USA.

Hercules, Joseph Oriolo, TV series, 1960's, 6 min., USA. This is a great example of how to cut costs and make a bad film.

Paladins of France, Emanuele Luzzati and Giulio Gianini, 1960, 12 min., Italy.

Do It Yourself Cartoon Kit, (Vera Linnecar, Keith Learner, Nancy Hanna, & Bob Godfrey) Biographic Films, 1961, 5 min., Great Britain. How to do an animated film.

Love Me, Love Me, Love Me, Richard Williams, 1962, 9 min. Canada/Great Britain. Written by Stan Hayward.

The Flying Man, George Dunning, 1962, 2 min., Canada/Great Britain. Painting on glass

The Critic, Ernest Pintoff, 1963, 3 min., USA. Mel Brooks as a critic. A. A. Winner

Love, Yoji Kuri, 1963, 4 min., Japan.

God Is Dog Spelled Backwards, Dan McLaughlin, 1963, 3 min., USA. First complete film in Kinestasis (fig. 6-7).

Claude, Dan McLaughlin, 1963, 3 min., USA. First Place Chicago International Film Festival (figs. 1-2, 2-33).[7]

---

7. By the way, these two films are available for purchase under the title of *11 Films* by Dan McLaughlin available through Pyramid Films.

Game of Angels (Les Jeux des Anges), Walerian Borowczyk, 1964, 13 min., Poland/France. Polish concentration camps.

Canon, Norman McLaren, NFB of Canada, 1964, 9 min., Canada. A musical and visual canon.

Zid, Ante Zaninovic, Zagreb, 1965, 4min., Yugoslavia. A good example of the cycle structure.

Chromophobia, Raoul Servais, 1966, 9 min., Belgium.

Lapis, James Whitney, 1965/6, 10 min. , USA.

Breathe, Jimmy Murakami, 1967, 5 min. USA.

Windy Day, John and Faith Hubley, 1967, 9 min., USA. Improvisation with Emily and Georgia Hubley. A.A. Nominee

Pas De Deux, Norman McLaren, NFB of Canada, 1967, 14 min., Canada. A brilliant example of the use of the Optical Printer.

Walking, Ryan Larkin, NFB of Canada, 1968, 5 min., Canada. Resource for walking pencil test

Film, Film, Film, Fyodor Khitruk, 1968, 20 min., Russia.

Bambi Meets Godzilla, Marv Newland, 1969, 2 min., USA

The Further Adventures of Uncle Sam, Bob Mitchell and Dale Case, Habouscb Co., 1970, 13 min., USA.[8]

Rainbow Bear, Bill Melendez, 1970, 5 min., USA.

The Point, Fred Wolf, Murikami/Wolf, 1971, USA. First "feature" (55 min.) done for TV.

Karma Sutra Rides Again, Bob Godfrey, 1972, 8 min., Great Britain. Written by Stan Hayward. A.A. nominee.

Oni, Kihachiro Kawamoto, 1972, 8 min., Japan.

Frank Film, Frank Mouris, 1973, 9 min., USA. A. A. Winner Film.

Closed Mondays, Bob Gardiner and Will Vinton, 8 min., 1974 USA. Introduced 'Claymation', which is the process of using the rotoscoping technique on clay. A. A. Winner.

Diary, Nedeljko Dragic, Zagreb Studios, 1974, 8 min., Croatia.

Sisyphus, Marcell Jankovics, Hungarofilms, 1974, 2 min., Hungry. A. A. Nominee.

Kick Me, Bob Swarthe, 1975, 8 min., USA. Drawn on Film, A.A. Nominee.

Transformation, Paul De Nooijer, 1976, 3 min., Netherlands.[9]

The Street, Caroline Leaf, NFB of Canada, 1976, 10 min., USA/Canada. Painting directly on glass as the film is being shot. Based on a short story by Mordecai Richler. A.A. Nominee.

---

8. Some sources give the year as 1971.

9. Most online resources give the full title of this film as *Transformation* by Holding Time

The Landscape Painter, Jacques Drouin, 1976 NFB of Canada, 8 min., Canada. Pin screen.[10]

Animato, Mike Jittlov, 1977, 3 min., USA. An example of a very good film that is not in distribution.

Sunstone, Ed Emshwiller, 1979, 3 min., USA. Very early computer.

Getting Started, Richard Condie, 1979, 12 min., Canada. The hardest part of animation.

Tale of Tales, Yuri Norstein, 1979, 30 min., Russia.

The Wizard of Time and Speed, Mike Jittlov, 1979, 3 min., USA. Pixillation.

Opens Wednesday, Barrie Nelson, 1980, 4 min., USA. A spoof on the importance of film. [11]

Crac, Frederic Back, Societ Radio Canada, 1981, 15 min., Canada. Started as a story for his daughter by quite a man and an artist. A.A. Winner. [12]

The Strange Case of Mr. and Mrs. Donnybrook's Boredom, David Silverman, UCLA, 1982, 5 min., USA

Dimensions of Dialogue, Jan Svankmajer, 1982, 12 min., Czechoslovakia. Surreal puppets and anything else.

Jumping, Osamu Tezuka, 1984, 6 min., Japan.

Cuckoo, Velislav Kasalov, 1984, 3 min., Bulgaria.

High Fidelity, Randy Roberts and Robert Abel, 2 minutes, 1985? USA. This commercial is the first rastor computer animation.

Big Snit, Richard Condie, NFB of Canada, 1985, 10 min., Canada A. A. Nominee. Funny

Greek Tragedy, Nicole Van Goethem, CineTe pvba, 1985, 6 min., Belgium. A. A. Winner. What do caryatids think about?

Carnival, Susan Young, Royal College of Art, 1985, 8 min., UK.

Luxo Jr., John Lasseter, Pixar, 1986, 2 min., USA. A. A. Nominee. 3D Computer animation.

Propaganda Dance, Tom Sito, 1987, 5 min., USA.

The Man Who Planted Trees, Frederic Back, Societ Radio, 1987, 30 min., Canada. A. A. Winner.

Sand Dance, Richard Quade, UCLA, 1988, 3 min., USA. Animating directly under the camera by moving beach sand around.

Picnic on the Grass, Priit Pam, 1988, 25 min., Estonia. [13]

Technological Threat, Bill Kroyer, 1988, 5 min., USA. Tex Avery meets the computer. A. A. Nominee

10. Most online resources list Drouin's film from 1976 as *Mindscape/Le paysagiste*

11. Some sources say this film came out in 1981.

12. IMDB gives the year as 1980.

13. Online resources call this film *Breakfast on the Grass* and credit its year of production as 1987.

Balance, Christopher and Wolfgang Lauenstein, 1989, 8 min., Germany. A A Winner.

Hill Farm, Mike Baker, 1989, 18 min., Great Britain. A. A. Nominee.[14]

The Old Man and the Sea, Alexander Petrov, 1999, 20 min., Russia/Canada, A.A. Winner

Grey Wolf and Little Red Riding Hood, Garri Bardin, 1990, 27 min., Russia

Mona Lisa Descending a Staircase, Joan Grantz, 1992, 7 min., USA. A. A. Winner.

Wrong Trousers, Nick Park, 1993, 30 min., Great Britain. A. A. Winner

TV SERIES

Crusader Rabbit, Rocky and Bullwinkle, the Flinstones, Bevis and Butthead, South Park, Simpsons.

(fig. 7-2)

14. Some sources give the year of production as 1988.

ADDENDUM ONE

(fig. add 1-1)

A BRIEF SUMMARY OF COPYRIGHT LAW[1]

United States copyright protection is available for "original works of authorship" which are "fixed in a tangible medium of expressions" (fig. add1-1). Copyright law grants owners of copyright the sole right to do or allow others to do the following: to reproduce all or part of the work, to distribute copies, to prepare new versions based on the original work and to perform or display the work publicly. The Copyright Act of 1976 provides that copyright begins at the moment the work is created. Registration with the Copyright Office is not required for a work to be protected, although registration provides certain monetary advantages.[2]

The 1976 Copyright Act provides copyright protection for work created after Jan. 1, 1978, from date of creation to 90 years after the author's death. However, this time of protection may have been increased by subsequent amendments. Commissioned work or work done as an employee has different protection lengths, as does work copyrighted prior to 1978. Copyright protection covers both published and unpublished works. Unpublished works, such as scripts, are often registered with the Writers Guild to established date of completion. Another way suggested to establish date of completion of unpublished work is to mail the work to you in a sealed, registered letter that is kept unopened until it is needed.

Copyright does not include facts, ideas, procedures, processes, systems, concepts, principles or discoveries, although those may be protected under patent or trade secret laws. Only the form of expression of an idea is protected.

---

1. As mentioned in the Acknowledgements, the author completed the manuscript sometime around 2007 and the text has not been updated for accuracy. All statements reflect the belief of the author at the time of authorship and may, or may not, reflect current reality.
2. Basically see Copyright Basics Circular 1. U. S .Copyright Office.

As far as I know, a copyright for a character has to be on each different work that uses the character. An individual picture of Mickey Mouse used for publicity must have a copyright even though a film starring Mickey has a copyright.

Rights to Copyrighted Material

If you wish to use copyrighted material, either published or recorded, in a film that you plan to exhibit, you should get permission for two reasons. One, civil and criminal penalties may be imposed for copyright infringement and can include awarding monetary damages, attorney's fees, injunction against future infringement and destruction of the infringed copies. Second, it is a moral issue that you respect the creative work of others, as you would expect others to respect your created copyrighted work. There are exceptions in the Copyright Act called Fair Usage.

Getting permission for copyright could take money. There are people who secure copyrights for a fee, but unless you are doing a budgeted project they will probably be too expensive. These are some guidelines if you plan to get the permission yourself and hope not to pay a fee. For recorded music, two permissions are required. One is from the music publisher of the work and a second from the recording company. This information is usually on the work, but if the music publisher is not listed you can contact BMI (www.bmi.com) or ASCAP (www.ascap.com). The musicians on the recording and the composer may need to be compensated. For other recorded material -- voice recording, poetry reading, children's story and comedy record -- contact the entities printed on the label. For written material, you will go through the same process. When you are contacting people, the best person to contact is the artist, who may be sympathetic to your project and not charge you. Agents, whose job it is to see that artists get paid and get 10 percent or more for doing this, really do not want 10 percent of nothing, and publishers, who may have lawyers, will usually want money.

In your first contact with the copyright owners, you should let them know you are a student or the film is non-funded independent and not a commercial venture. Include a storyboard or some of the art with your request so that they can see the quality of your work. Try to convince the copyright owners that it would be beneficial to them to have their work in your film or your film about their work. You could provide them with a copy for their promotional use or offer to pay them a lump sum or a percentage if you get a commercial release and start making money. Think of ways the both of you can benefit. When making contact, come up with something unique to make your request stand out, especially if you are dealing directly with the artist. One of my students did this with an Elton John song she wanted to use. She gained his attention by leaving a stamped letter for him where he was working. The stamp was a beautiful stamp-size portrait of Elton that she had painted. He saw it, liked it and gave her the right to his song "I Gonna Be a Teen Age Idol." In return she gave him the rights, for a fee, to use her film to open his North American tour. He also invited her to be his guest of honor at the opening-night party in Los Angeles.[3]

Mention all the information on the plans for the finished work, such as festivals and distribution, so that you can be sure to get permission for those uses. Festival people, to protect themselves, will want a signed statement from you that you have secured and own the rights.

Start the process early as getting permission can take time. One of my students used a song by a well-known jazz musician. He wrote and wrote for permission, and after he had finished the film, they finally replied that the rights were tied up in an estate settlement and he could not get permission. Luckily a distributor who paid for a new sound track that was timed exactly like the original picked up the film. It is still a good idea to have all rights secured before production is started.[4] If the film is a success and you cannot get the rights, you have three choices: (1) limited or no distribution, (2) replace the copyrighted material with original material so there is no longer a copyright infringement or (3) pay a fee.

Options

Another way of attaining copyright is an option for use for a limited time. You would pay a smallish amount of money for the rights, the option, to, say a novel, for six months. This would give a window to raise the funds for production. If a deal is made for production, then the author is paid full copyright value. This is normally done when a feature or series is the final production goal.

If you become involved in an option for your work, make sure that the original rights are returned to you if the option is not picked up, even if the optioning party has put a lot of effort into reworking the project. Put this into the contract. If you do not do this, the optioning party will need to be paid for the work they put into it and thereby, in effect, killing any future life of the project.

Fair Usage of Existing Material

Fair usage is a complex issue. It is always best to consult a lawyer on how the doctrine of "Fair Use" under the U. S. copyright law applies in the specific instance that involves you. Here are some examples of "Fair Usage" that may be helpful.

A student should be able to use copyrighted material as part of a project for a class and show

---

3. A Billboard article 11/2/1974, *Acts Spend Thousands on Ultimate Visual/Aural Presentation* by Johnny Sippel mentions that Elton John's tour would feature a four-minute animated cartoon by Peggy Okeya. Currently in IMDb she is listed as working under the name of Peggy Yamamoto.

4. This one, I have no idea who it is.

it as part of the course requirements. However, any screening must be part of the class. This student use of the copyrighted material is often the "right" granted by the copyright owner when giving permission. If they do not grant you other uses, such as festivals, in essence they are giving you a right you already have.

How does copyright protection apply to satire or parody? If your work is a satire or a parody, you have the right as an artist in the United States to parody or satirize existing material. A work cannot claim copyright protection against satire or parody as they take that risk when a work is presented to the public. Mad Comics is a good example of satire. Still, it is always best to check with a lawyer who knows this area of the law when you undertake a satire or parody of a popular icon. Make sure that the parody or satire is glaringly obvious in case there is a lawsuit. A recent example (2003) is the ruling that Mattel Inc. stepped over the line when it sued a Utah artist who photographed naked Barbie dolls stuffed into a blender. The court ruled that the toy maker ought to pay the artist's legal fees and that "the benefits to the public in allowing such use -- allowing artistic freedom and expression and criticism of a cultural icon -- are great."[5]

Non-Copyright Material

Material that had no copyright or the copyright is no longer in force is in the public domain and copyright free. The music of Beethoven is copyright free, but the performance, recording, and distribution may still be under copyright protection. Make sure the work is truly in the public domain as public domain material can be altered into a new version and be copyrighted by the new owners. An example is the taking of a black and white film and colorizing it and becoming a new owner of a film classic. The song "Happy Birthday" is copyrighted. It came from an old tune, "Good Morning Dear Teacher," which is in the public domain, but new words were added and then it was copyrighted as a new song.

Original Material

To avoid the whole copyright permission issue, it is best to use your original material, especially music. Original music is usually better as it is written for film and the composer should be able to give you exactly the exact mood and timing you need.

Your Copyright

On the film, the copyright normally is physically represented by a symbol, a small c with a circle around, which is followed by your name and the year (© by Dan McLaughlin 2002). The copyright should be part of the title sequences, whether in the opening titles, the end titles or the last title on the film. Put the copyright where it would be difficult to cut off as this will deter thievery and slow down the practice of TV, especially cable, of getting rid of

---

5. Mattel, Inc. v. Walking Mountain Productions

any credits and copyrights but their own. Even if a non-registered copyright is automatic at the completion of the work, there never should be a public screening without a copyright logo on the film. This lets potential thieves know you are aware of the copyright laws. After the film is done, you should register your film with the copyright office. The details are on the web, www.copyright.gov. Everything you need to know is on the menu under Register a Copyright. You will be entitled to more damages if you registered your film and someone tried to steal it from you. If the film is completed late in the year, sometimes the next year's date is put down to give the film another year on the festival circuit. Have signed releases from all your talent to ensure complete copyright protection.[6] Below is a sample talent release:

TALENT RELEASE AGREEMENT

PRODUCERS:_____   TALENT:_____

This Release confirms that _____(TALENT) (hereinafter "Releaser"), for good and valuable consideration, the receipt and sufficiency of which is hereby acknowledged, has granted permission to Producers and their successors, assignees and licensees to use Releaser's contributions including any interview with Releaser or Releaser's name and/or likeness (hereinafter "Performance") as such Performance appears in connection with or is related to Producer's project entitled_____(hereinafter "The Project") or in connection with advertising, publicizing, exhibiting, and exploiting The Project by any and all means, media, devices, processes and technology now or hereafter known or devised without limitation as to time or locality. Releaser hereby acknowledges that Producers shall have no obligation to utilize Releaser's Performance in The Project.

Producer's exercise of the rights granted herein shall not violate or infringe any rights of any third party. Releaser understands that Producers have been induced to proceed with production, distribution, and exploitation of "The Project" in reliance upon this Agreement.

Releaser hereby releases Producers, their successors, assignees and licensees from any and all claims and demands arising out of or in connection with such use, including without limitation, any and all claims for invasion of privacy, infringement of Releaser's right of publicity, defamation (including libel and slander), false light and any other personal and/or property rights.

This Talent Release Agreement shall be governed and interpreted by the laws of the State of California and the Courts of this State shall have exclusive jurisdiction over any disputes that may arise under this Agreement.

IN WITNESS WHEREOF, this Agreement has been executed and delivered as of the date set forth below.

Dated:_____

TALENT_____   RELEASER_____

---

6. Have I made it clear that a. the author was not a lawyer, and b. this section is pretty much as he wrote it sometime about 10 years ago? Well, take that into account. I am including this section as it reflects his opinions of legal issues, rather than for his expertise of legal affairs.

Any original score or song in the film could also be copyrighted either by the composer and/or songwriter. There may be residual income for the music or song. Please consult an appropriate source for copyrighting music.

FINAL THOUGHTS ON COPYRIGHT

For the filmmaker, the copyright law is applicable at least once (your copyright) and perhaps twice (using copyright material) for the film. A copyright logo is an essential part of your completed film and is normally done as part of the titles. Copyright could be a consideration when you are developing your idea and plan to use copyrighted material in your film. On any question regarding copyright, it is always wise to consult the appropriate laws or a copyright lawyer.

(fig. 6-14)

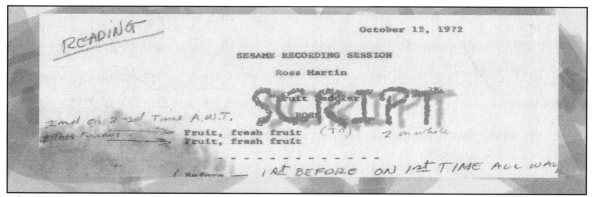

ADDENDUM TWO

(fig. 5-52)

SCRIPTWRITING FOR A TV SERIES[1]

A screenwriter for a TV series is a person who writes the script for one show for the production company that is doing that series. This section deals with the process of writing such a script. The dream of many writers and animators in TV animation is to sell and have produced a TV series that they created. If nothing, else this can mean more money. Selling a series is not the purpose of this section, but it is dealt with briefly at the end of this section.

To prepare yourself to be a screenwriter in television animation, you should study the history of animation and the current animated series on TV. There are very few, if any, classes or books on screenwriting for animation. You will have to make do with classes or books for live-action screenwriting, adapting the live-action screenwriting techniques to the special strengths and needs of animation, especially in creating the visual content. If you plan to write for comedy (most American animation is comedic), study comedians, read humor, take classes in stand-up comedy or write some funny short stories. To keep writing and get moral support, join a local writers group. To find out what is going to happen in TV animation, read the Hollywood trades. Analyze what kinds of series, comedy, action or others appeal to you and decide in which area you want to write. Then get some existing scripts of those series. The Writers Guild of America (WGA) has a script library where you can read scripts. Try calling a series production office and ask them nicely to send you a script. Sending them a stamped, self-addressed envelope won't hurt. If you know a writer ask her to get you a script as there are plenty floating around. There even may be some on the web. Look at these scripts

---

1. As mentioned in the acknowledgements, the author completed the manuscript sometime around 2007 and the text has not been updated for accuracy. All statements reflect the belief of the author at the time of authorship and may, or may not, reflect current reality.

to understand the content, structure, characters and dialogue for a series. See if you can get the series bible. A series bible is a written document that contains the premise and description of the series, all the characters and their relationships. It is an outline, writing guide and template for the series and should have example scripts in it.

Format

Live-action scripts run about one page per minute, but animated scripts, unlike live-action scripts, are almost two pages per minute due to the addition of a description of the visual action and the shot and camera selection. A half-hour show that is 22 minutes of show (with eight minutes of advertising) is about 35 to 40 pages. If the half-hour breaks down into two 11-minute shows, each show will be about 18 pages in length. Most of the writing is for low-budget limited animation programming and should be written accordingly, i.e., no 10,000 stampeding drunken dinosaurs. On the other hand, you should have enough action so that you do not end up with a radio show and talking heads. To stop this from happening, Hanna Barbera once had a rule that no more than two lines of dialogue could accompany any one shot.

Write scripts for practice. A good practice script is a spec script, which are unsolicited scripts written on pure speculation for an existing series. For formatting a spec script, compare a page from your script to a page from an existing script. Do they look alike? Why not? Change it so that it has a professional format, which can help you write and look professional. Spec scripts hardly ever sell because they do not reflect what is actually happening with the series, what ideas have been worked on or what ideas have been rejected. However, doing spec scripts is good experience and most beginning writers do them. Most important, do some written premises, which are discussed in the next section.

The Common Steps in Writing a Script

Make sure that your idea follows the concept and premise of the series. Your idea should be both visual and verbal. The first three chapters of this book will apply to this stage. Research what has been done and not done in TV animation. This is tough because TV has gobbled up a lot of story ideas over the years. Know the age of your audience; a typical audience for a network children's show is two to 11 years old. Networks can be very touchy about this; for example, Jay Ward Productions (*Rocky and Bullwinkle, George of the Jungle, Dudley Do-Right*) ignored the network suggestions on how to write animated shows for children. Their programs were very successful and are considered classics today, but because they did not follow the networks' dictums, the networks stopped buying them. *Fang the Wonderdog*, one of their pilots for a new series that was turned down, was the funniest animated show I have ever seen on TV. Of course, this was before cable, which can do shows for different age groups without the restrictions of network TV.

Premise

When you have the idea, it is best to write it down in the form of a premise. The premise is normally one to four double-spaced pages. The structure of the premise should have a beginning, middle and end; its conflicts and twists are clearly established. The premise must follow the concept and character personalities of the series. Keep in mind that all the way through this process you will need to think visually and be able to describe the visuals. You could submit several premises at a time, as on the average only one out of three good premises are accepted. Do not turn in two bad ones and one good one to make sure the good one will be accepted (you can bet one of the bad ones will be chosen). If you are making a verbal pitch of the premise, check out the storyboard chapter section in this book on presentation. The key of a good verbal pitch is that it be told succinctly, visually and, most important, it makes your audience laugh (a comedy) or cry (drama). If you do not sell right away, find out what they liked about it, what you are doing wrong, find new directions to go and then resubmit. When a premise is accepted, the people responsible for the show will want changes, sometimes small, sometimes sweeping. Sometimes so sweeping that only a small part of your premise will be taken to form a new premise. Normally, once your premise has been accepted, you will start the outline, as most shows require an outline.

Outline

For the outline, the premise is broken down into scenes and acts, with all the action, details, description and gags (if the show is funny) filled in. A long outline can run 10 pages or more. Some shows may only require a beat outline, which is the main beats or points of the premise without the details. It is possible you may be asked to write an outline from someone else's premise. You would commonly get a week to write an outline, unless there is an impending deadline. Your contract may require one rewrite, but after the outline has been read and you have been given the written comments for changes, there is usually not enough time for a rewrite so you will have to go right into the script stage.

Script

Follow the required script format. The script contains all of the dialogue. Your contract should contain how many drafts you will have to write (around three are the customary number). Sometimes you will do a draft or two and the story editor will take it and do the final polish. You should have two to three weeks to do the first draft. The changes for the rewrites will come in the form of notes from the story editor, the producer, the studio and network executives, Broadcast Standards and Practices, sponsors and their children. I hope that these notes are not too contradictory and there are not too many from the network executives, who, as Fred Allen once said, "Are the only people who could turn mountains in molehills."[2] The moral climate is more open now, but the network Standards and Practices' people and the clients will still be on the lookout for objectionable material. If a toy line is involved, you may be asked to do certain changes to sell more toys. Sometimes getting all the various groups to agree is the hardest part.

Storyboard

The storyboard is the final form of the script for production, when the images are added to the script. The writer is normally not involved at this stage. Some feel that the writer should be, as he or she could improve the show at this or a later stage. Some series like *The Simpsons* have done this with success. There is also a growing desire to start with storyboards and develop the show with the script (writer) and storyboard (artist) working together in the traditional way and do away with the script format.

Two People Whom You Meet Along the Way

The story editor is the person on the series who coordinates all the scripts. The duties of the story editor include: reading and rereading every script, doing rewrites from a minor polish to a major revision, creating premises and writing scripts at their discretion. Story editors should be the conduit and interpreter for notes from the production company and the networks as, well as their own comments to the writer. A good story editor can be a positive buffer between the writer and the clients, and is the one person, along with the producer, who keeps the show moving in the right direction.

The producer is the person who has the final say as he/she has the money, complete overview and final responsibility. Because of this,, producers will often rewrite.

Hopefully, they were former writers.

---

2 Well not quite. According to http://www.azquotes.com/quote/904519 , "A molehill man is a pseudo-busy executive who comes to work at 9 AM and finds a molehill on his desk. He has until 5 PM to make this molehill into a mountain. An accomplished molehill man will often have his mountain finished before lunch".

Voice Recording

The voices are recorded before production begins and writers are not normally involved at this stage. An executive in charge of voice recording who has to be approved by the networks may direct these recordings. A director or producer could also be present.

HOW TO GET STARTED

Agents

It is up to you if you want an agent. Some writers feel it is not important to have an agent in animation as the wages are low and the TV series are limited to a number of local producing units that are relatively easy to contact. Often, you can make a cold call. A cold call is when you call without knowing the person and ask him or her to read your scripts or hear your pitch. After you are established, you could get by with the contacts you have made. On the other hand, agents can make it easier to get the jobs and to negotiate contracts. Their 10 percent will allow you to concentrate on your writing. Normally scripts come into a producing studio through agents. There are a few agencies that specialize in animation, and only about a dozen agencies that have an agent specializing in animation. The WGA's Directory of Animation Writers not only carries a list of writers but also their agents, if they have one.[3] Check out as much as you can about an agent before you call him. If he has a bad reputation, do not call. This may be self-evident, but I have heard so many people say, "I knew he had a bad rep but I went with him anyway, I figured it couldn't be that bad, and boy, was I wrong. He was even worse."

Contacts

It seems that quite a few people, after they have done their preparation, get into the business of TV animation writing through contacts. Contacts, or networking, are very important in the field. Once you get your foot in the door, personal contacts can be a very major source of employment. After you are successful, you may want to pass along your experience to the beginning writers.

Partners

Whether or not to have a partner is a decision you will need to make. Some people write better with a partner. A partner is someone you can kick ideas, gags, whatever around with; a part-

3. This information can be found in what is now known as the Animation Writers Caucus, http://www.wga.org/the-guild/going-guild/caucuses/animation.

ner can make writing less lonely, less boring, can make an assignment shorter; and when one person is down or tired, the other could be up and full of vim and vigor. When you start, if you can team up with a writer who is already established, it will make you entreé much easier.

Submissions

When you have some writing samples, spec scripts, premises, etc., that you like, contact agents, a story editor or someone who can make decisions, and submit your writing for review. If your material gets read you will get feedback, and if the timing is right someone may be impressed by your writing and hire you to do a premise or some writing for them. Keep doing this until you start selling. It may take awhile, but be persistent, do not take rejection personally and do not give up. Be aware that if you send unsolicited material without a contact, the production house may return it unopened. The reason is their concern over potential lawsuits involving the perceived stealing of the ideas in the material.

Pay

The going rate today is about $6,000 and up for a 22-minute script with two to four drafts. You should get one-third of the $6,000 ($2,000) for the outline. The pay is about $3,500 for an 11-minute script. For a pilot, the going rate is from $8,000 to $25,000. MPSC 839 minimum unit rates for a half-hour show are $1,106.50 for synopsis and outline and $3,888.33 for a script (storyboard only $1,956.07). There usually is no pay for the premise. The payoff is in the acceptance of the premise and the money that comes in writing the script. The sad news is that unlike in live action, so far there are no residuals for reruns in animation. Residuals could generate a substantial amount of money over the years if you write for a successful series. There are around 300 to 400 animation writers working on a regular basis who are not getting residuals. One reason you see so many associate producers on some shows is that they are writers who were able to get associate producer credit so that they can get residuals.

OTHER CONSIDERATIONS

Union or Guild

The MPSC 839 has represented animation writers. Traditionally, animation writers have not been represented by the Writers Guild of America (WGA), which represents writers for live-action films. That is changing. In 1994, the Animation Writers Caucus (AWC) of the WGA was formed. It is an organization for people who have written professionally at least one half-hour of produced animation. Since its conception, it has grown from 42 members to over 300. The AWC has signed up several companies, making WGA the representative of animation writers for those companies. This gives these animation writers the same health and welfare benefits that live action writers enjoy and will one day provide residuals. Check and see what the situation is today as there is a jurisdiction dispute between unions.

Syndication

Most series, even though they may originally be for only 13 weeks, 13 shows or half a season, try to end up with 65 shows so they can go into syndication. Ideally, syndication in animation means that a new program is shown every day, five days a week, usually after school for 13 weeks, which equals 65 shows. However, some syndication may be for a shorter time.

Creating Your Own Series

You start by pitching (selling) a series concept to a production company or network. Make certain what you are developing is not something old in a new suit. Be positive that it is good, original and right for the target audience. Everyone knows what has been around and what is coming up. If it sells, be sure that you have a financial and production stake. Be sure to have business and/or legal representation. Especially for network programming, there are censorship issues. There is far less censorship in cable. Be prepared to wait a long time for someone to give the final yes or no, and read the section in copyright on options.

Good luck.

Courtesy of the Dan F. McLaughlin, Jr Collection

CHANGING EXPRESSION TO LAUGH OR SMILE WITH BREAKDOWNS FOR MORE EFFECT
FIRST A DOUBLE BLINK THEN THE LAUGH- WHICH GIVES ANTICIPATION AND MORE EMPHASIS

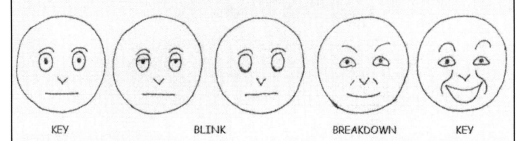

KEY   BLINK   BREAKDOWN   KEY

CHANGING EXPRESSION TO SMILE WITH BREAKDOWN FIRST OF EYES

THEN JAW DROPS- THEN SMILE- RATHER THAN GO FROM KEY TO KEY
THIS GIVES ANTICIPATION AND MORE CHARACTER

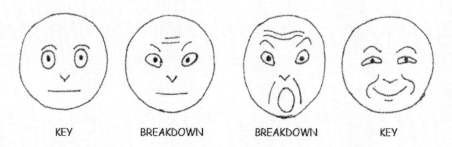

KEY   BREAKDOWN   BREAKDOWN   KEY

CHANGING EXPRESSION TO ANGER WITH BREAKDOWNS FOR
MORE EMPHASIS- FIRST THE EYES- THEN MOUTH OPEN- THEN ANGER

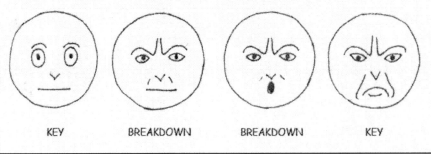

KEY   BREAKDOWN   BREAKDOWN   KEY

(fig. 7-13)

INDEX

Please note that items in bold are in the book *Animation Rules!: Book Two: Art*.

101 Dalmatians (1961) - 54
    SEE ALSO Davis, Marc; Disney (studio); Feature films
180 degree rule - 39, 98, 101-102: **fig. 2-28**
2D Animation SEE Animation, 2D
2001: A Space Odyssey (1968) - 139, 253, 306
3D Animation SEE Animation, 3D
3D Studio Max (animation software) - 265, 271
    SEE ALSO Animation, computer
7-Up (commercial) - **Fig. 12-2**
    SEE ALSO Mitchell, Bob; Commercials
9 (animation, experimental) (2005) - 45
    SEE ALSO Acker, Sean; Animation, experimental; UCLA Animation Workshop
9 (film) (2009) - 45
SEE ALSO Acker, Sean; Animation, experimental; Feature films; UCLA Animation Workshop

Abel, Robert - 361
    Works
        High Fidelity (1985) - 361
    SEE ALSO Roberts, Randy
Absolute animation SEE Animation, absolute
Academy Awards - 137, 223, 256, 294, 357
    SEE ALSO *Balance* (1989); *Big Snit, The* (1985); *Closed Mondays* (1974); *Crac!* (1981); *Critic, The* (1963); *Flowers and Trees* (1932); *Frank Film* (1973); *Gerald McBoing Boing* (1950) *Greek Tragedy* (1985); *Kama Sutra Rides Again* (1972); *Kick Me* (1973); *Luxo Jr.* (1986); *Man Who Planted Trees, The* (1987); *Mona Lisa Descending a*

Staircase (1992); *Neighbors* (1952); *Old Man and the Sea, The* (1999); *Peace on Earth* (1939); *Sisyphus* (1985); *Street, The* (1976); *Technological Threat* (1988); *Three Little Pigs, The* (1933); *Two Mouseketeers, The* (1952); *Wallace and Gromit* (1989,2005); *Wild Hare* (1940); *Windy Day* (1967)
Acker, Shane - 45
    Works
        9 (animation, experimental) (2005)- 45; *9* (film) (2009) - 45
    SEE ALSO UCLA Animation Workshop
Acting exercise SEE Exercises, acting
Action drawings SEE Quick Sketches
Adventures of an * (1957) - 3, 50, 359: **Fig. 2-36**
    SEE ALSO Animation, experimental; Hubley, Faith; Hubley, John
Advertising SEE Commercials
Adventures of Prince Achmed, The (1926) - 137, 357
    SEE ALSO Feature films; Reiniger, Lotte
Aeschylus - 43
Aesop's Fables - 47
After Effects (animation software) - 265
    SEE ALSO Animation, computer
Alexeieff, Alexander - 73, 94, 137, 358
    Works
        Night on Bald Mountain (1933) - 73, 94, 137, 358
    SEE ALSO Animation, experimental, Parker, Claire
Alice Comedies SEE *Little Alice* (1924)
Alice in Cartoonland SEE *Little Alice* (1924)
All-Aflutter (1997) – 136; **Fig. 6-2**
    SEE ALSO Animation, experimental; Wells, Brian; UCLA Animation Workshop
Allegretto (1936) - 17, 50, 58, 101, 358
SEE ALSO Animation, experimental; Fischinger, Oskar

Allen, Fred - 372
Anchors Away SEE *Anchors Aweigh* (1945)
Anchors Aweigh (1945) - 138, 250, 252, 358
    SEE ALSO Feature films; Kelly, Gene; Metro-Gold-
wyn-Mayer (studio); *Tom and Jerry* (1940-1958); Visual
effects
Andy Panda (1939-1949) - 358
    SEE ALSO *Knock, Knock* (1940); Shorts (theatrical);
Universal (studio); Woody Woodpecker (character)
Animal Farm - 47
Animal Locomotion SEE *Animals in motion*
Animal walk cycles SEE Exercises, walks and other
forms of locomotion
Animals in Motion SEE Muybridge, Eadweard
*Animated Cartoons: How They Are Made: Their Origin
and Development* SEE Lutz, Edward George
Animatics - 11, 41, 65, 72, 74, 75-76, 80, 81, 82, 85, 86,
104-105, 115, 141, 142, 143, 144, 164, 184, 236, 254, 258,
259, 260, 261, 313, 320, 330, 342, 352
SEE ALSO Storyboard, animatic
Animation
    2D - 9, 36, 51, 53, 135, 136-137
    3D - 9, 36-37, 51, 53, 135, 137-139, 144, 211, 214, 231, 232-
248, 259; **Fig. 10.1**
        Articulated models - 233-247
            Animation techniques - 235-238, 242
            Effects - 243
                SEE ALSO Animation, effects
            Cameras for - 238-241-242
            Computers and - 243
    Lenses for - 241
            Light meters - 242
            Lighting - 243-247
            Sets SEE Backgrounds
        Categories of - 232-233
        Non-articulated models, everyday items, etc. -
247-248
        Pixilation - 138-139, 233, 248
        Semi-flat objects - 248
        SEE ALSO *Automatic Moving Company, The* (1912);
Cameraman's Revenge, The (1912); *Chairy Tale, A* (1957);
Closed Mondays (1974); *Dimensions of Dialogue* (1982);
Mental Block (1985); *Mona Lisa Descending a Staircase*
(1992); *Neighbors (1952); Nightmare before Christmas,
The* (1993); *Oni* (1972); *Pappa Oh Mama* (1974); *Puppe-
toons* (1932-1971); *Quay, Brothers; Swat the Fly* (1916);
Transformations by Holding Time (1976); *Tubby the Tuba*
(1947); *Wallace and Gromit* (1989-2005); *Wizard of

Speed and Time, The (1979)
    Absolute - 17, 358
        SEE ALSO Fischinger, Oskar
Administrative elements - 128-129, 201; **Fig. 5-47**
Basic categories of - 9
    Basic components of - 150-151
    Basic principles of - 205-206, 231
        SEE ALSO Exercises
    Basis, theoretical - 204-205, 281
    Censorship SEE Censorship
    Character - 185-186, 327
        SEE ALSO Animation, drawing and; Character,
design
    Commercial aspects SEE Distribution
    Commercials SEE Commercials
    Computer - 9, 41, 59, 76, 132, 135, 139-140, 142, 143,
144, 150, 158, 174, 178,
186-187, 211, 231, 232, 238, 243, 257-270, 323, 326, 328, 337
    2D animation, assisting - 257-259
    2D motion graphics - 263-264
    Animation vs. rotoscoping - 262-263
    Backgrounds - 261-262
    Character animation - 259-261
    Hardware and software - 264-266
        SEE ALSO Animation, materials
    Lighting - 261
    Tool, as, thoughts on - 269
    Vs. live action - 262
    Warnings - 263
    SEE ALSO 3D Studio Max (animation software);
After Effects (animation software); Animation,
interactive; C++ (programming language); Emsh-
willer, Ed; Final Cut Pro (animation software); Flash
(animation software); High Fidelity (1985); Luxo
Jr. (1986); Massachusetts Institute of Technology;
Maya (animation software); Photoshop (animation
software); Pixar (studio); Premiere (animation
software); ProMAX (animation software); Saxenian;
Softimage (animation software); Shrek 2 (2004);
Sunstone (1979); Visual effects, computers and;
Wacom (drawing tablet); XSI (animation software)
    Cranes - 119-120, 121, 123,126, 130-131, 132, 136-137, 139,
140, 141, 202, 215, 252,
253, 259, 278-279, 282, 309, 311, 315, 318, 333-334, 343-
344; **Fig. 5-42; Fig. 7-3; Fig. 7-81**
        SEE ALSO Layout, technical aspects of; Pans
Crime and criminals SEE Crime and Criminals
    Definitions of - 7-9

Display of Pose – 191; **Fig. 7-66**

Drawing and – 185; **Fig 2-10; Fig. 7-33; Fig. 7-62**

SEE ALSO Animation, character

Economic aspects - 24, 27, 54, 55, 84, 136, 215, 221, 227-228, 266, 273, 279, 328; **Fig. 5-50**

SEE ALSO Distribution

Effects - 195-197; **Fig. 7-71; Fig. 7-72; Fig. 7-73; Fig. 7-74; Fig. 7-75**

Ethical aspects SEE Plagiarism

Exercises SEE Exercises

Experimental - 17, 27, 38, 42, 44, 57-60, 203, 211, 328

WORKS *9* (animation, experimental) (2005) – 45; *All-Aflutter* (1997) – 136; *Allegretto* (1936) - 17, 50, 58, 101, 358; *Adventures of an* * (1957) - 3, 50, 359; *Animato* (1977) – 361; *Automatic Moving Company, The* (1912) - 138, 248; *Bad Dream Girl* (2009) – 137; *Balance* (1989) - 47, 61, 74, 94, 362; *Bambi Meets Godzilla* (1969) – 360; *Begone Dull Care* (1949) - 17, 50, 58, 88, 101, 138, 204, 358; *Big Snit, The* (1985) - 101, 361; *Breakfast on the Grass* (1987) – 361; *Breathe* (1967) - 360 *CALM anti-perspirant* (commercial) (1971) – 146; *Cameraman's Revenge, The* (1912) - 138, 235, 357; *Canon* (1964) - 137, 256, 360; *Carmen* (1933) – 358; *Carnival* (1985) – 361; *Celery Stalks at Midnight* (1937) – 137; *Chairy Tale, A* (1957) - 138, 248, 359; *Chasing the Light* (2014) – 116; *Chromophobia* (1966) – 360; *Claude* (1963) - i, 3, 4, 17, 38, 45, 63, 359; *Closed Mondays* (1974) - 237, 238, 360; *Connection, The* (1961) – 27; *Crac!* (1981) - 47, 101, 136, 361; *Critic, The* (1963) - 55, 137, 359; *Cuckoo* (1984) - 74, 94, 361; *Diary* (1974) – 360; *Dimensions of Dialogue* (1982) - 58, 138, 248, 361; *Do-It-Yourself Cartoon Kit* (1961) - 137, 359; *Dot and the Line, The* (1965) - 50, 55; *Epiphanies* (1968) – 136; *Experimentations* (1970s); *Fantasmagorie* (1908) - 51, 58, 136, 321, 357; *Film, Film, Film* (1968) – 360; *Flying Man, The* (1962) - 136, 359; *Fossils* (1999) - 58, 59; *Frank Film* (1973) - 50, 137, 360; *Fire Safety Spot* (1960) – **Fig. 2-68; Fig 5-5;** *Frog He Would A-wooing Go, A* (1990) – 136; *Furies* (1975) - 59, 79, 136; *Further Adventures of Uncle Sam, The* (1970) – 360; *Getting Started* (1979) – 361; *Gerald McBoing Boing* (1950) - 36, 47, 358; *Gertie the Dinosaur* (1914) - 51, 101, 136, 161, 197, 340, 357; *God is Dog Spelled Backwards* (1967) - 17, 21, 42, 58, 101, 137, 301, 303, 311, 359; *Greek Tragedy* (1985) – 361; *Grey Wolf and Little Red Riding Hood* (1990) – 362; *Harry* (n.d.) - 3-4, 24; *Hello* (1984) – 136; *Hen Hop* (1942) - 138, 358; *High Fidelity* (1985) – 361; *Hill Farm, The* (1988) - 321, 362; *if my wings had dreams* (2002) – 50; *Jumping* (1984) - 157-158, 337, 361; *Kama Sutra Rides Again* (1972) – 360;

Katzenjammer Kids: Still Stranded, The (1995) – 152; *Kick Me* (1973) - 138, 360; *L'Idee* (1932) - 135, 136; *La Jetée* (1962) - 152, 359; *La Poulette Grise* (1947) – 136; *Landscape Painter, The* (1976) – 137; *Lapis* (1966) - 20, 42, 57, 58, 211, 360; *Les Jeux des Anges* (1964) - 47, 119, 136, 153, 359-360; *Lines: Vertical* (1960) – 58; *Little Nemo* (1911) – 321; *Lost World, The* (1925) - 26, 357; *Love* (1963) – 359; *Luxo Jr.* (1986) – 361; *Madame Tutli-Putli* (2007) – 45; *Madcap* (1991) – 138; *Man Who Planted Trees, The* (1987) - 50, 136, 361; *Mental Block* (1985) – 236; *Microsecond* – **Fig. 9-1;** *Mindscape/Le paysagiste* (1976) - 137, 361; *Mona Lisa Descending a Staircase* (1992) - 137, 248, 362; *Mothlight* (1963) – 136; *Muratti cigarettes* (commercial) – 146; *Mystery Box, A* (2001) – 59; *Mystery of Easter Island* (n.d.) - 3, 168; *Neighbors* (1952) - 138, 248, 359; *Night on Bald Mountain* (1933) - 73, 94, 137, 358; *Nine O'Clock News* (1968) – Fig. 7-9; *No Idea* (2000) – 17; *Old Man and the Sea, The* (1999) - 136, 362; *One Final Encore* (2016) – 140; *Oni* (1972) - 138, 232, 360; *Open Wednesday* (1980) – 361; *Optical Poem* (1938) – 58; *Paladins of France, The* (1960) - 137, 359; *Pappa Oh Mama* (1974) – 248; *Pas de deux* (1968) - 139, 256, 360; *Portrait of Jason* (1967) – 27; *Propaganda Dance* (1987) – 361; *Preludes in Magical Time* (1988) – 59; *Prisoner, The* (1973) – 197; *Rainbow Bear* (1970) – 360; *Rainbow Dance* (1936) - 59, 358; *Red/Green* (1985) - 58, 105; *Roadkill Redemption* (2013) – 139; *Russia, March to November, 1917* (1959) - **Fig. 2-12;** *Sand Dance* (1988) - 74, 94, 101, 137, 311, 361; *Scratch Film #1* (1989) – 59; *Screen* (1969) – 138; *Shapes of Movement* (1996) – 251; *Sisyphus* (1985) - 45-46, 360; *Song of the Prairie* (1949) - 73, 94, 358; *Spring Blanket* (circa 1986) – 136; *Star Spangled Banner* (1968) – **Fig. 2-64;** *Starlore* (1983) – 136; *Strange Case of Mr. and Mrs. Donnybrook's Boredom, The* (1981) - 73, 94, 361; *Street, The* (1976) - 25-26, 47, 50, 98, 137, 360; *Street Works* (1988) - 58, 59; *Study series* (1929-1934) – 55; *Sunstone* (1979) – 361; *Swimming* (1986) – 136; *Symphonie Diagonale* (1924) - 58, 357; *Ta-Daa* (2016) – 9; *Tale of Tales* (1979) – 361; *Technological Threat* (1988) - 74, 94, 361; *Transformations by Holding Time* (1976) - 139, 248, 360; *Walking* (1968) - 61, 138, 349, 360; *Where's Poppa?* (1970) - 66, 256; *Windy Day* (1967) – 360; *Wizard of Speed and Time, The* (1979) - 138-139, 248, 361; *Yantra* (1955) - 58, 211; *Zid (The Wall)* (1965) - 46, 360

Feature films SEE Feature films

Festivals - 64, 88, 138, 217, 220-223, 225, 226, 299-300, 365, 367; **Fig. 9-2; Fig. 9-3; 9-6**

SEE ALSO Ann Arbor Film Festival; Chicago

International Film Festival; L.A. Animation Celebration; Spike and Mike's Sick and Twisted Festival of Animation; Athens International Film Festival; Cinestud (International Festival of Student-Made Films); Sacramento Film Festival; Sacramento Film Festival; Newport Beach Film Festival; San Francisco Art Institute Film Festival
Filming - 202-203
Final check - 202
Full SEE Animation, types of
    Future of - 146-147
Genre - 145-145
    History - 8, 40-41, 71, 75, 81, 82, 89-90, 112, 116, 136, 145-146, 153, 154, 155, 158, 168, 174, 193, 195, 200, 201, 205, 224-225, 232, 234, 237, 244, 256, 262, 268, 272-273, 279, 280-281, 289, 306-307, 326, 334, 335, 340, 341-342, 351
        SEE ALSO Animation, Stories of/about
Interactive - 9, 135, 140, 231, 232, 270-276, 326, 328
    Delivery systems for - 273
    Job prospects in - 273
        SEE ALSO Animators, vocational aspects
    Static vs. dynamic - 271
    SEE ALSO Animation, computer; Storyboards, interactive; Thankamushy, Sunil
    International - 40, 56, 146, 279-280, 285, 293, 295, 311, 339
    Japanese - 11, 40, 80, 81, 146, 157-158, 279-280, 295, 337
    Key/posed SEE Animation, methods of
    Levels - 197-198
    Limited SEE Animation, types of
    Materials - 153-154, 159, 170, 203, 210-211, 232, 233, 234, 238, 239, 241, 242, 243-244, 264, 265-266, 277-282, 309-310, 311, 334; **Fig. 7-4; Fig. 11-1; Fig. 11-2**
    Suppliers - 278, 350
    SEE ALSO Animation, computer, hardware and software
    Methods of - 151-152
    Paper SEE Animation, materials
    Process - 184
    Program (academic) - 236-239
    Production stages of SEE Production
    Rubber hose - 170, 201; **Fig. 7-81**
    Scripts SEE Sound, dialogue
Series SEE Television series
    Shorts SEE Shorts (theatrical)

    Stories of/about - 19, 27, 33, 34, 37, 41-42, 46, 53, 54, 56, 57, 61-62, 65, 67, 75, 81, 82-83, 85, 89-90, 112, 116, 120, 125, 138, 151, 153, 154, 156, 159, 163, 168, 182, 185, 186, 193, 195, 197, 205, 217, 222, 226, 234, 236, 238, 240, 247, 257, 262, 280-281, 285, 286, 287, 288, 289, 298, 310, 311, 320, 332, 334, 335, 340, 341-342, 370
    Straight-ahead SEE Animation, methods of
    Style – 145; **Fig. 2-35**
Techniques - 135-147
Testing - 198-199
Time - 38, 101 **Fig. 2-26**
Types of - 152-153; **Fig. 7-1. Fig. 7-2**
Vs. live-action - ii, 10-11, 20, 25-26, 39-40, 46, 48, 50, 55, 69, 80, 89, 89-90, 93, 98, 235, 321
    SEE ALSO Visual effects
Animation Celebration - 294
    SEE ALSO UCLA Animation Workshop
Animation Guild Local 839 IATSE SEE Unions and guilds
Animation: Learn How to Draw Animated Cartoons - 183, 194, 315, 355
    SEE ALSO Blair, Preston
Animation Magazine - 293, 356
Animation World Network - 356
Animato (1977) - 361
    SEE ALSO Animation, experimental; Jittlov, Mike; UCLA Animation Workshop
Animators
    Copyright and SEE Copyright
    Educational aspects - 11, 12, 150, 153-184
    Ethical aspects - 63, 64, 219-220, 298-305
    Hollywood and - 21, 226-227
        SEE ALSO Animators, vocational aspects; Distribution, contracts
    Vocational aspects - 11, 255, 267, 273, 283-308
        Areas of work - 294-295
        Avoiding being taken advantage of - 284, 287, 292, 299
        Employment trends - 306-307
        Freelancing - 283, 285, 286, 289-290, 307
        Independent filmmaking - 283, 284-286
        Notes and - 295-296
        Portfolios - 296-298
        Studio ownership - 283, 286-288
        Unemployment - 289, 292-294
        Unions SEE Unions and guilds
        SEE ALSO Animators, wages
    Wages - 287, 289, 290, 291-292, 374

SEE ALSO Animators, vocational aspects
SEE ALSO Animation, Stories of/about
Animator's block SEE Ideas, generating
Animator's Survival Kit, The SEE Williams, Richard
Animatrix (Peroidical) - 261
SEE ALSO UCLA Animation Workshop
Animatronics SEE Visual effects
Ann Arbor Film Festival - 138
SEE ALSO Animation, festivals; Denslow, Phil;
Madcap (1991)
Anonymous - 13, 31, 207
Anticipation exercise SEE Exercises, Anticipation
Antheil, George - 308
Arcade games SEE Animation, interactive
Aristotle - 18, 43
Armature SEE Animation, 3D, Articulated Models
Artificial Intelligence - 28
ASIFA-Hollywood - 9, 221, 297, 356
Association Internationale du Film d'Animation SEE
ASIFA-Hollywood
Asterisk exercise SEE Exercises, asterisk
Athens International Film Festival - **Fig. 9-3**
Atlantis: The Lost Empire (2001) - 140
SEE ALSO Disney (studio); Feature films
Automatic Moving Company, The (1912) - 138, 248
SEE ALSO Animation, 3D, Animation, experimental;
Bosetti, Romeo
Avery, Tex - 15, 21, 27, 28, 41-42, 96, 166, 168, 344, 358;
Fig. 1-7
Works
Bad Luck Blackie (1949) - 186, 358; *Porky's Duck
Hunt* (1937) – 358; *Red Hot Riding Hood* (1941) – 94; *Wild
Hare (1940)* - 358
SEE ALSO Bugs Bunny (character); Daffy Duck
(character); Porky Pig (character); Shorts (theatrical);
Warner Brothers (studio)

Babbitt, Art - 151, 194
Works
Dumbo (1941) - 17, 49; *Fantasia* (1940) - 58, 73, 79,
135, 186; *Pinocchio* (1940) - 17, 33-34, 44, 94, 137, 179, 180;
Playful Pluto (1943) - 186, 193, 313, 352; *Snow White and
the Seven Dwarfs* (1937) - 16, 17, 44, 49, 50, 57, 65, 101,
118, 128, 145, 193, 197, 268
SEE ALSO Disney (studio)
Backgrounds - 33, 39, 50, 51, 53, 54, 91, 92, 97-98, 105,
106-107, 109, 112, 113, 114, 115, 116, 119, 123, 124, 128-129,

133, 136, 141, 142, 143, 144, 165, 174, 176, 197-198, 199, 201-
202, 234-235, 238, 243, 246, 250, 251, 258, 259, 261-262,
267, 273, 277, 278, 288, 290, 295, 296, 303, 325, 328, 343,
349; **Fig. 5-12; Fig 5.25; Fig. 5-26; Fig. 7-80**
SEE ALSO Animation, computer, backgrounds;
Layout, composition
Bad Dream Girl (2009) – 137; *Fig. 6-8*
SEE ALSO Animation, experimental; Mercer, Celia
Bad Luck Blackie (1949) - 186, 358
SEE ALSO Avery, Tex; Metro-Goldwyn-Mayer (studio);
Shorts (theatrical)
Back, Frédéric - 26, 29, 47, 136, 362
Works
Crac! (1981) - 47, 101, 136, 361; *Man Who Planted
Trees, The* (1987) - 50, 136, 361
SEE ALSO Animation, experimental
Baker, Mark - 321, 362
Works
Hill Farm, The (1988) - 321, 362
SEE ALSO Animation, experimental
Bakshi, Ralph - 138, 192
SEE ALSO Rotoscoping
Balance (1989) - 47, 56, 61, 74, 94, 362
SEE ALSO Academy Awards; Animation, experi-
mental; Lauenstein, Christoff and Wolfgang
Baloo (character) - 82-83
SEE ALSO *Disney Animation: The Illusion of Life*;
Disney (studio); Harris, Phil; *Jungle Book, The* (1967)
Bambi (1942) - 17, 23
SEE ALSO Blair, Preston; Davis, Marc; Disney (studio);
Feature films; Johnston, Ollie; Salten, Felix
Bambi Meets Godzilla (1969) - 360
SEE ALSO Animation, experimental; Newland, Marv
Band Concert, The (1935) - 314, 352
SEE ALSO Disney (studio); Disney, Walt; Mickey
Mouse (character); Shorts (theatrical)
Bar sheets - 39, 62, 75, 80, 81, 82, 85, 86, 87, 104, 141, 142,
143, 310, 324, 342: **Fig. 2-62**
Barbera, Joseph - 359
Works
Two Mouseketeers, The (1952) - 359
SEE ALSO Hanna, William; Hanna-Barbera (studio)
Bardin, Garri - 362
Works
Grey Wolf and Little Red Riding Hood (1990) - 362
SEE ALSO Animation, experimental
Barret, Earl - 45
Bart Simpson (character) - 50

Bartosch, Berthold - 135
    L'Idee (1932) - 135, 136
    SEE ALSO Animation, experimental
Basic walk cycle SEE Exercises, walks and other forms of locomotion
Beavis and Butt-Head (1993-2011) - 362
    SEE ALSO Television series
Beck, Jerry - 3, 356
    SEE ALSO *Jerry Beck's Cartoon Research*
Begone Dull Care (1949) - 17, 50, 58, 88, 101, 138, 204, 358
SEE ALSO Animation, experimental; McLaren, Norman
Beethoven, Ludwig van - 26, 106, 275, 303, 313, 352, 366
Bell, Margie SEE Champion, Marge
Benchley, Robert - 220, 300
Benny, Jack - 76
Betty Boop in Snow White SEE *Snow-White* (1933)
Big Cartoon Database - 356
Big Snit, The (1985) - 101, 361
    SEE ALSO Academy Awards; Animation, experimental; Condie, Richard; National Film Board of Canada
Bill Melendez Productions (studio) - 285, 360
    Works
        Rainbow Bear (1970) - 360
    SEE ALSO Melendez, Bill
Biographic (studio) - 137, 359
    Works
        Do-It-Yourself Cartoon Kit (1961) - 137, 359
    SEE ALSO Animation, experimental; Godfrey, Bob; Hanna, Nancy; Learner, Keith; Linnecar, Vera
Bird beak animation SEE Sound, dialogue
Black Orpheus (1959) - 103
Blaiklock, Andy - 46
    SEE ALSO UCLA Animation Workshop
Blair, Preston - 183, 194, 312, 315, 351, 355
    Works
        Animation: Learn How to Draw Animated Cartoons - 183, 194, 315, 355; *Bambi* (1942) - 17, 23; *Fantasia* (1940) - 58, 73, 79, 135, 186; *Flintstones, The* (1960-1966) - 21, 125, 362; *Pinocchio* (1940) - 17, 33-34, 44, 94, 137, 179, 180; *Red Hot Riding Hood* (1941) - 94
    SEE ALSO Disney (studio); Hanna-Barbera (studio); Metro-Goldwyn-Mayer (studio); Universal (studio)
Blake, William - 29
Blanc, Mel - 56, 298
    SEE ALSO Brown, Treg; Bugs Bunny (character); Daffy Duck (character); Foghorn Leghorn (character); *Knock, Knock* (1940); *Porky's Duck Hunt* (1937);

Rabbit Fire (1951); Tweety and Sylvester; Warner Brothers (studio); *What's Opera, Doc?* (1957); *Wild Hare* (1940)
Book of Kells, The - 110
Bookkeeping SEE Layout, administrative elements
Borowczyk, Walerian - 47, 119, 136, 359-360
    Works
        Les Jeux des Anges (1964) - 47, 119, 136, 153, 359-360
    SEE ALSO Animation, experimental
Bosetti, Romeo - 248
    Works
        Automatic Moving Company, The (1912) - 138, 248
Bouncing ball exercise SEE Exercises, bouncing ball
Brakhage, Stan - 136
    Works
        Mothlight (1963) - 136
    SEE ALSO Animation, experimental
Brando, Marlon - 263
Breakfast on the Grass (1987) - 361
    SEE ALSO Animation, experimental
    SEE ALSO Parn, Priit
Breathe (1967) - 360
    SEE ALSO Animation, experimental; Murakami, Jimmy
Brooks, Mel - 55, 359
    SEE ALSO *Critic, The* (1963)
Brown, Treg - 89, 298
    SEE ALSO Blanc, Mel; Warner Brothers (studio)
Budgets SEE Animation, economic aspects
Bugs Bunny (character) - 17, 25, 28, 49, 50, 54, 55, 187, 358
    SEE ALSO Avery, Tex; Blanc, Mel; Jones, Chuck; *Rabbit Fire* (1951); Shorts (theatrical); Warner Brothers (studio); *What's Opera, Doc?* (1957); *Wild Hare* (1940)
Bus (Sesame Street spot) (circa 1974) – 317; **fig. 13-3**
    SEE ALSO McLaughlin, Dan F., Jr.; *Sesame Street* (1969-present); Shorts, theatrical
Butterfly walk cycle SEE Exercises, walks and other forms of locomotion
Buonarroti, Michelangelo - 13, 20, 109, 296

C++ (programming language) - 272, 274
    SEE ALSO Animation, computer
CALM anti-perspirant (commercial) (1971) – 146; **Fig. 6-14**
    SEE ALSO Animation, experimental; Commercials; Mitchell, Bob
Camera view SEE Design, By camera view
    SEE ALSO Layout, Camera

Cameraman's Revenge, The (1912) - 138, 235, 357
SEE ALSO Animation, 3D; Animation, experimental; Starewicz, Ladislaw
Campbell, Glen *SEE Smothers Brothers Summer Show, The*
Campbell, Joseph - 45
Canadian Film Board SEE National Film Board of Canada
Candle flame animation SEE Animation, effects
Cannon, Robert - 358
    Works
        Gerald McBoing Boing (1950) - 36, 47, 358
    SEE ALSO UPA (studio)
Canon (1964) - 137, 256, 360
SEE ALSO Animation, experimental; McLaren, Norman; National Film Board of Canada; Visual effects
Cantwell, Colin - **Fig. 13-4**
    SEE ALSO UCLA Animation Workshop
Canyon Cinema - 225
    SEE ALSO Distribution
Carmen (1933) - 358
    SEE ALSO Animation, experimental; Reiniger, Lotte
Carnival (1985) - 361
    SEE ALSO Animation, experimental; Royal College of Art; Young, Susan
Cartoon adult character of the author walking with a beer and a slight up-and-down motion SEE Exercises, walks and other forms of locomotion
Cartoon character run cycle SEE Exercises, walks and other forms of locomotion
Cartoon Colour SEE Animation, materials, suppliers
Cartoon dog walk cycle SEE Exercises, walks and other forms of locomotion
Cartoon with springs for legs walk cycle SEE Exercises, walks and other forms of locomotion
Cartooning – **Fig. 2-39**
    SEE ALSO McLaughlin, Dan F., Jr.
Cary, Joyce - 70
Case, Dale - 360
    Works
        Further Adventures of Uncle Sam, The (1970) - 360
    SEE ALSO Animation, experimental; Haboush Company (studio); Mitchell, Bob
Cassidy, Chris - 289
Categorical imperative - 305
    SEE ALSO Kant, Immanuel
Celery Stalks at Midnight (1937) - 137
    SEE ALSO Animation, experimental; Whitney, John

Cels, Layers of – **Fig. 5-1; Fig. 5-47**
Censorship - 63-64, 275, 303, 375
    SEE ALSO Animators, ethical aspects
Cézanne, Paul - 26, 275
Chairy Tale, A (1957); - 138, 248, 359
    SEE ALSO Animation, experimental: McLaren, Norman; National Film Board of Canada
Chicago International Film Festival - 359
    SEE ALSO Animation, festivals; *God is Dog Spelled Backwards (1967);* McLaughlin, Dan F., Jr.
Champion, Marge - 128, 193
    SEE ALSO Snow White (character); *Snow White and the Seven Dwarfs* (1937)
Channel Four - 284
Chaplin, Charlie - 61, 65, 73, 147, 179, 350
Character - 16, 48-55
    Design - 52-54; 187-190: **Fig. 2-46; Fig. 2-47; Fig.2-49; Fig. 2-50; Fig. 7-35; Fig. 7-36; Fig. 7-37; Fig. 7-38; Fig. 7-39; Fig. 7-40; Fig. 7-41; Fig. 7-42; Fig. 7-43; Fig. 7-44; Fig. 7-45; Fig. 7-46; Fig. 7-47; Fig. 7-48; Fig. 7-49; Fig. 7-50; Fig. 7-51; Fig. 7-52; Fig. 7-53; Fig. 7-54; Fig. 7-55; Fig. 7-56; Fig. 7-58; Fig. 7-59; Fig. 7-60; Fig. 7-82**
    Marketing - 55
    Name - 61-62: **Fig. 2-51**
    Personality - 48-50
    Story, and - 56-57
    SEE ALSO Animation, character; Movement, character
Charlie Brown (film and television franchise) - 294
Chasing the Light (2014) – 116; **Fig. 5-29**
    SEE ALSO Shipman, Jay; Animation, experimental; UCLA Animation Workshop
Chiang, Doug - 236
    Works
        Mental Block (1985) - 236
    SEE ALSO Animation, experimental
Chouinard Art Institute - 185
    SEE ALSO Davis, Marc
Chromophobia (1966) - 360
    SEE ALSO Animation, experimental; Servais, Raoul
Chuck Amuck: The Life and Times of an Animated Cartoonist SEE Jones, Chuck
Cinderella (1950) - 17
    SEE ALSO Davis, Marc; Disney (studio); Feature films; Johnston, Ollie; Kimball, Ward
Cinedoc – **Fig. 9-9**
Cinestud (International Festival of Student-Made Films) – **Fig. 9-2; Fig. 9-4**
Cinethics SEE McLaughlin, Dan F. Jr., ethical con-

cerns AND Hollywood, ethical aspects AND Animators, ethical aspects

City of Gold (1957) - 137, 146, 153, 359

SEE ALSO Koenig, Wolf; Low, Colin; National Film Board of Canada; Shorts (theatrical)

Classical Gas SEE *God is Dog Spelled Backward* (1967)

Clarke, Shirley - 27, 217, 284, 285

Works

Connection, The (1961) – 27; *Portrait of Jason* (1967) – 27

Claude (1963) - i, 3, 4, 17, 38, 45, 63, 359: **Fig. 1-2; Fig 2-9; Fig. 2-33; Fig. 2-66; Fig. 5-1; Fig. 5-19; Fig. 5-20; Fig. 5-21; Fig. 5-22; Fig. 5-28; Fig. 7-77; Fig. 8-2; Fig. 9-4; Fig. 9-7; Fig. 9-8**

SEE ALSO Animation, experimental; McLaughlin, Dan F., Jr.; UCLA Animation Workshop

Claymation SEE Animation, 3D, articulated models

Clip shows - 81

Closed Mondays (1974) - 237, 238, 360

SEE ALSO Academy Awards; Animation, 3D; Animation, experimental; Gardiner, Bob; Rotosoping; Vinton, Will

Clutch Cargo (1959-1960) - 194

SEE ALSO Television series

Cohen, Karl - 284

SEE ALSO San Francisco State University

Cohl, Emile - 58, 136, 194, 357

Works

Fantasmagorie (1908) - 51, 58, 136, 321, 357

Color - 32, 34-35, 37, 51, 53, 54, 57, 62, 64, 92, 103, 106, 107, 111-115, 116, 118, 140, 141, 142, 144, 163, 165, 189, 196, 197, 199, 201, 204, 214, 234, 244, 245, 251-252, 253, 255, 257, 258-259, 260-261, 277, 278, 279, 288, 296, 310, 324, 328, 341, 343, 366: **Fig. 2-48; Fig. 5-23; Fig. 5-24; Fig. 5-27**

Cards - 58, 204, 252; **Fig. 7-84**

Use in Model sheets - 52, 115, 116, 343; **Fig. 2-45**

SEE ALSO Character, design; Layout, composition

Comedy SEE Humor

Commercials - 27, 59, 72, 75, 99-100, 140, 146, 221, 253, 257, 285, 289, 290, 295, 300-301, 302: **Fig. 2-48; Fig. 7-2; Fig. 5-15**

SEE ALSO CALM anti-perspirant (commercial) (1971); *High Fidelity* (1985); *Muratti cigarettes* (commercial); *Rainbow Dance* (1936); *Tiger Paws* (n.d.); *National Lumber* (Commercial) (Circa 1985); *Pittsburgh Paint* (commercial) (n.d.); *7-Up* (n.d.) (commercial)

Computer animation SEE Animation, computer

Computer-assisted animation SEE Animation, computer

Computer games SEE Animation, interactive

Condie, Richard - 361

Works

Big Snit, The (1985) - 101, 361; *Getting Started* (1979) - 361

SEE ALSO Animation, experimental; National Film Board of Canada

Connection, The (1961) - 27

SEE ALSO Animation, experimental; Clarke, Shirley

Copyright - 22, 62, 69, 84, 218, 363-368; **Fig. add-1**

Fair usage - 365-366

Courage to Create, The SEE May, Rollo

Courses SEE Syllabi

Crac! (1981) - 47, 101, 136, 361

SEE ALSO Academy Awards; Animation, experimental; Back, Frédéric

Creating 3D Animation SEE Lord, Peter and SEE Sibley, Brian

Creativity SEE Ideas, creativity and

Crime and criminals - 21, 300, 301

SEE ALSO *Glen Campbell Summer Show, The; Smothers Brothers Summer Show, The*

Critic, The (1963) - 55, 137, 359

SEE ALSO Academy Awards; Animation, experimental; Brooks, Mel; Pintoff, Ernest

Criticism - 63, 303; **Fig. 9-7**

Crusader Rabbit (1950-1979) - 362

SEE ALSO Television series

Cuckoo (1984) - 74, 94, 361

SEE ALSO Animation, experimental; Kazakov, Velislav

Cyclone animation SEE Animation, effects

Daffy Duck (character) - 16, 25, 49, 50, 55, 62, 358

SEE ALSO Avery, Tex; Blanc, Mel; *Daffy's Southern Exposure* (1942); *Duck Amuck* (1953); Jones, Chuck; *Porky's Duck Hunt* (1937); *Rabbit Fire* (1951); Shorts (theatrical)

SEE ALSO Warner Brothers (studio)

Daffy's Southern Exposure (1942) - 16

SEE ALSO Daffy Duck (character); Jones, Chuck; McCabe, Norm; Shorts (theatrical); Warner Brothers (studio)

Davis, Marc - 185, 296; **fig. 7-34**

Works

101 Dalmatians (1961) - 54; *Bambi* (1942) - 17, 23; *Cinderella* (1950) – 17; *Peter Pan* (1953) - 33, 114, 275;

Sleeping Beauty (1959) – 17; *Snow White and the Seven Dwarfs* (1937) - 16, 17, 44, 49, 50, 57, 65, 101, 118, 128, 145, 193, 197, 268

    SEE ALSO Chouinard Art Institute; Disney (studio)

De Nooijer, Paul - 139, 248, 360

    Works

        Transformations by Holding Time (1976) - 139, 248, 360

    SEE ALSO Animation, experimental

Denslow, Phil - ii, 1, 3, 138, 197, 256; **Fig. 6-9; Fig. 7-76**

    Works

        Madcap (1991) – 138; *Prisoner, The* (1973) - 197

    SEE ALSO Animation, experimental; Ann Arbor Film Festival; L.A. Animation Celebration; UCLA Animation Workshop

Der Fuehrer's Face (1943) - 49

    SEE ALSO Disney (studio); Donald Duck (character); Shorts (theatrical)

Design

    Best structure for abstract film - 58

    By camera view - 34-39: **Fig. 2-13; Fig. 2-17; Fig. 2-18; Fig. 2-19; Fig. 2-20; Fig. 2-21; Fig. 5-30; Fig. 5-31; Fig. 5-32**

    By composition of shot – 37: **Fig. 2-24**

    By size of shot - 35-36: **Fig. 2-14**

    By time of shot SEE Pacing

    Screen direction – 39: **Fig. 2-30; Fig. 2-31**

    Timeline SEE Timelines

    X direction exercise – 37: **Fig. 2-25**

Dewey, John - 22

Dialogue SEE Sound, dialogue

Diamond, Ron - 293

Diary (1974) - 360

    SEE ALSO Animation, experimental; Dragic, Nedeljko; Zagreb Studios

Dick Clark Show, The - 300

    SEE ALSO McLaughlin, Dan F., Jr.

Dickson, Bob - 3

    SEE ALSO UCLA Animation Workshop

Dimensions of Dialogue (1982) - 58, 138, 248, 361

SEE ALSO Animation, experimental; Svankmajer, Jan

Disney Animation: The Illusion of Life - 17, 82-83, 185, 194, 283, 355

    SEE ALSO Baloo (character); Harris, Phil; Johnston, Ollie; *Jungle Book, The* (1967); Thomas, Frank

Disney (studio) - 3, 17, 26, 34, 37, 41, 50-51, 53, 75, 81, 94, 104, 116, 124, 136, 137, 140, 145, 151, 152, 163, 168, 185, 192-193, 195, 205, 257, 279, 286, 290, 294, 296, 306, 314, 349, 351, 353, 357, 358; **Fig. rt-1**

Works

    101 Dalmatians (1961) – 54; *Atlantis: The Lost Empire* (2001) – 140; *Bambi* (1942) - 17, 23; *Band Concert, The* (1935) - 314, 352; *Cinderella* (1950) – 17; *Der Fuehrer's Face* (1943) – 49; *Dumbo* (1941) - 17, 49; *Fantasia* (1940) - 58, 73, 79, 135, 186; *Flowers and Trees* (1932) – 357; *Jungle Book, The* (1967) – 82; *Lion King, The* (1994) - 50, 140, 257; *Little Alice* (1924) - 26, 250; *Mary Poppins* (1964) – 139; *Night on Bald Mountain* (1940) - 73, 94; *Peter Pan* (1953) - 33, 114, 275; *Pinocchio* (1940) - 17, 33-34, 44, 94, 137, 179, 180; *Plane Crazy* (1928) – 99; *Playful Pluto* (1943) - 186, 193, 313, 352; *Robin Hood* (1973) - 85, 306; *Silly Symphonies* (1929-1939) – 79; *Skeleton Dance* (1929) - 61, 357; *Sleeping Beauty* (1959) – 17; *Snow White and the Seven Dwarfs* (1937) - 16, 17, 44, 49, 50, 57, 65, 101, 118, 128, 145, 193, 197, 268; *Steamboat Willie* (1928) - 90, 357; *Three Little Pigs, The* (1933) - 45, 358; *Who Framed Roger Rabbit* (1988) - 26, 139, 250, 306

    SEE ALSO Babbitt, Art; Baloo (character); Blair, Preston; Davis, Marc; *Disney Animation: The Illusion of Life*; Disney, Walt; Donald Duck (character); Dopey (character); Dumbo (character); Gillett, Burt; Honest John (character); Iwerks, Ub; Johnston, Ollie; Kimball, Ward; Mickey Mouse (character); Mickey Mouse Sound; Pederson, Con; Peter Pan (character); Pluto (character); Smith, Webb; Snow White (character); Stepmother (character); Stromboli (character); Thomas, Frank

Disney, Walt - 11-12, 26, 33, 41, 56, 61-62, 65, 168, 283, 284, 286, 341-342, 357

Works

    Band Concert, The (1935) - 314, 352; *Fantasia* (1940) - 58, 73, 79, 135, 186; *Flowers and Trees* (1932) – 357; *Little Alice* (1924) - 26, 250; *Plane Crazy* (1928) – 99; *Skeleton Dance* (1929) - 61, 357; *Steamboat Willie* (1928) - 90, 357; *Three Little Pigs, The* (1933) - 45, 358

    SEE ALSO Disney (studio); Mickey Mouse (character)

Distribution - 11, 55, 141, 142, 143, 144, 145, 217-229; **Fig. 9-1; Fig. 9-8; Fig. 9-9**

    Avenues - 223-225

Contracts - 218-219, 226-227

    SEE ALSO Animators, Hollywood and

    SEE ALSO Animators, vocational aspects

    Festivals SEE Animation, festivals

    History - 224-225

Revenue streams - 227-228

    Promotion - 218-220

    Reels - 228-229

Screenings, invited - 218
Venues - 225-226
SEE ALSO Animation, economic aspects; Canyon Cinema; Copyright; Film-Makers' Cooperative
Do-It-Yourself Cartoon Kit (1961) - 137, 359
SEE ALSO Animation, experimental; Biographic (studio); Godfrey, Bob; Hanna, Nancy; Learner, Keith. Linnecar, Vera
Dog walk cycle SEE Exercises, walks and other forms of locomotion
Donald Duck (character) - 25, 49, 62, 185
SEE ALSO *Der Fuehrer's Face* (1943); Disney (studio); Shorts (theatrical)
Donovan's Brain SEE Siodmak, Curt
Doors, The - 263
Dopey (character) - 49
SEE ALSO Disney (Studio); Snow White and the Seven Dwarfs (1937)
Dot and the Line, The (1965) - 50, 55
SEE ALSO Animation, experimental; Jones, Chuck; Metro-Goldwyn-Mayer (studio)
Double take - 168, 193, 237; **Fig. 7-12**
Dover Boys, The (1942) - 101, 358
SEE ALSO Jones, Chuck; Shorts (theatrical); Warner Brothers (studio)
Dr. Seuss SEE Geisel, Theodor
Dragic, Nedeljko - 360
Works
Diary (1974) - 360
SEE ALSO Animation, experimental; Zagreb Studios
Drama-Logue (Periodical) - 82
Drawing the Head and Figure SEE Hamm, Jack
DreamWorks (studio) - 257
Works
Shrek 2 (2004) - 257
Drouin, Jacques - 137, 361
Works
Mindscape/Le paysagiste (1976) - 137, 361
SEE ALSO Animation, experimental; National Film Board of Canada
Duck Amuck (1953) - 101, 359
SEE ALSO Jones, Chuck; Shorts (theatrical); Warner Brothers (studio)
Dudley Do-Right (character) SEE *Rocky and Bullwinkle Show, The* (1959-1964)
Dumbo (1941) - 17, 49
SEE ALSO Babbitt, Art; Disney (studio); Dumbo (character); Feature films; Kimball, Ward

Dumbo (character) - 17, 49, 53
SEE ALSO Disney (studio); *Dumbo* (1941)
Dune (1984) - 253, 302-303
SEE ALSO Rotoscoping
Dunning, George - 136, 138, 194, 303, 359
Works
Flying Man, The (1962) - 136, 359; *Yellow Submarine* (1968) - 128, 138, 194, 303
SEE ALSO Animation, experimental

Eames, Charles - 207
Eames, Rae SEE Eames, Ray
Eames, Ray – 288
Easter Island SEE *Mystery of Easter Island*
Easy walk cycle SEE Exercises, walks and other forms of locomotion
Editing - 11, 25, 35, 37-38, 58, 68, 76, 80, 85, 86-88, 93, 97, 100-106, 120-121, 132, 141, 142, 143, 144, 164, 203, 209, 210-212, 213, 238, 265, 274, 280-281, 282, 297, 314, 328, 342, 353
Terms - 38
Time - 38
SEE ALSO Reshooting; Sound, editing
Edwards, Richard - ii
SEE ALSO UCLA Animation Workshop
Effects, Special SEE Visual Effects
Effects, Visual SEE Visual Effects
Eggeling, Viking - 58, 357
Works
Symphonie Diagonale (1924) - 58, 357
Einstein, Albert - 77
Eliot, T.S. - 13
Electric Company, The (1971-1977) - 285
SEE ALSO Hubley, Faith; Hubley, John
Elements of Color, The SEE Itten, Johannes
Elmer Fudd (character) - 49, 55
SEE ALSO Shorts (theatrical); Warner Brothers (studio)
Emotion SEE Exercises, facial expressions
SEE ALSO Character, design
Emshwiller, Ed - 361
Works
Sunstone (1979) - 361
SEE ALSO Animation, computer; Animation, experimental
Engles, Steve - ii, 1
SEE ALSO UCLA Animation Workshop

Epiphanies (1968) – 136; **Fig. 6-2**
  SEE ALSO Animation, experimental; McLaughlin, Dan F., Jr.; UCLA Animation Workshop
Esquire (Periodical) - **Fig. 9-7**
Exaggeration - 162, 178-179, 235; **Fig. 7-85**
Exercises - 153-184, 312-314, 318, 333-353
  Acting - 167-169; **Fig. 7-10**
  Anticipation - 166, 312-313, 344-345, 351; **Fig. 7-63; Fig. 14-4; Fig. extra-1**
  Asterisk - 158-162, 312, 338-341, 351
  Bouncing ball - 153-158, 312, 334-338, 351; **Fig. 7-5, Fig. 7-6; Fig. 14-1**
  Exposure sheet - 183-184, 350
    SEE ALSO Exposure sheets
  Facial expressions - 313, 346-347, 351-352; *Fig. 7-13*
    SEE ALSO Character, design
  Punch - **Fig. extra-2**
  Storyboard for final project - 162-165, 341-342
    SEE ALSO Storyboards
  Walks and other forms of locomotion - 169-183, 313, 347-350, 351
    Basic walk cycle - 170-173, 347-348
    Birds - 182-183; **Fig. 7-27; Fig. 7-28; Fig. 7-30**
    Butterfly cycle – 182; **Fig. 7-29**
    Cartoon adult character of the author walking with a beer and a slight up-and-down motion – 173; **Fig. 7-16**
  Cartoon character run cycle – 177; **Fig. 7-22**
  Cartoon character walk forward in perspective in place cycle – 176; **Fig. 7-21**
  Cartoon dog walk cycle – 182; **Fig. 7-24**
  Cartoon female walk in place – 175; **Fig. 7-18**
  Cartoon male walk in place – 175; **Fig. 7-17**
  Cartoon with springs for legs walk cycle – 175; **Fig. 7-20**
  Easy walk cycle – 175; **Fig. 7-19**
  Inchworm in space – 183; **Fig. 7-31**
  Female adult walk cycle – 173; **Fig. 7-14**
  Horse walk cycle – 182; **Fig. 7-26**
  Human character run cycle – 177; **Fig. 7-23**
  Male adult walk cycle – 173; **Fig. 7-15**
  Naturalistic dog walk cycle – 182; **Fig. 7-25**
  Other animals - 183
  Paddle wheel with up-and-down-head walk cycle – 175; **Fig. 14-5**
  Walk in place - 173-175, 348-349
    SEE ALSO Walk cycles
  SEE ALSO Animators, educational aspects
  SEE ALSO Animation, basic principles of

Existentialism - 305
  SEE ALSO Kierkegaard, Søren
Experimental films SEE Animation, Experimental
Experimentations (1970s) - 137
  SEE ALSO Animation, experimental; Oren, Tsvika
Explosion animation SEE Animation, effects
Exposure sheet exercise SEE Exercises, exposure sheet
Exposure sheets - 11, 39, 80, 87, 92, 120, 121-122, 126, 127, 128, 131-132, 141, 142, 143, 151, 159, 162, 164, 165, 166, 167, 169, 182, 183-184, 200, 202, 236-237, 258, 265, 277, 310, 314-315, 317, 324, 338-341, 342, 343, 345, 346, 350; **Fig.5-52, passim**
  SEE ALSO Exercises, exposure sheet
Eye blinks SEE Eyes
Eyeballs SEE Eyes
Eyes - 35, 93, 97, 102, 113, 114, 160, 165, 167-169, 188, 193, 234, 236, 346; **Fig. 7-11; Fig. 7-13; Fig. 6-61; Fig. 7-63**
  SEE ALSO Character, design; *Dune* (1984); Exercises, acting

Falling Lizard Weekend - i, 7, 138, 232: **Fig. intro-1**
  SEE ALSO *Mystery Box, A* (2001); *Pirates vs. Ninjas* (circa 2011); UCLA Animation Workshop
Fang the Wonderdog (n.d.) - 370
  SEE ALSO Television series; Ward, Jay
Fantasia (1940) - 58, 73, 79, 135, 186
  SEE ALSO Babbitt, Art; Blair, Preston; Disney (studio); Disney, Walt; Feature films; Johnston, Ollie; Kimball, Ward
  SEE ALSO *Night on Bald Mountain* (1940)
Fantasmagorie (1908) - 51, 58, 136, 321, 357
SEE ALSO Animation, experimental; Cohl, Emile
Faroudja, Phil – 3; Fig. 7-1
  SEE ALSO UCLA Animation Workshop; *Katzenjammer Kids: Still Stranded* (1995); Animation, experimental
Feature films
  101 Dalmatians (1961) – 54; *9* (film) (2009) – 45; *Adventures of Prince Achmed, The* (1926) - 137, 357; *Anchors Aweigh* (1945) - 137, 250, 252, 358; *Atlantis: The Lost Empire* (2001) – 140; *Bambi* (1942) - 17, 23; *Cinderella* (1950) – 17; *Dumbo* (1941) - 17, 49; *Fantasia* (1940) - 58, 73, 79, 135, 186; *Incredibles, The* (2004) – 132; *Jungle Book, The* (1967) – 82; *King Kong* (1933) - 139, 232, 233, 234, 250, 357; *Lion King, The* (1994) - 51, 140, 257; *Little Nemo: Adventures in Slumberland* (1989) – 75; *Mary Poppins* (1964) - 139; *Nightmare before Christmas, The*

(1993) – 232; *Peter Pan* (1953) - 33, 114, 275; *Pinocchio* (1940) - 17, 33-34, 44, 94, 137, 179, 180; *Point, The* (1971) - 136, 360; *Robin Hood* (1973) - 85, 306; *Shrek 2* (2004) – 257; *Sleeping Beauty* (1959) - 17; *Snow White and the Seven Dwarfs* (1937) - 16, 17, 44, 49, 50, 57, 65, 101, 118, 128,145, 193, 197, 268; *Toy Story* (1995) - 25, 140; *WALL-E* (2008) – 16; *When the Wind Blows* (1986) – 139; *Who Framed Roger Rabbit* (1988) - 26, 139, 250, 306; *Yellow Submarine* (1968) - 128, 138, 194, 303

Feedback SEE Criticism

Felix in Hollywood (1923) SEE *Felix the Cat* (1919-1930)

Felix the Cat (1919-1930) - 262, 357

    SEE ALSO Messmer, Otto; Shorts (theatrical); Sullivan, Pat

Female adult walk cycle SEE Exercises, walks and other forms of locomotion

Field charts - 92, 120-121, 77, 334; **Fig. 5-36; Fig. 5-37**

    SEE ALSO Layout

Flash (animation software) - 272, 273-274

    SEE ALSO Animation, computer

Film festivals SEE Animation, festivals

Film, Film, Film (1968) - 360

    SEE ALSO Animation, experimental; Khitruk, Fyodor

Film News (Periodical) – **Fig 9-1**

Film preservation SEE Post-production, storage

Film-Makers' Cooperative – 225; **Fig. 8-2**

    SEE ALSO Distribution

Filming SEE Animation, filming

Final check SEE Animation, final check

Final Cut Pro (animation software) - 76, 266

Fire animation SEE Animation, effects

Fire Safety Spot (1960) – **Fig. 2-68; Fig. 5-5**

    SEE ALSO McLaughlin, Dan F., Jr.; Animation, Experimental

Fischinger, Oskar - 17, 26, 50, 55, 57, 58, 89, 137, 146, 152, 194, 358

    Works

        Allegretto (1936) - 17, 50, 58, 101, 358; *Muratti cigarettes* (commercial) - 146; *Optical Poem* (1938) – 58; *Study series* (1929-1934) - 55

    SEE ALSO Animation, absolute; Animation, experimental

Flags SEE Sine curve

Flames SEE Animation, effects

Fleischer, Dave SEE Fleischer (studio)

Fleischer, Max SEE Fleischer (studio)

Fleischer (studio) - 41, 128, 136, 201, 306, 357-358, 358

    Works

        Popeye the Sailor Meets Ali Baba's Forty Thieves (1937) - 136, 358; *Snow-White* (1933) - 201, 357-358

    SEE ALSO Koko (character); Natwick, Grim; Sears, Ted

Flight cycles SEE Exercises, walk cycles and other forms of locomotion

Flintstones, The (1960-1966) - 21, 125, 362

    SEE ALSO Blair, Preston; Hanna-Barbera (studio); Television series

Flowers and Trees (1932) - 357

    SEE ALSO Academy Awards; Disney, Walt; *Silly Symphonies* (1929-1939); Shorts (theatrical)

Flying Man, The (1962) - 136, 359

    SEE ALSO Animation, experimental; Dunning, George

Foghorn Leghorn (character) - 49

    SEE ALSO Mel Blanc; Shorts (theatrical); Warner Brothers (studio)

Folders SEE Animation, materials

Foley stage SEE Sound, recording

Foray, June - **Fig. 15-1**

Ford, John - 93

Forrest Gump (1994) - 250, 254

Fossils (1999) - 58, 59: **Fig. 2-56**

    SEE ALSO Animation, experimental; Mercer, Celia; UCLA Animation Workshop

Frank Film (1973) - 50, 137, 360

    SEE ALSO Academy Awards; Animation, experimental; Mouris, Frank

Frog He Would A-wooing Go, A (1990) – 136; **Fig. 6-1**

    SEE ALSO Animation, experimental; Tsark, Tami; UCLA Animation Workshop

Fruit Peddler (Sesame Street spot) (circa 1974) - **Fig 2-51**

Fugitive Sensations (1987) - **Fig. 15-1**

    SEE ALSO McLaughlin, Dan F., Jr.

Furies (1975) - 59, 79, 136

    SEE ALSO Animation, experimental; Petty, Sara

Further Adventures of Uncle Sam, The (1970) - 360

    SEE ALSO Animation, experimental; Case, Dale; Haboush Company (studio); Mitchell, Bob

Furniss, Maureen - 3

GameCube SEE Animation, interactive, delivery systems for

Game of the Angels, The SEE *Les Jeux des Anges* (1964)

Gardiner, Bob - 238, 360

Works

    Closed Mondays (1974) - 237, 238, 360

SEE ALSO Academy Awards; Animation, 3D; Vinton, Will

Geisel, Theodor - 47, 358

    Works

        Gerald McBoing Boing (1950) - 36, 47, 358; *How the Grinch Stole Christmas!* (1966) - 294

SEE ALSO Animation, experimental

Gerald McBoing Boing (1950) - 36, 47, 358

SEE ALSO Academy Awards; Animation, experimental; Cannon, Robert; Geisel, Theodor; UPA (studio)

Gertie the Dinosaur (1914) - 51, 101, 136, 161, 197, 340, 357

SEE ALSO Animation, experimental; McCay, Winsor

George of the Jungle (1967) - 44, 370

SEE ALSO Television series; Ward, Jay

Getting Started (1979) - 361

SEE ALSO Animation, experimental; Condie, Richard; National Film Board of Canada

Gianini, Giulio - 137, 359

    Works

        Paladins of France, The (1960) - 137, 359

SEE ALSO Animation, experimental; Luzzati, Emanuele

Gillett, Burt - 358

    Works

        Flowers and Trees (1932) - 357

        Three Little Pigs, The (1933) - 45, 358

SEE ALSO Disney (studio)

Gilligan, Carol - 305

Glen Campbell Summer Show, The - 21

SEE ALSO Crime and criminals; *God is Dog Spelled Backwards* (1967); McLaughlin, Dan F., Jr.

Gloves SEE Animation, materials

Golden Age of Animation SEE Animation, history

God is Dog Spelled Backwards (1967) - 17, 21, 42, 58, 101, 137, 301, 303, 311, 359: **Fig. 1-3; Fig 2-32; Fig 2-54; Fig 6-7; Fig. 8-2; Fig. 9-8**

SEE ALSO Animation, experimental; Chicago International Film Festival; Glen Campbell Summer Show, The; Kinestasis; McLaughlin, Dan F., Jr.

SEE ALSO UCLA Animation Workshop

Godfrey, Bob - 359, 360

    Works

Do-It-Yourself Cartoon Kit (1961) - 137, 359; *Kama Sutra Rides Again* (1972) - 360

SEE ALSO Animation, experimental; Biographic

(studio); Hanna, Nancy; Learner, Keith; Linnecar, Vera

Gone with the Wind (1939) - 61

Grantz, Joan - 137, 248, 362

    Works

        Mona Lisa Descending a Staircase (1992) - 137, 248, 362

SEE ALSO Animation, experimental

Graves, Robert - 70

Greek Tragedy (1985) - 361

SEE ALSO Academy Awards; Animation, experimental; Van Goethem, Nicole

Grey Wolf and Little Red Riding Hood (1990) - 362

SEE ALSO Animation, experimental; Bardin, Garri

Gymnastics SEE *Shapes of Movement* (1996)

Haboush Company (studio) - 360

    Works

        Further Adventures of Uncle Sam, The (1970) - 360

SEE ALSO Case, Dale; Mitchell, Bob

Hamm, Jack - 355

Hands - 150, 179, 187, 188, 189-190, 236, 260

Hanna, Nancy - 359

    Works

Do-It-Yourself Cartoon Kit (1961) - 137, 359

SEE ALSO Animation, experimental; Biographic (studio); Godfrey, Bob; Learner, Keith; Linnecar, Vera

Hanna, William - 358

    Works

        Two Mouseketeers, The (1952) - 359

SEE ALSO Barbera, Joseph; Hanna-Barbera (studio)

Hanna-Barbera (studio) - 34, 153, 279, 286, 370; **Fig. 11-3**

    Works

        Flintstones, The (1960-1966) - 21, 125, 362

        Johnny Bravo (1997-2001) - 226

SEE ALSO Blair, Preston; Shorts (theatrical); Television series

Harman, Hugh - 358

    Works

        Peace on Earth (1939) - 358

SEE ALSO Metro-Goldwyn-Mayer (studio); Shorts (theatrical)

Harper's Magazine (Periodical) - Fig. 9-7

Harris, Phil - 82-83

SEE ALSO *Disney Animation: The Illusion of Life; Jungle Book, The* (1967); Baloo (character)

Harry (n.d.) - 3-4, 24: **Fig. 1-6; Fig. 2-1; Fig 2-6; Fig 2-7;**

Fig. 2-13; Fig. 2-41; 2-43; Fig. 2-44; Fig 2-45; Fig. 2-46; Fig.2-49; Fig.2-50; Fig. 5-3; Fig. 5-13; Fig. 5-39; Fig. 5-50; Fig. 7-35; Fig. 7-36; Fig. 7-37; Fig. 7-38; Fig. 7-39; Fig. 7-40; Fig. 7-41; Fig. 7-42; Fig. 7-43; Fig. 7-44; Fig. 7-45; Fig. 7-46; Fig. 7-47; Fig. 7-48; Fig. 7-49; Fig. 7-50; Fig. 7-51; Fig. 7-52; Fig. 7-55; Fig. 7-56; Fig. 7-60

    SEE ALSO Animation, experimental; McLaughlin, Dan F., Jr.

Hayward, Stan - 355, 359, 360
    Works
        Kama Sutra Rides Again (1972) - 360
        Love Me, Love Me, Love Me (1962) – 359
    SEE ALSO Shorts (theatrical); Animation, experimental

Hedonism - 305

Hellbent for Election (1944) - 358
    SEE ALSO Hubley, John; Jones, Chuck; Shorts (theatrical); UPA (studio)

Help (Sesame Street spot) (circa 1974) – Fig. 6-15
    SEE ALSO Shorts (threatical), McLaughlin, Dan F. Jr., *Sesame Street* (1969-present)

Hello (1984) - 136
    SEE ALSO Animation, experimental; Hubley, Faith

Hen Hop (1942) - 138, 358
    SEE ALSO Animation, experimental; McLaren, Norman; National Film Board of Canada

Hercules SEE *Mighty Hercules, The* (1963-1966)

Hero With A Thousand Faces, The SEE Campbell, Joseph

High Fidelity (1985) - 361
    SEE ALSO Abel, Robert; Animation, computer; Animation, experimental; Commercials; Roberts, Randy

Hill Farm, The (1988) - 321, 362
    SEE ALSO Animation, experimental; Baker, Mark

Hippocrates - 77

Hitchcock, Alfred - 93

Hitler, Adolph - 27, 49

Hollywood
    Economic aspects - 24, 130
    Ethical aspects - 27, 222, 226-227, 298-301
    Stories of - 17, 18, 21, 27, 67, 76, 85, 130, 146, 161, 220, 222, 226-227, 249, 263, 268, 288, 289, 299, 300, 301, 302
    Techniques for dealing with - 68, 218-220, 222, 370, 226-227, 298-303

Holmes, Adam - 3

Fig, 2-43; Fig. 2-44;Fig. 2-45; Fig. 2-46; Fig. 2-49; Fig. 2-50; Fig. 5-3; Fig. 5-16; Fig. 5-19; Fig. 5-20; Fig. 5-21;

Fig. 5-22; Fig. 7-35; Fig. 7-36; Fig. 7-37; Fig. 7-38; Fig. 7-39; Fig. 7-40; Fig. 7-41; Fig. 7-42; Fig. 7-43; Fig. 7-44; Fig. 7-45; Fig. 7-46; Fig. 7-47; Fig. 7-48; Fig. 7-49; Fig. 7-50; Fig. 7-51; Fig. 7-52; Fig. 7-53; Fig. 7-54: Fig. 7-55; Fig. 7-56; Fig. 7-58; Fig. 7-59; Fig. 7-60; Fig. 7-61

    SEE ALSO UCLA Animation Workshop

Homer - 43

Honest John (character) - 33-34, 180
    SEE ALSO Disney (studio); *Pinocchio* (1940)

Honeymooners, The (1955-1956) - 21

Hopkins, Willie - 233
    Works
        Swat the Fly (1916) - 233

Horse walk cycle SEE Exercises, walks and other forms of locomotion

Horse's Mouth, The SEE Cary, Joyce

Holy Family, The (c. 1504) – 109; Fig. 5-22

How the Grinch Stole Christmas! (1966) - 294
    SEE ALSO Geisel, Theodor; Jones, Chuck; Metro-Goldwyn-Mayer (studio); Shorts (theatrical)

Hubley, Emily - 3, 285, 358, 360

Hubley, Faith - 3, 47, 58, 136, 285, 286, 359, 360; **Fig. 2-34; Fig. 2-36**
    Works
        Adventures of an * (1957) - 3, 50, 359; *Electric Company, The* (1971-1977) – 285; *Hello* (1984) – 136; *Starlore* (1983) – 136; *Windy Day* (1967) - 360
    SEE ALSO Animation, experimental

Hubley, Georgia - 360

Hubley, John - 47, 285, 358, 359, 360; **Fig. 2-36**
    Works
        Adventures of an * (1957) - 3, 50, 359; *Electric Company, The* (1971-1977) – 285; *Hellbent for Election* (1944) – 358; *Windy Day* (1967) - 360

SEE ALSO Animation, experimental

Human character run cycle SEE Exercises, walks and other forms of locomotion

Human Figure in Motion, The SEE Muybridge, Eadweard

Humor - 23, 28, 42, 43, 46, 48, 49, 51, 52, 53, 55, 60-61, 65, 67, 68, 72, 76, 83, 84, 89, 145-146, 163, 166, 168, 177, 179, 186, 189, 218, 220, 222, 248, 285, 342, 349, 369, 371: **Fig. 2-61**
    SEE ALSO Puns

Hungarofilms (studio) - 360
    Works
        Sisyphus (1985) - 45-46, 360
    SEE ALSO Jankovics, Marcell

Hurtz, Bill - 75

Works
   Little Nemo: Adventures in Slumberland (1989) - 75
   SEE ALSO Feature films
Huston, John - 18
Huxley, Aldous - 262

Ideas - 15-30, 141, 142, 143, 144, 145, 260
   Creativity and - 18-19, 26
   Definition of - 15-16
   Generating - 21, 64
   Intuition and - 18-19
   Limits of - 27
   Problem-solving - 22-24
   Provides themes for film - 42
   Quality of - 24
   Sound, and - 81
if my wings had dreams (2002) – 50; **Fig. 2-37**
   SEE ALSO Animation, experimental; Mercer, Celia
Iliad SEE Homer
Incredibles, The (2004) - 132
   SEE ALSO Feature films; Pixar (studio)
Ink and paint - 51, 75, 116, 129, 131, 136, 140, 141, 142, 143, 165, 201, 257, 259, 265, 277, 295, 325, 343; **Fig. 6-3**
   SEE ALSO Animation, computer
Interactive animation SEE Animation, interactive
International Animated Film Association SEE ASIFA-Hollywood
Invisible Moving Company, The SEE *Automatic Moving Company, The* (1912)
Internet – 222, 224; **Fig. 9-5**
Iota - 356
Iris wipe - 38, 105; **Fig. 2-27**
Itten, Johannes - 114
Iwerks, Ub - 99, 357
   Works
      Plane Crazy (1928) – 99; *Skeleton Dance* (1929) - 61, 357; *Steamboat Willie* (1928) - 90, 357
   SEE ALSO Disney (studio); Shorts, theatrical

James Bond (film franchise) - 294
Jankovics, Marcell - 45-46, 360
   Works
      Sisyphus (1985) - 45-46, 360
   SEE ALSO Hungarofilms (studio)
Jason and the Argonauts (1963) - 45
Jay Ward Productions (studio) - 286, 370

Works
   George of the Jungle (1967) - 44, 370; *Rocky and Bullwinkle Show, The* (1959-1964) - 44, 153, 362, 370
SEE ALSO Ward, Jay
Jerry Beck's Cartoon Research - 356
   SEE ALSO Beck, Jerry
Jim Keeshen Productions (studio) - 285
Jittlov, Mike - 138-139, 147, 248, 299-300, 361; **Fig. 6-16**
   Works
      Animato (1977) – 361; *Wizard of Speed and Time, The* (1979) - 138-139, 248, 361
John, Elton - 2, 364-365
Johnny Bravo (1997-2001) - 226
   SEE ALSO Hanna-Barbera (studio); Television series
Johnston, Ollie - 17, 57, 82-83, 183, 185, 355: Fig. 2-53
   Works
      Bambi (1942) - 17, 23; *Cinderella* (1950) – 17; *Fantasia* (1940) - 58, 73, 79, 135, 186; *Peter Pan* (1953) - 33, 114, 275; *Pinocchio* (1940) - 17, 33-34, 44, 94, 137, 179, 180 *Snow White and the Seven Dwarfs* (1937) - 16, 17, 44, 49, 50, 57, 65, 101, 118, 128, 145, 193, 197, 268
   SEE ALSO *Disney Animation: The Illusion of Life*: Disney (studio)
Jones, Chuck - 16, 45, 46, 48, 52, 55, 56, 71, 98, 101, 355, 358, 359: **Fig. 1-1; Fig 2-40**
   Works
Daffy's Southern Exposure (1942) – 16; *Dot and the Line, The* (1965) - 50, 55; *Dover Boys, The* (1942) - 101, 358; *Duck Amuck* (1953) - 101, 359; *Hellbent for Election* (1944) – 358; *How the Grinch Stole Christmas!* (1966) – 294; *Rabbit Fire* (1951) - 55, 61, 358; *One Froggy Evening* (1955) - 45, 46, 61, 359; *What's Opera, Doc?* (1957) - 359
   SEE ALSO Animation (experimental); Warner Brothers (studio); Bugs Bunny (character); Daffy Duck (character); Porky Pig (character); Pepé le Pew (character); Road Runner and Wile E. Coyote; Road Runner (character) Shorts (theatrical); Wile E. Coyote (character)
Joyce, James - 26
Jumping (1984) - 157-158, 337, 361
   SEE ALSO Animation, experimental; Tezuka, Osamu
Jungle Book, The (1967) - 82
   SEE ALSO Baloo (character); *Disney Animation: The Illusion of Life*; Disney (studio); Feature film; Harris, Phil

Kama Sutra Rides Again (1972) - 360
    SEE ALSO Academy Awards; Animation, experimental; Godfrey, Bob; Hayward, Stan
Kane, Helen - 357-358; **Fig. 15-1**
    SEE ALSO *Snow-White* (1933)
Kant, Immanuel - 305, 331
    SEE ALSO Categorical imperative
Katzenjammer Kids: Still Stranded, The (1995) - 152; **Fig. 7-1**
    SEE ALSO Animation, experimental; UCLA Animation Workshop
Kawamoto, Kihachiro - 15, 138, 232, 360
    Works
        Oni (1972) - 138, 232, 360
    SEE ALSO Animation, experimental
Kazakov, Velislav - 74, 94, 361
    Works
        Cuckoo (1984) - 74, 94, 361
    SEE ALSO Animation, experimental
Keaton, Buster SEE Keaton, Joseph Frank "Buster"
Keaton, Joseph Frank "Buster" - 147
Kelly, Gene - 138, 250, 252, 358
    SEE ALSO *Anchors Aweigh* (1945)
Khitruk, Fyodor - 360
    Works
        Film, Film, Film (1968) - 360
    SEE ALSO Animation, experimental
Kick Me (1973) - 138, 360
    SEE ALSO Academy Awards; Animation, experimental; Swarthe, Robert
Kierkegaard, Søren - 305
    SEE ALSO Existentialism
Kimball, Ward - 37, 104; **Fig. 5-17**
    Works
Cinderella (1950) – 17; *Dumbo* (1941) - 17, 49; *Fantasia* (1940) - 58, 73, 79, 135, 186; *Peter Pan* (1953) - 33, 114, 275; *Pinocchio* (1940) - 17, 33-34, 44, 94, 137, 179, 180; *Snow White and the Seven Dwarfs* (1937) - 16, 17, 44, 49, 50, 57, 65, 101, 118, 128, 145, 193, 197, 268
SEE ALSO Disney (studio); Feature Films
Kinestasis - 21, 137, 226, 301, 359
    SEE ALSO *God is Dog Spelled Backwards* (1967); McLaughlin, Dan F., Jr.
King Kong (1933) - 139, 232, 233, 234, 250, 357
    SEE ALSO Wray, Fay; Feature films; King Kong (character); O'Brien, Willis; Visual effects
King Kong (character) - 234
    SEE ALSO *King Kong* (1933)

King of the Hill (1997- 2010) - **Fig. 5-47**
Klasky Csupo (studio) - 286
Klee, Paul - 15, 109, 159, 339, 355
Knock, Knock (1940) - 358
    SEE ALSO *Andy Panda* (1939-1949); Blanc, Mel; Lantz, Walter; Shorts (theatrical); Universal (studio); Woody Woodpecker (character)
Koko (character) - 62, 128
    SEE ALSO Fleischer (studio); Rotoscoping
Koenig, Wolf - 137, 359
    Works
        City of Gold (1957) - 137, 146, 153, 359
    SEE ALSO National Film Board of Canada
Kohlberg, Larry - 305
Kroyer, Bill and Sue - 74, 94, 361
    Works
        Technological Threat (1988) - 74, 94, 361
    SEE ALSO Animation, experimental
Kuri, Yoji - 359
    Works
        Love (1963) - 359
    SEE ALSO Animation, experimental
Kurtz, Bob - 27

L.A. Animation Celebration - 138, 294
    SEE ALSO Animation, festivals; Denslow, Phil; *Madcap* (1991)
L'Idee (1932) - 135, 136
    SEE ALSO Animation, experimental; Bartosch, Berthold
La Poulette Grise (1947) - 136
    SEE ALSO Animation, experimental; McLaren, Norman
La Jetée (1962) - 152, 359
    SEE ALSO Animation, experimental, Marker, Chris
Landscape Painter, The (1976) SEE *Mindscape/Le paysagiste* (1976)
Lantz, Walter - 40, 358
    Works
        Knock, Knock (1940) - 358
    SEE ALSO UCLA Animation Workshop; Universal (studio); Walter Lantz Productions; Woody Woodpecker (character)
Lao-tzu - 13
Larkin, Ryan - 138, 349, 360
    Works

Walking (1968) - 61, 138, 349, 360
    SEE ALSO Animation, experimental; Rotoscoping
Lapis (1966) - 20, 42, 57, 58, 211, 360
SEE ALSO Animation, experimental, Whitney, James
Lam, David - **Fig. 13-4**
    SEE ALSO UCLA Animation Workshop
Lasseter, John - 361
    Works
        Luxo Jr. (1986) - 361
    SEE ALSO Pixar (studio)
Lauenstein, Christoff and Wolfgang - 74, 94, 362
    Works
        Balance (1989) - 47, 61, 74, 94, 362
    SEE ALSO Animation, experimental
Layout - 91-133, 141, 142, 143, 253, 328, 342-343: **Fig. 5-1; Fig. 5-2; Fig. 5-10; Fig. 5-13; Fig. 5-16; Fig. 14-3**
    Bookkeeping SEE Animation, administrative elements
    Background SEE Backgrounds
    Camera - 93-98; **Fig 5-7; Fig. 5-8**
    Color SEE Color
    Composition - 106-111; Fig. 5-15
    Computers and - 132
        SEE ALSO Animation, computer
    Continuity - 101-103
    Design - 92-93
    Editing SEE Editing
    Exposure sheets SEE Exposure sheets
    Fades - 125-127
    Film vs. video - 116-117
    Lighting - 118
    Line - 108-109: **Fig. 5-19; Fig. 5-20; Fig. 5-21; Fig. 5-22**
    Multipass - 128
    Movement - 98-100
    Pans SEE Pans
    Pantographic movement - 127-128; **Fig. 2-64; Fig 5-43; Fig. 5-44**
    Perspective - 117-118; **Fig. 5-6; Fig. 5-33; Fig. 5-34; Fig. 5-35; Fig 5-41**
    Production planning - 130-131
    Props – 115; **Fig. 5-28**
    Rotations - 127
    Rotoscoping SEE Rotoscoping
    Size - 109
    Space - 109-110
    Special effects SEE Visual effects
    Spins – 127; **Fig. 5-40**
    Style - 115-116

    Technical aspects of - 119-122
    Time - 115
    Titles - 129-130
    Transitions - 105-106
    Value - 110
    Wipe-offs - 127
Le Garde-meuble automatique SEE *Automatic Moving Company, The* (1912)
Leaf, Caroline - 25-26, 47, 50, 98, 137, 204, 360
    Works
        Street, The (1976) - 25-26, 47, 50, 98, 137, 360
    SEE ALSO Animation, experimental
Learner, Keith - 359
    Works
Do-It-Yourself Cartoon Kit (1961) - 137, 359
    SEE ALSO Animation, experimental; Biographic (studio); Godfrey, Bob; Hanna, Nancy; Linnecar, Vera
Leica reel SEE Animatics
Les Jeux des Anges (1964) - 47, 119, 136, 153, 359-360
    SEE ALSO Animation, experimental; Borowczyk, Walerian
Lettera, Valerie - ii, 3
    SEE ALSO UCLA Animation Workshop
Levant, Oscar - 220, 300
Lightning animation SEE Animation, effects
Line quality - 198
Lines: Vertical (1960) - 58
SEE ALSO Animation, experimental; McLaren, Norman
Linnecar, Vera - 359
    Works
Do-It-Yourself Cartoon Kit (1961) - 137, 359
    SEE ALSO Animation, experimental; Biographic (studio); Godfrey, Bob; Hanna, Nancy; Learner, Keith
Libeled Lady (1936) - Fig. 5-4
Lion King, The (1994) - 50, 140, 257
    SEE ALSO Disney (studio); Feature films
Lippi, Fra. Filippo - 107
Lip sync SEE Sound, dialogue
Littlejohn, Bill - 99-100, 136; **Fig. 5-14; Fig. 6-6**
    Works
        Tiger Paws (n.d.) - 99, 136
    SEE ALSO Commercials
Little Alice (1924) - 26, 250
    SEE ALSO Disney (studio); Disney, Walt; Shorts (theatrical); Visual effects
Little Nemo (1911) - 321
    SEE ALSO Animation, experimental; McCay, Winsor
Little Nemo: Adventures in Slumberland (1989) - 75

SEE ALSO Feature films; Hurtz, Bill
Live-action SEE Animation vs. live-action
SEE ALSO Visual effects
Local 839 SEE Unions and guilds
Lord of the Rings, The (2001-2003) - 253
Lord, Peter – 355
Los Angeles Free Press (Periodical) – **Fig. 2-39**
SEE ALSO Sibley, Brian
Lost World, The (1925) - 26, 357
SEE ALSO Animation, experimental; O'Brien, Willis;
Visual effects
Love (1963) - 359
SEE ALSO Animation, experimental; Kuri, Yoji
Love Me, Love Me, Love Me (1962) - 359
SEE ALSO Hayward, Stan; Shorts (theatrical);
Williams, Richard
Low, Colin - 137
Works
City of Gold (1957) - 137, 146, 153, 359
SEE ALSO National Film Board of Canada
Lucht, Bernie - 70
Lucy in the Sky with Diamonds SEE *Yellow Submarine*
(1968)
Lutz, Edwin George - 207, 355
Luxo Jr. (1986) - 361
SEE ALSO Academy Awards; Animation, computer;
Animation, experimental; Lasseter, John; Pixar (studio)
Luzzati, Emanuele - 137, 359
Works
Paladins of France, The (1960) - 137, 359
SEE ALSO Animation, experimental; Gianini, Giulio
Lye, Len - 59, 204, 311, 358
Works
Rainbow Dance (1936) - 59, 358
SEE ALSO Visual effects

Madame Tutli-Putli (2007) - 45
SEE ALSO Animation, experimental; National Film
Board of Canada
Mad Comics SEE *Mad Magazine*
Mad Magazine (Periodical) - 366
Madcap (1991) – 138; Fig. 6-9
SEE ALSO Animation, experimental; Ann Arbor Film
Festival; Denslow, Phil; L.A. Animation Celebration;
UCLA Animation Workshop
Madonna with Child and Two Angels (c. 1465) – 107; **Fig. 5-19**
Male adult walk cycle SEE Exercises, walks and other
forms of locomotion
Maltese Falcon, The (1941) - 18-19
Man Ray - 138
Man Who Planted Trees, The (1987) - 50, 136, 361
SEE ALSO Academy Awards; Animation,
experimental; Back, Frédéric
Marker, Chris - 359
Works
La Jetée (1962) - 152, 359
SEE ALSO Animation, experimental
Marketing SEE Character, marketing; Distribution;
Animators, economic aspects
Marx Brothers - 89, 179, 350
Marx, Groucho SEE Marx Brothers
Mary Poppins (1964) - 139
SEE ALSO Disney (studio); Feature films; Visual
effects
Massachusetts Institute of Technology - 158, 262, 337
SEE ALSO Animation, computer; Saxenian
Master shot - 36, 94, 95-96, 97-98, 314, 353: **Fig. 2-16**
Matte shot - 125, 196-197, 251-252, 255; **Fig. 10-2**
Mattel Inc. - 366
Maura (character) - 2, 61, 128, 201 SEE A
SEE ALSO Weber, Maura
May, Rollo - 64, 355
Maya (animation software) - 259, 263, 265, 266, 271, 272
SEE ALSO Animation, computer
Maya Embedded Language SEE Maya (animation
software)
McCabe, Norm - 16
Works
Daffy's Southern Exposure (1942) - 16
SEE ALSO Warner Brothers (studio)
McCay Split System SEE McCay, Winsor
McCay, Winsor - 51, 136, 149, 161, 194, 197, 340, 357
Works
Gertie the Dinosaur (1914) - 51, 101, 136, 161, 197,
340, 357; *Little Nemo* (1911) - 321
SEE ALSO Animation, experimental
McLaren, Norman - 11-12, 17, 26, 50, 58, 59, 89, 101, 136,
137, 138, 149, 194, 204, 248, 256, 358, 359, 360
Works
Begone Dull Care (1949) - 17, 50, 58, 88, 101, 138, 204,
358; *Canon* (1964) - 137, 256, 360; *Chairy Tale, A* (1957)
- 138, 248, 359; *Hen Hop* (1942) - 138, 358; *La Poulette
Grise* (1947) – 136; *Lines: Vertical* (1960) - 58; *Neighbors*
(1952) - 138, 248, 359; *Pas de deux* (1968) - 139, 256, 360
SEE ALSO National Film Board of Canada; Animation,

experimental
McLaughlin, Dan - 1-4, 251
*McLaughlin, Dan F., Jr. - i-ii, 1-4, 25, 93, 120, 136, 137, 173, 186, 197, 214, 215, 219; **Fig. rt-1; Fig. intro-2; Fig. 1-2; Fig. 1-3; Fig1-4; Fig 1-5; Fig. 1-6; Fig. 1-7; Fig. 1-8; Fig. 2-1; Fig 2-2; Fig 2-5; Fig 2-6; Fig 2-7; Fig 2-8; Fig 2-9; Fig 2-10; Fig. 2-13; Fig. 2-12; Fig. 2-14 Fig. 2-16; Fig. 2-17; Fig. 2-18, Fig. 2-19, Fig. 2-20, Fig. 2-21, Fig. 2-24, Fig. 2-25; Fig. 2-26; fig. 2-28; fig. 2-29; Fig. 2-32; Fig. 2-33; 2-35: Fig. 2-39; Fig. 2-41; Fig, 2-42; Fig. 2-43; Fig. 2-44; Fig. 2-45; Fig. 2-46; Fig. 2-47; Fig. 2-48; Fig. 2-49; Fig. 2-50; Fig. 2-51; Fig 2-52; Fig 2-54; Fig. 2-55; Fig. 2-58: Fig. 2-62; Fig. 2-63; Fig. 2-64; ; Fig. 2-66; Fig. 2-68; Fig. 2-69; Fig. 3-1: Fig. 4-1; Fig. 5-1; Fig. 5-2; Fig. 5-3; Fig. 5-4; Fig. 5-5; Fig. 5-6; Fig. 5-7; Fig. 5-8; Fig. 5-9; Fig. 5-13; Fig. 5-16; Fig. 5-19; Fig. 5-20; Fig. 5-21; Fig. 5-22; Fig. 5-23; Fig. 5-24; Fig. 5-25; Fig. 5-26; Fig. 5-27; Fig. 5-28; Fig. 5-30; Fig. 5-31; Fig. 5-32; Fig. 5-30; Fig. 5-31; Fig. 5-32; Fig. 5-33; Fig. 5-34; Fig. 5-35; Fig. 5-39; Fig. 5-40; Fig. 5-41; Fig. 5-45; Fig. 5-50; Fig. 6-2; Fig 6-7; Fig. 7-3; Fig. 7-5; Fig. 7-6; Fig/ 7-7; Fig 7-8; Fig. 7-10; Fig. 7-11; Fig. 7-12; Fig. 7-13; Fig. 7-13; Fig. 7-15; Fig 7-16; Fig. 7-17; Fig. 7-18; Fig. 7-19; Fig. 7-20; Fig. 7-21; 7-22; Fig. 7-23; Fig. 7-24; Fig. 7-25; Fig. 7-26; Fig. 7-27 Fig. 7-28; Fig. 7-29; Fig. 7-30; Fig. 7-35; Fig. 7-36; Fig. 7-37; Fig. 7-38; Fig. 7-39; Fig. 7-40; Fig. 7-41; Fig. 7-42; Fig. 7-43; Fig. 7-44; Fig. 7-45; Fig. 7-46; Fig. 7-47; Fig. 7-48; Fig. 7-49; Fig. 7-50; Fig. 7-51; Fig. 7-52; Fig. 7-55; Fig. 7-56; Fig. 7-60; Fig. 7-62; Fig. 7-63; Fig. 7-64; Fig. 7-65; Fig. 7-66; Fig. 7-67; Fig. 7-68; Fig. 7-69; Fig. 7-70; Fig. 7-71; Fig. 7-72; Fig. 7-73; Fig. 7-74; Fig. 7-75; Fig. 7-77; Fig. 7-78; Fig. 7-79; Fig. 7-80; Fig. 7-81; Fig. 7-82; Fig. 7-83; Fig. 7-85; Fig. 8-1; Fig. 8-2; Fig. 9-1; Fig. 9-2; Fig. 9-3; Fig. 9-4; Fig. 9-5; Fig. 9-6; Fig. 9-7; Fig. 9-8; Fig. 9-9; Fig. 9-10; Fig. 12-1; Fig. 14-1; Fig. 14-2; Fig. 14-4; Fig. 14-5; Fig. 15-1; Fig. add-1; Fig. extra-1**

Works - 17, 38, 42, 45, 58, 63, 66, 136;
Bus (Sesame Street spot) (circa 1974) – 317; *Claude* (1963) - i, 3, 4, 17, 38, 45, 63, 359; *Epiphanies* (1968) – 136; *Fire Safety Spot* (1960) - **Fig. 2-68, Fig 5-5**; *Fugitive Sensations* (1987) **Fig. add-1;** *God is Dog Spelled Backwards* (1967) - 17, 21, 42, 58, 101, 137, 301, 303, 311, 359; *Harry* (n.d.) - 3-4, 24; *Microsecond* (1970) – **Fig. 9-1**; *Mystery of Easter Island* (n.d.) - 3, 168; *Nine O'Clock News* (1968) – **Fig. 7-9**; *No Idea* (2000) – 17; *Peace* (1970) – 3; *Red/Green* (1985) - 58, 105; *Russia, March to November, 1917* (1959) - **Fig. 2-12;** ; *Shapes of Movement* (1996) – 251; *Second Will and Testament* (n.d.) – **Fig. 5-24**; *Star Spangled Banner* (1968) – **Fig. 2-64;** *Where's Poppa?* (titles) (1970) - 66, 256; **Fig. 10-3**
   Crimes against - 21, 300, 301
   Ethical concerns - i-ii, 62-63, 219-220, 222, 298-305
Hollywood and - 65, 93, 249, 288, 301, 303, 305-306
   Nigeria - 7
   Quotes - 6, 13, 29, 207, 215, 332
   Stories - 25, 28, 37, 47, 54, 63-64, 65, 66, 67, 75, 89, 110-111, 120, 159, 185, 186, 197, 214, 220, 222, 223, 226, 240, 247, 249, 257, 268, 285, 286, 287, 288, 296, 297, 300, 301, 304, 305-306, 310, 320, 339, 364-365, 365, 373
   Teaching philosophy/techniques - 3, 7, 104, 119, 153-184, 259, 267-268, 270, 282, 298, 309-332
   Thoughts on tool maker and tool user - 269
   UCLA Animation Workshop - 7
   SEE ALSO Animation, experimental; Chicago International Film Festival; Dick Clark Show, The; Glen Campbell Summer Show, The; Kinestasis; Smothers *Brothers Summer Show, The*; UCLA Animation Workshop
Meet Me in St. Louis (1944) - 294
MEL SEE Maya Embedded Language
Melendez, Bill - 360
   Works
      Rainbow Bear (1970) - 360
   SEE ALSO Bill Melendez Productions (studio)
Melodrama - 23, 37; **Fig. 1-5**
Memoirs of Josephine Mutzenbacher SEE Salten, Felix
Mercer, Celia - ii, 1, 3, 50-51, 58, 59, 136, 137, 311, 321; **Fig. 2-37; Fig. 2-38; Fig. 2-56; Fig. 2-59; Fig. 2-60; Fig. 6-4; Fig 6-7**
   Works
      Bad Dream Girl (2009) - 137; *Fossils* (1999) - 58, 59; *if my wings had dreams* (2002) – 50; *Mystery Box* (2001) – 59; *Scratch Film #1* (1989) - 59; *Street Works* (1988) - 58, 59; *Swimming* (1986) - 136
   SEE ALSO Animation, experimental; UCLA Animation Workshop
Messmer, Otto - 357
   Works
      Felix the Cat (1919-1930) - 262, 357
   SEE ALSO Sullivan, Pat
Menger, Bill - 48
Mental Block (1985) - 236
   SEE ALSO Animation, 3D; Animation, experimental; Chiang, Doug

Metro-Goldwyn-Mayer (studio) - 136, 138, 288, 358, 359
  Works
        Anchors Aweigh (1945) - 137, 250, 252, 358; *Bad
Luck Blackie* (1949) - 186, 358; *Dot and the Line, The*
(1965) - 50, 55; *How the Grinch Stole Christmas!* (1966)
– 294; *Peace on Earth* (1939) – 358; *Red Hot Riding Hood*
(1941) – 94; *Tom and Jerry* (1940-1958) - 17, 138, 252, 358,
359; *Two Mouseketeers, The* (1952) - 359
  SEE ALSO Blair, Preston; Harman, Hugh
MGM (studio) SEE Metro-Goldwyn-Mayer (studio)
Michelangelo SEE Buonarroti, Michelangelo
Mickey Mouse (character) - 25, 54, 55, 61-62, 168, 178,
189, 364
  SEE ALSO Disney (studio); Shorts (theatrical);
Steamboat Willie (1928)
Mickey Mouse Sound - 90
  SEE ALSO Sound
Microsecond (1970) - **Fig. 9-1**
  SEE ALSO McLaughlin, Dan F., Jr.; Animation,
experimental; UCLA Animation Workshop
Mighty Hercules, The (1963-1966) - 180, 317, 359
  SEE ALSO Television series
Mill, John Stuart - 305
  SEE ALSO Utilitarianism
Milton, John - 320
Mindscape/Le paysagiste (1976) - 137, 361
  SEE ALSO Animation, experimental; Drouin,
Jacques; National Film Board of Canada
MIT SEE Massachusetts Institute of Technology
Mitchell, Bob - ii, 146, 300-301, 360: **Fig. 2-48; Fig.
5-46; Fig. 6-14; Fig. 12-1; Fig. 12-2; Fig. 14-5**
  Works
        CALM anti-perspirant (commercial) (1971) – 146;
Further Adventures of Uncle Sam, The (1970) – 360;
Yellow Submarine (1968) - 128, 138, 194, 303; *Pittsburgh
Paint* (commercial) (n.d.) – Fig. 2-48; *7-Up* (commer-
cial) - Fig. 12-2
SEE ALSO Case, Dale; Haboush Company (studio)
Mitchell, Thomas - 25, 220
Mitchell, William - 139, 256
  Works
        Zebu (1987) - 256
  SEE ALSO UCLA Animation Workshop
Model sheets - 32, 50, 51, 52, 53, 54, 65, 82, 92, 97, 115,
116, 141, 142, 143, 163, 165, 167, 181, 184, 186, 189, 192, 341,
343, 346: **Fig, 2-42; Fig, 2-43; Fig. 5-17: Fig. 7-60**
  SEE ALSO Character, design; Color, Use in Model
sheets

Model animation SEE Animation, 3D
Models SEE Animation, 3D
Mokhberi, Emund - 261
  SEE ALSO UCLA Animation Workshop
Mona Lisa Descending a Staircase (1992) - 137, 248, 362
  SEE ALSO Academy Awards; Animation, experi-
mental; Grantz, Joan
Monty Python's Flying Circus (1969-1974) - 179, 350
Moore, Gordon - 266
Moore's Law SEE Moore, Gordon
Morrison, Jim - 263
Mostel, Zero - 285
Motion capture SEE Rotoscoping
  SEE ALSO Animation, computer
Mother and Child (1926) – 108; **Fig. 5-21**
Mothlight (1963) - 136
  SEE ALSO Animation, experimental; Brakhage, Stan
Motion capture SEE Rotoscoping
Mouris, Frank - 50, 137, 360
  Works
        Frank Film (1973) - 50, 137, 360
  SEE ALSO Animation, experimental
Movement - 194
Character - 190-192
        SEE ALSO Character, design
  Speed - 99-100, 150-151, 154, 155-156, 157, 160, 161, 171,
336, 337-338, 339, 348; **Fig. 7-6**
Mr. Magoo (character) - 49
  SEE ALSO Shorts (theatrical); UPA (studio)
MTV - 284
Murakami, Jimmy - 139, 360
  Works
        Breathe (1967) – 360; *When the Wind Blows* (1986)
- 139
  SEE ALSO Feature films
Murakami-Wolf Productions - 136, 360
Works
  Point, The (1971) - 136, 360
SEE ALSO Wolf, Fred
Muratti cigarettes (commercial) - 146
  SEE ALSO Animation, experimental; Commercials;
Fischinger, Oskar
 Music SEE Sound, music
Muybridge, Eadweard - 177, 180, 182, 183, 313, 351
Mystery Box, A (2001) - 59: Fig. 2-60
  SEE ALSO Animation, experimental; Falling Lizard
Weekend; Mercer, Celia; UCLA Animation Workshop
Mystery of Easter Island (n.d.) - 3, 168: **Fig 2-5; Fig. 2-35;**

Fig. 2-47; Fig. 3-1; Fig 5-40; Fig. 7-10; Fig. 7-12
SEE ALSO Animation, experimental; McLaughlin, Dan F., Jr.

Narration SEE Sound, narration
Narrative - 43-48
    Animation - 46-48
    Cultural elements - 48
History of - 43
Music and - 83
Structural elements of - 43-46
National Center for Film and Video Preservation – Fig. 8-2
National Film Board of Canada - 26, 45, 47, 137, 285, 358, 359, 360, 361
    Works
        Big Snit, The (1985) - 101, 361; *Canon* (1964) - 137, 256, 360; *Chairy Tale, A* (1957) - 138, 248, 359; *City of Gold* (1957) - 137, 146, 153, 359; *Getting Started* (1979) – 361; *Hen Hop* (1942) - 138, 358; *Madame Tutli-Putli* (2007) – 45; *Mindscape/Le paysagiste* (1976) - 137, 361; *Neighbors* (1952) - 138, 248, 359; *Pas de deux* (1968) - 139, 256, 360; *Street, The* (1976) - 25-26, 47, 50, 98, 137, 360; *Walking* (1968) - 61, 138, 349, 360
    SEE ALSO Condie, Richard; Drouin, Jacques, Koenig, Wolf, Larkin, Ryan, Leaf, Caroline; Low, Colin; McLaren, Norman, Animation, experimental
National Lumber (Commercial) (Circa 1985) – **Fig. 7-2**
Naturalistic dog walk cycle SEE Exercises, walks and other forms of locomotion
Natwick, Grim - 193, 357; **Fig. 15-1**
    Works
        Snow-White (1933) - 201, 357-358
    SEE ALSO Fleischer (studio)
Neighbors (1952) - 138, 248, 359
    SEE ALSO Academy Awards; Animation, experimental; McLaren, Norman; National Film Board of Canada
Nelson, Barrie - 285, 361
    Works
        Open Wednesday (1980) - 361
    SEE ALSO Animation, experimental
Neutral shot - 38, 97, 102; **Fig. 5-9**
Newland, Marv - 360
    Works
        Bambi Meets Godzilla (1969) - 360
    SEE ALSO Animation, experimental

Newport Beach Film Festival – **Fig. 9-6**
Newsweek (Periodical) – **Fig. 9-7**
Next Stop Judgement Day (2016?) – 10; **Fig. intro-4**
    SEE ALSO Shipman, Jay
Nietzsche, Friedrich - 332
Nigeria – 7; **Fig. intro-1**
Night on Bald Mountain (1933) - 73, 94, 137, 358
    SEE ALSO Animation, experimental; Alexeieff, Alexander; Parker, Claire
Night on Bald Mountain (1940) - 73, 94
    SEE ALSO Disney (studio); Fantasia (1940); Shorts (theatrical)
Nightmare before Christmas, The (1993) - 232
    SEE ALSO Animation, 3D; Feature films
Nine O'Clock News (1968) – **Fig. 7-9; Fig. 8-2**
    SEE ALSO McLaughlin, Dan J,; Animation, experimental; UCLA Animation Workshop
Nixon, Richard – 3; **Fig. 1-8**
NFB, Canada SEE National Film Board of Canada
No Idea (2000) – 17: **Fig. 1-4; Fig. 8-1**
    SEE ALSO Animation, experimental; McLaughlin, Dan F., Jr.; UCLA Animation Workshop
Norstein, Yuri - 361
    Works
        Tale of Tales (1979) - 361
    SEE ALSO Animation, experimental
NY Film-Makers' Coop SEE Film-Makers' Coop

O'Brien, Willis - 139, 233, 357
    Works
        King Kong (1933) - 139, 232, 233, 234, 250, 357; *Lost World, The* (1925) - 26, 357
    SEE ALSO Feature films
O'Neill, Pat - 59, 138, 139, 256
    Works
        Screen (1969) - 138
    SEE ALSO Animation, experimental; Visual effects
Object animation SEE Animation, 3D
Odyssey SEE Homer
Okeya, Peggy SEE Yamamoto, Peggy
Old Man and the Sea, The (1999) - 136, 362
    SEE ALSO Academy Awards; Animation, experimental; Petrov, Alexander
One Froggy Evening (1955) - 45, 46, 61, 359
    SEE ALSO Jones, Chuck; Shorts (theatrical); Warner Brothers (studio)
One Final Encore (2016) – 140; **Fig. 6-12**

SEE ALSO Animation, experimental; Shipman, Jay
"One person, one film" - 7, 147
    SEE ALSO UCLA Animation Workshop
Oni (1972) - 138, 232, 360
    SEE ALSO Animation, 3D; Animation, experimental;
Kawamoto, Kihachiro
Open Wednesday (1980) - 361
    SEE ALSO Animation, experimental; Nelson, Barrie
Optical Poem (1938) - 58
    SEE ALSO Animation, experimental; Fischinger,
Oskar
Oren, Tsvika - 137
    Works
        Experimentations (1970s)
    SEE ALSO Animation, experimental
Oriolo, Joseph - 359
    Works
        Mighty Hercules, The (1963-1966) - 180, 317, 359
    SEE ALSO Television series
Overlapping action SEE Exercises, anticipation

Pacing SEE Timing
Paddle wheel with up-and-down-head walk cycle SEE
Exercises, walks and other forms of locomotion
Paint on film SEE Animation, 2D
Pal, George - 138, 232, 233, 236
    Works
        Puppetoons (1932-1971) – 233; *Tubby the Tuba*
(1947) - 138, 232
    SEE ALSO Animation, 3D; Shorts (theatrical)
Paladins of France, The (1960) - 137, 359
    SEE ALSO Animation, experimental; Gianini,
Giulio; Luzzati, Emanuele
Pans - 38-39, 94, 97, 98, 105, 117, 118, 119, 120, 122, 123-125,
127, 129, 132, 152, 155, 165, 174, 196, 198, 200, 201, 236,
239, 240, 278, 313, 337, 342, 343, 348-349, 350, 352; **Fig.
5-39; 5-40**
Pappa Oh Mama (1974) - 248
    SEE ALSO Animation, 3D; Animation, experimental;
Woluluk, Jon
Paradise Lost SEE Milton, John
Park, Nick - 138, 232, 362
    Works
        Wallace and Gromit (1989-2005) - 19, 138, 232, 362
    SEE ALSO Animation, 3D
Parker, Claire - 73, 94, 137, 358
    Works

Night on Bald Mountain (1933) - 73, 94, 137, 358
    SEE ALSO Animation, experimental; Alexeieff,
Alexander
Parker, Dorothy - 21
Parn, Priit - 361
    Works
        Breakfast on the Grass (1987) - 361
    SEE ALSO Animation, experimental
Pas de deux (1968) - 139, 256, 360
    SEE ALSO Animation, experimental; McLaren, Nor-
man; National Film Board of Canada; Visual effects
Peace (1970) – 3; **Fig. 1-8**
    SEE ALSO McLaughlin, Dan F., Jr.
Peace on Earth (1939) - 358
    SEE ALSO Academy Awards; Harman, Hugh; Met-
ro-Goldwyn-Mayer (studio); Shorts (theatrical)
Pedagogical Sketchbook SEE Klee, Paul
Pederson, Con - 254, 312, 351
    SEE ALSO Disney (studio)
Pencil tests – 198; **Fig. 7-79**
Pencils SEE Animation, materials
Perry Como Show, The - 303
Perspective - 97, 99, 110, 117-118, 157, 161-162, 176, 187, 236,
296, 312, 314, 328, 340, 350, 351, 353; **Fig. 7-21; Fig. 7-79**
    SEE ALSO Layout, perspective in
Peter Pan (1953) - 33, 114, 275
    SEE ALSO Davis, Marc; Disney (studio); Feature
films; Johnston, Ollie; Kimball, Ward; Peter Pan
(character)
Peter Pan (character) - 33, 65
    SEE ALSO *Peter Pan* (1953); Disney (studio)
Pepé le Pew (character) - 49
    SEE ALSO Jones, Chuck; Shorts (theatrical); Warner
Brothers (studio)
Petrov, Alexander - 136, 362
    Works
        Old Man and the Sea, The (1999) - 136, 362
    SEE ALSO Animation, experimental
Petty, Sara - 59, 79, 136
    Works
        Preludes in Magical Time (1988) – 59; *Furies* (1975)
- 79, 136
    SEE ALSO Animation, experimental; UCLA Anima-
tion Workshop
Phil Roman (studio) – 286
PhotoKem - **Fig. 8-1**
Photoshop (animation software) - 116, 255, 265
Picasso, Pablo - 20, 29, 178

Picnic on the Grass SEE *Breakfast on the Grass* (1987)
Pink Panther Show, The (1969-1980) - 56, 89, 294
    SEE ALSO Shorts (theatrical)
Pinocchio (1940) - 17, 33-34, 44, 94, 137, 179, 180
    SEE ALSO Babbitt, Art; Blair, Preston; Disney (studio);
Feature films; Honest John (character); Johnston,
Ollie; Kimball, Ward; Stromboli (character)
Pintoff, Ernest - 55, 137, 359
    Works
        Critic, The (1963) - 55, 137, 359
    SEE ALSO Animation, experimental
Pirates vs. Ninjas (circa 2011) - 138, 232; Fig. 6-10
    SEE ALSO Falling Lizard Weekend; UCLA Anima-
tion Workshop
Pittsburgh Paint (commercial) (n.d.) – **Fig. 2-48**
Pixar (studio) - 16, 361
    Works
        Incredibles, The (2004) – 132; *Luxo Jr.* (1986) – 361;
Toy Story (1995) - 25, 14; *WALL-E* (2008) - 16
    SEE ALSO Lasseter, John; Stanton, Andrew
Plagiarism SEE Animators, ethical aspects
Plane Crazy (1928) - 99
    SEE ALSO Disney (studio); Disney, Walt; Iwerks,
Ub; Shorts, theatrical
Playful Pluto (1934) - 186, 193, 313, 352
    SEE ALSO Babbitt, Art; Disney (studio); Pluto
(character); Shorts (theatrical)
PlayStation 3 SEE Animation, interactive, delivery
systems for
Pluto (character) - 186, 193, 313, 352
    SEE ALSO Disney (studio); *Playful Pluto* (1934)
Plympton, Bill - 285
Poetics SEE Aristotle
Poetry – **Fig. 2-69**
    SEE ALSO McLaughlin, Dan F., Jr.
Point, The (1971) - 136, 360
    SEE ALSO Feature films; Murakami-Wolf Productions
(studio); Wolf, Fred
Pointing – 190; **Fig. 7-65; Fig. 7-66**
Popeye the Sailor Meets Ali Baba's Forty Thieves (1937)
- 136, 358
    SEE ALSO Fleischer (studio); Shorts (theatrical)
Porky Pig (character) - 62, 358
    SEE ALSO Avery, Tex; Jones, Chuck; *Porky's Duck
Hunt* (1937); Shorts (theatrical); Warner Brothers
(studio)
Porky's Duck Hunt (1937) - 358
    SEE ALSO Avery, Tex; Blanc, Mel; Daffy Duck (char-
acter); Porky Pig (character); Shorts (theatrical);
Warner Brothers (studio)
Portfolios SEE Animators, vocational aspects
Portrait of Jason (1967) - 27
    SEE ALSO Animation, experimental; Clarke, Shirley
Post-production - 11, 209-215
    Answer print - 210, 214
    Distribution - 210, 215
        SEE ALSO Distribution
        SEE ALSO Animation, festivals
    Duplication - 210, 214-215
    Editing SEE Editing
    Final sound mix - 209, 211
    Interlock - 209, 212-213
    Locking - 209, 213
    Negative cut - 209, 213
    Optical track - 210, 213
    Reshoots - 209, 210, 211
    Screening - 210, 214
    Storage - 210, 215
    Viewing - 209, 210
    SEE ALSO Production
Powell, Marilynn - ii, 2
Preludes in Magical Time (1988) - 59
    SEE ALSO Animation, experimental; Petty, Sara;
UCLA Animation Workshop
Premiere (animation software) - 76, 116, 265
    SEE ALSO Animation, computer
Prince Achmed (1926) SEE *Adventures of Prince Achmed,
The* (1926)
Principles of animation SEE Animation, basic prin-
ciples of
    SEE ALSO Exercises
Prisoner, The (1973) – 197; **Fig. 7-76**
    SEE ALSO Animation, experimental; Denslow,
Phil; UCLA Animation Workshop
Production - 10-11, 140-145
    Distribution SEE Distribution
Post-production - 11
        SEE ALSO Post-production
    Pre-production - 11, 130-131
    Schedule - 131, 141, 142, 143, 144, 324-325; *Fig. 5-51*
Stages of - 11
    Visual effects and - 254-255
Propaganda Dance (1987) - 361
    SEE ALSO Animation, experimental; Sito, Tom
Proportions SEE Character, design
ProMAX (animation software) - 266

SEE ALSO Animation, computer
Ptolemy - 204-205, 280-281
Punch SEE Exercises, Punch
Puns - 61
SEE ALSO Humor
Puppet animation SEE Animation, 3D

Quade, Richard - 74, 94, 137, 311, 361
    Works
        Sand Dance (1988) - 74, 94, 101, 311, 137, 361
    SEE ALSO Animation, experimental; UCLA Animation
Workshop
Quay, Stephen SEE Quay, Brothers
Quay, Timothy SEE Quay, Brothers
Quay, Brothers - 235
    SEE ALSO Animation, 3D; Animation, experimental
Quick Sketches – 185; **Fig. 7-33; Fig. 7-62**

Rabbit Fire (1951) - 55, 61, 358
    SEE ALSO Blanc, Mel; Bugs Bunny (character); Daffy
Duck (character); Jones, Chuck; Shorts (theatrical)
    SEE ALSO Warner Brothers (studio)
Rain animation SEE Animation, effects
Rainbow Bear (1970) - 360
    SEE ALSO Animation, experimental; Melendez,
Bill; Bill Melendez Productions (studio)
Rainbow Dance (1936) - 59, 358
SEE ALSO Animation, experimental; Commercials;
Lye, Len
Red/Green (1985) - 58, 105: **Fig. 2-55; Fig. 9-3; Fig. 9-10**
    SEE ALSO Animation, experimental; McLaughlin,
Dan F., Jr.; UCLA Animation Workshop
Red Hot Riding Hood (1941) - 94
    SEE ALSO Avery, Tex; Blair, Preston; Metro-Gold-
wyn-Mayer (studio); Shorts (theatrical)
Reel SEE Portfolio
Reiniger, Lotte - 137, 357, 358
    Works
        Adventures of Prince Achmed, The (1926) - 137, 357;
Carmen (1933) - 358
    SEE ALSO Animation, experimental; Feature films;
Silhouettes
Rembrandt SEE Van Rijn, Rembrandt
Reshooting - 106, 202, 203, 209, 210, 212, 236, 237, 238,
252
    SEE ALSO Post-production, reshoots

Rhythm & Hues (studio) - 286
Richler, Mordecai - 25, 47, 360
    SEE ALSO *Street, The* (1976)
Rivera, Diego - 108
Road Runner and Wile E. Coyote - 16, 18, 44, 50, 51, 56,
61, 71, 72, 89, 118, 128, 138, 150, 166
    SEE ALSO Jones, Chuck; Road Runner (character);
Shorts (theatrical); Warner Brothers (studio); Wile E.
Coyote (character)
Road Runner (character) - 19, 44
    SEE ALSO Jones, Chuck; Road Runner and Wile E.
Coyote; Shorts (theatrical); Warner Brothers (studio)
Roadkill Redemption (2013) - 139
    SEE ALSO Animation, experimental; Hadrika, Karl
Roberts, Randy - 361
    Works
        High Fidelity (1985) - 361
    SEE ALSO Abel, Robert
Robin Hood (1973) - 85, 306
    SEE ALSO Disney (studio); Feature films; Thomas,
Frank
Rocky and Bullwinkle Show, The (1959-1964) - 44, 153,
362, 370
SEE ALSO Scott, Bill; Television series; Ward, Jay
Roget, Peter Mark - 205, 281
Rotoscoping - 128, 138, 150, 180, 183, 186, 192-193, 194,
195, 238, 253, 262-263, 302-303: **Fig. 5-45**
    SEE ALSO Animation, computer, animation vs.
rotoscoping; *Closed Mondays* (1974); *Dune* (1984)
Royal College of Art - 361
    Works
        Carnival (1985) - 361
    SEE ALSO Young, Susan
Rubber hose animation SEE Animation, rubber hose
Run cycle SEE Walk cycles
    SEE ALSO Exercises, walks and other forms of
locomotion
Russia, March to November, 1917 (1959) - **Fig. 2-12**
    SEE ALSO McLaughlin, Dan F., Jr.; UCLA Animation
Workshop; Animation, experimental

Sacramento Film Festival – **Fig. 9-3**
Saks, Ron - 3
    SEE ALSO UCLA Animation Workshop
Salkin, Leo - 288
Salten, Felix - 23
    Works

Bambi (1942) - 17, 23

San Francisco Art Institute Film Festival – **Fig. 9-10**
SEE ALSO Animation, festivals

San Francisco State University - 284
SEE ALSO Cohen, Karl

Sand Dance (1988) - 74, 94, 101, 137, 311, 361
SEE ALSO Animation, experimental; Quade, Richard; UCLA Animation Workshop

Santa Fe Film Festival Web Cast – **Fig. 9-5**

Santayana, George - 16, 59-60

SAS - 331, 356

Savenick, Phil - 81
SEE ALSO UCLA Animation Workshop

Saxenian - 158, 337
SEE ALSO Animation, computer; Massachusetts Institute of Technology

Schmitt, Michael - 3-4: **Fig. 2-16; Fig. 2-17; Fig. 2-18, Fig. 2-19, Fig. 2-20, Fig. 2-21, Fig. 2-24; Fig. 2-30; Fig. 2-31; Fig. 2-48; Fig. 5-6; Fig. 5-7; Fig. 5-8; Fig. 5-10; Fig. 5-12; 5-13; Fig. 5-16Fig. 5-19; Fig. 5-20; Fig. 5-21; Fig. 5-22; Fig 5-23; Fig. 5-27; Fig. 5-30; Fig. 5-31; Fig. 5-32; Fig. 5-33; Fig. 5-33; Fig. 5-34; Fig. 5-35**

Scott, Bill - 44, 46, 48, 308: **Fig. 2-61**
SEE ALSO *Rocky and Bullwinkle Show, The* (1959-1964); Ward, Jay

Scratch Film #1 (1989) – 59: **Fig. 2-59**

SEE ALSO Animation, experimental; Mercer, Celia; UCLA Animation Workshop

Screen (1969) - 138
SEE ALSO Animation, experimental; O'Neill, Pat

Scriptwriting for Animation SEE Hayward, Stan

Scriptwriting for television - 369-375 **Fig. 2-51**
Format - 370
Getting started - 373-374
Steps - 370-372
SEE ALSO Sound, dialogue

Sears, Ted - 41
SEE ALSO Fleischer (studio) – 41

Second Will and Testament (n.d.) – **Fig. 5-24**
SEE ALSO McLaughlin, Dan F., J.

Self Portrait as a Young Man (1634) – 107; **Fig. 5-20**

Servais, Raoul - 360
Works
Chromophobia (1966) - 360
SEE ALSO Animation, experimental

SEPARATE - 49

Sesame Street (1969-present) - 113, 120, 146, 285, 287, 317: *Fig. 2-51; Fig. 6-15*

SEE ALSO *Bus* (Sesame Street spot) (circa 1974); McLaughlin, Dan. F., Jr.; Television series; *Help* (Sesame Street spot) (circa 1974) – (Fig. 6-15); *Fruit Peddler* (Sesame Street spot) (circa 1974) - **Fig 2-51**

Shadow animation SEE Animation, effects

Shakespeare, William - 26, 43

Shapes of Movement (1996) – 251; **Fig. 4-1; Fig. 7-78; Fig. 9-5**
SEE ALSO Animation, experimental; McLaughlin, Dan; UCLA Animation Workshop

Shipman, Jay - 3, 9, 10, 116, 139: **Fig. intro-3; Fig. intro-4; Fig. 5-29; Fig. 6-12**
Works
Chasing the Light (2014) - 116; *Next Stop Judgement Day* (2016?) - 10; *One Final Encore* (2016) - 140; *Ta-Daa* (2015) - 9

SEE ALSO UCLA Animation Workshop

Shorts (experimental) SEE Animation, experimental

Shorts (theatrical)
Andy Panda (1939-1949) – 358; *Bad Luck Blackie* (1949) - 186, 358; *Bus* (Sesame Street spot) (circa 1974) – 317; *City of Gold* (1957) - 137, 146, 153, 359; *Daffy's Southern Exposure* (1942) – 16; *Der Fuehrer's Face* (1943) – 49; *Dover Boys, The* (1942) - 101, 358; *Duck Amuck* (1953) - 101, 359; *Felix the Cat* (1919-1930) - 262, 357; *Flowers and Trees* (1932) – 357; *Hellbent for Election* (1944) – 358; *Help* (Sesame Street spot) (circa 1974) – **Fig. 6-15;** *How the Grinch Stole Christmas!* (1966) – 294; *Knock, Knock* (1940) – 358; *Little Alice* (1924) - 26, 250 *Love Me, Love Me, Love Me* (1962) – 359; *Night on Bald Mountain (1940)* - 73, 94; *One Froggy Evening* (1955) - 45, 46, 61, 359; *Peace on Earth* (1939) – 358; *Pink Panther Show* (1969-1980) - 56, 89, 294; *Plane Crazy* (1928) – 99; *Playful Pluto* (1943) - 186, 193, 313, 352; *Popeye the Sailor Meets Ali Baba's Forty Thieves* (1937) - 136, 358; *Porky's Duck Hunt* (1937) – 358; *Rabbit Fire* (1951) - 55, 61, 358; *Red Hot Riding Hood* (1941) – 94; *Road Runner and Wile E. Coyote* - 16, 18, 44, 50, 51, 56, 61, 71, 72, 89, 118, 128, 138,150, 166; *Silly Symphonies* (1929-1939) – 79; *Skeleton Dance* (1929) - 61, 357; *Snow-White* (1933) - 201, 357-358; *Steamboat Willie* (1928) - 90, 357; *Swat the Fly* (1916) – 233; *Three Little Pigs, The* (1933) - 45, 358; *Tom and Jerry* (1940-1958) - 17, 138, 252, 358, 359; *True Story of the Civil War, The* (1957) – 146; *Tubby the Tuba* (1947) - 138, 232; *Tweety and Sylvester* - 17; *Two Mouseketeers,* The (1952) – 359; *Wallace and Gromit* (1989-2005) - 19, 138, 232, 362; *What's Opera, Doc?* (1957) – 359; *Wild Hare* (1940) - 358

SEE ALSO Bugs Bunny (character); Daffy Duck (character); Donald Duck (character); Elmer Fudd (character); Foghorn Leghorn (character); Hanna-Barbera (studio); Mickey Mouse (character); Mr. Magoo (character); Pepé le Pew (character); Porky Pig (character); Road Runner (character); Wile E. Coyote (character)

Shrek 2 (2004) - 257
    SEE ALSO Animation, computer; Dreamworks (studio); Feature films

Shull, Bill SEE Shull, William

Shull, William - ii, 25, 207; **Fig. 13-4**
    SEE ALSO UCLA Animation Workshop

Sibley, Brian - 355
    SEE ALSO Lord, Peter

SIGGRAPH - 293, 356

Silhouettes - 137, 175, 177, 189, 191; **Fig. 7-67**

SEE ALSO Reiniger, Lotte

Silly Symphonies (1929-1939) - 79
    SEE ALSO Disney (studio); *Flowers and Trees* (1932); Shorts (theatrical); *Skeleton Dance* (1929); *Three Little Pigs, The* (1933)

Silverman, David - 2, 73, 94, 311, 334, 361: **Fig. 2-67; Fig. 13-1; Fig. 15-1**
    Works
        Simpsons, The (1989-present) - 2, 25, 46, 50, 187, 295, 306, 311, 334, 362, 372; *Strange Case of Mr. and Mrs. Donnybrook's Boredom, The* (1981) - 73, 94, 361
    SEE ALSO Animation, experimental; *Tracey Ullman Show, The;* UCLA Animation Workshop

Simonides of Ceos - 70

Simpsons, The (1989-present) - 2, 25, 46, 50, 187, 295, 306, 311, 334, 362, 372
    SEE ALSO Bart Simpson (character); Silverman, David; Television series

Sine curve - 192, 313, 352; **Fig. 7-68; Fig. 7-69**

Sine wave SEE Sine curve

Siodmak, Curt - 21

Sisyphus (1985) - 45-46, 360
    SEE ALSO Academy Awards; Animation, experimental; Hungarofilms; Jankovics, Marcell

Siti, Tom - ii
    SEE ALSO UCLA Animation Workshop

Sito, Tom - 292, 292-293, 361
    Works
        Propaganda Dance (1987) - 361
    SEE ALSO Unions and guilds

Situational ethics - 305

Skeleton Dance (1929) - 61, 357
    SEE ALSO Disney (studio); Disney, Walt; Iwerks,

Ub; *Silly Symphonies* (1929-1939); Shorts (theatrical)

Sky Captain and the World of Tomorrow (2004) - 254

Sleeping Beauty (1959) - 17
    SEE ALSO Davis, Marc; Disney (studio); Feature films

Slugging SEE Storyboards, slugging

Smith, Webb - 41
    SEE ALSO Disney (studio)

Smoke animation SEE Animation, effects

Smothers Brothers Summer Show, The - 301, 303
    SEE ALSO McLaughlin, Dan F., Jr., crimes against

Snow animation SEE Animation, effects

Snow White (character) - 44-45, 49, 50, 128, 193, 197
    SEE ALSO Champion, Marge; Disney (studio); *Snow White and the Seven Dwarfs* (1937)

Snow White and the Seven Dwarfs (1937) - 16, 17, 44, 49, 50, 57, 65, 101, 118, 128, 145, 193, 197, 269
    SEE ALSO Babbitt, Art; Davis, Marc; Disney (studio); Dopey (character); Feature films; Johnston, Ollie; Kimball, Ward; Snow White (character); Stepmother (character)

Snow-White (1933) - 201, 357-358; Fleischer (studio); Kane, Helen; Natwick, Grim; Shorts (theatrical)

Society for Animation Studies SEE SAS

Softimage (animation software) - 265, 271
    SEE ALSO Animation, computer

Song of the Prairie (1949) - 73, 94, 358
    SEE ALSO Animation, experimental; Trnka, Jirí

Sophocles - 43

Sound - 39-40, 79-90, 141, 142, 143, 144
    Dialogue - 55-56, 79, 193-194; **Fig. 4-1; Fig. 7-70**
    Drawing on film - 88
    Editing - 80, 86-88, 89
        SEE ALSO Post-production
    Effects - 40, 80
    Mixing SEE Sound, editing
    Music - 39-40, 79, 81, 83, 84
    Narration - 79
    Negative cut and - 87-88
    Production stages of - 80
    Reading - 80, 87
    Recording - 80-85
    Tempo - 88
    Timing SEE Timing, sound and
    Transfer - 86
    Voice - 39-40, 79, 81, 82-83, 84, 85
    SEE ALSO Mickey Mouse Sound

South Park (1997-present) - 25, 140, 265, 362
    SEE ALSO Television series

Special effects SEE Visual effects
Spielberg, Steven - 275
Spike and Mike's Sick and Twisted Festival of
Animation - 225, 294
    SEE ALSO Animation, festivals
Spin - 127-128; **Fig, 5-41; Fig 5-52**
Springs - 175, 350
    SEE ALSO Cartoon with springs for legs walk cycle
Stanford, Leland - 182
Stanton, Andrew - 16
    Works
    Toy Story (1995) - 25, 140; WALL-E (2008) - 16
    SEE ALSO Pixar (studio)
Star Spangled Banner (1968) – **Fig. 2-64 Fig. 8-2;**
    SEE ALSO McLaughlin, Dan F., Jr.; Animation,
experimental: UCLA Animation Workshop
Star Wars (1977) - 45, 100, 254
Starewicz, Ladislaw - 138, 235, 357
    Works
      Cameraman's Revenge, The (1912) - 138, 235, 357
    SEE ALSO Animation, 3D; Animation, experimental
Starlore (1983) - 136
    SEE ALSO Animation, experimental; Hubley, Faith
Stars animation SEE Animation, effects
Steamboat Willie (1928) - 90, 357
    SEE ALSO Disney (studio); Disney, Walt; Iwerks,
Ub; Mickey Mouse (character); Shorts (theatrical)
Stepmother (character) - 16, 44, 45
    SEE ALSO Disney (studio); *Snow White and the
Seven Dwarfs* (1937)
Stitchman (character) - 56-57
    SEE ALSO UCLA Animation Workshop
Stoicism - 305
    SEE ALSO Zeno
Stop-motion animation SEE Animation, 3D
Story SEE Narrative
Storyboards - 20, 31-41, 64-69, 81, 141, 142, 143, 144, 145,
319-322, 327, 341-343: **Fig. 1-6; Fig. 2-1; Fig 2-3; Fig 2-4;
Fig 2-5; Fig 2-6; Fig 2-7; Fig 2-8; Fig 2-9**
    Animatic SEE Animatics
    Computers and - 41, 76
Design elements SEE Design, by camera view
    History - 34, 40-41
    Interactive - 275
    Materials - 32-33, 51; **Fig. 5-48**
    Panels - 32, 33, 34, 41; **Fig. 2-11**
    Presentation - 64-68, 320, 322, 342: **Fig. 2-12**
    Production board vs. presentation board - 34, 64-65

    Slugging - 40
    Style - 50-52
    Thumbnails - 20, 22, 32
    When possible to skip - 40
SEE ALSO Exercises, Storyboard for final project;
Syllabi, Storyboard course
Storyboard reel SEE Animatic
*Strange Case of Mr. and Mrs. Donnybrook's Boredom,
The* (1981) - 73, 94, 361: **Fig. 2-67**
    SEE ALSO Silverman, David; Animation, experi-
mental; UCLA Animation Workshop
Street, The (1976) - 25-26, 47, 50, 98, 137, 360
    SEE ALSO Academy Awards; Animation, exper-
imental; Leaf, Caroline; National Film Board of
Canada; Richler, Mordecai
Street Works (1988) - 58, 59; **Fig. 2-38**
SEE ALSO Animation, experimental; Mercer, Celia;
UCLA Animation Workshop
Stromboli (character) - 34, 179
    SEE ALSO *Pinocchio* (1940); Disney (studio)
Structure SEE Design
Study series (1929-1934) - 55
    SEE ALSO Animation, experimental; Fischinger,
Oskar
Sturges, Preston - 17-18
Subjective point of view - 36, 96
Sullivan, Pat - 357
    Works
      Felix the Cat (1919-1930) - 262, 357
    SEE ALSO Messmer, Otto
Sunstone (1979) - 361
    SEE ALSO Animation, computer; Animation,
experimental; Emshwiller, Ed
Surrealism – 58: **Fig. 2-58**
Svankmajer, Jan - 26, 58, 138, 235, 248, 361
    Works
      Dimensions of Dialogue (1982) - 58, 138, 248, 361
    SEE ALSO Animation, experimental
Swarthe, Robert - 138, 204, 360
    Works
      Kick Me (1973) - 138, 360
    SEE ALSO Animation, experimental
Swat the Fly (1916) - 233
    SEE ALSO Animation, 3D; Hopkins, Willie; Shorts
(theatrical)
Swimming (1986) - 136; **Fig. 6-4**
    SEE ALSO Animation, experimental; Mercer, Celia
Syllabi - 314-326

Beginning course - 314-318
Storyboard course - 319-322
Production course (two semesters) - 322-326
Symphonie Diagonale (1924) - 58, 357
SEE ALSO Animation, experimental; Eggeling, Viking

Ta-Daa (2015) - 9: **Fig. intro-3**
SEE ALSO Animation, experimental; Shipman, Jay
Table top animation SEE Animation, 3D
Tale of Tales (1979) - 361
SEE ALSO Animation, experimental; Norstein, Yuri
Tati, Jacques - 147
Tea kettle exercise SEE Exercises, anticipation
Technological Threat (1988) - 74, 94, 361
SEE ALSO Academy Awards; Animation, experimental; Kroyer, Bill and Sue
Television series
Beavis and Butt-Head (1993-2011) – 362; *Clutch Cargo* (1959-1960) – 194; *Crusader Rabbit* (1950-1979) – 362; *Fang the Wonderdog* (n.d.) – 370; *Flintstones, The* (1960-1966) - 21, 125, 362; *George of the Jungle* (1967) - 44, 370; *Johnny Bravo* (1997-2001) – 226; *Mighty Hercules, The* (1963-1966) - 180, 317, 359; *Puppetoons* (1932-1971) – 233; *Rocky and Bullwinkle Show, The* (1959-1964) - 44, 153, 362, 370; *Sesame Street* (1969-present) - 113, 120, 146, 285, 287, 317; *Simpsons, The* (1989-present) - 2, 25, 46, 50, 187, 295, 306, 311, 334, 362, 372; *South Park* (1997-present) - 25, 140, 265, 362
SEE ALSO Scriptwriting for television
Tezuka, Osamu - 157-158, 183, 337, 361
Works
Jumping (1984) - 157-158, 337, 361
SEE ALSO Animation, Japanese
Tezuka School of Animation, Vol. 2: Animals in Motion SEE Tezuka, Osamu
Thankamushy, Sunil - 275-276
SEE ALSO Animation, interactive; UCLA Animation Workshop
Theory SEE Animation, basis, theoretical
Three Little Pigs, The (1933) - 45, 358
SEE ALSO Academy Awards; Disney (studio); Disney, Walt; Gillett, Burt; Shorts (theatrical); *Silly Symphonies* (1929-1939)
Thomas, Frank - 17, 57, 82-83, 183, 355: **Fig. 2-53**
Works
Robin Hood (1973) - 85, 306
SEE ALSO *Disney Animation: The Illusion of Life;*

Disney (studio)
Tiger Paws (n.d.) - 99, 136; **Fig. 5-15; Fig. 6-6**
SEE ALSO Commercials; Littlejohn, Bill
Timelines – 62: **Fig. 2-61**
Time sheets - **Fig. 11-3**
Timing - 62, 71-77: **Fig. 3-1**
Animatics SEE Animatics
Areas of - 72
Bar sheets SEE Bar sheets
Determining - 72-73
Patterns - 73-74
Sound and - 74-75
SEE ALSO Animation, basics of
Title cards SEE Titles
Titles - 61-62, 200; **Fig. 2-28; Fig 5-49; Fig 10-4**
SEE ALSO Layout, titles
Tom and Jerry (1940-1958) - 17, 138, 252, 358, 359
SEE ALSO *Anchors Aweigh* (1945); Jones, Chuck; Metro-Goldwyn-Mayer (studio); Shorts (theatrical); *Two Mouseketeers, The* (1952)
Toy Story (1995) - 25, 140
SEE ALSO Feature films; Pixar (studio)
Trace back cycles - 108, 160, 166, 196, 160-161, 340; **Fig. 7-7**
Tracey Ullman Show, The - 311, 334
SEE ALSO Silverman, David; *Simpsons, The* (1989-present)
Transformations by Holding Time (1976) - 139, 248, 360
SEE ALSO Animation, experimental; de Nooijer, Paul
Trnka, Jirí - 73, 94, 358
Works
Song of the Prairie (1949) - 73, 94, 358
SEE ALSO Animation, experimental
Trucks - 33, 36, 94, 97, 98, 99, 119, 121-122, 132, 152, 155, 165, 184, 202, 239-240, 142, 313, 337, 342, 350, 352: **Fig. 2-15; Fig. 5-38**
True Story of the Civil War, The (1957) - 146
SEE ALSO Shorts (theatrical)
Tsark, Tami- 3, 136; Fig. 6-1
Works
Frog He Would A-wooing Go, A (1990) - 136
SEE ALSO UCLA Animation Workshop; Animation, experimental
Tubby the Tuba (1947) - 138, 232
SEE ALSO Animation, 3D; Pal, George; Shorts (theatrical)
TV Series SEE Television series
Tweety and Sylvester - 17
SEE ALSO Blanc, Mel; Shorts (theatrical); Warner

Brothers (studio)
Two Mouseketeers, The (1952) - 359
SEE ALSO Academy Awards; Barbera, Joseph; Hanna, William; Metro-Goldwyn-Mayer (studio) Shorts (theatrical); *Tom and Jerry* (1940-1958)

UCLA Animation Workshop - 4, 7, 25, 207, 146, 301, 312, 331; **Fig. 1-1; Fig. 7-83; Fig. 13-4; Fig. 13-5**
Works
9 (animation, experimental) (2005) – 45; *9* (film) (2009) – 45; *All-Aflutter* (1997) – 136; *Animato* (1977); *Chasing the Light* (2014) – 116; *Claude* (1963) – i, 3, 4, 17, 38, 45, 63, 359; *Epiphanies* (1968) – 136; *Frog He Would A-wooing Go, A* (1990) – 136; *Fossils* (1999) - 58, 59; *God is Dog Spelled Backwards* (1967) - 17, 21, 42, 58, 101, 137, 301, 303, 311, 359; *Katzenjammer Kids: Still Stranded, The* (1995) – 152; *Madcap* (1991) – 138; *Microsecond* – **Fig. 9-1**; *Mystery Box, A* (2001) – 59; *Next Stop Judgement Day* (2016?) – 10; *Nine O'Clock News* (1968) – **Fig. 7-9**; *No Idea* (2000) – 17; *One Final Encore* (2016) – 140; *Pirates vs. Ninjas* (circa 2011) - 138, 232; *Prisoner, The* (1973) – 197; *Russia, March to November, 1917* (1959) - Fig. 2-12; *Sand Dance* (1988) - 74, 94, 101, 137, 311, 361; *Scratch Film #1* (1989) – 59; *Shapes of Movement* (1996) – 251; *Spring Blanket* (circa 1986) – 136; *Strange Case of Mr. and Mrs. Donnybrook's Boredom, The* (1981) - 73, 94, 361; *Star Spangled Banner* (1968) – **Fig. 2-64**; *Street Works* (1988) - 58, 59; *Ta-Daa* (2015) – 9; *Wizard of Speed and Time, The* (1979); *Zebu* (1987) - 256
SEE ALSO Acker, Sean; Animation Celebration; Animatrix; Blaiklock, Andy; Cantwell, colin; Denslow, Phil; Dickson, Bob; Edwards, Richard; Engels, Steve; Falling Lizard Weekend; Faroudja, Phil; Holmes, Adam; Lantz, Walter; Lam, David; Lettera, Valeria; Mercer, Celia; Mitchell, Bill; Mokhberi, Emund; Petty, Sara; Quade, Richard; Saks, Ron; Savenick, Phil; Shipman, Jay; Shull, William; Silverman, David; Siti, Tom; Stitchman (character); Thankamushy, Sunil; Tsark, Tami; Vilppu, Glenn; Walter Lantz Productions; Ward, Doug; Wells, Brian; Yamamoto, Peggy
UFVA - 223, 331, 356
Unions and guilds - 8, 291, 292, 292-293, 297, 374-375
SEE ALSO Sito, Tom; Writers' Guild of America
United Producers of America SEE UPA (studio)
Universal (studio) - 40
Works

Andy Panda (1939-1949) – 358; *Knock, Knock* (1940) - 358
SEE ALSO Blair, Preston; Lantz, Walter
University Film and Video Association SEE UFVA
UPA (studio) - 36, 47, 97, 98, 118, 153, 174, 358
Works
Gerald McBoing Boing (1950) - 36, 47, 358; *Hellbent for Election* (1944) - 358
SEE ALSO Cannon, Robert; Mr. Magoo (character)
Upstaging SEE Layout, camera
Utilitarianism - 305
SEE ALSO Mill, John Stuart

Van Goethem, Nicole - 361
Works
Greek Tragedy (1985) - 361
SEE ALSO Animation, experimental
Van Rijn, Rembrandt - 107, 296
Venezia, Tony - 256
SEE ALSO Visual effects
VFX SEE Visual effects
Video games SEE Animation, interactive
Vilppu Drawing Manual, The SEE Vilppu, Glenn
Vilppu, Glenn - ii, 185, 355
SEE ALSO UCLA Animation Workshop
Vinton, Will - 238, 360
Works
Closed Mondays (1974) - 237, 360
SEE ALSO Academy Awards; Animation, 3D; Gardiner, Bob
Visual effects - 9, 26, 118, 135, 139, 231, 232, 249-256
NOTE: This section refers to animation used to embellish an otherwise entirely
live-action work. The process for animating effects such as rain, explosions, or snow in an all-animation work is found under Animation, effects.
Complete film - 256
Computers and - 251, 253, 254, 255
Motion control - 253
Production stages - 254-255
Techniques - 252-253
Types of - 250-251
Vs. special effects - 249-250
Visual transitions - 38-39
SEE ALSO *Anchors Aweigh* (1945); *Canon* (1964); *King Kong* (1933); *Little Alice* (1924); *Mary Poppins* (1964); *Pas de deux* (1968); Rotoscoping; *Where's Poppa?*

(titles) (1970); *Who Framed Roger Rabbit* (1988); *Zebu* (1987)

Voices SEE Sound, voices

Wacom (drawing tablet) - 265

    SEE ALSO Animation, computer

Walk cycles - 88, 161, 169-183, 340

    References - 183

    SEE ALSO Exercises, Walks and other forms of locomotion

Walk in place SEE Exercises, walks and other forms of locomotion

Walking (1968) - 61, 138, 349, 360

    SEE ALSO Animation, experimental; Larkin, Ryan; National Film Board of Canada; Rotoscoping

WALL-E (2008) - 16

    SEE ALSO Feature films; Pixar (studio); Stanton, Andrew

Wallace and Gromit (1989-2005) - 19, 138, 232, 362

    SEE ALSO Academy Awards; Animation, 3D; Park, Nick; Shorts (theatrical); Wallace (character)

Wallace (character) - 19

    SEE ALSO *Wallace and Gromit* (1989-2005)

Walter Lantz Digital Animation Studio - 146-147

    SEE ALSO Lantz, Walter; UCLA Animation Workshop; Woody Woodpecker (character)

Ward, Doug - ii, 1, 125; **Fig. intro-2; Fig. 5-38; Fig. 5-42; Fig. 7-83;**

    SEE ALSO UCLA Animation Workshop

Ward, Jay - 44, 153, 286, 370

    Works

        Fang the Wonderdog (n.d.) – 370; *Rocky and Bullwinkle Show, The* (1959-1964) - 44, 153, 362, 370; *George of the Jungle* (1967) - 44, 370

    SEE ALSO Jay Ward Productions; Scott, Bill

Warner Brothers (studio) - 16, 17, 45, 51, 61, 67, 75, 88, 136, 298, 358, 359

    Works

        Daffy's Southern Exposure (1942) – 16; *Dover Boys, The* (1942) - 101, 358; *Duck Amuck* (1953) - 101, 359; *One Froggy Evening* (1955) - 45, 46, 61, 359; *Porky's Duck Hunt* (1937) – 358; *Rabbit Fire* (1951) - 55, 61, 358; *Road Runner and Wile E. Coyote* - 16, 18, 44, 50, 51, 56, 61, 71, 72, 89, 118,128, 138, 150, 166; *What's Opera, Doc?* (1957) – 359; *Wild Hare* (1940) - 358

    SEE ALSO Brown, Treg; Bugs Bunny (character); Daffy Duck (character); Elmer Fudd (character); Foghorn Leghorn (character); Pepé le Pew (character); Porky Pig (character); Wile E. Coyote (character); Tweety and Sylvester; Avery, Tex; Blanc, Mel; Jones, Chuck; McCabe, Norm; Shorts (theatrical); Warner, Jack

Warner, Jack (1892-1978) - 18

    SEE ALSO Warner Brothers (studio); *Maltese Falcon, The*

Waves SEE Sine curve

Wayne, John - 263

Maura, Weber – 2; **Fig. 15-1**

Wells, Brian - 3, 136; **Fig. 6-3**

    Works

        All-Aflutter (1997) - 136

    SEE ALSO UCLA Animation Workshop

West, Mae - 283

Weston Woods (studio) - 153

WGA SEE Writers' Guild of America

What's Opera, Doc? (1957) - 359

    SEE ALSO Blanc, Mel; Bugs Bunny (character); Jones, Chuck; Shorts (theatrical); Warner Brothers (studio)

When the Wind Blows (1986) - 139

    SEE ALSO Feature films; Murakami, Jimmy

Where's Poppa? (titles) (1970) - 66, 256; **Fig. 10-2**

    SEE ALSO Animation, experimental; McLaughlin, Dan F., Jr.; Visual effects

Whitney, James - 20, 26, 42, 57, 58, 137, 200, 211, 360

    Works

        Celery Stalks at Midnight (1937) – 137; *Lapis* (1966) - 20, 42, 57, 58, 211, 360; *Yantra* (1955) - 58, 211

SEE ALSO Animation, experimental

Whitney, John - 137

    Works

        Celery Stalks at Midnight (1937) - 137

    SEE ALSO Animation, experimental

Who Framed Roger Rabbit (1988) - 26, 139, 250, 306

    SEE ALSO Disney (studio); Feature films; Visual effects; Williams, Richard

Wild Hare (1940) - 358

    SEE ALSO Academy Awards; Avery, Tex; Blanc, Mel; Bugs Bunny (character); Shorts (theatrical); Warner Brothers (studio)

Wilder, Gene - 285

Wile E. Coyote (character) - 16, 42, 44, 50, 71, 72, 118, 166

SEE ALSO Jones, Chuck; *Road Runner and Wile E. Coyote*; Road Runner (character); Shorts (theatrical);

Warner Brothers (studio)
Williams, Mason SEE *Classical Gas*
    SEE ALSO *Smothers Brothers Summer Show, The*
Williams, Richard - 128, 138, 150, 183, 355, 359
    Works
        Animator's Survival Kit, The - 183, 355; *Love Me, Love Me, Love Me* (1962) – 359; *Who Framed Roger Rabbit* (1988) - 26, 139, 250, 306
    SEE ALSO Animation, experimental; Short (theatrical)
Wind animation SEE Animation, effects
Windy Day (1967) - 360
    SEE ALSO Academy Awards; Animation, experimental; Hubley, Emily; Hubley, Faith; Hubley, Georgia; Hubley, John
Wizard of Speed and Time, The (1979) - 138-139, 248, 361; **Fig. 6-16**
    SEE ALSO Jittlov, Mike, Animation, Pixilation; UCLA Animation Workshop
Wolf, Fred - 360
    Works
        Point, The (1971) - 136, 360
    SEE ALSO Murakami-Wolf Productions (studio)
Woluluk, Jon - 248
    Works
        Pappa Oh Mama (1974) - 248
    SEE ALSO Animation, 3D; Animation, experimental
Women in Animation - 356
Wooden, John - 207
Woody Woodpecker (character) - 358
    SEE ALSO *Andy Panda* (1939-1949); *Knock, Knock* (1940); Lantz, Walter; Walter Lantz Productions
Wray, Fay (- 234
    SEE ALSO *King Kong* (1933)
Writers' Guild of America - 369, 373, 373-374
Wrong Trousers, The (1993) SEE Wallace and Gromit (1989-2005)

Xbox SEE Animation, interactive, delivery systems for
XSI (animation software) - 265, 271
    SEE ALSO Animation, computer

Yamamoto, Peggy - 364-365
    SEE ALSO UCLA Animation Workshop
Yantra (1955) - 58, 211

SEE ALSO Animation, experimental; Whitney, James
Yeats, William Butler - 26
Yellow Submarine (1968) - 128, 138, 194, 303; **Fig. 5-46; Fig. 12-1**
    SEE ALSO Dunning, George; Feature films; Rotoscoping; Mitchell, Bob
Young, Susan - 361
    Works
        Carnival (1985) - 361
    SEE ALSO Animation, experimental; Royal College of Art

Zagreb Studios - 46, 360
    Works
        Diary (1974) - 360
Zid (The Wall) (1965) - 46, 360
    SEE ALSO Dragic, Nedeljko
Zaninovic, Ante - 46, 360
    Works
        Zid (The Wall) (1965) - 46, 360
    SEE ALSO Animation, experimental
Zebu (1987) - 256
    SEE ALSO Mitchell, William; Visual effects
Zeno - 305
    SEE ALSO Stoicism
Zid (The Wall) (1965) - 46, 360
SEE ALSO Animation, experimental; Zagreb Studios; Zaninovic, Ante

73587719R00228

Made in the USA
Columbia, SC
13 July 2017